CLARENDON LIBRARY OF LOGIC AND PHILOSOPHY

General Editor: L. Jonathan Cohen, The Queen's College, Oxford

TRUTH, FICTION, AND LITERATURE

The *Clarendon Library of Logic and Philosophy* brings together books, by new as well as by established authors, that combine originality of theme with rigour of statement. Its aim is to encourage new research of a professional standard into problems that are of current or perennial interest.

General Editor: L. Jonathan Cohen, The Queen's College, Oxford.

Also published in this series

TRUTH, FICTION, AND LITERATURE

A Philosophical Perspective

PETER LAMARQUE

and

STEIN HAUGOM OLSEN

CLARENDON PRESS · OXFORD
1994

Oxford University Press, Walton Street, Oxford OX2 6DP

Oxford   New York   Toronto
Delhi   Bombay   Calcutta   Madras   Karachi
Kuala Lumpur   Singapore   Hong Kong   Tokyo
Nairobi   Dar es Salaam   Cape Town
Melbourne   Auckland   Madrid
and associated companies in
Berlin   Ibadan

Oxford is a trade mark of Oxford University Press

Published in the United States
by Oxford University Press Inc., New York

British Library Cataloguing in Publication Data
Data available

Library of Congress Cataloging in Publication Data
Lamarque, Peter.
Truth, fiction, and literature : a philosophical perspective /
Peter Lamarque and Stein Haugom Olsen.
—(Clarendon library of logic and philosophy)
Includes bibliographical references (p.) and index.
1. Literature—Philosophy.   2. Literature—Aesthetics.
3. Narration (Rhetoric).   4. Fiction.   5. Truth in literature.
6. Reality in literature.   I. Olsen, Stein Haugom, 1946–
II. Title.   III. Series.
PN45.L316   1994   801'.953—dc20   93–37773
ISBN 0–19–824082–1

1 3 5 7 9 10 8 6 4 2

Typeset by Graphicraft Typesetters Ltd., Hong Kong
Printed in Great Britain
on acid-free paper by
Bookcraft (Bath) Ltd.
Midsomer Norton, Avon

Preface

ONE of the useful purposes served by a book's preface, other than introducing a welcome personal element, is to guide librarians in how to catalogue the book. Authors usually describe in their prefaces what kind of book they think they have written; this is sometimes done overtly, sometimes by recounting the history of how the book came to be written and the influences on it.

In our own case the problem of the book's classification is particularly pressing, being interdisciplinary in both subject-matter and authorship, so a few authorial reflections on how it came about might be especially helpful.

We have often been asked how two people can write a book, not least when the two people live in different countries and work, and teach, in different subject areas. The practicalities have presented few difficulties, indeed we have made the most of having an irresistable excuse for international travel. In the early years of our friendship, at the beginning of the 1980s, P.L. was teaching a course on Philosophy and Literature at Stirling to which S.H.O. frequently contributed as a visitor to the university. It became clear from this and subsequent exchanges of papers and letters, that the work we were doing more or less independently—S.H.O. on literary aesthetics, P.L. on fiction—was complementary in many respects. We both came to modify the views we held in the light of what we learned from the other.

It was not long before we came to believe that the combined ideas promised a powerful and coherent framework for explaining, among other things, the cultural significance of literature. But we never let one set of ideas become subsumed into the other and it is no coincidence that a central argument in the book is that the concepts of fiction and of literature are distinct and call for separate analyses. What we came to see is that these separate analyses can follow very similar lines and furthermore that no adequate account of the cognitive values of literary fiction could be complete without providing both a theory of fiction and a theory of literary aesthetics. The idea of the book was conceived to develop just such an account. Nowhere else, to our knowledge, has such an attempt been made. Accounts of fiction and accounts of literature abound but no account of both together, with the inevitable consequence that the fiction theories seem weak on literature and the literature theories weak on fiction.

In writing the book we have merged together the modified views that have evolved in our own thinking through a decade of discussion. For those who know our work it should be obvious how the labour was divided; for those who do not, and are interested, P.L. was responsible principally for Chapters 1–9 and Chapter 14, while S.H.O. was responsible principally for Chapters 10–13 and 15–17. However, the responsibility is shared for the entire finished product, in many parts of which the origin of the ideas is a joint effort or at least unclear.

Whatever else it is, this is an interdisciplinary book, a book on philosophy-and-literature, though that appellation could and does mean many different things. Philosophical methods underlie the whole approach and do not emanate from one author in particular (we both draw on a philosophical training)—there runs throughout a strong commitment to analytical argument, careful and explicit reasoning, though without undue recourse to a technical vocabulary. The literary element is harder to specify. There is some discussion of particular works of literature (and of fiction) though this is primarily for illustrative purposes rather than being literary criticism for its own sake. Also although there is plenty of *theorizing about literature*, in the sense that literature provides the substantial subject-matter of the debate, this is not a book in or about *literary theory* as that field is currently defined. In fact we are often critical of the broad enterprise that goes by that name, much of which, surprisingly, has been hostile to philosophy. Those expecting 'literary theory' will be disappointed, not least because central areas in that enquiry—psychoanalysis, cultural materialism, new historicism, feminism, and others—are left out of account altogether.

Nor is the book a survey or an attempt to give a comprehensive account of literature or fictionality. It is a focused study of a specific problem, that of literature's relation to truth (or truth-telling). The conclusions drawn are often unusual and polemical, with far-reaching consequences in the wider debate of cultural values. We will return to that in a moment. The topic of 'truth in art' is of course a staple diet in aesthetics, in fact one which has acquired a certain staleness after so many centuries of wearisome to-ing and fro-ing. Certainly the book is a contribution to aesthetics and to that old familiar topic. But qualifications are again advisable so as not to raise unwarranted expectations. We are not concerned with art in general but only the rather special case of literature where the question of truth is at its most pronounced and most hotly defended (novels, unlike sculptures and symphonies, seem as if they *must* yield truths). Nor do we attempt to give a history of the problem, in spite of the fact that the history of 'poetry and truth' is long and intriguing. As will be evident from the length of this study, there is enough to say about the foundations of the problem, mapping its intellectual ramifications, quite apart from exploring its chequered past. Needless to say, though, figures from the past inevitably make an appearance. Our own approach is foundational—we examine practices and concepts, we attempt to give more or less precise formulations for intuitions that are often vague and unformed, we examine the consequences of holding different points of view, and of course above all we offer our own suggestions on the best way of explaining cognitive values.

It might surprise those not directly involved to know that literature and literary study are under serious attack both from outside and from within academic institutions. The status of literature or literary criticism as an academic discipline in schools and universities is a matter of widespread, and public, controversy. Curiously, many of the very people who teach literature have been at the forefront of those seeking to undermine it. It should be said, though, that doubts about the teaching of literature—how it is done, what it seeks to achieve, what justification there is for it—are by no means new. Ever since literature (other than classical texts and philology) was introduced into university syllabuses, at the beginning of the century, it has been controversial. The problem was always *what* to teach and *how*. There has always been a residual, even mildly guilt-ridden, self-consciousness associated with reading novels and poems as a kind of *work*. That sentiment itself of course has a history, which is where the more insidious attacks on literature have their roots. For there has been a persistent tendency, in trying to justify the study of literature, to make it seem something that it is not, something other than literature—a branch of philosophy, perhaps, or psychology or linguistics or 'cultural studies'.

Although we are not offering a 'defence of literature' in

anything like the traditional sense we do believe that the standard
attacks on it are misguided and ill-founded and that this is dem-
onstrable. The view we develop has clear consequences for the
teaching of literature, for those seeking a rationale for having
literature on the curriculum, though we have little to say directly
on this practical debate. Ours is a non-reductionist account, it
(unfashionably) acknowledges the autonomy of literature and literary criticism; it does not seek to reduce the study of literature
to rhetoric, *belles-lettres*, philology, ethics, civic studies, or whatever. Nor does it suppose that literary criticism is either a science
or mere 'intuition'. Literary appreciation can be taught and developed; it can be more or less well-informed, intelligent, and per-
ceptive, and is governed by its own conventions and concepts.
Literature does not need to be justified as a source of moral
precepts or an adjunct to philosophy or the social sciences. It is its
own justification, providing its own rewards. No adequate study of
a culture can ignore its literary tradition, for in studying that
tradition one comes to understand the literary development of the
culture's central concerns and interests. Nor are there grounds for
disparaging literary works for their fictionality as if that somehow
weakens their claim to seriousness; the thinking here almost
certainly stems from a misunderstanding of what fictionality is,
what its aims are.

The idea of a literary tradition, even a literary canon, must be
respected and that in itself will have consequences for how literature is taught (though it plainly does not have the consequence
that only canonical works should be taught). It is simply unintelligible to eschew value judgements and suppose that just
any work is equal to any other, particularly on the weak grounds
that it is always possible to find someone who prefers work *a* to
work *b*. But it is equally wrong to think there is much political
baggage attached to the idea of literary canons, even though the
debate often takes a political turn. Canonical works in a tradition
are those that most clearly define and develop significant ideas in
that tradition. External—perhaps political or ideological—questioning of those ideas is perfectly valid but does little to disrupt
either the tradition or the canon that defines it. These issues,
though, will be taken up in detail later.

We offer the book to all those with an interest in the cognitive
values of literature, particularly those who like philosophical

bearings in their thinking. Other than that we have no more direct
advice to librarians.

For stylistic simplicity we have used the pronouns 'he' and 'him'
throughout with, where relevant, the meaning of 'he or she' and
'him or her'.

P.L.
S.H.O.

Acknowledgements

ONE of the added pleasures of working with Stein Olsen has been coming into contact with the friendly and intellectually lively community of aestheticians in Scandinavia. For many years I have attended, and given papers at, their conferences. Their hospitality and generosity have been unbounded and I have learnt much from their comments and advice. For particular encouragement, from those working in similar areas, I must thank Göran Sörbom, Göran Hermerén, Lars-Olof Åhlberg, Jeanette Emt, Torsten Pettersson, Anders Pettersson, and Ole-Martin Skilleås.

Many friends in the American Society of Aesthetics have also been a constant source of inspiration and critical stimulus. I have never failed to benefit from lengthy discussions with Kendall Walton, Susan Feagin, Noël Carroll, Ben Tilghman, and David Novitz. Encouragement and help in all kinds of ways from Peter Kivy, Jerry Levinson, Judith Tormey, Jenefer Robinson, Nicholas Wolterstorff, Don Crawford, and Peter McCormick have always been welcome.

In the UK the person I learnt most from about fiction was the late Flint Schier, who in the early stages of the project read and discussed everything I wrote on the subject, with unfailing insight. I must thank also Peter Hobbis, who as my teacher first introduced me to Philosophy and Literature and set standards I fear I have not always lived up to. Denis Pollard, Terry Diffey, Malcolm Budd, and Martin Warner have been consistently supportive.

At Stirling, my colleagues in the English Department, Alastair Macrae and Lance Butler, with whom I taught a Philosophy and Literature course throughout the 1980s, demonstrated the subtlety and richness of literary criticism at its best. And my Philosophy colleagues showed endless patience with what must have seemed a single-tracked obsession for many years.

Finally, nearer home, I must record my warmest thanks to my wife Mary who knows far more about fiction than I do, as a writer, teacher of writing, and avid reader. Her perceptiveness on practical and theoretical topics alike has constantly steered me to clearer thinking.

I will dedicate the book to the memory of my father who died in 1979, several years before the project began, but whose unsurpassed intellectual breadth and integrity have been an enduring example.

Parts of the book are drawn from previously published material of mine. Chapter 5 includes passages from 'Reasoning to What is True in Fiction', *Argumentation*, 4 (1990), 99–112. Chapter 6 draws on 'In and Out of Imaginary Worlds', in D. Knowles and J. Skorupski (eds.), *Virtue and Taste: Essays on Politics, Ethics and Aesthetics in Memory of Flint Schier* (Oxford, 1993). And Chapter 7 makes use of 'Narrative and Invention: The Limits of Fictionality', in C. Nash (ed.), *Narrative in Culture* (London, 1990). I thank the publishers for permission to use this material.

PETER LAMARQUE

Edinburgh
February 1993

SOME of my own material in this book has been presented at the yearly meetings of the Scandinavian Society of Aesthetics and I would like to thank my fellow members for comments and discussions on these occasions, in particular Tore Nordenstam, Göran Sörbom, Lars-Olof Åhlberg, Torsten Pettersson, and Anders Pettersson. A special thanks is due to Kjell S. Johannessen who has supported and encouraged me in my work from the very beginning.

Among my colleagues at the University of Oslo, Olav Lausund deserves special mention for unfailing support over many years and critical comments on all the material I have asked him to look at. I should also mention Bjorn Tysdahl and Odd Inge Langholm who have always been willing to discuss my arguments and offer criticism.

I would like to dedicate the book to my parents who have always supported me and encouraged me to be independent in my work.

Parts of Chapter 16 have previously been published as 'Thematic Concepts—Where Philosophy Meets Literature', in Stein

Haugom Olsen, *The End of Literary Theory* (Cambridge, 1987). I would like to thank Cambridge University Press for permission to use this material.

STEIN HAUGOM OLSEN

Oslo
February 1993

Contents

1

Setting the Scene

Literature and truth

Stated baldly, in what follows we present a 'no-truth' theory of literature.[1] That is, we will argue, *inter alia*, that the concept of truth has no central or ineliminable role in critical practice. The point is not, of course, that critics have no concern with true judgements but only that there is no significant place for truth as a critical term applied to works of literature. The rejection of truth as an essential facet of literature is hardly original; indeed versions of 'no-truth' theories probably have wider support in the critical community at present than do 'pro-truth' theories. So why return again to such well-worn ground?[2]

Part of the answer—the positive part—is that a new paradigm is needed, replacing the standard truth/world axis which still dominates the debate, for explaining the values of literature and the nature of fiction. It is not enough just to throw out truth as a critical term and hope that its popular currency will somehow wither away. A clear alternative to the truth-paradigm must be found which will do justice to the powerful and persistent intuitions

---

[1] The term 'no truth theory' comes from R. K. Elliott, 'Poetry and Truth', *Analysis*, 27 (1967), 77.

[2] The topic has been much debated by philosophers, as well as literary critics, in the past thirty years. A typical sample would be: Monroe C. Beardsley, *Aesthetics: Problems in the Philosophy of Criticism* (2nd edn.; New York, 1981), ch. 11; John Hospers, 'Implied Truths in Literature', *Journal of Aesthetics and Art Criticism*, 19 (1960), 37–46; Morris Weitz, 'Truth in Literature', *Revue internationale de philosophie*, 9 (1955), 116–29; repr. in John Hospers (ed.), *Introductory Readings in Aesthetics* (New York, 1969); F. E. Sparshott, 'Truth in Fiction', *Journal of Aesthetics and Art Criticism*, 26 (1967), 3–7; D. H. Mellor, 'On Literary Truth', *Ratio*, 10 (1968), 150–68; Jerry S. Clegg, 'Some Artistic Uses of Truths and Lies', *Journal of Aesthetics and Art Criticism*, 31 (1972), 43–7; Peter Mew, 'Facts in Fiction', *Journal of Aesthetics and Art Criticism*, 31 (1973), 329–37; Mary Sirridge, 'Truth from Fiction?', *Philosophy and Phenomenological Research*, 35 (1974–5), 453–71; Richard W. Miller, 'Truth in Beauty', *American Philosophical Quarterly*, 16 (1979), 317–25; Peter McCormick, 'Moral Knowledge and Fiction', *Journal of Aesthetics and Art Criticism*, 41 (1982–3), 399–410.

which motivate it in the first place. The bulk of this book will be devoted to that task.

But there is another, more polemical, reason for taking up again the old debate about literature and truth. The most prominent arguments currently advanced against 'literary truth' are, so we believe, radically misconceived. These characteristically lie at the convergence of two lines of thought: an undermining or wholesale rejection of a humanistic conception of literature and the importation of contentious, and only dubiously relevant, metaphysical theses into literary theory. Our own approach to the issue of truth and literature is totally at odds with the approach epitomized by these lines of thought.

First of all, it is no part of our argument against 'literary truth' to reject a humanistic conception of literature. On the contrary, we will offer a vigorous defence of the humanistic conception, along with its concomitant notions of value, tradition, creative imagination, even mimesis, in the conviction that no other coherent concept of literature is at hand. Those who reject the humanistic conception are not usually proposing an alternative way of looking at *literature* but rather proposing to do away with the idea of literature altogether.[3] But their arguments, such as they are, either presuppose spurious metaphysical views about reality, truth, and fiction or stem from overtly political or ideological doctrines. The interesting issue is not whether literature is a humanistic concept, or indeed whether the concept is desirable in some way, but rather how this humanistic concept relates to truth and, more generally, how works of literature relate to works with paradigmatically truth-seeking aims.

So it is, secondly, that we will expose as irrelevant a whole body of 'theory' which purports to derive conclusions about literature from theses in metaphysics and epistemology. It is no coincidence that attacks on the humanistic conception of literature have gone hand in hand with the development of theses about truth, reality, expression, representation, fictionality, and so on, for such attacks rest on the assumption that the idea of truth is integral to the humanistic conception. Thus we find literary theorists spending a great deal of effort, for example, criticizing realism, both literary and metaphysical, or challenging the notion of

[3] A good example would be Terry Eagleton, *Literary Theory: An Introduction* (Oxford, 1983).

an objeotive world, or undermining the idea of a subject of experience or knowledge, or 'deconstructing' the distinction between
philosophy and fiction, or impugning the ideas of reference and
representation, and so forth. But if there is no essential link between literature and truth then all this intellectual enterprise can
make only a marginal contribution to *literary theory* conceived as
theorizing about *literature.*

The fundamental mistake is to suppose that you need a well-
developed epistemological or metaphysical theory—about truth
or the world or the self—before you can pronounce on the values
of literature or, in a more theoretical vein, assess the merits of
'no-truth' or 'pro-truth' conceptions of literature. Current support
among literary theorists for 'no-truth' theories of literature derives far more from a fashionable scepticism about truth and
reality (there is no such thing as truth, the world, objectivity, self-
expression, etc.) than from a clear conception of literature itself.
Yet once the latter is in place the former can be seen to be beside
the point.

Thus it is that our own defence of a no-truth theory must be
sharply distinguished from those currently in favour. Our account
rests on no sceptical premisses, indeed on no particular metaphysical or epistemological premisses at all. We certainly do not
reject the idea of truth *per se*, a position that is basically incoherent, but we remain neutral as between different theories of
truth; we wish to retain some conception of an objective world
but without commitment to any epistemological stance concerning
that world, be it realist, idealist, constructivist, foundationalist, or
whatever; we will have much to say about the relation between
reference and fiction but the issues do not hang on the nature of
objects or objectivity; and far from undermining the humanistic
conception of literature our argument aims to strengthen it and in
doing so find a proper location for intuitions about literature's
'truth-telling' capacities.

It is no part of our argument, again in contrast to more familiar
no-truth theories, that works of literary fiction are 'mere play', or
'cut off from the world', or in other ways 'non-serious'. On the
contrary, we will show that being 'serious' is not restricted to stating
truths and that literary fictions can play a central, even indispensable, role in the development and understanding of fundamental ideas within the history of a culture.

One major problem with the age-old debate about literature

and truth lies in establishing just what relation between the two is expected or desired. The problem is compounded by the fact that at one level truth is all too easily connected to literature. The trouble is none of the obvious connections seem to satisfy the traditional pro-truth theorists. Although our own view rejects any essential link between truth and literature we do not hesitate to acknowledge a large number of non-essential, or contingent, links. The point is worth dwelling on at the outset because 'no-truth' theorists are sometimes treated as if they were denying the obvious. Indeed some 'no-truth' theories, particularly those in the structuralist tradition, *have* wanted to deny even the simplest links with truth, attempting apparently to cut off literary fictions altogether from the world of object and fact. We need, then, to clarify our own working assumptions.

First of all, the relation between truth and *fiction* turns out to be rather more complex than it might appear, as our analysis of fictionality will show. Fiction, in the relevant sense, is not *defined* in terms of truth (or the world or reality) so there need be no logical incompatibility between the two. Many simple observations relating to literary fictions bear this out: truths about actual people, places, or events often appear in works of fiction; presuppositions, about what things exist, what they are like, how they work, and so forth, arising from fictive descriptions can be true or false;[4] propositions brought to mind or entertained by a reader as a result of reading literary fictions can be true or false; and there can be truths about fictive events or characters, as formulated by a critic or reader, just as there can be truths of a descriptive or interpretative kind about literary works themselves. In the detailed account we will be giving later about the nature and conditions of fictionality we will seek only to explain, not to challenge, these commonplace relations with truth.

Second, coming nearer to the cognitive potentiality of literature, there are further, to our mind obvious, connections with truth and knowledge which it is no part of our 'no-truth' theory to challenge. *Of course* readers can pick up information about people, places, and events from works of fiction; *of course* readers can learn practical skills, historical facts, points of etiquette, insights

---

[4] L. B. Cebik, for example, emphasizes the importance of these presuppositions: see *Fictional Narrative and Truth: An Epistemic Analysis* (Lanham, Md., 1984), ch. 8.

into Regency England, etc., from literary works; *of course* writers of literary fiction often offer generalizations about human nature, historical events, political ideologies, and so forth, in their works; *of course* what readers take to be true (in the world) will affect how they respond to literary works, including how they understand the works;[5] *of course* readers often need to have background knowledge of a cultural, psychological, or historical kind, even moral or philosophical preconceptions, to understand some literary works.

The theoretical interest lies not in defending these commonplace observations but in integrating them into a satisfactory account of literature, literary value, and fictionality. For the important question regarding literature and truth is not whether any connections at all can be found between the two but whether there is anything integral to works of imaginative literature which makes the expression, embodiment, revelation, etc. of truths indispensable to their value, aesthetic or otherwise.

The limits of truth and falsity

Another fundamental difficulty with any discussion of literature and truth is setting acceptable limits on the notion of truth itself. This is not the same as providing a *theory* of truth, in the sense of adjudicating between correspondence, coherence, pragmatist views, and such like. There is a more basic level at which decisions must be made as to how the terms 'true' and 'false' are to be used. For example, if 'true' as applied to works of literature is used to mean 'sincere', as it sometimes is,[6] then the claim that literary works can be true or false amounts to no more than the claim that they can be sincere or insincere. There is always a danger in this debate of talking at cross purposes. We have no quarrel with those who want to use 'true' in this sense; after all the predicates 'true' and 'false' have many applications—true friend, true likeness, true

---

[5] This is a central point in R. K. Elliott's attack on 'no-truth' theories in 'Poetry and Truth'.

[6] See e.g. Dorothy Walsh, *Literature and Knowledge* (Middletown, Conn., 1969); I. A. Richards identifies 'acceptability' and 'sincerity' as the two most common senses of 'truth' in criticism; what he calls the 'scientific sense' defined in terms of 'references' and 'statements symbolizing references' he thinks is 'little involved by any of the arts', *Principles of Literary Criticism* (2nd edn.; London, 1926), 212–13.

beauty, false teeth, etc.—and no doubt there is a recognizable sense of 'true' as 'sincere'. Then the debate simply shifts elsewhere. If, more problematically, 'true' is used to mean 'true to life', in the sense of having 'verisimilitude' or being 'lifelike', then that notion needs careful explanation.[7] Whether literary value resides in being 'true to life' will depend at least partly on the explanation given. But is *truth* really at issue? Resemblance and similarity relations certainly do play an important role in understanding literary fictions, but they are not equivalent to truth. Clearly basic questions of terminology need to be settled early on for they determine how the debate will proceed.

Our principal debate is with those who want a 'stronger' sense of 'truth' and 'falsity' applied to literature; i.e. those who see the aim of literature as conveying or teaching or embodying universal truths about human nature, the human condition, and so on, in a sense at least *analogous* to that in which scientific, or psychological, or historical hypotheses can express general truths.[8]

What is this 'stronger' sense? And what are the paradigmatic bearers of truth in this sense? The safest, least controversial, place to start is with Aristotle's seemingly platitudinous dictum on truth: 'to say of what is that it is, and of what is not that it is not, is true'.[9] Everyone would agree with that. Although it remains neutral as to any substantive theory of truth, Aristotle's dictum at least serves to delimit a central and familiar sense of 'true'. It is that sense that we will engage in what follows.

We find a similar sense in Tarski's 'semantic conception of truth', which develops at least the spirit of Aristotle's account. Tarski showed how the necessary and sufficient conditions for the truth of any given sentence can be specified by the simple expedient of 'disquotation': in his own well-worn example, 'snow is white' is true if and only if snow is white.[10] It has been suggested that an

---

[7] A seminal modern discussion of 'true to' is in John Hospers, 'Literature and Human Nature', *Journal of Aesthetics and Art Criticism*, 17 (1958–9), 45–57.

[8] According to Peter McCormick, there is a 'hermeneutic perspective' on the issue which simply *takes it for granted* that 'literary artworks present truths . . . about persons . . . and about their actions': see Peter McCormick, *Fictions, Philosophies and the Problems of Poetics* (Ithaca, NY, 1988), 87.

[9] Aristotle, *Metaphysics* (1011^b25–8).

[10] Alfred Tarski, 'The semantic conception of truth and the Foundation of Semantics', *Philosophy and Phenomenological Research*, 4 (1944); repr. in H. Feigl and W. Sellars (eds.), *Readings in Philosophical Analysis* (New York, 1949).

adequacy condition for any theory of truth is that it satisfy a schema of this kind, the so-called 'equivalence schema'.[11] More radically, it has also been argued, with considerable force, that a 'minimal theory', which rests entirely on the generalized schema 'It is true that p if and only if p', is sufficient 'to explain *all* the facts involving truth'.[12]

The 'minimal theory', drawing on the Aristotelian truism, is congenial for our purposes in that, whatever questions it might leave unanswered about truth, it still captures a simple, core sense of 'true' which it would be difficult for anyone to dispute. It might well be, as the minimalist would argue, that the traditional problems supposedly 'about truth' turn out on examination to be centrally about something other than truth: for example, how to *discover* it, why it matters to *belief*, what *facts* are or the *objective world*, whether *realism* is a tenable theory, how *meaning* relates to truth, whether *progress* towards truth is an aim of science, whether *literature* seeks truth, and so forth.

Tarski emphasized the point that his semantic conception remained neutral on epistemological questions, for example about how truth was arrived at, or known, or about the conditions under which a sentence like 'Snow is white' is to be asserted:

we may accept the semantic conception of truth without giving up any epistemological attitude we may have had; we may remain naïve realists, critical realists or idealists, empiricists or metaphysicians—whatever we were before. The semantic conception is completely neutral toward all these issues.[13]

This idea fits well with our own belief that the outcome of the debate about literature and truth does not hang on any particular epistemological stance. The attraction of the 'equivalence schema' is that in effect it diverts attention away from truth as a problematic concept. Of course there are related problems—indeed some of the most intractable in philosophy—but perhaps they are not problems about truth as such. Nevertheless, even if we can avoid

[11] See Michael Dummett, *Truth and Other Enigmas* (London, 1978), p. xx; also Michael Devitt, *Realism and Truth* (Princeton, NJ, 1984), 24, and Simon Blackburn, *Spreading the Word* (Oxford, 1984), 226.
[12] Paul Horwich, *Truth* (Oxford, 1990), 7.
[13] Tarski, 'The Semantic Conception of Truth', 71; for a useful account of the commitments (epistemological and otherwise) of Tarski's theory, see Susan Haack, 'Realism', *Synthese*, 73 (1987), 275–99.

getting embroiled in theories of truth, that is not at the price of accepting just any conception of truth, or of so weakening the term 'true' that it becomes merely a generalized term of approbation. After all, 'is sincere', 'is highly regarded', 'is profound', 'is brilliantly lifelike', for example, are not substitutable for 'is true' in the equivalence schema.

Aristotle's simple dictum is by no means without content. One implication, for example, is that truth is a property of *sayings* or *something said* (in Tarski's case, sentences in a language). It is not a property of objects or facts, nor is it something 'out there' in the world.[14] We do not strictly speaking 'discover truths', in the sense in which we discover hidden treasure, rather we discover facts in the world (or, more neutrally, how things are) which verify our sayings; we discover, or find out, that our sayings are true. Of course further qualifications are needed. It is not only sayings that are true or false, even if they are paradigmatic; we are not moving far from Aristotle's intuition if we include beliefs and thoughts as bearers of truth, and even pictures or other representations, at least in so far as they have something akin to predicative structure. Nor are just any sayings candidates for truth; statements can be true or false but not questions and commands. And individual concepts—chair, mountain, goodness, beauty—cannot in themselves be true or false, though of course when applied to objects—the picture is beautiful, the chair is comfortable—they can become components of truths. Finally, the idea of 'saying' (and by extension 'writing') has a multiple ambiguity. It can mean the act of saying (the uttering of a sentence), the thing said (the sentence uttered), and the content of the saying (the meaning of the sentence or the proposition it expresses).

We will follow normal, i.e. pre-theoretical, usage (albeit departing from Tarski) in supposing that it is the content, specifically the *propositional content*, of what is said, and by analogy what is stated, believed, or thought, that is the proper bearer of truth. Although this appears to incur a commitment to propositions, which are often thought to be ontologically dubious entities, it does not entail any particular theory of propositions. We will have more to say later about propositional content when characterizing 'fictive

---

[14] The allusion is to Richard Rorty, *Contingency, Irony, and Solidarity* (Cambridge, 1989), ch. 1, who makes much of the fact that truth is not 'out there': in our Ch. 8 we give a detailed discussion of Rorty's view of truth.

content'. For the present it is important to note that assigning truth to propositional content does not beg the question about the applicability of truth to works of literary fiction. Inasmuch as such works do (at least in part) have propositional content they remain as *candidates* for truth. The definition of truth does not rule out the application of truth to the content of works of literature.

The pre-theoretical ground-clearing cannot quite end here. For one thing, any adequate conception of truth must accommodate the fact that truth is something speakers *aim for* in some (most) of the things they say. As Michael Dummett puts it, 'it is part of the concept of truth that we aim at making true statements', in much the same way that 'it is part of the concept of winning a game that a player plays to win'.[15]

Simon Blackburn makes a similar point and connects it with the 'redundancy theory' of truth. According to the redundancy theory, which draws on the equivalence schema, truth is not a genuine property of statements because there is nothing more to saying that a statement is true than simply making the statement itself. Asserting that p is true is equivalent to asserting that p. In the words of F. P. Ramsey, an early exponent of the theory:

'It is true that Caesar was murdered' means no more than that Caesar was murdered, and 'It is false that Caesar was murdered' means that Caesar was not murdered.[16]

In this way, apparently, the predicate 'is true' can be eliminated altogether.

Blackburn, however, argues that this seeming redundancy does not itself count against the possibility of a more substantive account of truth:

Truth is *internal* to judgement in the sense that to make or accept a judgement is to have it as an aim. So how could there be a difference between making a judgement on the one hand, and describing the judgement as meeting the aim, on the other? Consider some parallels. In a game there is an equivalence between making a move and judging that the move is a good one. . . . It would be redundant to add, when moving . . . that the move is one that promotes winning. This is already implicit in the choice. But this redundancy does not suggest that we have

[15] Dummett, *Truth and Other Enigmas*, 2.
[16] F. P. Ramsey, 'Facts and Propositions', in George Pitcher (ed.), *Truth* (Englewood Cliffs, NJ, 1964), 16.

no conception of what it is to win . . . The analogy is that since truth counts as success in judgement, making a judgement and describing it as true are evidently equivalent. But for all that we may have a substantive conception of what that success is.[17]

Now the question becomes: what counts as success in judgement-making? This is where the familiar candidates can be wheeled in: *corresponding with reality, belonging to a harmonious system of beliefs, being verified in ideal conditions, facilitating successful behaviour*, and so forth.[18] For our purposes, though, we do not need to pursue that line of enquiry. What the connection between truth and judgement principally establishes—giving support to the redundancy view and complying with the equivalence schema—is the simple fact that truth matters, that speakers are not indifferent to the truth of what they say; truth is something to aim for. It would be impossible to conceive of a language-community for whom speaking the truth made no difference. Communication, as it is normally understood, rests on a convention of truth-telling. This incidentally also sheds light on the connection between truth and sincerity; a sincere judgement aims for truth. The reason why we cannot accept truth as *equivalent* to sincerity, in the paradigmatic sense, is that sincere judgements can sometimes be false.

We must be careful not to misconstrue the idea that 'truth is internal to judgement'. Although the idea of judgement (or assertion) necessarily invokes the idea of truth, the connection in the other direction, of truth with judgement, is somewhat looser. A proposition can be true regardless of whether it is asserted as true in an act of judgement; it might, for example, appear as the unasserted antecedent of a conditional or as a supposition or the content of a propositional attitude. Likewise, in connection with literary fiction it is not sufficient to eliminate fictional sentences from truth assessment merely to show that they are not asserted.

However, it is important to note the close connection between truth, judgement, and belief. Belief, like judgement, aims at truth; to believe that p is to believe that p is true. In turn, judgement (or assertion) is conventionally, if defeasibly, associated with the expression of belief. In these and other ways belief contrasts with other psychological attitudes, in particular with imagination.

---

[17] Blackburn, *Spreading the Word*, 231.
[18] The list is drawn from Horwich, *Truth*, 9–11.

Imagination does not aim at truth. We can imagine, ponder, entertain thoughts, or speculate about something without any commitment to the truth of our ruminations. Finally, truth, as an aim of judgement and belief, is paradigmatically identifiable with certain human practices, notably practices of enquiry, argument, discovery, testing, verification, investigation, and so on.

Aristotle's dictum on truth, with the further refinements we have added, provides an important constraint in discussions of literature and truth. 'To say of what is that it is' is not equivalent to saying (implying, showing, suggesting, etc.) that something is *like* something or that something is *about* something. Similarity relations and referential relations, about which we will have a great deal to say in subsequent chapters, are not interchangeable with truth. To establish the *likeness* of fictive events to facts or to establish that certain fictive descriptions are *about* items in the world falls well short of establishing truth. These considerations already indicate how truth—on the simple Aristotelian model—begins to fade in importance when talking of literary fictions. More interesting and more complex 'relations with the world' are at hand.

The diffuseness of 'literary truth'

It is possible at this point that 'pro-truth' theorists might object that we have simply legislated 'literary' or 'imaginative' truth out of existence, that by constraining so tightly the concept of truth and making so many disarming concessions about where truth does intersect with literature we have made the 'no-truth' position trivially, or at least definitionally, true. But the objection need not cause us much concern. First of all, the constraints we have presented are merely procedural, they do not by any means decide the issue of whether literary works can be bearers of truth, and, second, these procedural constraints are not remotely controversial in philosophical terms but amount to perfectly standard fare on the subject. If 'pro-truth' theorists find themselves on the defensive it is most likely because their conception of truth is nonstandard; it is they who are seeking controversial extensions to a notion which in common applications is pretty straightforward. If literary works are true—*but not in the sense in which statements, hypotheses, historical treatises, etc. are true*—then special explanations are in order. Our own view is that once these explanations are forthcoming it will become clear that conceptions other than truth assume far greater significance and interest.

In fact even the most cursory look at the general kinds of theories that traditionally have made appeal to 'truth' in 'defences' of literature shows the diffuseness of the intuitions that motivate 'pro-truth' theorists, and also the tenuous connection in many of them with truth *per se*. It is possible to distinguish at least five general clusters of such theories, which could be labelled 'mimetic', 'epistemological', 'moral', 'integrity', and 'affective'. It is clear that no uniform adherence to any one conception of truth is involved in these theories and that many go well beyond our Aristotelian paradigm. Sometimes so weak a conception of truth is involved that the term has become merely honorific. Our aim, however, is not to throw out these theories *tout court* but to recast what seems to be right about them in terms other than truth.

Mimetic theories of fiction (and art in general) take many forms. Works of fiction have been supposed to 'imitate' or 'mirror' the world in different ways, sometimes through similarity (verisimilitude of character and incident), sometimes through embodying universal truths, often in other ways besides. Where 'mimesis' means 'representation' the connection with truth is made through the idea that sentences (or thoughts or beliefs) are true in virtue of 'representing states of affairs'. But representation is much less clear a notion than truth itself and there are conceptions of artistic representation which make no reference to truth. Certainly mimesis, in its different interpretations, need not be confined to semantic or semiotic correspondence between sign and object or proposition and fact. It might be associated, for example, with the idea of internal coherence or 'acceptability', of 'ringing true', in colloquial usage, rather than being true.[19] The traditional conception of mimesis relies as much on relations between mental images (in artists and spectators) as on relations between images and objects.[20] And in a recent treatment, by Kendall Walton, mimesis ceases to be a relation of any kind (certainly far removed from truth) and is defined in terms of culturally based 'functions' and roles in games

---

[19] See Richards, *Principles of Literary Criticism*, 212–13.
[20] Göran Sörbom emphasizes this point in 'Imitation and Art', in Richard Woodfield (ed.), *Proceedings of the xith International Congress in Aesthetics* (Nottingham, 1990).

of make-believe.[21] We ourselves will attempt to preserve the core idea of a 'mimetic value' in literature, though again without tying mimesis to truth.

Epistemological theories emphasize knowledge and belief and the idea of 'learning from fiction'. In different versions this learning might or might not be propositional, in the sense of involving the grasp of truths. Knowledge acquired from reading literary works could be 'knowledge how' as well as 'knowledge that'; what we learn could be skills, cognitive or otherwise, as well as facts.[22] Where 'knowledge how' is at the centre of the cognitive defence of fiction neither truth nor propositions need be involved. The question remains, however, not whether it is *possible* for works of literature to impart knowledge—that can be trivially conceded, if only at a causal level—but what role such knowledge plays in literary appreciation.

Moral theories offer moral truths or moral knowledge as the primary cognitive contribution of literary works. Although in unsophisticated versions 'the moral of the story' is encapsulated in a general proposition 'implied' or 'suggested' by the work, it is more common to find 'moral truths' conceived in more diffuse forms, for example as special kinds of beliefs.[23] Again the central issue is not whether literature can have 'moral content', from which readers might learn something, but rather the form this content takes and its relation to truth and value.

The first three clusters of theories at least allow for a propositional conception of truth, albeit without express commitment to any substantive view. However, integrity and affective theories seem to move well away from the paradigm of propositional truth and although the term 'truth' is used in connection with them, it is soon evident that rather different considerations are at stake.

Integrity theories concentrate, for example, on the sincerity of an author as a mark of 'truthfulness' or the authenticity of an artistic presentation.[24] We have already acknowledged that there are perfectly acceptable (i.e. commonplace) senses of 'true' where it

---

[21] See Kendall Walton, *Mimesis as Make-Believe* (Cambridge, Mass., 1990), ch. 1.

[22] The point is emphasized in David Novitz, *Knowledge, Fiction and Imagination* (Philadelphia, 1987), ch. 6.

[23] See McCormick, 'Moral Knowledge and Fiction'.

[24] Again a good example of this would be Walsh, *Literature and Knowledge*, ch. 8.

simply means sincere or authentic or genuine. Correspondingly, sentimentality, one manifestation of a lack of authenticity, is often associated with falsity.[25] If a 'pro-truth' theorist is using one of these senses then so be it; there is little point in debating terminology and the focus of debate then turns to the status of sincerity and authenticity among criteria of literary value. These are indeed interesting and important issues but we will touch on them only inasmuch as they bear on the characterization of 'content'.

Affective theories appeal to the effects wrought by works of fiction, some of which will be seen as cognitive. There is likely to be an overlap here with other theories, particularly those classed as epistemological. Truth might enter the picture in so far as works of fiction might causally induce true beliefs. But supporters of affective theories will more often appeal to broader kinds of psychological effects such as heightened awareness or sensibility, 'seeing as', or varieties of empathetic response as constituting a work's cognitive content. We will be carefully examining affective theories in connection with both the notion of 'subjective knowledge' and also that of 'metaphorical truth', two applications where these theories have had most prominence in recent philosophical debate.

This brief survey of cognitive or 'truth' theories shows the broad nature of support for 'literary truth' but also its lack of cohesion. It shows too that post-structuralist attacks on metaphysical and literary realism or the idea of an objective world or a 'privileged discourse' are not sufficient to disarm 'pro-truth' sympathizers. For, however diffuse their conceptions of truth, few of these theories involve metaphysically controversial commitments.

Fictionality

Many of the central problems in the debate about literature and truth concern fictionality. The tendency to see deep metaphysical issues at stake in literary theory often arises from confusions about the nature of fiction. In the course of the book we will offer a detailed account of fiction in the sense appropriate to literary fictions. We will show how metaphysical worries about the nature

---

[25] See Laurence Lerner, *The Truest Poetry* (London, 1960), ch. 8.

of objects, reality, the world, truth, and so forth, arise in connection with fiction but how they can be dispelled—often shown to be irrelevant—in the context of literary criticism or theory. The basic argument is this: that the level at which philosophers speak of objects as 'constructs' or 'fictions' or 'mind-dependent' is quite different from that at which readers of stories notice that characters and events are 'made up', 'fictional', or 'unreal'. There is no merit in blurring such differences. Indeed the kind of 'making' involved in 'making up a story' turns out, on examination, to have little or nothing in common with the 'making' that, for example, constructivists in epistemology see as basic in cognition. But the matter is undoubtedly controversial and goes against a powerful trend in literary theory which precisely encourages a weakening of such differences. To establish these points, and thus remove the almost endemic confusions, requires a careful investigation of different senses of 'fiction', as well as the role of narration and the role of imagination in cognitive processes.

Meanwhile, a certain amount of preliminary ground-clearing is again in order. The term 'fiction' has a wide use, yielding such diverse conceptions as literary, legal, logical, mathematical, and epistemological fictions, among others. It is easy to get seduced by the topic, as perhaps did one of fiction's best-known theoreticians, Hans Vaihinger, and come to see fictions as inescapable in all enquiry. Vaihinger used the label 'fiction' to include: inventions, conceits, figments of the brain, fantasies, imagination, conceptual aids, expedients, devices, artifices, chimera, deceptive ideas, unjustified methods, schemata, heuristic ideas, regulative ideas, and much more besides.[26] He distinguished numerous categories of fictions: abstractive, schematic, paradigmatic, utopian, type, symbolic, juristic, personificatory, summational, heuristic, practical (ethical), and mathematical. And he offered a fine medley of instances: an immortal god, the virgin birth, atoms, the materialistic conception of the world, vital force in biology, an original social contract, human freedom, and so on, and so on.

Our own task is not to attempt a taxonomy of fictions so much as an analysis of various central conceptions of fiction. In spite of the diversity of Vaihinger's lists he himself saw a unifying rationale,

[26] Hans Vaihinger, *The Philosophy of 'As If'*, trans. C. K. Ogden (2nd edn.; London, 1935), 96–7.

within a 'philosophy of "as if" ', for linking together his many examples. We will be looking at the 'as if' conception of fiction in due course, though we will give reasons why it is not adequate to explain literary fictions. Indeed, somewhat against the spirit of Vaihinger's enterprise, we will argue that there is no substantive unitary conception of fiction covering both the general areas that concerned him, particularly the role of fictions in logic and cognition, and the more humble, if familiar, notion of 'work of fiction' as employed by publishers, bookshop managers, and literary critics. It is that humble notion that we are seeking to explain.

There is of course *some* unitary concept of fiction which, although inadequate to provide a significant theoretical unity to all conceptions, should at least be acknowledged at the start. Basic etymology reminds us that fiction involves 'fabrication' or 'making', that which is 'fashioned or formed', a creation of some kind. It is important to keep in mind this core idea of *making* or *creating*, though on its own it affords only the barest starting-point. There is a great deal of 'making', even of an intellectual or imaginative kind, which is not appropriately described as 'fiction' and within recognizable limits of the fictional there is a diversity of 'makings', both in kinds and aims. We will give reasons for resisting too generous an assimilation of different kinds and aims of imaginative making, although we will be careful not to forsake the core conception. The dangers of over-generalization soon become apparent in the light of a fundamental ambiguity in the idea of 'fiction': between object and description senses of the term.

Object and description senses

We speak of fictions sometimes as kinds of objects or things, such as Sherlock Holmes, average families, or perpetual motion machines, and sometimes as kinds of descriptions, such as *The Hound of the Baskervilles*, Jones's statement to the police, or the story of Adam and Eve. A fictional character is a fiction in the object sense, a work of fiction is a fiction in the description sense. To say of a thing that it is fictional is to suggest that it does not exist, the implied association being between what is fictional and what is *unreal*. To say of a description that it is fictional is to suggest that it is not true, the implied association being between what is fictional and what is *false*.

Unfortunately these familiar associations with *unreality* and *falsity* cannot, at least in any simple way, yield definitive characteristics common to all kinds of fiction. Being made and being real are clearly not incompatible categories. And in an investigation of fiction and truth it would be rash too early on to invoke truth-values in a definition of descriptive fictions. Again being made (or made up) and being true are not logically incompatible. Even Jones's lying statement to the police might contain a few shreds of truth; indeed it is possible to make up a story and have the intention to deceive while inadvertently speaking the whole truth.

A further distinction, between *content* and *mode* of utterance, is connected to, but not identical with, the object/description ambiguity. The content of an utterance might be fictional even though its mode of utterance is non-fictional (perhaps asserted with the intention to deceive or asserted in the mistaken belief that it is non-fiction). Whether someone is speaking fictively is not determined solely by the content of what they say. A person might retell the story of *20,000 Leagues Under the Sea* firmly believing it to be historically accurate; the content is fictional, but not the telling. Likewise, when Konrad Kujau forged the Hitler Diaries he made up the content, which it would be reasonable to describe as fictional, but we should surely hesitate to call the finished product a 'work of fiction' given the mode of its presentation. Conversely, someone might recount the events of the Entebbe Raid believing them to be pure fiction; here the content is non-fiction, while the telling is in the fictive mode. One reason why content and mode of utterance can pull apart in this way lies in the fact that those who tell (fictional) stories have not always made up the stories themselves. Making and telling are distinct. Another reason stems from an ambiguity in 'story', somewhat akin to the ambiguity in 'saying' noted earlier. By 'story' is sometimes meant *what is told* (the content), sometimes the *telling* of it. To say, for example, 'The story is entirely true' is to refer to the story-content, to say 'The story took ten minutes' is to refer to the story-telling.

The content/mode distinction is close to the object/description ambiguity because content normally consists in the characterization of objects, fictional or otherwise, broadly conceived (i.e. including events, places, people), and mode of utterance applies to fiction in the description sense. But the distinctions are not identical because fictions in both object and description senses might be included under content. Also, 'making' or 'making up' does not apply uniformly across the different cases. While making applies to both objects and descriptions, and generally to content, it does not apply directly to mode of utterance. An utterance is fictive (in the fictive mode) not in virtue of being made up, or in having a made-up content, but in virtue of its role or purpose. These subtle distinctions will be further developed in later chapters.

Finally, there is a pronounced divergence of connotation, positive and negative, in the term 'fiction' which reveals itself in both object and description senses. On the positive side, we think of fiction as something creatively constructed or imagined, a product of an active and inventive mind. On the negative side, we think in terms of falsity, non-existence, unreality, a failure of some kind, something to be avoided.

This positive/negative polarity cuts across the object/description ambiguity. Thus the object sense of fiction can have both positive and negative connotations. The object can be praised as a product of the imagination, a creative invention, or denigrated as non-existent or unreal. The pejorative connotation of unreality is often suspended when the positive connotation of fiction is invoked. Similarly, the description sense of 'fiction' can elicit favour for being imaginative, for example *The Hound of the Baskervilles*, or invite censure for being false, for example Jones's statement. Again, the association with falsity is played down, if not removed altogether, under the positive connotation.

Fiction and metaphysics

Once these familiar ambiguities have been recognized it is easy to see how metaphysical and epistemological issues get drawn into discussions of fiction. And this makes the need all the more pressing to sort out the distinctive kind of 'making', be it of object or description, involved in literary fictions.

The object sense of 'fiction', for example, seems to lead naturally and inevitably to an enquiry about existence and reality, even the idea of 'object' itself. This is the realm of metaphysics or ontology. Certain conceptions of fiction, in the object sense, have played a prominent role in philosophy, as well as more recently in literary theory, and undoubtedly have served to weaken the distinction between a fiction, so conceived, in the object sense, and a (real) object. The romantic (empiricist) tradition in epistemology, encouraged by a positive conception of fictions as imaginative constructions, sees the empirical world of objects as itself a kind of construct of the mind. 'Constructivist' theories of knowledge go back at least as far as Kant but much of twentieth-century analytical philosophy has also followed in the same vein: phenomenalists and logical positivists described ordinary objects as 'logical constructions', Quine famously compared physical objects with the gods of Homer and spoke of both as 'myths',[27] and more recently Nelson Goodman has described science as 'worldmaking'.[28] If we think of fictions in the object sense only in terms of intellectual or imaginative *making* and we see making as a fundamental process in epistemology then there will inevitably be a tendency to blur the distinction between the fictional and the real. Many literary theorists have pursued similar lines of thought within their own terms of reference, casting doubt on the idea of a 'given' objective world standing in sharp contrast to the imaginative 'made-up' worlds of the novelist or playwright. Correspondingly, this has inclined some theorists to play down the distinction between different modes of writing, the literary, the philosophical, the scientific, and so on, although that takes us more into the description sense of fiction.

If we are to avoid dragging these metaphysical questions into literary criticism then it will be necessary to show just how different is the literary critic's conception of fiction, in the object sense, from those conceptions found in epistemology, and elsewhere. In fact there is a world of difference between the 'constructs' of science and the imaginative 'fictions' of the story-teller. In later chapters we will offer a detailed examination of different conceptions of fiction, as well as the nature of 'worldmaking' in epistemology; and we will show, among other things, that the role of the imagination in the acquisition of knowledge is fundamentally different from the use of the 'fanciful imagination' in the creation of art and literature.

The description sense of 'fiction' also invites metaphysical speculation, this time about the nature of truth and facts. The

---

[27] W. V. O. Quine, 'Two Dogmas of Empiricism', in *From a Logical Point of View* (2nd rev. edn.; New York, 1961), 44; see also 18.

[28] Nelson Goodman, *Ways of Worldmaking* (Brighton, 1978).

pressures we have already noted on the distinction between fiction and (real) object are reflected in similar pressures on the distinction between fiction and truth. We have seen that the positive connotations of 'fiction', applied to the description sense of the word, tend to play down the association of fiction and falsity. Once again, if the idea of construction or making is emphasized in theories of knowledge, and if the empirical world is seen as in some sense a product of the mind, then it is a short step to Goodman's conceit of the 'fabrication of facts' or to Rorty's of truth as 'man-made'. All this seems to weaken not only the distinction between what is 'made up' and what is 'found out' but also the very idea of truth itself. If facts are 'fabricated' (or 'made up') then what becomes of 'correspondence'? Certainly we could no longer distinguish kinds of descriptions—fictional and factual—merely in terms of whether they 'make up' a world or correspond to a 'given' world. Nor could fictional descriptions be judged as false merely in virtue of failing to mirror this objective 'given' world.

Again what is needed is a clear account of different conceptions of fiction, in the description sense. The descriptive fictions relevant to the literary critic can and should be defined in metaphysically neutral terms, without reference to notions like correspondence, facts, truth, or the world. Nothing of much importance, as far as literary criticism is concerned, hangs on defending, for example, a correspondence conception of truth. Whatever (reputable) theory of truth is maintained it is not going to make any significant difference to the distinctions that matter: between fictive and other kinds of story-telling, between the kinds of 'correspondence' or referential relations that pertain in works of fiction, and between the kinds of value judgements that bear on literary fictions.

Only by exploring the basic conventions (the constitutive rules) of story-telling can we come to understand fictionality in the sense relevant to works of literature. It is not semantic—referential or truth-based—properties that identify literary fictions nor any metaphysically conceived 'relations with the world'. Fictive story-telling is distinct from the stories told by historians or scientists but the distinction is rooted in human practices whose institution-ally based rules give them their salient features.

A fundamental mistake in discussions of fiction in the description sense is to misinterpret the prevalence of narration, or story-telling, in intellectual enquiry. Narration is undoubtedly widespread

and there are interesting questions both about the formal modes
of narration and, more generally, why the temporal presentation
of information should be predominant. But story-telling is not the
same as fiction. In discussions of literary fictions the interesting
issue rests not with the mere presence of the narrative form but
with the distinctive uses to which it is put and the conventions by
which it is governed.

Theoretical allegiances

In a debate as longstanding as that concerning literature and truth
there is a danger of positions becoming stereotyped and unwarranted assimilations being imposed. In terms of traditional alle-
giances our own stance in defence of a humanistic conception of
literature, though without appeal to 'literary truth', is anomalous.
The rejection of literary truth might point towards aestheticism or
structuralism or might indicate a broader, perhaps pragmatist,
attitude to truth itself, while the humanistic view of literature would
normally be associated with a conception of literature as knowledge and perhaps a romantic blurring of the imaginative and the
cognitive. We hope to resist these false associations, albeit at the
cost of alienating those with whom in many respects we are in
sympathy.

When we reject literary truth we do not reject literary value,
even of a cognitive kind, properly understood. The age-old charge
against works of literature (or poetry), drawing on the negative
connotations of 'fiction', is that they are tainted with falsehood
and deceit. The age-old reply appeals to the positive connotations
of imagination and creative thought. In the case of romantic
'defences of poetry' the imagination is elevated to the pinnacle of
cognitive endeavour, becoming the supreme source of knowledge,
and the value of poetry proclaimed to lie in the 'imaginative truths'
it can impart. Our simple argument—in part a response to this
debate—is that inasmuch as literature needs 'defending' for its
fictionality it is pointless to try and do so in terms of truth; the
hopelessness, and counter-productiveness, of this move is soon
evident in the inevitable fudging of the idea of truth. 'Imaginative'
or 'literary' truth always turns out to be something less than truth
itself and the case falters from then on. It is much more rewarding
to try and explain the interest and value of works of literary fiction

without looking over one's shoulder at science or philosophy. Literary works can contribute to the development and understanding of the deepest, most revered of a culture's conceptions without advancing propositions, statements or hypotheses about them.

There is no commitment whatsoever in the rejection of literary truth to an arid aestheticism or to 'cutting literature off from the world' (a notion virtually incomprehensible). It merely takes seriously the idea of the special nature of literary value, as not reducible to the values of history, philosophy, or science. The intended contrast is with prevailing attitudes in structuralism or post-structuralism which tend to be reductionist: literary works are *no more than* instances of language, discourse, rhetoric, the 'play of signifiers', and so on.

It is the special, non-reductive, nature of literary value which is at the core of the humanistic conception of literature. That conception is only weakened by appeal to the supposed truth-telling capacities of literature, which suggests that *au fond* literature is not all that different from, say, philosophy. At its simplest, what needs to be explained is why so many (perhaps all) of the major cultures have developed a tradition of imaginative writing, or oral narrative, which is more or less overtly *fictional*. What special value is attributed to these works, which frequently coexist with traditions of more or less overtly *non-fictional* writing or narrative? No doubt the boundaries are not always sharp, no doubt there are complex sociological and psychological explanations of particular cases. But it will not do to suppose a priori that there must be some univocal notion of truth binding together these different endeavours. There is at least a *prima facie* case for supposing that there is some distinctive—even if in a broad sense 'cognitive'—function for creations of the fanciful imagination.

A reaction among literary theorists (and philosophers) has already set in against post-structuralism, with its sceptical, anti-humanist, reductionist attacks on literature. The humanistic conception of literature and literary value is being revived and redefined, as evidenced, for example, by the recent work of Graff, Nuttall, Nussbaum, Novitz, Falck, Ellis, and others.[29] But

---

[29] See Gerald Graff, *Literature Against Itself: Literary Ideas in Modern Society* (Chicago, 1979); A. D. Nuttall, *A New Mimesis: Shakespeare and the Representation of Reality* (Oxford, 1983); Martha Craven Nussbaum, *The Fragility of Goodness:*

unfortunately this revival is often developed through a renewed association of literature and truth (or at least knowledge), i.e. at precisely the point where the humanistic conception is at its weakest. This is most evident in Nussbaum, Novitz, and Falck; the latter, for example, is uncompromising: '[l]iterature ... gives us our purest and most essential way of grasping reality or truth', 'the connection between art [including poetry and literature] and ontological truth [is] a necessary and definitional one'.[30] Plainly not all pro-humanistic defences of literature are equivalent and they should not be run together.

Nor are all attacks on post-structuralism equivalent. Certain critics seem to be against any form of theorizing about literature or fundamental principles of criticism.[31] Rejection of theory is sometimes prompted by no more than a vague intuition of critical pluralism, but it is often also a reaction to specific arguments by literary theorists. Our own position is not antagonist to theorizing as such about literature, which after all is what this book engages in. But we will not offer detailed arguments against post-structuralist theory; our central contention is not that post-structuralism is *wrong* but that for the most part it is beside the point. Sceptical worries about the nature of reality or the mind or language certainly have their place in philosophical debate but the connection with literature is often remote. A clearer conception of such core notions as fiction, reference, and literary value will enable us to bypass many of the arguments of the post-structuralists.

The fictional dimension and the literary dimension

Up to now we have characterized our subject-matter in general terms as 'literary fiction' and have made no special effort to discriminate 'work of literature' and 'work of fiction'. However, as we move on to closer analyses in the chapters to come the distinction

---

Luck and Ethics in Greek Tragedy and Philosophy (Cambridge, 1986); Novitz, *Knowledge, Fiction and Imagination*; Colin Falck, *Myth, Truth and Literature* (Cambridge, 1989); John Ellis, *Against Deconstruction* (Princeton, NJ, 1990).

[30] Falck, *Myth, Truth and Literature*, p. xii and 74.

[31] F. R. Leavis often gave the impression he was against theorizing, a stance still reflected among his followers, though his own work seems to imply otherwise: see F. R. Leavis, *The Critic as Anti-Philosopher: Essays and Papers*, ed. G. Singh (London, 1982). See also W. J. T. Mitchell (ed.), *Against Theory* (Chicago, 1985).

between literature and fiction, or between the literary dimension and the fictional dimension of particular works, will assume increasing importance. The *concepts* of literature and fiction are logically distinct, not least because the former, unlike the latter, is essentially evaluative. Certainly it is possible, as we will show, to give an independent analysis of the two concepts. To explain what makes a work fictional is not the same as to explain what makes it literary. The interesting issue is how fictionality can be used in the creation of works of literature.

On the question of truth we find a curiously paradoxical situation. On the face of it, it might seem natural to suppose that fiction is inimical to truth, given its associations of unreality and falsity, while literature, with its humanistic associations of cognitive value, seems positively congenial to truth. Indeed, the root of the problem we are addressing is precisely how works of literature, so revered in a culture, can at the same time be mere *fictions*. But our own enquiry will produce a surprising reversal of these commonplace assumptions. For it will turn out that the fictional dimension, fiction *per se*, is perfectly hospitable to truth while the literary dimension—that which gives a work the status of literature—is resistant to evaluation in terms of truth.

The shift of paradigm we mentioned at the beginning applies both to the literary and fictional dimensions. Truth, understood on the Aristotelian model, is not part of the definition of either fiction or literature. In both cases the key relations are not semantic—between word and object—but, put simply, hold between people, for example between story-tellers and readers operating under the conventions of social practices. What vestiges remain of the semantic are explained via the crucially important notion of *aboutness*. Both the fictional and the literary dimensions exhibit aboutness, and in the two senses familiar to philosophers: the referential or quasi-referential sense and the sense introduced by Brentano, involving a species of content or 'intentionality'. We will explain in detail the way, or ways, in which works of fiction can be *about* something or other. But that does not exhaust the literary application. Works of fiction which are also works of literature give rise to a distinctive kind of aboutness. Literary aboutness is explained in terms of *themes* and *thematic content*. Not only are these notions (partially) constitutive of the literary dimension but they provide the theoretical grounding for a revised, and genuinely substantive, conception of literary mimesis or mimesis conceived as a literary value.

These, however, are several steps along the argument. We must begin with a characterization of the fictional dimension of literary fictions.

PART 1

Fiction and Truth

2

The Practice of Story-Telling

Preliminary identification of fiction

What distinguishes a work of fiction from works of other kinds? The philosophical question is not about a particular genre, where 'fiction' simply means 'novel' or 'popular novel' in contrast to drama or poetry. It concerns a more fundamental conception of fiction encompassing diverse forms of spoken or written narratives: novels, short stories, dramas, dramatic or epic poems, fantasies, fables, parables, legends, and sagas.[1] The label 'fictional', where appropriate, is not a literary critical classification but a description of a feature or dimension common to different instances of these narrative forms. A reformulated question might be: what is the nature of this feature or dimension in virtue of which certain works, but not others, are characterized as fictional?

We are posing the question at this stage in terms of works rather than in terms of descriptions or objects because it is the fictionality of whole works (or, more modestly, 'stories') that we are ultimately trying to explain. We will of course need to determine what makes a description fictional or an object fictional, in the sense introduced in Chapter 1, but which of these has priority in an account of fictional works should not be presupposed in advance. In the context of a discussion of fiction the term 'work' bears no particular theoretical weight, though it will acquire more significance when applied to literature. In the literary context, a 'work' must be contrasted with a 'text', and neither literariness nor fictionality is a property of texts, so we will argue. Meanwhile all that is required of 'work' applied to fiction is that it satisfies minimal conditions for being a narrative or story. A story, thus a work in this sense, might consist of a single sentence.

We are taking as paradigmatic 'works of fiction' a large class

---

[1] Peter McCormick distinguishes 'work of fiction' for the narrow, genre, sense and 'fictional work' for the broader, descriptive, sense: see McCormick, *Fictions*, 51.

of familiar cases: these include Aesop's Fables, the Parable of the Vineyard, The Decameron, *The Tempest*, *Lord of the Rings*, *Dynasty*, 'The Owl and the Pussy-Cat', *Carry On, Jeeves, King Kong*, and so on, and so on. The list of works that are indisputably fictional is enormous and could be added to with little difficulty by those who have given the matter no theoretical consideration. It is worth bearing this in mind because theorists of the subject often begin to worry too early on about cases like *In Cold Blood, Dead Certainties*, Plato's Dialogues, *Richard III*, the Book of Genesis, and so on, which are—and in some cases are deliberately meant to be—problematic. On the whole if you get it right about the first list the second list will look after itself (albeit requiring that different things be said about different items on the second list).

The fact that works of fiction, of the paradigmatic kind, are so easily recognized should not detract from the importance of making a distinction between fiction and non-fiction. Those who fail to draw the distinction in particular cases—the gullible listeners of Orson Welles's adaptation of *The War of the Worlds* or the more apocryphal backwoodsman who leapt on to the stage to 'save' Desdemona—are often figures of fun; but that is only because the distinction is so familiar and secure. The truth is that the classification of narrative into fiction and non-fiction is of the utmost significance; not only is it a precondition for making sense of a work but it determines how we should respond both in thought and action.

We can eliminate fairly swiftly some potential candidates for the constitutive feature (or features) of fictionality. For example, it is not a particular kind of language, as that would normally be understood. There is no 'language of fiction' as such. Not only can writers of fiction employ a host of different literary modes, they can also mimic other discursive forms, such as history, biography, letter-writing, psychologist's report, or whatever. And they can utilize all the stylistic and syntactic constructions available to the writer of non-fiction. The search for necessary and sufficient conditions among stylistic or formal features of language is doomed from the start, if only because of the sheer ingenuity of fiction-makers.

Perhaps literary critics and linguists will view this rejection of a 'language of fiction' as too hasty; after all, complex studies are made of the devices, modes, and rhetoric of fiction and it might seem presumptuous to rule out a priori the essentiality of this subject-matter.[2] But the point is not especially controversial given the kind of question we are asking about fiction. There are of course conventional characteristics of fictional writing, in all the narrative genres listed, and these are important both for classificatory purposes and more generally as guides in the recognition of fiction. But even an exhaustive description of the linguistic characteristics of all extant works of fiction would not necessarily determine the logical feature which explains fictionality *per se*.

Nor will subject-matter determine the logical distinction between fiction and non-fiction. Again, there are conventional characteristics: mathematical treatises, reports on town sewage systems, and car-maintenance manuals signal their non-fictionality through their subject-matter (at least partly). And no doubt a narrative that begins 'As Gregor Samsa awoke one morning from uneasy dreams he found himself transformed into a gigantic insect' carries the presumption of fictionality (i.e. invites a fictional reading). But there is nothing here on which to build a definition of the fictional. The presumptions can be overturned; sentences of the Gregor Samsa kind could have a non-fictional status, fulfilling different purposes, and there is no limit in principle on what a work of fiction might be about.

More interestingly, neither truth-value nor reference determine fictionality, at least in the literary application. Obviously this takes us to a central concern of the book and will need careful examination. But it seems clear enough to begin with that false sentences alone do not make a work fictional, nor do non-referring names. This is clear anyway for literary senses of 'fiction' even though there is a simpler sense where 'fiction' just means 'false'. Falsity and reference failure cannot be sufficient conditions for fictionality in the sense we are seeking. More problematic is whether they are necessary. Characteristically, descriptions in works of fiction do not depict actual states of affairs; and names of fictional objects—Superman, the Time Machine—do not denote real things. But once again it is not easy to extract defining conditions. After all, in the case of historical fiction all the names might bear their standard denotation and in the case of some simple fictions ('Once

---

[2] Cf. Wayne C. Booth, *The Rhetoric of Fiction* (Chicago, 1961); David Lodge, *The Modes of Modern Writing* (London, 1977); Michael Riffaterre, *Fictional Truth* (Baltimore, 1990).

upon a time, there was a young man who . . .') it might just be that all the descriptions turn out to be true.

The practice of fiction

In the next three chapters we will give a systematic account of truth and reference in the context of works of fiction. The relevant conception of fictionality will develop in the course of that discussion. Before then, though, it would be helpful to give a preliminary sketch of the conception in question, one which does not give prominence to these semantic notions. The controlling idea is this: *that the fictive dimension of stories (or narratives) is explicable only in terms of a rule-governed practice, central to which are a certain mode of utterance (fictive utterance) and a certain complex of attitudes (the fictive stance).* The task of the theorist is to identify the rules of the practice, specifically the contextual conditions governing fictive story-telling, the communicative, or other, purposes fulfilled, the appropriate range of attitudes and responses, the ways in which the practice intersects with other practices, and the many implications of the practice concerning, for example, reference and truth. The central focus is not on the structural or semantic properties of sentences but on the conditions under which they are uttered, the attitudes they invoke, and the role that they play in social interactions. Only these conditions are relevant to the status of the sentences as fictional. In fact the terms 'fictional sentence' and 'fictional name' should be used only derivatively, relative to the prior notion of a 'fictive utterance'. A work of fiction, in the philosophical sense, instantiates not a particular kind of language but a particular kind of utterance.[3] The explanatory work for defining the fictional dimension of stories appeals more to actions and attitudes than to words and things.

The perspective here is by no means new—most of the elements have been discussed and developed before[4]—but the position needs

[3] The term 'utterance' is familiar currency in philosophy of language, going back at least as far as H. P. Grice's early work. In our usage it is primarily shorthand for the production of spoken sounds or written symbols but as Grice used it it can stand for any token which can be assigned non-natural (or conventional) meaning, including gestures, movements, the deliberate alignment of objects, and so forth.

[4] Particularly influential in recent years has been the work of John R. Searle, Nicholas Wolterstorff, Kendall Walton, and Gregory Currie (see Bibliography);

to be consolidated and its truly radical implications for reference and truth, implications which undermine a whole strand of modern thinking about fiction, need to be properly assimilated. Defining fiction in terms of a *mode of utterance* located in a *social practice* involves rejecting certain persistent misconceptions about fiction: for example, the association of fiction with 'reference-failure', or the 'intransitivity of writing',[5] or the suggestion that fiction is 'cut off' from the world, or lacks 'correspondence' with the facts. The perspective also undermines the more refined post-structuralist theory that fictional discourse is somehow paradigmatic of all discourse, that the deliberate flouting of the link between language and reality, which is supposedly definitive of fiction, shows that that link itself is unstable or untenable.

Let us consider the perspective in more detail. Fictive utterance is made possible by the existence of a practice of story-telling. The basic idea of a social or cultural practice is just that of a regulated activity. Practices can vary enormously in complexity and theoretical interest. Shaking hands is a practice, as is wearing a tie, clapping at the end of a concert, drinking in pubs, playing hide-and-seek, or telling jokes. At the more weighty end, democratic government, international share dealing, High Mass, even art itself, are practices.[6] All games are practices and the analogy with games is often invoked with regard to story-telling.[7] But the games analogy in connection with fiction, however illuminating from a theoretical point of view, continues to be misconstrued as meaning 'non-serious', particularly by those not familiar with the Wittgensteinian idiom, and should probably be used sparingly in discussions of literary fiction. The notion of a practice does not need the games analogy.

The practice of fictive story-telling at the most fundamental level (making up, telling, appreciating, talking about stories) is relatively simple; it is mastered at an early age and is based largely on innate dispositions (imagination, make-believe, play, narrative structuring, and so forth). Learning the practice is learning to utilize these

our own position does not coincide completely with any of these, as will emerge in the discussion to come.

[5] As in Roland Barthes' essay 'Writing: An Intransitive Verb', in *Image-Music-Text*.

[6] On art as a practice, see Noël Carroll, 'Art, Practice and Narrative', *The Monist*, 71 (1988), 140–56.

[7] Kendall Walton's work is the most prominent example.

dispositions for specific communicative ends. Narrative skills can, of course, become highly complex both in mastery and apprecia- tion, particularly as fiction develops into art or literature. But the basic skills of making up stories, telling, repeating, and talking about stories, recognizing them as such, taking up attitudes to them, and responding in appropriate ways, all of which constitute the practice, are more like those of simple customs than of complex institutions.

Why speak of a practice of fictive story-telling? Does that not make the whole thing much more complicated than in fact it is? There are several reasons for invoking the idea of a practice. First of all, it serves to emphasize that fiction is grounded in *activities* of a certain kind not, for example, in *relations* of a certain kind (e.g. between language and the world). Second, it requires that this grounding is *social* (rather than, say, exclusively psychological), at least in the sense that works of fiction only become such given their role in social contexts. Fictive utterance is ultimately a kind of communication, involving an interaction between speaker (writer) and audience (reader). It is of course possible to make up a (fictional) story without *telling* it, but this possibility itself pre- supposes the social practice of story-telling which determines how such a story is to be *taken*, how it relates to other forms of reflec- tive thought or discourse, what intentions and purposes underlie it, and so on. Closely related to this, thirdly, the idea of a practice serves to distinguish fictive utterance (and thus fiction *per se*) from what might be called purely 'natural', or non-conventional, activities, such as imagining, day-dreaming, or make-believe. There is more to fiction than merely imagining, etc., that such-and-such is the case. Fiction—in the sense relevant to literary fiction—cannot be reduced without remainder to an individual's psychological states. Finally, the idea of a practice has normative implications; there are right and wrong ways of engaging in a practice and these can usually be formulated into rules (both constitutive and regu- lative, in John Searle's sense).[8] There are constraints on what can count as making up a story (or even an object or character within a story), and there are right and wrong ways of 'taking' fictional stories.

---

[8] On the distinction between constitutive and regulative rules in social practices, see John R. Searle, *Speech Acts: An Essay in the Philosophy of Language* (Cambridge, 1969), ch. 2.

Social practice vs. natural activity

Before we get down to the details of explaining just what fictive utterance and the 'fictive stance' are it is worth pausing to consider an objection to our grounding of fiction in social practices. As the idea of a practice (or later an 'institution') is going to run right through our account, including what we say about works of literature, it would be useful to confront early on a certain kind of resistance to the project. In fact we will be returning to it again in Chapter 9.

One form of resistance comes from the thought that because fiction involves *making* (in the mind?), the basic explanatory framework must involve psychological facts not social facts. The objection might be developed by saying that making up and telling stories, far from residing in a rule-governed practice, are in fact among the most fundamental and 'natural' human activities. Fiction should be explained, so the argument goes, not by appeal to conventions and social transactions but simply in terms of (perhaps even as an instance of) basic psychological acts such as narrating and imagining. C. G. Prado offers one version of this objection:

Production of fiction is traditionally seen as a special use of language, a use which violates the intrinsic referentiality of language.... Works of fiction are taken as products of a deliberate and specific activity, and appreciating fiction is likewise a special activity. Against this I am trying to realign things to show fiction as only an extreme case of a pervasive activity. According to the traditional view fiction is not possible except against a rich conceptual background; in my view it is only the largely honorific category of literature that requires such a background. The traditional view requires complexly motivated authors who set out to produce works having aesthetic worth and cognitive and emotive depth.... The special case is taken as the paradigm, and production of fiction is construed as a special, learned activity. The contrast is with refined natural activities. For instance, we all eat and speak, but gourmets and orators eat and talk in highly refined ways. Their training only enhances something; it does not teach anything new.[9]

It should be noted that there are several points in this characterization of the 'traditional view' which do not conform to our own

---

[9] C. G. Prado, *Making Believe: Philosophical Reflections on Fiction* (Westport, Conn., 1984), 131–2.

view: first, that what makes fiction 'special' is its violation of 'the intrinsic referentiality of language'; second, that fiction presupposes 'a rich conceptual background', as distinct from a background of a social practice; third, that story-tellers *ipso facto* 'set out to produce works having aesthetic worth', etc. However, we do hold that there is a special fictive use of language, constituted by a practice which has to be learned, albeit without much difficulty. So our view, if only by implication, is targeted in this passage.

Underlying the objection are two ideas: first, that literary fiction is just a simple extension of narration, and second, that narration is a fundamental and natural (unlearned?) mode of cognition. Essentially the same objection could be made on behalf of 'natural' activities other than narration which are also associated with fiction. Imagination would be an obvious candidate but others might qualify as well, such as imitating (the basis of Aristotle's account of *poesis*), or day-dreaming (Freud's model for creative writing).

It is no part of our reply to this class of objection that narrating or imagining, or whatever, are not in some sense 'natural' dispositions, even though the contrast between 'natural' and conventional is not particularly helpful in this context (there is nothing *un*natural about the practice of telling stories). Nor do we deny that these dispositions (and skills) will need to be incorporated into a full explanation of fictive story-telling. Nor indeed do we seek to play down the role of psychological states in an account of fiction (intentions, beliefs, attitudes, and so forth, are essential to an adequate account). But we do seek to explain what *more* is needed to move from the natural disposition to narrate or imagine to the conscious construction and appraisal of fictive stories. This is a crucial problem for precisely those theories that attribute a central cognitive function to narration or the imagination. If, as is so often claimed, narrative form is somehow integral to the structuring of experience, to making sense of the world, to the acquisition of knowledge, then some explanation is needed for those narratives that seem to have no such purpose, that are produced merely to amuse or divert. It is not enough simply to postulate 'natural' transitions: 'What begins as part of coping with experience, and is naturally extended in play, is first noticed, then exercised as an effort to determine events, and finally exercised for its own sake.'[10]

[10] Ibid. 134.

Any attempt to explain how fictive stories are told and enjoyed in a community, without deceit, without mistaken inference, and without inappropriate response, seems inevitably to require reference to co-operative, mutually recognized, conventions. Indeed Prado, whose version of the objection we have quoted, comes close to implying this. Fiction, he writes,

is just more of the same, more 'world-making' done for its own sake and *reinforced by the collaboration* of others. The difference is that *we know enough* not to attempt to act on the basis of these presentations or narratives, but knowing that does not preclude our enjoyment.[11]

The idea of *collaboration* is indispensable and calls for more explanation: 'the move from useful narratives to full-fledged stories is a function of collaboration'.[12] The best way of explaining the required collaboration, we suggest, is through the notion of an established practice with its underlying procedural rules.

The so-called 'traditional view' of fiction as a special use of language was charged with taking as its paradigm the complex conventions of literature. Our charge against 'naturalistic' accounts of story-telling grounded only on inner states is that they take the *soliloquy* as the paradigm, the narrative of the lone individual structuring experience. There is surely a more satisfactory paradigm mid-way between the literary institution and the private soliloquy, one which identifies fiction as a communicative act, an exchange between participants, governed by minimal conditions of intention and response. From that simple starting-point we can look forward to an account of more complex literary fictions and back to the special case of the solitary individual making up narratives in the pursuit of knowledge.

It might be that in the end there is not much difference between speaking of fiction as a practice and describing it as a 'refined natural activity'. After all neither account purports to explain the psychological or social origins of the practice. Certainly our own investigation is philosophical not scientific. It concerns, as it were, the logical space within which to locate fictions. But the ideas of a practice, of acts and intentions, of conventional or rule-governed activities, are well established in other areas of philosophy and their invocation in this context usefully connects with applications elsewhere.

---

[11] Ibid. 131. Italics added.   [12] Ibid. 127.

In trying to characterize the practice of fiction (i.e story-telling of a fictive kind) our enquiry is synchronic not diachronic. We are concerned to describe the practice as it now exists, in paradigmatic forms; we do not seek to recount the history of the practice. Practices, we acknowledge, are rarely static but change and evolve. In the case of fictive utterance there are no doubt significant variations across cultures and within the history of our own culture. In a systematic study of the development of the concept of fiction it would probably be useful to distinguish sub-practices within the general category of fictional story-telling, incorporating, for example, the many supplementary purposes of fiction: instruction, entertainment, propaganda, religious ceremony, or whatever. There are also numerous generic forms of fictive utterance which in turn are subject to historical evolution: drama, poetry, epic, saga, folk-tale, the novel, and the rest.

Even the line between fiction and non-fiction is subject to historical fluctuation. It would be a mistake to suppose that the concept of fiction or fictive utterance is so precise that the boundaries are always determinate. That is why we have resolved to begin with current undisputed cases. The history of fiction is replete with troublesome borderline cases—saints' lives, chronicles, sagas, (early) histories of the world—which involve some but not all elements of the current paradigm. It is common to find in such cases deliberate imaginative embellishment, of a kind we now associate with fiction, though without the attitudes of make-believe characteristic of a more recognizable practice of fiction. The period that produced saints' lives and sagas is transitional in the development of our current concept, though probably these special genres are more useful in shedding light on the history of *literature* or *literary* fiction than on the practice of fiction itself.

We call fiction a social practice not because it is an esoteric form found in some cultures not others, indeed it seems likely that all known cultures have used forms of make-believe story-telling for various ends, just as they have developed more or less structured games. However, it does not follow, for example, just in virtue of having a language, or being able to conceptualize, or use the imagination, that humans inevitably make up fictions, that they cannot but tell and respond to stories in forms we now take for granted. It is at least conceivable that a society should lack the practice of fictive story-telling but in other ways be recognizably human. We might even conceive of a society, by way of a thought-experiment, that possessed a language to a large extent similar to ours, and even created narratives very like those we label 'novels', 'dramas', 'folk-tales', yet still lacked the practice (our paradigmatic practice) of fictive utterance. We could suppose that members of the society used the narratives for very different social purposes, perhaps seeing them as historical reports of distant worlds, perhaps as divine revelations, perhaps as pernicious lies. In such circumstances we would not say that in this society the narratives are 'works of fiction' in the sense we are trying to capture.

The idea of a practice based on conventions of utterance and response provides an appropriate framework for distinguishing different kinds of story-telling or narrative. Narrative form is common to different discursive ends, including history, science, philosophy, and telling lies. But not all narrative is fictional, i.e. not all narrative conforms to the conventions of fictive utterance. Even if the subject-matter or narrative structures of fictive utterances were to overlap with those of other discourses that need not in itself blur the distinction between fiction and non-fiction; that distinction can be retained assuming that a sufficiently precise account can be given of the different narrative practices.

Another advantage of the appeal to a practice is that it directs attention away from the search for a 'semantics of story-telling'. Admittedly most work on the semantics or logic of fiction concerns not fictive utterance (the telling of stories) itself but reports about stories or their content, where questions of truth and reference do have a place.[13] But there is a residual temptation amongst theorists of fiction to seek semantic characterizations of sentences in fictive utterances. Apart from the most obvious conditions of falsity or reference-failure, one common and more subtle thought is that such sentences are implicitly prefixed by a logical operator which determines how the sentences are to be construed. Thus Samuel R. Levin, for example, speaking of poetry (he has in mind the fictive aspects of poetry), argues that 'implicit in every poem is a higher sentence which is subsequently deleted . . . "I imagine myself in and invite you to conceive a world in which" '.[14] Similarly

---

[13] See John Woods, *The Logic of Fiction: A Philosophical Sounding of Deviant Logic* (The Hague, 1974), David Lewis, 'Truth in Fiction', *American Philosophical Quarterly*, 15 (1978), 37–46, and Richard Routley, 'Some Things Do Not Exist', *Notre Dame Journal of Formal Logic*, 7 (1966), 251–76.

[14] S. R. Levin, 'Concerning What Kind of Speech Act a Poem Is', in Teun A. van Dijk (ed.), *Pragmatics of Language and Literature* (The Hague, 1976), 149.

Casteñada: 'all the sentences in a typical novel are . . . in the scope of an operator of the form 'In . . . (by . . .).'[15] More recently, Gregory Currie has proposed what he calls the 'standard logical form of a fictional story', i.e. a general characterization of the content of fictive utterances, which includes the postulation of a narrator telling the story.[16] Although the underlying motivation for such accounts might be sound, the location of these features in the content or structure of sentences is misplaced. It is more helpful to locate them within the conventions of the practice, as conditions, for example, governing appropriate response rather than as logical properties of the sentences uttered.

The decisive first step towards an understanding of the nature and values of fiction involves a shift away from talk of reference-failure or truth-values. By taking the act of story-telling and the attitudes appropriate to it as our starting-point we can go on to explain references, even truth, as they arise within the story-telling context. We also then have a framework for explaining and pre-serving the distinctions that matter: between fiction and non-fiction, the imaginary and the real, literature and history, and so on. And finally, not least, we will have the necessary detail to illustrate the different ends and achievements of the 'natural' activities of nar-rating and imagining.

Telling and making

The idea of 'fictive utterance', as we will use it, applies indiffer-ently to those utterances used in the creation of stories and those used merely to retell or repeat stories created elsewhere.[17] The term, however, does not apply to those utterances used to *report* the content of a story, as when a reader remarks that 'Othello mis-trusted Cassio' or '*Othello* is about jealousy'. Fictive utterance is a mode of speaking (writing), conforming to certain conditions, but it does not necessarily involve making. The distinction between

---

[15] Hector-Neri Castañeda, 'Fiction and Reality: Their Fundamental Connections', *Poetics*, 8 (1979), 44.

[16] Gregory Currie, 'Fictional Names', *Australasian Journal of Philosophy*, 66 (1988), 475.

[17] Gregory Currie restricts 'fictive utterance' to those utterances 'productive of fictional works': see *The Nature of Fiction* (Cambridge, 1990), 42.

telling and making is important even though the two, as might be expected in the fiction case, are closely related.

Perhaps the most fundamental point in an understanding of the fictional dimension is this: to say that a story (or an incident, event, character) is made or 'made up' is to say something about its *origin* not something about its *relation with the world*. By 'origin' is meant cause, or at least salient cause; a cause will no doubt be the product of earlier causes but it is not causal chains so much as determining causes which are at issue. The origin of a made-up story resides in a human act of some kind. Although the act must be intentional, it is not otherwise of necessity a mental act. It is common to suppose that the creation of fiction stems from an act of the imagination on the part of the author and no doubt as a matter of fact that will nearly always be the case. But logically speaking stories could be made up without the use of the imagination. It is not necessary, even if it is normally the case, for a story-teller to imagine the contents of a story while, or prior to, making it up. The crucial act is linguistic not psychological.

What linguistic act? The answer is: an act of description. Fiction, in the literary sense, involves the making of descriptions; by descriptions are meant predicates and as there cannot be predication without propositions, fiction-making is primarily propositional. The trouble is language-users other than fiction-makers also make, or make up, propositions: journalists, historians, biographers, philosophers, not to speak of liars. What sets the fictive story-teller apart are the conditions governing the way the descriptions are presented, the purposes they seek to fulfil, the responses they elicit, and so on; in other words the practice within which they play their part. So we are back to fictive utterance. Making up a fictive description involves making an utterance of the requisite kind. Notice, however, that although fictive utterance is necessary for fiction-making, it is not sufficient. Only fictive utterance which initiates, or is the origin of, descriptions of the appropriate kind can constitute 'making up a story'; fictive utterance which merely repeats or retells such descriptions can count as fictive story-telling but not as story-making.

In Chapter 1 we introduced a distinction between mode of utterance and content, suggesting that fictional content could be presented in a non-fictional mode just as non-fictional content might be presented in a fictional mode. What makes (propositional) content fictional or otherwise? Again, the answer must be something about its origin (not its truth-value). If the content, i.e. the predicative content, originated in a fictive act then the content itself can be counted fictional; if not, then not. Clearly a great deal more needs to be said about fictive content and we will return to it briefly at the end of this chapter and again in subsequent chapters. It will be valuable, though, to anticipate two points here and now.

The first concerns identity (or sameness) of content. If a story-teller is retelling a story then it would be reasonable to suppose that certain variations are possible in the telling while preserving basic content-identity. Normally identity of content would be taken to reside, broadly speaking, in identity of meaning (including reference). To establish identity of fictional content, however, something over and above meaning-identity is required: namely, connectedness to some original act of story-telling. In other words to establish that a story is a version of this fiction rather than that its content must be traceable to some original fictive utterance (if not to a specific story-teller at least to a determinate 'tradition'). We do speak loosely of the 'same story' cropping up in culturally isolated contexts but it would be misleading to suppose that fictional characters and incidents could be identified independently of specific descriptive acts which 'create' them. It is in this sense that fictive content must be causally grounded in acts of story-telling as well as determined by meaning.

The second point about content concerns the idea of 'making up a fictional object'. Normally whether content is fictional or not is determined by what it is *about*. Does it, or does it not, describe made-up objects, events, places, people, and so forth? If that question is relevant, as it seems to be, does it not reintroduce the idea of 'relations with the world' in characterizing fictive content and therefore fiction itself? Again, we will have more to say later about what fictional objects (or fictional characters) are. But in the present context of distinguishing making and telling, the crucial point is simply this: that 'making up a fictional object' cannot be explained independently of 'making up a fictional description'. To speak of a fictional object (or character) is just a way of speaking of a certain kind of descriptive content; it does not involve reference to what does or does not exist in the world. A fictional object (or character) is an intensional object originating in a fictional description, such that the characteristics of the object are determined by the way it is described. What is important is origin not reference.

So the order of explanation to unravel the complexities of fictive stories and their content is this: fictional content is explained in terms of fictional objects (events, places, etc.) which themselves are explained in terms of fictional descriptions. Fictional descriptions are explained in terms of fictive utterances. These latter can either be original or repeats; repeated (or borrowed) fictive utterances are those, in the requisite mode of presentation, whose content is traceable, both through meaning-relations and causal connectedness, to an original act of fictive utterance. It is, then, these original acts, rooted in a practice of story-telling, that are the bedrock of explanation.

Fictive utterance and the fictive stance

How are we to characterize the fictive mode of utterance? Certain features have already emerged. One is that fictive utterance is an *act* of a certain kind—at its simplest that of uttering sentences—carried out for a *purpose*, under the conventions of a *practice*. Fundamentally, the purpose is to invoke the conventions of the practice, thereby inviting an appropriate response to the sentences uttered. In turn the appropriate response involves recognizing that the conventions of the practice are in operation and conforming to them. Although the substantive detail is yet to be worked out, concerning what the relevant conventions are, we already have the basic structure of a theory of (literary) fiction.

The fictive story-teller, making up a story, makes and presents sentences (or propositions, i.e. sentence-meanings) for a particular kind of attention. The aim, as a first approximation, is this:

for the audience to make-believe (imagine or pretend) that the standard speech act commitments associated with the sentences are operative even while knowing that they are not.

Attending to sentences in this way is to adopt the *fictive stance* towards them.[18] One consequence of adopting the fictive stance is

[18] The term 'fictive stance' comes from Nicholas Wolterstorff, *Works and Worlds of Art* (Oxford, 1980), 231–4. However, his definition 'the fictive stance consists of

that many (though probably not all)[19] inferences are blocked from a fictive utterance back to the speaker or writer, notably inferences about the speaker's or writer's beliefs. This disengagement from normal conversational commitments highlights the idea of 'cognitive distance' associated with fiction. The idea that fiction is 'distinct from fact' or that there is a 'gap' between fiction and reality can best be explained in terms of the cognitive distance, under the fictive stance, between what is said and what can be inferred. The reference to 'speech act commitments' is to acknowledge the fact that fictive utterances need not only be in the indicative mood; they might also involve, for example, interrogatives and imperatives. Thus with indicatives an audience is invited to make-believe that a narrator is asserting something, with interrogatives that a narrator is asking something, and so forth.[20]

It is one thing for a story-teller to intend that an audience adopt the fictive stance. But how could such an intention be realized? Story-tellers, of course, can be misunderstood; but that is not the point. In a community of speakers which lacks the practice of fictive story-telling it is hard to see how the intention could expect to be fulfilled. Perhaps we are locked hopelessly in an explanatory circle: fictive utterance presupposes the practice of story-telling but that practice is explained in terms of fictive utterance and response. The problem here is real though it is almost certainly an instance of a wider problem afflicting all theories of meaning: basically the problem of how, in principle, linguistic meaning could

presenting, of offering for consideration, certain states of affairs—for us to reflect on, to ponder over, to explore the implications of, to conduct strandwise extrapolation on' (233) is not sufficient to mark off fiction from other discursive functions.

[19] See e.g. Colin Lyas, 'The Relevance of the Author's Sincerity', in Peter Lamarque (ed.), Philosophy and Fiction: Essays in Literary Aesthetics (Aberdeen, 1983).

[20] Gregory Currie makes a similar point, though curiously offers his principal analysis of fiction in terms of an intention that an audience make-believe P. He claims that 'to make-believe P is the very same act (type) as to make-believe that someone is asserting P'. But that cannot be right, at least on a natural interpretation of make-believe, which parallels belief itself. To make-believe P is to imagine P as true, or to entertain the thought that P; nothing in that imagining or thinking requires the additional thought of a narrator. To entertain the thought that P is not equivalent to entertaining the thought that someone is asserting that P. Also it seems evident that when we make-believe to ourselves we do not need to make-believe that we (or anyone) are asserting anything. Gregory Currie, 'What is Fiction?', Journal of Aesthetics and Art Criticism, 43 (1985), 392, n. 8.

ever have arisen in the first place.[21] Two refinements of the intention go some way towards alleviating the problem.

The first is to make the intention a 'Gricean intention'.[22] According to H. P. Grice, a speaker's meaning-intention to bring about a required response (be it belief or action) to an utterance is rational not simply causal. It is rational in the sense that the speaker intends there to be a reason for the required response such that the utterance brings about that response for that reason. Applied to fiction, the primary reason for an audience to adopt the fictive stance would be recognition of the story-teller's intentions to speak (or write) fictively. Furthermore, to establish it as a genuine act of communication, avoiding the notorious counter-examples,[23] there must be a Mutual Belief[24] between the story-teller and audience that the story-teller intends the response to be achieved for that reason.

Although Grice introduced his theory of non-natural meaning as an account of one-off acts of communication, without presupposing the existence of conventions or practices, it does seem that the success of fictive utterance depends at least in part on the mutual knowledge of the participants that there is a practice of 'taking' utterances in the required way. A story-teller will rely on this knowledge, at least in part, to secure the audience's recognition of the original intention. Needless to say, there are all kinds of contextual features that can trigger this recognition: from children's cases of 'Once upon a time', tone of voice, occasion, etc., to more sophisticated cues in the utterances themselves.

So far, then, there are three main features of fictive utterance:

1. A Gricean intention that an audience make-believe (or imagine or pretend) that it is being told (or questioned or advised or

---

[21] See e.g. Jonathan Bennett, *Linguistic Behaviour* (Cambridge, 1976) and Stephen Schiffer, *Remnants of Meaning* (Cambridge, Mass., 1987).

[22] See H. P. Grice, 'Meaning', *Philosophical Review*, 66 (1957), 377–88, repr. in *Studies in the Ways of Words* (Cambridge, Mass., 1989), 213–24, and 'Utterer's Meaning and Intentions', *Philosophical Review*, 78 (1969), 147–77, repr. in *Studies in the Ways of Words*, 86–117. For a systematic application to fiction, see Currie, 'What is Fiction?', and *The Nature of Fiction*.

[23] See Stephen Schiffer, *Meaning* (Oxford, 1972).

[24] A and B have a Mutual Belief that p if and only if A believes that p, B believes that p, A believes that B believes that p, B believes that A believes that p, and so on.

warned) about particular people, objects, incidents, or events, regardless of whether there are (or are believed to be) such people, objects, incidents, or events;

2. The reliance, at least in part, of the successful fulfilment of the intention in (1) on mutual knowledge of the practice of story-telling;

3. A disengagement from certain standard speech act commitments, blocking inferences from a fictive utterance back to the speaker or writer, in particular inferences about beliefs.

What about the story-teller who makes up a story but has no intention of telling it to anyone else? To the extent that people can tell themselves stories (in a way that they cannot, for example, inform themselves of something) they can become their own audience, following their own instructions to make-believe. But it is also compatible with not intending to tell a story to anyone that a story-teller should intend that *were there to be an audience* that audience should make-believe, etc.[25] So it is no objection to the account that a story-teller should have no audience in mind.

In characterizing the fictive stance we have spoken indifferently of make-believe, imagination, and pretence. We shall have more to say about the appropriate psychological attitudes in the next two chapters. For the time being it should be emphasized that these are attitudes invited of an audience, not necessarily attitudes of the story-teller. A story-teller is, in J. L. Austin's terms, someone who does things with words, not necessarily with the mind.[26]

Props in games of make-believe

Kendall Walton, in *Mimesis as Make-Believe*, presents a theory of fiction which, on the face of it, seems radically opposed to the one on offer here.[27] For Walton fiction is not *essentially* connected with human action of any kind or with intention or making or communication. Rather 'to be fictional is ... to possess the function of

---

[25] This latter counterfactual condition is developed by Currie in *The Nature of Fiction*, 33–4.

[26] There can be story-telling in other media than words, of course—in pictures, dance, mime—but our own interest is with verbal fictions. The account could easily enough be extended to these other media.

[27] Walton, *Mimesis as Make-Believe*.

serving as a prop in games of make-believe'.[28] Walton's purpose is wider than ours, in addressing not merely the fictionality of literary fictions, but the fictionality of all kinds of representations (somewhat counterintuitively, the theory has the consequence that dolls, toys, mud pies, sculptures, and portraits turn out to be fictions). A prop in a game of make-believe is a generator of fictional truths but a fictional truth is not a special kind of truth, merely a fact about what is fictional. It is fictional that Jack climbed the beanstalk, that Toby is putting a pie in the oven, that, in *Las Meninas*, the Infanta Margarita is standing in front of the King and Queen. What makes a proposition fictional is that 'there is a prescription to the effect that it is to be imagined'.[29]

Walton's theory has revolutionized the way that philosophers think about fiction (and representation) and its profound insights should be welcomed by anyone working in this difficult area. In fact the differences between our own account and Walton's turn out to be somewhat less fundamental than at first appeared. We prefer to ground our theory in the idea of a *practice* rather than a *game*, partly because of the misleading connotations of the latter, partly because it seems to us a conceptual truth, at a literal level, that if participants in an activity do not believe they are playing a game then they are not playing a game. However, the idea that works of fiction prescribe imaginings (or make-believe) is an important point of overlap as is the insistence that fiction be defined independently of semantic notions like truth or reference.

Why, though, does Walton play down fiction-making and intention, both of which are at the heart of the account developed earlier? Here is what he says:

[t]he institution of fiction centers not on the activity of fiction makers but on objects—works of fiction or natural objects—and their role in appreciators' activities, objects whose function is to serve as props in games of make-believe. Fiction making is merely the activity of constructing such props.[30]

The key question, then, is: how does an object acquire the function of serving as a prop in a game? The implication of the theory is that an object need not be *made* as a prop by any human action (or intention); of course some objects—like pictures, mud pies,

[28] Ibid. 102.   [29] Ibid. 61.   [30] Ibid. 88.

written texts—*might* be made as props but that need not be so. This split between fiction and making is undesirable (given the etymology of 'fiction', if for no other reason) but also unnecessary in Walton's own terms. For *assigning an object a role* in a game of make-believe is as much a kind of making—and intentional action—as the construction of a prop in a more literal sense. Walton's examples of the 'naturally occurring story' (the cracks in the rock that by coincidence spell out 'Once upon a time there were three bears') and the 'natural objects' like clouds and constellations which we often treat as representations do not establish the case against making and intention.[31] It is not until someone deliberately does something with these natural phenomena, at least adopt an appropriate stance towards them, that they become fictions. They are *made* into fictions by this purposive attitude on a specific occasion. It is not enough for something to possess the function of serving as a prop in a game that there be 'a tradition or common practice or convention . . . of using it or things like it for that purpose'.[32] For all that establishes is that things of that kind are good candidates for being pressed into service as props, not that they already have that function regardless of how anyone views them at a specific time. Even to speak of a 'naturally occurring story' is misleading, for the cracks are not a *story* as such until they are appropriated to that end.

Gregory Currie, in pressing a similar objection against Walton, rightly insists on a distinction between something's *being fiction* and something's *being treated as fiction*.[33] Normally the latter is not sufficient for the former. Nevertheless, it does seem that in certain cases the distinction collapses. For there are circumstances in which the act of treating an object or text as a fiction can constitute the act of making the object or text into a fiction. The cracks in the rocks seem to be just such a case. They cannot count as a work of fiction, we have agreed, until they are utilized in a certain way; but that use, grounded in the intention that the fictive stance be adopted, just is the creation of a work of fiction.

The point can be generalized towards an important conclusion. A work of fiction must be the product of a specific intention (of the kind described). However, some objects or texts have been

---

[31] Ibid. 86–8.   [32] Ibid. 52.   [33] Currie, *The Nature of Fiction*, 36.

subject to more than one determining intention. Take Picasso's *Bull's Head*, which consists of a bicyle seat and handlebars in the configuration of a head with horns. The seat and handlebars were originally produced, by a bicycle manufacturer, with the intention that they perform specific functions on a bicycle. Picasso took the very same objects and presented them with different intentions, namely that they represent a bull's head. We would say of Picasso not merely that he treated the objects *as if* they were a representation but that he had *made* a representation out of them. So it is with certain works of fiction. Material initially produced with one set of intentions can be appropriated by the fiction-maker under a different set of intentions. In that way a new work can come into being, not just an old work treated in a new way.

Walton in this context raises the thorny question of ancient myths and legends. He is tempted by the familiar notion that these might be 'nonfiction for the Greeks but fiction for us', albeit acknowledging the modern tendency to respect, and seek out, original purposes.[34] Here is his explanation, in a footnote, how a myth, non-fiction in origin, might become fiction:

One might say either that the *original* myth, which is not fiction even by our lights, was replaced by a homologous story which is, or that there is but one enduring myth which was nonfiction for its originators and is fiction for us. In any case the original *tellings* of the story were supposedly straightforward truth claims, but contemporary tellings are fiction instead, i.e., they have the function of serving as props in games of make-believe.[35]

The only way to establish the point that the content *becomes* fiction, rather than being merely *treated as* fiction, is to insist not only that there are separate *tellings* (with separate intentions) but that there are in effect separate *works*: those works of fiction we tell each other and those supposed truth-claims told by the ancient Greeks. That is what appropriation requires; that is how fiction retains its sense of making. What makes the myths fictions is not just that stories of the *kind* told by the Greeks have acquired the function of being props in games of make-believe but that particular instances have actually been appropriated and retold with the fictive intent.

---

[34] Walton, *Mimesis as Make-Believe*, 91–2.
[35] Ibid. 95, n. 28.

Mode and content

Before we leave fictive utterance and the practice of story-telling there remains a nagging worry that accounts such as ours, in terms of intention, fictive stance, and so forth, supply only necessary but not sufficient conditions for the fictional dimension of works of fiction. Currie, for example, believes so because of worries about content. Suppose the content of a story is resolutely non-fictional. Can fictive utterance and the fictive stance make it fictional? The problem is similar to that posed by the status of Greek myths and, on the face of it, seems merely to beg the question about fictional content. But the matter is complex and important so let us consider Currie's cases:[36]

[1] Someone may write a strictly autobiographical account of his or her life (perhaps a life full of highly unlikely events), adopting as he or she does certain stylistic devices usually indicative of fictional discourse. The author might intend that the audience make-believe the story, and reasonably expect that the audience will understand that this is the intention. But it is doubtful whether such a work is genuinely fiction.[37]

[2] Jones finds a manuscript m which he takes to be fictional and which he determines to plagiarize. He produces his own text, exactly recounting the events in m, but written in a somewhat different way. But m was, unknown to Jones, nonfiction. Surely Jones's text is nonfiction . . .[38]

[3] Jones experiences certain events which he represses. He then writes a story, recounting those events, but which he takes to be a fiction invented by himself. Again. Jones's text is surely nonfiction . . .[39]

The intuition in each case, though Currie does not put it in this way, is that the texts are non-fiction because their content is not 'made up'. The problem, it should be stressed, is not that the content is *true*, because Currie readily concedes that there could be genuine works of fiction each sentence of which, as it happens, turns out to be true.[40] He has offered—on different occasions— two ways of eliminating cases such as these. The first stipulates that a text, to be fictional, must not be 'related by an information-preserving chain to a sequence of actually occurring events',[41]

---

[36] These are drawn from 'What is Fiction?' but very similar cases appear in *The Nature of Fiction*, 42–5.

[37] Currie, 'What is Fiction?', 388.   [38] Ibid.

[39] Ibid.   [40] Ibid.; Currie, *The Nature of Fiction*, 48.

[41] Currie, 'What is Fiction?', 389.

the second stipulates' that 'if the work is true, then it is at most accidentally true'.[42]

There are problems with the first, earlier version which perhaps led Currie to the second, later one. In particular there is a problem arising from classical empiricist psychology (notable in Hume) which claims that all imaginative creation draws on, and is causally derived from, prior experience. Currie must either show that his 'information-preserving chains' are of a different kind from these experience-based relations or he must produce independent arguments against the empiricist view of the imagination. The second version, requiring that any truth in a work of fiction be merely accidental, might well be right but still seems unnecessarily *ad hoc.*

What is needed to determine that a work (or a story) is fictional is that its content be fictional as well as its mode of presentation. But content and mode of presentation, we have seen, are closely related. Content is fictional, so we earlier suggested, if it originates in a fictive utterance. We can now go further. While propositional content in general consists of the characterization of objects, events, places, people, and so on, content is *fictional* just in case what is true of those objects, events, etc. is dependent on the fictive descriptions which characterize them in the first place. It is in that sense that fictional objects are intensional objects; what they are, and what is true of them, is determined by the way they are described in certain kinds of utterances. Because the content requirement of fiction can be defined in terms of origin, there is no need for any reference to 'accidental truth' or 'information-preserving chains'. Fictional content is such that *how things are (in the fiction) is determined by how they are described to be in a fictive utterance.* This points up the contrast with truth because *how things are (in the world)* is not determined by any kind of utterance. The ontological dependence of the fictional on modes of presentation is crucial to the distinction between fiction and non-fiction.

Returning to Currie's cases, we can see that the autobiographical content in (1) does not meet the condition that what is true in the work is dependent on the fictive utterances which introduce the content. But autobiography can, of course, provide material for fiction; what once were real people become fictional characters

---

[42] Currie, *The Nature of Fiction*, 46.

in virtue of being presented (characterized) in a certain way and subject to a certain kind of attention. In the case of (2), Jones is *retelling* a story rather than initiating it; if it is the *same* story then the status of the original telling will affect the status of the content. But whether the story is the same is far from obvious; it is not clear, for example, that it is *about* the same things as the original and if it is not then the story itself is different and might well count as fiction. Finally, case (3) is most problematic of all, particularly for those sympathetic to Freudian views of creativity, in that one might suppose that many fictions do, unconsciously, recount actual experiences in the author's life. But again whether the content can be considered fictional or not rests both on its origin in a fictive utterance and the dependence of its objects (broadly conceived) on the mode of description and characterization. It is by no means a foregone conclusion that the resulting work is non-fiction.

What emerges from all this is that some constraint on content is required for a work (or a story) to be fictional. But no more resources are needed to explain this than are already on offer. The content must originate in a fictive utterance, not only in the sense that it is characterized by fictive descriptions (those conforming to the conventions of utterance and response) but also that those descriptions determine the nature of the content, what it is about, what inferences can be drawn from it, and so forth. When modern story-tellers appropriate the ancient Greek myths and make fictions of them the reason that new works are thereby created is that the content in this retelling now becomes dependent on the modes of its characterization in a way that could not have been true of the original, assuming the original to be non-fictional. What this case shows is that truth, even accidental truth, is not at the heart of the fiction/non-fiction distinction.

3

Truth-Value and Pretence

The falsity thesis

The idea that fictional stories are comprised (largely) of false sentences (or propositions) has had wide currency. Thus Bertrand Russell, for example, speaking of *Hamlet*: '[t]he propositions in the play are false because there was no such man.'[1] Goodman similarly holds that '[a]ll fiction is literal, literary falsehood',[2] 'literal' because he believes that some fiction can be metaphorically true, and 'literary' because he believes falsity alone is not sufficient for fictionality. Goodman concedes that works of fiction generally contain a mixture of truths and falsehoods and thus that 'pure fiction' is rare. He concludes that the distinction between fiction and non-fiction is in practice a matter of degree, determined by percentages of truths and falsehoods.[3]

The thesis that 'pure fiction', by definition, consists of false sentences (the falsity thesis) has some initial plausibility. If descriptive fictions are made up or invented it is unlikely that they will 'correspond to the facts' and the expression 'pure fiction' is often colloquially used to mean 'completely false'. But the theory is not satisfactory and discovering precisely why not will yield a better understanding of literary fictions. The simplest objection is this: that a work of fiction might consist entirely of non-declarative sentences—interrogatives, imperatives, exclamations—which do not admit of truth assessment, in which case falsity could not be necessary for fictionality. Goodman himself admits the falsity condition is not sufficient. Even where declaratives are involved, as Walton observes, '[w]e did not have to compare George Orwell's *1984* with the events of that year to decide whether it is fiction or nonfiction'.[4]

---

[1] Bertrand Russell, *An Inquiry into Meaning and Truth* (London, 1962), 277.
[2] Nelson Goodman, *Of Mind and Other Matters* (Cambridge, Mass., 1984), 124; also 'Fiction for Five Fingers', *Philosophy and Literature*, 6 (1982), 162.
[3] Goodman, *Of Mind*, 126; 'Fiction for Five Fingers', 164.
[4] Walton, *Mimesis as Make-Believe*, 74.

There is a deeper problem, though, which shows that the truth-value of individual sentences in fictive utterances has little to do with their status as fiction. The first point is that different kinds of sentences, even among declaratives, appear in works of fiction; the second is that truth-valuation of these sentences depends on different modes of construal.

Consider the following simple examples:

(A) John worked in the fields
(B) He found it tiring
(C) There was once a young man who worked in the fields
(D) Working in the fields is tiring.

Suppose each sentence appears in a work of fiction. First of all, it would seem that (C) and (D), unlike (A) and (B), are open to truth-assessment on what might be called a *non-contextual construal*, that is a construal independent of information about the circumstances of utterance. Because they express general propositions, they are true just in case the predicate in the existential claim (C) is instantiated and the generalization in (D) holds good by and large. These might be examples for Goodman of truths, bits of non-fiction, which appear in works of fiction.

On Goodman's view no work of *fiction* could consist of sentences only of the (C) and (D) kind, which turn out, in the (C) case merely incidentally, to be true. The reason that must be wrong is not just, following Currie, that the truth is accidental, but because it ignores the appropriate *contextual construal* of such sentences. If (C) is offered as part of a (fictional) story then the incidental instantiation of the predicates is of no account; what matters is the fact that within the fiction some *particular* young man is being described, not anyone who happens to fit the descriptions. To account for particularity of reference in a fictional context is no easy matter and belongs in a systematic theory of what fictional works can be 'about'. But it seems plain enough that construing the sentence in context requires attention to its *characterizing* function (in general its role in the story) rather than whatever non-contextual, incidental, truth-value it might possess.

The case of (D) is more controversial because we must not beg the question against Goodman by simply assuming that an utterance of (D) can count as genuinely fictive, rather than, say, an assertion appearing in a fictional work. But what we can note is that construed contextually, i.e. as part of a work of fiction, (D) might be subject to a different truth-assessment from that of a non-contextual construal merely as a universal generalization. The fictional context might, for example, offer grounds for reversing the non-contextual truth-value. As with sentences of the (C) kind, the question to ask of (D) is what purpose the sentence is intended to serve in its context. To attain the status of fiction a necessary condition is that it be uttered with a fictive purpose, i.e. not only inviting the fictive stance, but again, in the most general terms, having the aim of characterizing a fictional setting (or background), thereby licensing further inferences about the fictional 'world'. The important theoretical point—in opposition to Goodman's view—is that such a purpose is quite compatible with the sentence's being true, and being intended to be true.

The contrast between contextual and non-contextual construal is much more striking in the case of (A) and (B), which involve singular and anaphoric reference. No truth-value is assignable to these sentences on a non-contextual construal. It is not sufficient to construe (A), non-contextually, as expressing a general proposition, 'someone named "John" (or one and only one person named "John") worked in the fields', for normally proper names are used 'rigidly' to designate a specific individual. It would be strange to say that (A) is non-contextually true just in case someone or other named 'John' worked in the fields. But are (A) and (B) *false* on a contextual construal, as sentences uttered fictively (being about fictional characters)? Clearly Russell believes so, and so it seems does Goodman. But on what basis do we make a truth-valuation in these cases?

The plausibility of the falsity thesis seems to rest on the following counterfactual: *many sentences in works of fiction are such that were they to be uttered with assertoric force they would turn out to be false (about the actual world).* The intuitively sensible idea is that because there is no such person as John (in (A)) there can be no fact that John worked in the fields, therefore (A) is false. On a simple application of Russell's theory of descriptions, a sentence is false if its existential implications are false.

But the counterfactual is more problematic than this suggests.

For the most reasonable (contextually sensitive) construal of (A) *uttered assertorically* is something like:

(E) According to the fiction, John worked in the fields

Now an assertion of (E), as we shall see, is (or is likely to be) *true* not false. The existential implication attached to the proper name is blocked by the prefixed operator so the falsity of the implication does not affect the truth-value of the whole sentence. The suggestion is not that sentences in works of fiction are in fact disguised assertions having the form of (E). Indeed it seems wrong to suppose that such sentences involve any kind of assertion. The point is only that were someone to assert the declarative sentences of the story (in accordance with the antecedent of the counterfactual) the assertions would probably take the form of (E) and as such would at least be candidates for truth.

Defenders of the falsity thesis might insist that their counterfactual requires the assertion of (A) *simpliciter* which, so they would say, would make the assertion false. But what would be asserted in asserting (A) *simpliciter,* independent of a context of utterance? On a causal or non-descriptivist theory of names, whereby a necessary condition for the meaningfulness of a sentence containing a name is that the name denotes, (A) would have no meaning (express no proposition) and therefore could not be true or false. But even on a descriptivist theory, what content would an assertion of (A) have, prior to a specific designation for the proper name 'John'? If the sentence is simply taken as equivalent in content to 'Someone named "John" worked in the fields' then again it is likely to be true rather than false. If the name is assigned a fuller descriptive sense there is a problem of determining what that sense should be (on a non-contextual construal it cannot be the sense assigned the name in the fiction). It seems we must say either that the asserted sentence has a variable content according to different specifications of the reference, in which case the truth-value itself will be variable, or that the sentence has no content as such, non-contextually, in which case it has no truth-value. Either way we find no clear support for the falsity thesis. It is even harder to see what truth-value an assertion of (B)—with its open variables—could have on a non-contextual construal; certainly, again, there is no clear motivation for designating it as false.

The no-truth-value thesis

A common alternative to the falsity thesis, which seems to accommodate some of these problems, is the no-truth-value view of fictive utterance. There are at least three versions of this:

1. Sentences in works of fiction are neither true nor false because their (existential) presuppositions are false;
2. Sentences in works of fiction are neither true nor false because the sentences are not asserted;
3. It is inappropriate (mistaken, etc.) to ascribe truth or falsity to sentences in works of fiction.

Version (1) rests on a theory of presupposition hinted at by Gottlob Frege and developed by P. F. Strawson, whereby (on Strawson's account) if statement S presupposes statement S′ and S′ is false then S will have no truth-value.[5] Applied to fiction, the theory seeks to show that as the existential presuppositions of (many) sentences in works of fiction are false (there are no real objects corresponding to the fictional names or descriptions) then the sentences themselves lack truth-values. As with the falsity thesis, this version of the no-truth-value thesis applies only to some, not all, sentences in works of fiction, notably sentences of the (A) or (B) variety.

Nevertheless, even for the appropriate kinds of sentences it is not clear that the theory has any proper application. The relevant presuppositions just do not seem to be present. Neither a storyteller nor an informed audience presupposes—in the sense of *believes* or *takes for granted*—that the fictional singular terms have an intended non-fictional reference. Indeed to suppose that they do marks a failure to grasp the practice of story-telling. The presupposition of reference is one of the beliefs suspended by those engaged in the practice. If this is right then there are no (existential) presuppositions which 'fail' in fictive utterance.

It won't do to say, in reply to this, that the sentences themselves bear the presuppositions. For one thing that conflicts with Strawson's theory which requires that only sentences-in-use or statements bear presuppositions. But even if we suppose, against

[5] See P. F. Strawson, *Introduction to Logical Theory* (London, 1952); 'On Referring', *Mind*, 59 (1950), repr. in P. F. Strawson, *Logico-Linguistic Papers* (London, 1971), 1–27; 'Identifying Reference and Truth-Values', *Theoria*, 30 (1964), repr. in *Logico-Linguistic Papers*, 75–95.

Strawson, that presuppositions are semantic features of sentence-types it still seems that these are precisely the kind of features that are cancelled or suspended in fictive utterance. It is no more helpful here than in the falsity thesis to be told that the presuppositions *would* be present and *would* fail were the sentences to be uttered assertively. Once again the assertions would either be *about the fiction*, in which case the presuppositions would not be present, or the asserted content would be distinct from the fiction, in which case the presuppositions would not be relevant.

Version (2) of the no-truth-value thesis appeals directly to a theory of assertion and does not depend on a theory of presupposition. One argument goes like this:

(a) Only an assertion (or statement) can have a truth-value;
(b) Sentences in fictive utterances are not used to make assertions (or statements);
(c) Therefore, sentences in fictive utterances have no truth-value.

There are some subtle distinctions here which need to be marked. For example, we should not run together a no-truth-value view with a no-assertion view. The latter belongs with speech-act accounts of fiction which we will return to later, along with premiss (b). It is possible to accept (b) but reject (c) (assuming the argument is formally valid, this involves rejecting (a)). Monroe Beardsley takes this line, holding both that 'a fiction . . . is a discourse in which the Report-sentences are not asserted' but also that these sentences 'may still be true or false', even though 'the writer is not claiming that they are true'.[6]

J. O. Urmson defends a no-truth-value view on what looks like version (2): 'I assert nothing when I make up a story as fiction, so *a fortiori* I do not assert something that is true or false, even by coincidence'.[7] Urmson, however, also holds that 'in typical works of fiction there are assertions that are true or false'.[8] His idea here, reminiscent of Goodman's, is that not all sentences in works of fiction are fictive utterances.

The argument for version (2) is not sound. The first premiss, for example, must be rejected. It is simply not the case that only assertions bear truth-values. When, for example, we conjecture or surmise or hypothesize that p, in contrast to asserting that p, there

---

[6] Beardsley, *Aesthetics*, 420–1.
[7] J. O. Urmson, 'Fiction', *American Philosophical Quarterly*, 13 (1976), 155.
[8] Ibid. 154.

is no doubt that the truth-value of p is at issue. Similarly, component sentences in disjunctions and conditionals are not asserted but still possess truth-values. It is a separate matter whether a speaker in uttering a non-asserted sentence is *committed* to its truth or *believes* it or *intends* others to believe it. These are attitudes we take to sentences with truth-values, and as such have a bearing on the force, assertive or otherwise, of utterances, but they are not to be confused with the truth-values themselves.

We should also reject the conclusion of the argument, that sentences in fictive utterances, by definition, have no truth-value. On the contrary, we have seen even from our simple examples that such sentences could be true or false or truth-valueless. Curiously, Urmson himself—in arguing against the falsity thesis—recognizes that some genuinely fictional sentences have truth-value: he gives the example 'There was . . . many years ago a little girl who lived with her grandmother on the edge of a large forest',[9] which he admits might just turn out to be true. In fact we have seen, following Currie, that in the extreme case, not countenanced by Urmson, all sentences of a work of fiction might, in a similar fashion, turn out to be true. Fictional status is determined by origin not by truth.

The idea of appealing to appropriate response to fictive utterance is invoked in version (3) of the no-truth-value thesis: this is the suggestion that, regardless of what truth-value might as a matter of fact obtain, it is nevertheless inappropriate to *ascribe* truth-values to fictive utterances. Urmson blurs this version with the last for he speaks of the 'utter absurdity' of 'raising the question of truth', this being a question which 'does not arise' in the fictional context.[10] A more committed proponent of this version is Richard Gale, who wants to retain unequivocal truth-values for fictional sentences while still rejecting the practice of making truth assessments in fictional contexts:

what a story-teller says might be patently false, e.g. that the fastest man in the world ran a mile in ten seconds, and still we would not want to ascribe a truth value to it. . . . [T]o say that what a person said is false reflects adversely on this person, viz. that he spoke carelessly, without any grounds, or insincerely, etc. Since the person who uses a sentence fictively does not perform an assertive illocutionary act, the pragmatic implication of non-fictive use of this sentence, viz. that he believes what he says, is

---

[9] Ibid. 155.   [10] Ibid.

cancelled. Thus it would be unfair to charge him with saying something false. And since we would not be willing to charge him with saying something false, neither would we be willing to honour him with having said something true. But all of this is quite consistent with his saying things that are true or false.[11]

Gale bases his discussion on a distinction between locutionary and illocutionary acts.[12] But the point can be made independently of speech act theory.[13] At root the idea concerns the kind of responses appropriate to fiction. Although, as acknowledged by Urmson,[14] readers of fiction are sometimes invited to attend to the truth-value of what they read—and even acquire beliefs of a general or specific nature about the world—nevertheless what is constitutive of fictive utterance is not belief but make-believe. It is a feature of the fictive stance, not a feature of referential or semantic properties of sentences, which makes certain kinds of responses inappropriate.

Sentences in fictive utterances when construed non-contextually might be true or false or lacking in truth-value. The fictive stance, not a theory of presupposition or assertion, determines how they are to be 'taken'. Truth and falsity are indifferent to what it is possible to imagine, entertain, or make-believe. Some sentences— notably those containing fictional singular terms—have no truth-values on a non-contextual construal but construed in context perform the function of characterizing objects and states of affairs whose very nature is determined by the descriptive content of the utterances themselves. The make-believe response involves bringing that content to mind, regardless of its truth-value.

Fictive utterance and pretence

The common association of fiction with play, make-believe, the imagination, 'as if', and so on, makes the connection with pretence

---

[11] Richard M. Gale, 'The Fictive Use of Language', *Philosophy*, 46 (1971), 328.

[12] Gale writes: 'In a fictive use of language the story-teller "says" in the locutionary sense things that are either true or false of the world, but he does not perform the illocutionary acts which are typically performed by the use of the sentences making up his story', 'The Fictive Use of Language', 325.

[13] See e.g. Wilfred Sellars, 'Presupposing', *Philosophical Review*, 63 (1954), 201–2.

[14] Urmson, 'Fiction', 154.

particularly attractive for theorists trying to explain fictionality. But the question is not whether pretence connects in some way or other with fiction but what precise place it does occupy in the practice of story-telling and what kinds of pretence there are.

Among different kinds of pretending it is helpful to distinguish at least the following: pretending *to be* something; pretending *to do* something; pretending *that* something is the case. Although these are not necessarily exclusive they provide a convenient focus for different kinds of theory. Pretending to be something involves projecting oneself into the pretence, while pretending that something is the case need not involve this. Pretending to do something is more like pretending to be something but draws attention more to the act performed than to the performer.

Pretending to be . . .

In one quite familiar sense of the term, actors pretend to be the characters they are portraying. Anyone who assumes a persona pretends to be a person of a certain kind. When story-tellers recite their stories they sometimes become like actors pretending to be the characters they have created (or which were created by others); for example, they assume special voices or mannerisms. In such cases there is no doubt that pretence, usually of a non-deceptive kind, is involved. But do story-tellers always pretend to be the characters in their story? No, surely not. A more subtle approach, however, has it that there is at least one character which story-tellers do always pretend to be, namely the narrator of the story. This seems to be David Lewis's view:

> Storytelling is pretence. The storyteller purports to be telling the truth about matters whereof he has knowledge. He purports to be talking about characters who are known to him, and whom he refers to, typically, by means of their ordinary proper names. But if his story is fiction, he is not really doing these things. Usually his pretence has not the slightest tendency to deceive anyone, nor has he the slightest intent to deceive.[15]

Lewis presents these claims as part of an account of our reasoning to what is true in fiction. This reasoning, he argues, involves invoking 'the worlds where the fiction is told, but as known fact rather than fiction'.[16] The story-teller pretends to be someone

---

[15] Lewis, 'Truth in Fiction', 40.   [16] Ibid.

telling the story as known fact. There are problems for Lewis with narrators who tell something less than 'known fact', but we will return to these in Chapter 4.[17] The question is whether Lewis has identified a necessary condition for fictive utterance.

There are two different issues here: one about pretence, the other about an implied narrator. Whether we need to distinguish a narrator, a figure within a fictional world, from the story-teller (or author) is independent of whether we must suppose that an author pretends to be such a narrator. Our view is that the latter does not play any fundamental role in understanding fictive utterance; and probably even Lewis's theory could be formulated without it. Apart from a certain heuristic plausibility in cases of first-person narration the idea of pretending to be a narrator only obscures the variety of narrative devices open to a story-teller. However, the postulation of a fictional narrator, explained independently of authorial pretence, does, as we have seen, play a significant part in the practice of telling stories. Not only does it serve as a focus for an audience's make-believe and for the attitudes and points of view projected in a narrative but it also helps account for the blocking of inferences back to the story-teller (for example, about the story-teller's beliefs). In the guise of the 'implied author' the fictional narrator is a commonplace in literary criticism but it does not entail any pretence in the story-teller.

Pretending to do . . .

The idea that a story-teller pretends *to do* something is associated with a certain kind of speech-act account of fiction. Searle's much debated theory is paradigmatic of this approach. 'The author of a work of fiction', Searle argues, 'pretends to perform a series of illocutionary acts, normally of the assertive type,' that is, 'statements, assertions, descriptions, characterizations, identifications, explanations, and numerous others.'[18] The pretending in question is a 'nondeceptive pseudoperformance' and for Searle it is a matter

[17] See also Peter Lamarque, 'The Puzzle of the Flash Stockman: A Reply to David Lewis', *Analysis*, 47 (1987).

[18] John R. Searle, 'The Logical Status of Fictional Discourse', in John Searle, *Expression and Meaning: Studies in the Theory of Speech Acts* (Cambridge, 1979), 65. Originally in *New Literary History*, 6 (1974).

of indifference whether we describe it as 'pretending' or 'acting as if', or 'going through the motions', or 'imitating'.[19]

Related theses help to clarify the central ideas in Searle's theory:

[1] [T]he pretended illocutions which constitute a work of fiction are made possible by the existence of a set of conventions which suspend the normal operation of the rules relating illocutionary acts and the world.[20]

[2] [T]he pretended performances of illocutionary acts which constitute the writing of a work of fiction consist in actually performing utterance acts with the intention of invoking the horizontal conventions that suspend the normal illocutionary commitments of the utterances.[21]

Thesis (2) emphasizes, surely rightly, that not all the author does is pretended. On Searle's view as outlined, only the illocutionary acts are pretended, not the 'utterance acts'. An utterance act is the act of 'uttering words (morphemes, sentences)', something one can do 'without performing a propositional or illocutionary act at all'.[22]

However, Searle offers two substantial qualifications to the idea that pretending to perform illocutionary acts constitutes the writing of fiction. First, he allows that 'serious (i.e. non-fictional) speech acts can be conveyed by fictional texts, even though the conveyed speech act is not represented in the text'.[23] In other words it is possible, according to Searle, to perform non-pretended illocutionary acts through fictive utterance, even though this is done indirectly. The idea is that a work of fiction might 'make a statement' or perhaps 'raise a question' as part of its overall purpose. Although this weakens the pretence view, it does seem to be right. Kendall Walton makes a similar point:

Assertions can be made in any number of ways: by producing a declarative sentence while delivering a lecture, by raising a flag, by honking a horn, by wearing a rose, by extending one's arm through a car window. There is no reason why, in appropriate circumstances, one should not be able to make an assertion by writing fiction. Indeed, there is a long tradition of doing just that. There is what we call *didactic* fiction—fiction used for instruction, advertising, propaganda, and so on. There is also the not

---

[19] Ibid. 65.   [20] Ibid. 67.   [21] Ibid. 68.
[22] Searle, *Speech Acts*, 24.
[23] Searle, 'The Logical Status of Fictional Discourse', 74.

uncommon practice, even in ordinary conversation, of making a point by telling a story, of speaking in parables.[24]

It is not only assertions that can be made through fictive utterance. It is often important to recognize other kinds of illocutionary intentions in a narrative: a writer might be *parodying* a sentimental style, *rejecting* liberal values, *pleading* for more tolerance in the world, *inviting* readers to take a certain view, as well as warning, cajoling, advising, entreating, requesting, or admonishing.[25] The crucial point, though, is that these are supplementary purposes behind fictive utterance; they are not in competition with, nor entail any weakening of, the fictive stance.

Searle's second qualification seems to raise further problems for the 'pretended speech acts' view of fiction. For he also allows that in works of fiction there can be genuine illocutionary acts not merely indirectly performed, as in the earlier examples, but directly so. He gives the example of the opening sentence of *Anna Karenina* which he describes as a 'genuine assertion'. This leads him to distinguish between a 'work of fiction' and 'fictional discourse', only the latter consisting of pretended (direct) illocutionary acts.

It is a perennial problem for theories of fiction how to give a satisfactory account of those sentences or passages in works of fiction which appear not to be 'fictional' in any paradigmatic sense, where an author seems to be speaking *in propria persona* about non-fictional matters. Familiar cases include Tolstoy's discourse on history in *War and Peace* or Melville's essay on whales in *Moby Dick* but the examples could easily be multiplied. Are we to say, with Searle and Goodman, that these are bits of non-fiction appearing in an otherwise fictional setting? Or should we say that they too are fiction—perhaps as pronouncements of a fictive speaker—or at least should be treated as such? The issue is important and by no means clear-cut but on it hangs the very notion of what a *work* of fiction might be. One or two observations should help bring the matter more sharply into focus.

[24] Walton, *Mimesis as Make-Believe*, 78; see also 'Fiction, Fiction-Making, and Styles of Fictionality', *Philosophy and Literature*, 7 (1983), 78–88.

[25] An argument of the relevance of authorial intention in literary criticism has been based on the presence of such illocutionary intentions: e.g. Quentin Skinner, 'Motives, Intentions and the Interpretations of Texts', *New Literary History*, 3 (1972); and A. J. Close, '*Don Quixote* and the "Intentionalist Fallacy"', *British Journal of Aesthetics*, 12 (1972).

First of all, we should recall our earlier discussion, on the falsity thesis, where we considered sentences like (D) ['Working in the fields is tiring'] which have a straightforward non-contextual construal under which they turn out to be true. We pointed out that it is a further—and no doubt more significant—question how the sentences should be construed in context and in particular what purposes they are fulfilling, and are intended to fulfil, *within the fiction*. A fictive purpose can be recognized where it is clear that the sentence is intended to make some contribution towards characterizing fictional states of affairs, or more specifically licensing inferences as to what can be taken as true within the fiction, thereby guiding what an audience is to make-believe.

We can extend this point by introducing an intuitive notion of 'being part of the story'. If a sentence or passage or utterance is part of a (fictive) story then it has a contributory role in characterizing the content of the story, what is and is not the case in the imaginary world; in other words, it must play a part in what an audience imagines or make-believes in adopting the fictive stance to the story's content. There are clear cases of utterances which, in spite of a physical occurrence within stories, are not part of the story in this sense. Suppose the phone rings when a parent is telling a story to a child. The utterance of 'That's the phone, I'll be back in a minute', albeit occurring in midstream as it were, is clearly not part of the story. It plays no role in the make-believe. Similarly, if the parent in retelling a fairy-story admits candidly 'I have forgotten what comes next' that utterance is likewise not part of the story; it can be treated in a straightforward way for what it is. These simple cases provide a paradigm of detachment against which to set the more interesting and familiar cases.

We must not lose sight of these paradigms when confronted with a certain style of *nouveau roman* which plays games with just the sorts of asides we have illustrated. When Italo Calvino begins *If on a Winter's Night a Traveler* as follows:

You are about to begin reading Italo Calvino's new novel, *If on a Winter's Night a Traveler*. Relax. Concentrate. Dispel every other thought. Let the world around you fade.

we are far more inclined to adopt the fictive stance, imagining a narrator (other than the author) addressing us, and so on, than we would be in the children's cases. These introductory exhortations are readily taken as 'part of the story'; they disengage from the standard commitments of non-fictional utterance, even though we might find ourselves acting on them. The first sentence is both true and fictional in intent.

So it is with the Melville and Tolstoy cases. Were a parent to say in mid-story 'let me pause here and tell you something about whales' that utterance is not performing a role in the story, nor inviting the fictive stance, but when Melville does something similar there is indeed a world of difference. Genre conventions (to do with the novel) and general conventions associated with the practice of fiction determine that a special kind of attention is demanded of apparent novelistic excursions into the non-fictional. Characteristics of the fictive response to such material are: a distancing of narrator and author, a search for meaning-connectedness with other fictional elements, particular attention given to the form that the descriptions take (why is it told in just this way?), the selection of facts for inclusion, the role of the descriptions in licensing inferences on the nature of fictional character and incident, and a disposition to imagine or reflect on the material in the specific context of other fictional content. In this the fictive response begins to merge with a more distinctively literary (or literary critical) response. Although, as we will be arguing later, the fictive stance is not identical to a literary response, nevertheless a literary treatment of these problematic passages would also resist taking them simply as authorial assertions. Searle's account of the opening sentence of *Anna Karenina*—seeing it as a 'genuine assertion'— is patently inadequate, even naïve, from the literary point of view, with its added dimensions of value and interpretation. The literary function of the sentence has little or nothing to do with trying to induce a belief in a reader about happy and unhappy families; it has far more to do with an initial characterization of a theme which gives focus and interest to the fictional content.

Perhaps the best solution to this perennial problem is, at least from the point of view of fiction (if not literature), to invoke the category of factual content subject to the fictive stance, that is, content of a factual nature presented in the fictive mode and integrated into a wider fictional content. Being fact-oriented the content is amenable to truth-assessment and might serve to impart belief, and be intended to do so; being subject to the fictive stance it occupies a distinctive role in reflection on fictional content and in the characterization of a fictional world. In effect what appear to be direct assertions are to be treated more on the model of the indirect assertions which we saw to be compatible with fictive utterance. Their information-imparting purposes are supplementary to, not in competition with, their distinctive fictive purposes. By speaking of factual content, rather than asserted content, thereby drawing on the distinction between content and mode of utterance, it is possible to retain the idea that adopting the fictive stance involves disengaging standard speech-act commitments. Searle's pretence theory, in which there is no middle ground between a 'genuine assertion' and a pretended assertion, is less flexible and is left in the uncomfortable position of having to suppose that authors switch in and out of pretence. Nor is the proposed solution an option for the falsity thesis for, if fiction is defined as a species of falsity, then sentences in works of fiction which are true (or candidates for truth or intended to be taken as true) must count as non-fiction *tout court*.

There is another kind of content in works of fiction which is more overtly fictive than the Tolstoy/Melville cases but which like them draws on, and probably is intended to convey, facts about the world. Here, for example, is a passage from David Lodge's *Small World*, describing London's Soho:

Soho seemed distinctly less sinful in the late morning sunshine. Admittedly the pornshops and the sex cinemas were already open, and had a few devout customers, but their façades and illuminated signs had a faded, shamefaced aspect. The streets and pavements were busy with people with jobs to do: dustmen collecting garbage, messengers on scooters delivering parcels, suited executives with briefcases, and young men pushing wheeled racks of ladies' dresses. There were wholesome smells in the air, of vegetables, fresh bread and coffee.[26]

Lodge is not making direct assertions about Soho (i.e. how it was at some particular time). The past tense used in the passage identifies not a real but a fictional time and the appearances depicted (the sights and smells) are attributed not to a real but to a fictional observer. For all those reasons the passage is unproblematically fictive. However, it is a short step to an inferred factual content: 'Soho seems distinctly less sinful in the late morning sunshine. . . .'. No doubt Lodge intended to give an accurate description of Soho and appreciation of the passage even under the fictive stance involves holding him responsible for its accuracy.

[26] David Lodge, *Small World* (Harmondsworth, 1984), 191.

Cases like this are commonplace in fiction where fictive events are characterized by means of descriptions directly applicable to items in the real world. Drawing on facts, intending to convey facts, being held responsible for 'getting the facts right', are all compatible with fictive utterance. Yet perhaps the difference between these passages and the *Anna Karenina/War and Peace/Moby Dick* cases is little more than stylistic and contextual, resting on things like verb-tenses, implied observers, and so forth. If so, this would be further grounds for not putting the 'apparent assertion' cases into a separate category of utterance.

Kendall Walton has suggested not only that fiction is compatible with full direct assertion but even that a genre of historical fiction is conceivable which consisted entirely of assertions: in which 'authors are allowed no liberties with the facts, and in which they are understood to be asserting as fact whatever they write'.[27] It is not easy to make sense of Walton's thought-experiment but it is comprehensible, if at all, only by supposing that the authors are engaged in two practices at the same time (the history 'game' and the make-believe 'game').[28] Perhaps a parallel might be a speaker's addressing a remark to two different kinds of audience at the same time with two different, even incompatible, meaning-intentions. An example might be a defendant in a political trial trying to ameliorate the judges by asserting that p (intending that they believe both p and that the speaker believes p) and simultaneously conveying to sympathizers the outright rejection of p (intending that they believe both not-p and that the speaker believes not-p). But nothing so radical is needed to explain the more familiar cases under consideration.

Other objections can be raised against Searle's pretence theory. Kendall Walton has argued, for example, that the idea of pretended illocutionary acts cannot be incorporated into a general theory of fiction as it fails to apply to (most) paintings and sculptures.[29] But even restricted to literary fictions, the idea of pretence (pretending to do something) is more misleading than helpful. For one thing, it is too negative, defining fiction in terms of what it is not: not a 'genuine' or 'serious' illocutionary act but a

---

[27] Walton, *Mimesis as Make-Believe*, 79.

[28] Currie offers an account of this possibility in terms of concurrent illocutionary acts: 'Works of Fiction and Illocutionary Acts', *Philosophy and Literature*, 10 (1986), 305. See also *The Nature of Fiction*, 35.

[29] Walton, *Mimesis as Make-Believe*, 82.

'pseudoperformance'. It is better to think of fictive utterance as an act (not necessarily an illocutionary act) with its own distinctive purposes defined within a practice of story-telling. In fact Searle's thesis (2) comes close to recognizing this when he appears to explain the relevant pretence in terms of something more positive: 'actually performing utterance acts with the intention of invoking the horizontal conventions that suspend the normal illocutionary commitments of the utterances'. If that is all there is to the pretence then the idea of pretence is redundant. If, on the other hand, the idea is meant to characterize the state of mind of a story-teller then it has some substance but is almost certainly false.

A deeper objection to Searle's pretence theory arises from his delimitation of pretence. According to Searle, pretence stops only at the level of 'utterance acts'. That cannot be right, for a writer is not merely uttering words but also conveying the sense of the words. There is no pretence in the content or sense of sentences uttered fictively. A story-teller is not pretending to express propositions. Searle includes 'descriptions', 'characterizations', and 'identifications' in his list of illocutionary acts that are pretended. Yet all of these seem to be integral to a story-teller's utterances. Perhaps Searle has in mind the idea of describing, identifying, etc. items *in the world*, with the implication that this is what is pretended in fiction. However, there is nothing in description or identification *per se* which ties them to non-fictive applications and even if we were to make that restriction there is no reason why fictive utterances should not describe and identify actual objects.

Pretending that . . .

There is a third kind of pretence theory which involves neither pretending to be a character (narrator) in a fictional world nor pretending to perform illocutionary acts. Instead it employs the notion of a story-teller's pretending *that* such-and-such is the case. Gilbert Ryle offers a theory of this kind. He claims, for example:

what Dickens did [in creating Mr Pickwick] was to compound a highly complex predicate and pretend that someone had the characters so signified.[30]

---

[30] Gilbert Ryle, 'Imaginary Objects', *Proceedings of the Aristotelian Society*, Suppl. Vol. 12 (1933), 18–43, repr. in *Collected Papers, ii: Collected Essays 1929–1968* (London, 1971), 78.

Although Ryle uses the notion of pretence throughout his discussion he sees it as interchangeable with imagining. Elsewhere we find: 'Dickens invented a composite description ... [and] ... simply imagined or pretended or "said" that it was true of someone'.[31] Significantly he insists on the propositional (*de dicto*) nature of imagining: '[i]magining is always imagining that something is the case'.[32] He uses the point to remove any possible ontological confusion about 'imaginary objects': '[w]here we seem to be imaginatively creating a thing or person, we are in fact imagining that someone or something has a complex of characters.'[33] For Ryle the pretence in fiction is strictly a pretence concerning existence or instantiation.

There are a number of things wrong with Ryle's account. First, it seems doubtful that all imagining is reducible to 'imagining that'. There is a difference between: (1) imagining that there is a squirrel in a tree, and (2) imagining a squirrel in a tree.[34] In their normal connotations (1) is satisfiable by imagining just some squirrel or other in a tree while (2) requires imagining some particular squirrel in a tree (though not necessarily imagining this of some real squirrel). No doubt there are readings of each where these connotations do not hold. But the difference, however rendered, is important in the discussion of fiction. Ryle's mistake, notoriously, is to suppose that the pretence or imagining in fiction is just that *something or other* instantiates the 'complex predicates' in fictional descriptions. So if by coincidence something (real) does happen to instantiate the predicates then the predicates cease to be fictive.[35] What is lost is the sense of the *particularity* of fictional creations. In a theory of fiction it is important to accommodate the appearance that what is being described in fictional characterization is in some sense unique, i.e. not merely a state of affairs of a general kind which might turn out to be instantiated in the real world. Lewis's theory meets this requirement by locating fictional beings in 'worlds where the story is told as known fact'; these worlds *ex hypothesi* do not include the real world.

---

[31] Ibid. 79.   [32] Ibid. 81.   [33] Ibid.

[34] The example and the distinction itself come from Walton, *Mimesis as Make-Believe*, 132 f.

[35] So if the descriptions in *Pickwick Papers* should turn out to be true of some actual person then 'we should say that while previously we had thought *Pickwick Papers* was only a *pretence* biography, we now find that, by coincidence, it is a real one'. Ryle, 'Imaginary Objects', 79. This passage is discussed further in Chapter 5.

Much of Ryle's insight, however, can be retained by transferring the pretence from story-teller to audience. Rather than saying that the story-teller pretends that there is someone who satisfies certain descriptions, it is more helpful to say that the audience pretends this, under instruction, as it were, from the story-teller. But to meet the particularity point something stronger is needed: the audience must pretend *that someone is telling them* about a particular person (object, incident, location, etc.). This captures the intuition behind Lewis's theory, the postulation of a narrator telling what he knows, without requiring any pretence on the part of the story-teller. It also captures something of Searle's theory (the idea of pretended tellings), but without requiring that the story-teller pretend to perform illocutionary acts. At this point it is better to drop the notion of pretence altogether, in favour of imagining or make-believe.

Fictive utterance and speech acts

Although Searle's theory could be called a speech-act theory of fiction, given its postulation of 'pretended illocutionary acts', there are other speech-act accounts which see fictive utterance as a special kind of speech act in its own right. As our own account makes essential use of the idea of an *act* of story-telling, subject to institutionally determined rules, is it not itself a kind of speech-act account? Let us see, then, finally, what speech-act theorists have to say about fiction.

One influential idea is that fictive utterance has the illocutionary force of *mimesis* or representation. Thus Richard Ohmann:

A literary work is a discourse whose sentences lack the illocutionary forces that would normally attach to them. Its illocutionary force is *mimetic*. By 'mimetic,' I mean purportedly imitative. Specifically, a literary work *purportedly imitates* (or reports) a series of speech acts, which in fact have no other existence.[36]

[36] Richard Ohmann, 'Speech Acts and the Definition of Literature', *Philosophy and Rhetoric*, 4 (1971), 14. Beardsley has developed a similar theory: the composition of a fictional text is the representation (i.e. depiction) of an illocutionary action, or series of them, in basically the same sense in which a painter depicts a cow, or an actor on the stage depicts an act of punching' (Beardsley, *Aesthetics*, p. xliv). See also: Monroe C. Beardsley, 'Fiction as Representation', *Synthese*, 46 (1981); 'Aesthetic Intentions and Fictive Illocutions', in P. Hernadi (ed.), *What is Literature?* (Bloomington, Ind., 1978).

Ohmann offers this as a definition of *literature* but with the clear implication that it is the fictive (rather than, say, evaluative) aspects that are being defined. The theory has features in common with pretence theories. Ohmann in fact states that '[t]he writer *pretends* to report discourse'[37] though, unlike Searle, he also thinks that '[t]he writer ... perform[s] the illocutionary act of writing a literary work'.[38] Like Lewis, Ohmann believes that postulating a fictional narrator is essential in understanding fictive utterance but unlike Lewis does not suggest that a writer pretends to be such a narrator. Ohmann locates the narrator as part of a reader's response: 'The reader constructs (imagines) a speaker and a set of circumstances to accompany the quasi-speech-act.'[39] Ohmann's theory allows that sentences in fictive utterances can be true or false but insists that no illocutionary acts, other than 'mimesis', appear in fictional works.

Thus Jane Austen does not *make* the statement, 'It is a truth universally acknowledged, that a single man ...'. The making of the statement is an imaginary illocutionary act. But in order to do his part in the mimesis, the reader must nonetheless consider whether the statement is true or false. Its falsehood is one tip-off to the fact that the imaginary narrator of the story is being ironic.[40]

There is much to be said for Ohmann's account: it emphasizes the reader's role in make-believe, it defines fiction in terms of conditions on utterance, and it certainly gives a better explanation of sentences like that from *Pride and Prejudice* than does Searle's of the opening sentence of *Anna Karenina*. However, Ohmann is wrong to suppose that the only illocutionary acts possible in works of fiction are imitative acts or acts of 'mimesis'. It is clear that a writer, via fictive utterance, can be parodying, describing, exaggerating, coaxing, etc. and also, in indirect ways, making assertions, giving advice, issuing warnings, and the rest. There is also little to be gained in Ohmann's account by appealing either to pretence or to a special kind of speech act (or illocutionary force).

The invocation of the literary notion of *mimesis*, explained in terms of the imitation (or purported imitation) of speech acts, is instructive but nevertheless gives too narrow an account of the traditional concept. First of all, it is hard to see how literary or

[37] Ohmann, 'Speech Acts', 14.   [38] Ibid. 13.
[39] Ibid. 14.   [40] Ibid. 14–15.

aesthetic value could be invested in such imitation and, secondly, it gives too much emphasis to the imitation of acts and not enough to the representational nature of content. In general, Ohmann needs a much clearer distinction between literature and fiction; while his account captures some important features of fiction *per se*, it does not provide much of a basis for explaining the peculiar evaluative notion of literature.

A variant of the mimetic theory suggests that telling a story consists of performing 'translocutionary' speech acts: '[t]he action of translocuting consists in the using of sentences (locuting) in order to attribute illocutions and/or perlocutions to dramatic speakers—the person(s) speaking the words which make up literary works.'[41] The theory is committed to the introduction of 'dramatic speakers' or narrators distinct from the author, though it does allow that authors may directly perform illocutionary acts.[42] What remains unclear, however, is exactly what counts as attributing a speech act to a (fictional) dramatic speaker. We know what it is to attribute a speech act to a real person. But a translocutionary act has to be understood not as a *report* of a speech act but as the *creation* of a speech act (along with a speaker). But an account of fiction which relies on the notion of *creating a fictional speaker* merely relocates, but does not solve, the problem of explaining fictionality.

A more promising account is that which emphasizes the special intentions of the fiction-maker. In his earlier work on this topic Gregory Currie has offered an analysis of fiction-making as a 'genuine illocutionary act' which, unlike the translocutionary view, does not presuppose the idea of a fictional speaker. Although he has more recently amended the definition so that it no longer refers to illocutionary acts, it is worth giving some consideration to his earlier analysis since it has been highly influential. The analysis is as follows:

---

[41] Marcia M. Eaton, 'The Truth Value of Literary Statements', *British Journal of Aesthetics*, 12 (1972), 170. The idea of a 'translocutionary act' is also discussed in her 'Good and Correct Interpretations of Literature', *Journal of Aesthetics and Art Criticism*, 29 (1970), 227–33, and 'Liars, Ranters and Dramatic Speakers', in B. R. Tilghman (ed.), *Language and Aesthetics: Contributions to the Philosophy of Art* (Lawrence, Kan., 1973).

[42] Eaton, 'Liars', 45.

U performs the illocutionary act of uttering fiction in uttering p if and only if

There exists ϕ such that U utters P intending that anyone who were to have ϕ

(1) would make-believe P;

(2) would recognize U's intention of (1);

(3) would have (2) as a reason for doing (1).[43]

When certain qualifications have been added this leads to a definition of a work of fiction.

Currie, in *The Nature of Fiction*, offers no reasons for abandoning the 'illocutionary act of uttering fiction', but he is right to have done so. First of all, the appeal to Gricean intentions does not commit the theory to postulating a special illocutionary act. The Gricean mechanism explains a kind of meaning or communication; irony, metaphor, conversational implicature, joke-telling, literary allusion, and satire might usefully be illuminated by Gricean intentions, though without supposing that each case involves a distinct illocutionary act. So it is with fiction. And normally the specification of illocutionary acts requires more than just Gricean intentions, including, for example, what Austin called 'felicity conditions'. The presence of Gricean intentions is not sufficient to determine a fictive illocutionary act.

An account which postulates a special illocutionary act of fiction-making needs to explain the relation between the illocutionary acts *conventionally* associated with the sentences in fictive utterances and the special act *in fact* being performed on this occasion (i.e. the fictive act). When Defoe utters the sentence 'My name is Moll Flanders' we know he is engaged in fiction but his sentence has all the appearance of an assertion (and is intended to have that appearance). How are the apparent assertion and the actual fictive act related? Currie does not address the question directly but seems to suggest that the relation is similar to that between uttering the indicative sentence 'It's hot in here', apparently making an *assertion,* while intending to issue the *command* 'Open the window'.[44] The problem with drawing this parallel is that it cuts the conventional link between the act apparently performed and the act in fact performed. On Searle's pretence theory, in contrast, this link is systematically preserved such that for any

---

[43] Currie, 'What is Fiction?', 387.   [44] Currie's own example, ibid. 387.

apparent act *A* (however finely specified) a fictive utterance always generates pretend-*A*. Currie's fictive illocutionary act, as defined, is curiously indifferent to the standard purposes of the sentence used in the performance of the act.[45] What Currie's view loses is that intimate connection between what sentences in works of fiction appear to be and what they actually are.

Also how literally are we to take the parallel with what Searle has called 'indirect speech acts'? For Searle the apparent speech act, let us say an assertion, remains operative even though it is the vehicle for an indirect speech act, let us say a command. Using one of Searle's own examples, if I utter 'Can you pass the salt' with the intention of requesting that you pass the salt, I have performed the speech act of 'asking a question' (literally about your ability to pass the salt) *as well as* the speech act of 'requesting'; the latter is primary, the former secondary.[46] But clearly we do not want a parallel consequence in the fiction case. We do not want to infer, even as a 'secondary' speech act, that Defoe is asserting that his name is Moll Flanders. The advantage of the pretence view is that this inference is automatically blocked (at least on the assumption that pretending to perform A is incompatible with actually performing A). There is nothing in the 'fictive illocutionary act' view which disengages the commitments of the apparent illocutionary acts in fictive utterances. Yet disengagement—a blocking of standard inferences—is an integral part of fictive utterance.

Although we are rejecting the notion that telling stories, or making up fictions, involves performing an illocutionary act of any kind, on the traditional Austin/Searle model, we do admit, of course, that it involves 'doing something with words'. A story-teller has a special kind of meaning-intention, using words (or,

[45] The point here raises issues similar to, but not identical with, those associated with what Currie calls the 'determination principle', i.e. the principle that 'the meaning of a sentence determines the kind of illocutionary act it is used to perform' (Currie, 'What is Fiction?', 385). Currie claims that Searle uses the principle against any theory postulating a distinct illocutionary act of fiction. But Currie himself rejects the principle on the ground that the same sentence can be used to perform different illocutionary acts. He also suggests that Searle's own theory of fiction contradicts the principle. Whatever the merits of this particular principle, it is clear that Searle's theory, unlike Currie's, conforms to a similar principle which requires some systematic relation between the standard speech acts associated with sentences in fiction and the acts, whatever they are, of the story-teller.

[46] See Searle, 'Indirect Speech Acts', in *Expression and Meaning*, 30–57.

more generally, other media) to elicit or encourage a certain sort of response. When the poet 'paints pictures with words' or the novelist 'creates imaginary worlds' what they are in fact doing is forming sentences (or other structured, sense-bearing, signs) with a propositional content which becomes the focus of a special kind of imaginative effort among participants. It is to that imaginative response which we now turn.

4

Content and Characters

Works of fiction might, of course, elicit any kind of response from their readers. These might be utterly idiosyncratic, resting on associations of ideas, personal recollections, emotional and psychological reactions, they might be dictated by expectations of genre and tradition, and in general they might involve different degrees of understanding and misunderstanding. In certain respects there might also be gender-relative and culture-relative responses. But it is helpful to distinguish those responses constitutive of fiction *per se* from those merely connected causally to particular works or those associated with specific genres or specific kinds of readers. The responses we aim to characterize are those *conventionally determined* by the practice of fiction, responses 'appropriate' to fiction. We should be careful too to distinguish those attitudes peculiar to the fictive stance and those arising from the distinctive literary dimension of works of fiction. A 'literary reading' goes well beyond what is required by the practice of fiction. We will be giving close consideration in later chapters to the conventions of literary response.

The most basic constitutive response to fictive utterance includes (at least) the following: grasping, and reflecting on, the sense of the sentences uttered; constructing an imaginative supplementation of that sense; and making-believe that actual particulars, facts, events, places, and so forth, are being described (even where it is known they are not). A reader is invited to partake in a distinctive kind of imaginative involvement with the content of a story-teller's utterances. The imagination is also invoked in attitudinal responses, for example, sympathy, revulsion, amusement, fear, or disapproval.

We might summarize this fictive stance towards propositional content, in the most general terms, by saying that a reader is invited to *entertain* sense and *make-believe* truth and reference. This simple notion captures the fundamental elements in a reader's response within the practice of fiction even if it needs qualification on several counts; for example, it requires that the entertainment of sense also involves supplementation, as well as other non-cognitive attitudes, and it needs the proviso that not all truth and reference is make-believe in works of fiction.

Fictional content

Consider the following sentences, from the opening of George Moore's novel *Esther Waters*:

She stood on the platform watching the receding train. The white steam curled above the few bushes that hid the curve of the line, evaporating in the pale evening. A moment more and the carriage would pass out of sight, the white gates at the crossing swinging slowly forward to let through the impatient passengers.

These sentences are uttered fictively. The singular terms 'she', 'the platform', 'the receding train', 'the white steam', etc. do not identify actual individuals, though a reader is invited to make-believe that they do. The make-believe status of the references (and truth-values) does not affect a reader's ability to grasp the sense of the sentences. Having grasped the sense a reader comes to imagine (but not believe) that these events are real. Supplementation of the sentential content will help make the imaginings vivid.

These same sentence-types could be used in other contexts. What we need to capture is that element of meaning common to different applications of the sentences. It is helpful to distinguish weak and strong identity of content. Take the sentence:

1. She stood on the platform watching the receding train.

A speaker could utter the sentence-type (1) with the intention of recounting an actual event unrelated to George Moore's novel. The references of the singular terms would have no bearing on those in the fictive use. We might call this a *coincidental* use of (1). Now the coincidental use of (1) clearly shares some common content with Moore's fictive use. We will say that the two utterances of the same sentence-type have a weak identity of content, that is they share the same *sense*, characterized in general terms, but not the same *reference*. Note that not all utterances of the same sentence-type even share a weak identity of content: ambiguous sentences—'He has lost his case', 'Visiting dignitaries can be boring'—might be used in (at least) two different senses.

Other utterances of sentence-type (1) might share a strong identity of content. They not only express the same sense but do so in the same *application*. In non-fictional utterances this strong identity of content requires the identity of reference as well as sense. In fictional cases the sameness of application might occur under two kinds of circumstances. First, the sentence could be used by someone other than the author to repeat or retell the story; this would be a continuation of fictive utterance. Second, the sentence could be used to *report* the content of the story. Genuine assertive claims, assessable as true or false, *about the content of a story* can be made with the same sentence-types that appear in the story. This assertive use will be the topic of the next section. Strong identity of content can be retained in fictive utterance, in the retelling of a story, and in assertions about a story, on the condition that all three applications are related in an appropriate way to the initial presentation of the content. Again that is a topic for later.

Finally, there could be a *misinformed* use of sentence-type (1) by a speaker under the mistaken belief that actual, non-fictional, events are being described. Such a speaker, intending to report the events in question, tries but fails to make an assertion about the world. Here only a weak identity of content is retained with the original fictive utterance. In such cases, and only in such cases, can we speak of reference-failure.

How should we characterize the sense or content of sentence-types which appear either in fictive utterances or in informed readers' assertive reports? There is no special problem with regard to those sentences which do not contain proper names as, for example, in the passage from *Esther Waters*. The sense of the sentences is identical with that of a coincidental non-fictional use, and is specifiable in general terms as the conditions under which the sentences would be true. Sense is not affected by fictionality or mode of utterance.[1]

The case of sentences containing proper names requires closer

---

[1] Obviously a fictional context *might* propose a special sense for its terms or sentences and this would need to be recognized by a reader. But there is nothing peculiar to fiction about this; non-fictional contexts might also generate non-standard senses.

attention. Sentences in fictive utterances and readers' reports (about fictions) often contain the names of both extra-fictional objects —'London', 'Napoleon', 'The Second World War'—and fictional objects—'Esther Waters', 'Casterbridge', 'The Time Machine'. What is the sense of sentences containing proper names of these kinds?

Our thesis is that in both such cases (extra-fictional and fictional) the names themselves must bear a descriptive sense which contributes to the overall sense, and content, of the sentences in which they appear. This does not commit us to a view about the semantics of proper names in non-fictional contexts. There are special reasons why proper names in fiction must have senses and these reasons do not apply outside fiction.

Let us take first the case of extra-fictional names. It is helpful in a discussion of proper names to distinguish different aspects under which proper names can be identified or categorized. First of all, ordinary proper names occupy a distinct syntactic category; only certain syntactic functions can be performed by proper names. We can speak of 'syntactic proper names' to mark this syntactic role independently of denotative function. Everyone can agree that fictional proper names are names in this syntactic sense. Second, proper names can be individuated by inscription-type: 'Jones' is a different inscription-type from 'Jonah'. Third, proper names can be individuated by denotation (what they *stand for*): the single inscription-type 'Jones' might denote different people and in that sense different tokens can count as separate, though homonymous, names. Conversely, although 'Hesperus' is a different inscription-type from 'Phosphorus' they both have the same denotation (they *name* the same object). The question is, do we need to mark some further aspect of proper names, their 'sense' or 'connotation'? Are there discriminations that we need beyond those of syntactic category, inscription-type, and denotation?

It is at least arguable that in non-fictional contexts there is no need to invoke the *sense* of a name over and above the other discriminations. But certain peculiarities of the fictive stance provide powerful reasons for invoking sense—or connotation or content—to explain the functioning of proper names in fiction. The main reason is that the fictive stance generates something like a non-extensional context: only 'something like' because strictly this is just an analogy. The common tests for extensionality are (1) substitutivity of co-referential terms *salva veritate*, and (2) applicability of the rule of existential generalization (the inference from '*a* is F' to 'something is F'). Although extra-fictional names in fictive utterances do submit to existential generalization they are subject to something analogous to failure of substitutivity *salva veritate*. As truth is not at issue, let us speak instead of *salva fictione*. In short, *story-identity is not preserved under some substitutions of co-referential singular terms* in fictive utterances. To take a trivial example, if the sentence 'Holmes returned to London' appears in a Conan Doyle story we have not preserved the story, or its content, if we substitute a sentence equivalent in truth-value and reference, such as 'Holmes returned to the Smoke' or even 'Holmes returned to the city where Mrs Thatcher lives'.[2] No doubt the conditions of story-identity are difficult to state precisely but the application of this simple substitutivity test is clear enough. We have changed the sense of the sentence and it is sense that determines fictive content.

In Chapter 5 we will be following up the implications of the substitutivity test in relation to reference and 'aboutness'. But for the moment we can draw certain conclusions about the function of extra-fictional names in fiction. One is that the names, in fictive utterances, do not function in a fully transparent or extensional manner and thus cannot be purely denotative. Because only *salva fictione* not *salva veritate* is concerned we need not modify our claim in earlier chapters that there are no special *semantic features* of fictive utterances. Indeed truth might be preserved even where narrative is not.

We could make the point in a slightly different way by saying that, in our example, it is not London *per se* that figures in the Holmes narrative but only London *under certain aspects*, those aspects licensed by the narrative. It is precisely for this reason that we cannot take the name 'London', or any extra-fictional proper name, to be functioning as a pure denotative expression in fictive utterances and thus why we need to invoke another dimension of the proper name, its sense or connotation. Whatever view we take

---

[2] It should be noted that the point does not rest only on the different times at which Holmes and Mrs Thatcher lived in London. We have not preserved the story even if we substitute the sentence 'Holmes returned to the city where Mrs Thatcher was later to live'. The reference to Mrs Thatcher is simply not licensed by the Holmes stories.

of such names in non-fictional contexts, we need to postulate a sense for the names in fiction, which captures all and only the relevant aspects of the objects named. Not any available sense will do. The narrative itself will supply (or authorize) the senses of its extra-fictional names and these senses will comprise the aspects under which the objects are presented. The London of, say, *Tom Jones* is presented under different aspects from the London of, say, *Bleak House*; so the sense (or descriptive content) of the name will be different in the two novels, even though both the denotation and the inscription-type are the same.

The case for postulating senses for names in fictive utterances is even stronger when we turn to fictional names. For these names, outside the fictional context, have no denotation and neither syntactic category nor inscription-type will provide adequate individuation.

Broadly speaking there are two alternative approaches to sentences containing fictional names. According to the first, we must say that strictly the sentences have no sense (express no proposition) because the names are 'empty'. Hence, Kendall Walton: 'If there is no Gulliver and there are no Lilliputians, there are no propositions about them; there is no such thing as the proposition that Gulliver was captured by the Lilliputians.'[3] The underlying justification for this view is (a) that the very significance of a proper name depends upon its having a referent and (b) that if a sentence contains a name without a referent then the sentence too lacks significance.[4] The second approach has it that it is only the sense, not the reference, of a name that determines whether or not a sentence containing the name expresses a proposition.

Our view is that the second approach is to be favoured, *at least in the case of fictive utterance*. It provides the most straightforward

---

[3] Walton, *Mimesis as Make-Believe*, 391. Also 'Do We Need Fictional Entities? Notes Towards a Theory', in *Aesthetics: Proceedings of the Eighth International Wittgenstein Symposium* (Vienna, 1984), 182.

[4] Gareth Evans introduced the notion of a Russellian singular term, among which he included fictional proper names:

a term is a Russellian singular term if and only if it is a member of a category of singular terms such that nothing is said by someone who utters a sentence containing such a term unless the term has a referent—if a term is empty, no move has been made in the 'language-game'. To say that nothing has been said in a particular utterance is, quite generally, to say that nothing constitutes *understanding* the utterance. (*The Varieties of Reference* (Oxford, 1982), 71)

way of explaining how readers understand fictive utterances (grasping their sense) and it does not require any exceptional theoretical presuppositions. However, it does assume that a satisfactory account can be given of the sense —or content—of fictional names.

Happily such an account is available for we need only help ourselves to some version of descriptivist theories of names which best fits the fictional application. And we can do so with a clear conscience as regards, for example, rival causal/historical theories, even if we are persuaded that in non-fictional cases causal/ historical theories are preferable. In fact, as we shall see, a causal element is involved, and integrally so, in a full explanation of what it is to use fictional names. In general we can say this:

the sense of a fictional name is given by those descriptions in, or derivable from, a source text which introduces the name, such that the descriptions identify the referent of the name internal to the fictional world depicted in the text.

Thus the sense of the name 'Esther Waters' is given by such descriptions as: the girl named 'Esther Waters', who became pregnant, who was forced from her job as a domestic servant, who lived in poverty, who married a man who gambled on the Derby, and so on. It is the source text, some original set of sentences uttered fictively (in this case George Moore's novel), which provides the grounding for the identification of the fictional referent; it is somewhat akin to the initial 'baptism' to which, according to causal theories, subsequent uses of a name must be causally related.

More needs to be said about the idea of reference 'internal to a fictional world' and, in general, about the nature of the descriptive content which gives sense to fictional names. These matters will be pursued later when we consider the identity conditions for fictional objects and the whole question of 'fictional reference'. For the time being we should simply note that what we call fictional names refer *within a fiction* to actual objects (or, to put it another way, a reader make-believes that there are actual objects referred to by the names). The name 'Esther Waters' refers *within the novel* to a person satisfying a certain description. Only from the external perspective are the names 'fictional' or identify fictional characters. The sense of a fictional name is given by those descriptions which *within a fiction* identify objects. In the next section we will explain what is meant by the locution 'within a fiction'.

In specifying the sense of a fictional name why do we need a cluster of descriptions? Why won't some simple description, such as 'the person named "Esther Waters"', suffice? The answer is that *individuating* descriptions are needed. There might be more than one character named 'Esther Waters' and we need to be able to say *which* Esther Waters we mean. As it is possible for there to be two almost identical fictional characters with the same name in the same work of fiction (or fictive utterance) in principle a complete set of characterizing predicates might be needed to disambiguate sentences containing the name.

Recall again why we need to introduce senses of fictional names. A work of fiction which introduces a fictional name will need to give sense to the sentences in which the name appears. It is that sense which a reader entertains in reflecting on the fictional content and it is also that sense which helps to guide the make-believe reference. But the sentence cannot have a sense (express a proposition) unless some semantic role is given to the fictional name; as the name has no extra-fictional referent its semantic role cannot be one of denotation so it must lie in its descriptive content. If a name were to be introduced in a fiction without any descriptive support a reader would not be able to make sense of sentences (in the fiction)[5] using the name nor be able to make-believe that the name has a reference. The descriptive sense of a fictional name— like the sense of whole sentences in a fiction—gives content to a reader's make-believe.

'In the fiction . . .'

We have seen that when readers (or other speakers) make reports about the content of stories they sometimes use the same sentence-types as appear in the stories themselves. More characteristically, they use either sentences of their own which summarize the explicit content of the story or sentences which expand on the explicit content. We turn now to one fundamental class of such reports,

[5] This applies only to fictive utterances. Suppose the name is 'Aniopolis'. Someone could speak meaningfully, at a second-order level, by saying: 'Aniopolis is that mysteriously unexplained character in novel X.'

those which are amenable to treatment as falling under the intensional operator 'In the fiction . . .'.[6]

Let us return to our sample sentence.

1. She stood on the platform watching the receding train.

A reader could report this fictive event by using (1). According to the view at hand what the reader *means* by uttering (1) with the aim of making such a report can be made explicit by (2):

2. In the fiction, she stood on the platform watching the receding train.

Sentence (2) signals *what a speaker means* in a certain context of utterance using the sentence-type (1); it does not record any semantic property of (1) itself.[7] There are fundamentally different pragmatic features attaching to the fictive utterance of (1) in the novel (or in a retelling of the novel) and the reportive utterance of (1) with the meaning of (2). The fictive utterance is not asserted, it engages the practice of fiction, it invites the response of make-believe, and it has no truth-value. The reportive utterance, by contrast, is asserted, it conforms to the standard conditions of assertion, it invites not make-believe but belief, and it has a truth-value.

The notion of 'In the fiction . . .' as an intensional operator governing reports of fictive content is now so common in theoretical writing on fiction that appeal to it does not need special defence. But its familiarity should not undermine its fundamental importance nor the distinct theoretical benefits it bestows on discussions of fiction. What are these benefits?

First of all, it removes any mystery as to how a speaker can speak the truth about fictive events and also hold true beliefs about them. Although not everything a speaker says or believes about fictions can be paraphrased into sentences of the form 'In the fiction, p'—we will be looking at other cases shortly—a significant class of assertions and beliefs do fall into this category. Part of the reason why the mystery is removed is that sentences of the form (2) bear no unwelcome ontological commitments. There

---

[6] This is a general form which should be taken to cover such variants as 'In the novel', 'In the play', etc. as well as specific locutions like 'In *Esther Waters*'. Kendall Walton has invented the idiom 'It is fictional that' for this purpose.

[7] A similar point is made by Kent Bach in *Thought and Reference* (Oxford, 1987), 216–17.

is no need to postulate a special class of entities—fictional, non-existent, etc.—to make sense of (2) or the occurrence of singular terms in (2). Of course those philosophers who do not find such commitments unwelcome do not need to avail themselves of the 'In the fiction . . .' device.[8] All that the device shows is that the commitments to fictitious entities are not *required* in our talk about the content of stories.

Sentences of the form 'In the fiction, p' share the same semantic features with sentences governed by other intensional operators, particularly those involving propositional attitude verbs: 'X believes that p', 'X imagines that p', 'X thinks that p.' The parallels are instructive but it would be wrong to infer that the operator 'In the fiction . . .' has its basis in any psychological state. Reports about stories are not reports about states of mind, for example about what anyone imagined, fantasized, dreamt, and so forth. Of course readers can, and should, engage states of mind—imagining, make-believe—with regard to fictional content. But it is not these states of mind that are reported in simple reports of the form (2).

The important parallels arise in the generation of intensional contexts. These contexts, for example, block existential generalization. We cannot infer from 'John dreamt that a gremlin was chasing him' that there is some gremlin which was chasing him (or of which he dreamt). Likewise, from 'In the fiction, Esther Waters lived in poverty' we cannot infer that there is (or was) someone named 'Esther Waters' who lived in poverty. The intensional context generated by 'In the fiction . . .' provides a clear explanation of the distance or 'remoteness' of fictional 'worlds' from the real world. The prefixed operator insulates fictional content from inferences regarding the real world. This primarily affects reference and truth. From 'In the fiction, p' we cannot infer p. And from 'In the fiction, a is F' we cannot infer that anything is F or even that 'a' exists. Let us explore in more detail this gap between the fictional and the real.

The gap occurs not just in reports about fictions but also in story-telling (i.e. fictive utterance) itself. Fictive utterance blocks inferences not in virtue of creating an intensional context but by suspending the standard commitments of assertive or truth-telling

---

[8] Several philosophers have defended the thesis that there are 'non-existent entities': e.g. Routley, 'Some Things Do Not Exist', 251–76; Terence Parsons, *Nonexistent Objects* (New Haven, Conn., 1980).

discourse. The fictive utterance of p implies neither p nor the speaker's belief that p and the fictive utterance of 'a is F' cancels the implication that the speaker is referring to, and characterizing, an actual object. However, although these implications are blocked it might nevertheless be the case that p is true and that the speaker is referring to an object. It is in this sense that fictive utterance is neutral with respect to truth and reference.

We can get a good idea of what fictional objects (or characters) are by reflecting on the way that fictional names operate either in the context of fictional reports or in fictive utterances. The starting-point is the simple observation made in the previous section: In the fiction, Esther Waters is a person; in the real world, Esther Waters is a fictional character. Esther Waters is not, of course, a fictional character *in the fiction*. To say that she is a fictional character (*only* a fictional character) is to say what she is, as it were, for us. In the fiction, for her fellows, she is a person, an actual flesh-and-blood human being, capable of being referred to, possessing a name that denotes, etc. *The intensional operator 'In the fiction . . .' turns a person (internally speaking) into a character (externally speaking).* Under the scope of the operator we can describe Esther Waters just as we would a normal human being. So too can the author speaking in the fictive mode of utterance. How is this reflected in the functioning of names?

Internal to the (world of the) fiction, 'Esther Waters' functions as the name of a person. Readers make-believe that there is an actual particular denoted by the name, whose story is being told. External to the (world of the) fiction, in either a fictional report or a fictive utterance, the name literally has a characterizing, rather than a denotative, function. It serves to give sense to—or characterize—a proposition, either presented fictively by the author or reported by a reader. Frege's theory about the function of names in contexts of propositional attitudes provides a useful analogy for the semantics of fictional names.[9] According to Frege, a proper

[9] We describe this as only an 'analogy' with Frege's thesis in 'Über Sinn und Bedeutung' because if the sense of a name, for Frege, is literally the mode of presentation of the object named then it is not clear how the 'name' (if there could be such) of a fictional object could have a sense. In later work Frege introduced the idea of a *mock sense* or *mock thought* in relation to fiction: see *Posthumous Writings*, ed. Hans Hermes, Friedrich Kambartel, and Friedrich Kaulbach (Oxford, 1979), 130 f. Tensions within Frege's own view of fictional names are well brought out in Evans, *The Varieties of Reference*, ch. 1.

name appearing in such contexts loses its 'customary reference' and takes on an 'indirect reference' which he identified as its 'customary sense'. We might think of the 'customary reference' of a fictional name as the reference it has internal to a fiction (i.e. the person Esther Waters). That reference is transformed into an 'indirect reference' when the name appears under the scope of either the story-teller's fictive utterance or the 'In the fiction...' operator. In other words only the sense of the name survives in these 'external' contexts; reference (i.e. reference to objects) stays in the realm of make-believe.

The picture we have so far is this. A story-teller, speaking under the conventions of the practice, presents propositions as the subject-matter for a reader's make-believe or imaginings. A reader in turn can report the contents of the make-believe by presenting propositions under the scope of the intensional operator 'In the fiction ...'. Both fictive utterance and fictional reports create a gap between the content described and the actual world. The gap is primarily inferential; in presenting a story, or reporting it, a speaker blocks inferences from the fictional content to how things are in the world. There will of course be connections between fictional content and the world, just as connections obtain between belief-content and the world, but the barrier of the non-extensional context limits inferential access to these connections.

So far we have concentrated only on the role of names in fictional contexts and their contribution to the propositions in fictive utterances and fictional reports. But there are important features too in the predicative content of fiction. It is not, as it were, incidental how fictive states of affairs are presented in fictive utterances. They are presented 'under a description' but more than that they are *constituted* by the predicative content of the descriptions.

Fictive states of affairs (including objects, events, places, characters) owe their identity to their mode of presentation. In this sense they are intensional objects whose nature and very existence are dependent logically on the descriptions in some originating fictive utterance. This is a simple consequence of the non-extensionality of fictive content and the redirection of attention from reference to sense entailed by the fictive stance. The predicative content of fictive utterances identifies and defines the aspects that characterize fictive states of affairs.

But these predicates will have more than merely descriptive

content. They will also (normally) incorporate attitudes of various kinds, notably values, points of view, and connotations, as well as such extensions of meaning as implicatures, symbolism, imagery, metaphoric content, and so forth. The complex network of attitudes and aspects embodied in the predicative content of fictive utterances constitutes the 'world' of the work. Readers are invited not just to reflect passively on propositional content but also to recognize and take up attitudes to that content. To a large extent how a reader responds to some aspect of a work of fiction is controlled by the way the fictive content is presented, that is, what attitudes are conveyed by the predication. We will return to this 'aspectival' view of fictive content in the next two chapters.

The supplementation of content

An integral part of responding to fiction involves a reader's imaginative supplementation of the explicit content of the fictive utterances. Readers 'fill in', or just take for granted, an enormous amount of detail which is not explicitly given. A general assumption, for example, is that if characters are human beings then, unless reasons are given to doubt this, they are *like* ordinary human beings in obvious respects. Inferences are licensed about their physical and, albeit more controversially, their psychological nature beyond what is made explicit.

Much of the pleasure of reading fiction derives from the imaginative 'filling in' of character and incident. But what are the principles on which this supplementation rests? Readers often fantasize with fictive content, 'filling in' as the whim takes them, and no doubt some genres of fantasy actively encourage this kind of whimsical response. But for a clear grasp of fictional narrative *per se*, we need the notion of an *authorized* response.[10] This involves a 'filling-in' process *authorized* by the content itself and its presentation, where the relevant authority resides not only with the author but with the genre, literary tradition, historical context, and so on. A reader sensitive to authorized response will attempt,

---

[10] Kendall Walton introduces the idea of an *authorized game of make-believe* to capture a similar constraint: see *Mimesis as Make-Believe*, 51, 397 f. Also 'Do We Need Fictional Entities?', 180–1.

through imaginative reflection on the content, to construct the 'world' of the work. Many of the controversial, and interesting, issues surrounding authorized response, to do with judgements and attitudes 'appropriate' to a work, will rest on literary critical sensibilities. We will deal in Part 3 with some of the complex constraints governing response to literary works. But more basic matters arise for fiction itself.

David Lewis has proposed that reasoning to what is true in a work of fiction—in the sense of what supplementations are authorized—is very like counterfactual reasoning. His suggestion is that we should ask *what would be the case in the world where the story is told as known fact.*[11]

Lewis takes us through a progression of three analyses which are increasingly sensitive to constraints arising from literary criticism. They are as follows:

ANALYSIS 0: A sentence of the form 'In fiction f, ϕ' is true iff ϕ is true at every world where f is told as known fact rather than fiction.[12]

ANALYSIS 1: A sentence of the form 'In the fiction f, ϕ' is non-vacuously true iff some world where f is told as known fact and ϕ is true differs less from our actual world, on balance, than does any world where f is told as known fact and ϕ is not true. It is vacuously true iff there are no possible worlds where f is told as known fact.[13]

ANALYSIS 2: A sentence of the form 'In the fiction f, ϕ' is non-vacuously true iff, whenever w is one of the collective belief worlds of the community of origin of f, then some world where f is told as known fact and ϕ is true differs less from the world w, on balance, than does any world where f is told as known fact and ϕ is not true. It is vacuously true iff there are no possible worlds where f is told as known fact.[14]

Analysis (0) rules out any reasoning to what is true in a work of fiction beyond what is explicitly given in the content of the sentences in the work. Lewis is right to reject this analysis as too restricted. Both literary critics and ordinary readers take it for granted that inferences beyond what is explicit are indispensable in understanding fiction.

Analyses (1) and (2) are offered as genuine alternatives, though the latter, Lewis thinks, conforms better to critical sensibilities. What they have in common is the idea that truth in fiction is a

---

[11] Lewis, 'Truth in Fiction'.   [12] Ibid. 41.
[13] Ibid. 42.   [14] Ibid. 45.

product of two sources: the explicit content of sentences in the relevant text and a background against which we reason *beyond* that content. In analysis (1) this background consists of facts about the actual world. In analysis (2) it consists of beliefs 'overt in the community of origin' of the fiction. Analysis (2) is offered as a way of eliminating the use of esoteric facts about the actual world (unknown perhaps to the author and readers of the text) to reason to what is true in the fiction.

Lewis's counterfactual basis for explaining our reasoning about fiction is in many ways highly attractive. It is easy to think of fictional narratives as describing what *would be the case if* . . . They speak, for the most part, of the *possible*, not the actual. They describe worlds, often similar, but not identical to, our own world. We can reason about what we are to take as true in a fiction, beyond its explicit content, because we read fiction against a presupposed background. All this is nicely captured by Lewis's account.

But there are several substantive reasons why the account is not adequate to explain the actual processes of supplementation that readers engage in. The fundamental objection, around which the others revolve, concerns the introduction of 'worlds', in particular *possible worlds*. We do speak colloquially of 'fictional worlds' or the 'worlds' of particular novels or authors but these are not the possible worlds of modal logic. The colloquial sense of 'fictional world' is that of fictional 'setting', which determines a (limited) range of specific, salient features. When we speak of the 'world' of a particular author (Iris Murdoch's world or John Le Carré's) we are alluding to certain characteristic features that recur in different novels by that author.

The trouble with possible worlds is that they bear *too much content*. They are 'complete', not only closed under deduction but determinate in detail. Fictional 'worlds' or fictional settings, in contrast, are incomplete; they leave a large number of details in-determinate, simple features, for example, of the physical setting (the weather or temperature on a certain day, the weight or height of a character, the distance between places). Although we can infer that 'In the fiction, these details are determinate' (normally internal to a fiction there will not be widespread vagueness of fact) we cannot infer that in the fiction these details are determinate *in this way or that*.

Lewis attempts to explain these indeterminacies by suggesting that each fiction (novel, text, etc.) sustains not a single possible world but a set of worlds.[15] There is a truth-value gap in the fiction, according to Lewis, where a detail obtains in some worlds of the set but does not obtain in others. Although Lewis is surely right about there being truth-value gaps in those cases where we have no better reason to infer 'In the fiction, p' than 'In the fiction, not-p', the point does not rely on the introduction of (sets of) possible worlds.

It is helpful to speak of truth-value gaps in cases of indeterminacy in physical detail (it is neither true nor false that Esther Waters was born, say, on a Monday), but it is less helpful in cases where we are concerned with character motivation or thematic development. In these cases, again, the idea of possible worlds is not illuminating. When a literary critic analyses some lines from *Macbeth* by observing that

with Macduff's statement about his birth, the naked babe rises before Macbeth as not only the future that eludes calculation but as avenging angel as well[16]

it is no use trying to give the truth-conditions of the claim in terms of worlds in which it is true. At best, this is a truth about the character *relative to a thematic interpretation*. What the example shows is that many of a reader's responses to fiction (and they need not only be 'literary' responses) are to do with *meaning*, with making sense of a work, or finding patterns and themes. Talk of possible worlds is of no help in explaining such responses.

The point can be pressed further against Lewis's model of reasoning about fiction. The starting-point for Lewis is the world (or worlds) where the story is 'told as known fact'. The assumption is that the act of narration and the 'facts' narrated are independent of each other, consequently that the very same facts could have been narrated in other ways. Now *in the fiction* it is no doubt true that the narrator could have told the tale using different words (some novels exploit the device of the same facts being related from different points of view). But from the external perspective of author or reader the mode of telling and the tale itself are not independent. We have seen that it is a peculiarity of fictional

[15] Ibid. 42–3.
[16] Cleanth Brooks, *The Well-Wrought Urn* (2nd edn.; London, 1968), 38.

narrative that it does not simply depict a world, it depicts a world-under-a-description. Acts of story-telling generate intensionality in fictional content; there are not just facts reported but facts-as-described.

Lewis rightly emphasizes the importance of the act of story-telling in identifying fictions:

Different acts of storytelling, different fictions. When Pierre Menard re-tells *Don Quixote*, that is not the same fiction as Cervantes' *Don Quixote* —not even if they are in the same language and match word for word.[17]

Acts of story-telling are individuated not just by story-tellers but by the mode of telling. If Cervantes had retold his story with slight variations that would have been a different act and would have generated a different fiction (or 'world'). The predicates in fictive sentences are not externally but internally related to the situations they characterize, in the sense that the particular aspects, attitudes, and values embodied in the predicates help to constitute the situations (events, characters, etc.) depicted. In Jorge Luis Borges' story what makes Menard's *Quixote* a different fiction from Cervantes' is not merely that they are told by different people but that the connotations and attitudes conveyed *by the very same words* differ in the two tellings.

What we learn about a fictional world derives not just from *what is said*, as determined by truth-conditions, but from *how it is said*, where style, connotation, tone, and point of view, must also be taken into account. A reader's task is to reconstruct this world by identifying and weighing the aspectival (connotative, evaluative, etc.) qualities in the fictive descriptions. This involves much more than simply accepting as true, or as 'known fact', what is explicitly reported. Information about fictional worlds is presented through a series of narrative filters. Even at the level of explicit content readers must determine not only what sentences to accept at face value (recognizing unreliable narration, irony, hyperbole, speaker's point of view, etc.) but also what paraphrases of the content of those sentences are licensed (recognizing connotative features, tone, figurative usage, satire, allusion, etc.). If fictional worlds are given under-a-description this places severe constraints on which *redescriptions* of fictional content—for example in readers'

---

[17] Lewis, 'Truth in Fiction', 39.

reports—accurately record the 'facts'. We can only discover what is true in a fiction through a clear grasp of the manner in which the fiction is presented. There is no escape from the introduction of an interpretative element right at the start of our reasoning about fictional worlds.

All this suggests that we should move away from the model of fictional 'worlds' as possible worlds and think of them more as imaginative constructs intimately connected to the linguistic forms by which they are characterized. The supplementation of content requires not the setting of one world against a background world—there is too much extraneous content involved in *worlds* and too little attention to modes of presentation—but rather the more subtle assessment of what information can legitimately be invoked in grasping and going beyond the content given. Not just any information about the actual world (Lewis's analysis (1)) nor about the 'collective belief worlds of the community of origin' (Lewis's analysis (2)) will be authorized by a fictive presentation. Certainly in many cases an appeal to the collective beliefs of the community of origin will be helpful in guiding the supplementation of content. But not always. Obvious counter-examples would be cases where an author challenges received ideas. Thomas Hardy's *Jude the Obscure* might be a simple instance. An ordinary reader of the time who shared the collective beliefs about how young ladies should behave and what attitudes were appropriate to marriage might well have attributed selfish and unreasonable motives to Sue Bridehead. We are not explicitly told that she was selfish or inconsiderate or that she deserved her fate (the opposite, of course, is strongly implied in the tone of the presentation) but it seems that whether or not she was, or did, should not be decided merely by appeal to a general moral consensus in Hardy's Britain. It also seems clear that what we say about Sue Bridehead's intentions and motives is going to be determined, in part at least, by some overall perspective we as readers take on the novel.

The question of what imported information is authorized by a fiction cannot be answered by any simple formula.[18] At the most basic level it is probably helpful, heuristically, to appeal to a *principle of verisimilitude*. Fictional states of affairs (objects, events,

---

[18] Kendall Walton, driven by somewhat different considerations, arrives at a similar conclusion when he speaks of the 'disorderly behavior of the machinery of generation [of fictional truths]': *Mimesis as Make-Believe*, 184.

personages) can be assumed to be like ordinary states of affairs (objects, events, personages) failing indications to the contrary. This is a useful guide at the ground level of physical and circumstantial detail. It is likely to play a significant role in a reader's imaginative response. But all the theoretical interest lies in what might count as 'indications to the contrary'. Here the crucial factor is what constitutes a correct, appropriate, or informed *understanding* of a work. All that can be said in general is that with regard to constraints in understanding fiction there is no clear line between those concerned with the importation of *facts about the world* and those concerned with *meanings* or *literary conventions*.

Make-believe response is guided as much by knowledge of genre conventions or implied meanings or narrative tone (and at a higher level by the practice of literary interpretation) as by knowledge of the extra-fictional world. When we read a whodunit, for example, we know, through genre expectations, that the prime suspect early on in the narrative is unlikely to be the guilty party; that knowledge overrides, or at least teasingly conflicts with, our knowledge about human nature that anyone acting in such-and-such a manner is, on the contrary, likely to be guilty.

We spoke earlier of a gap between fictive content and the real world, blocking inferences from what is the case *in the fiction* to what is the case (in the world). But now we have seen that inferences going the other way are not always blocked: we can infer what is true in fiction from what is true. Invocation of information about the world—about matters of fact, about beliefs, about other fictions, about meanings—contribute substantially to authorized supplementations of fiction. An author's fictive utterances provide not only the basic subject-matter of a reader's make-believe but also, in effect, a set of implicit instructions for how to supplement that subject-matter with extra-fictional information. Anyone who supposes that fictions are radically cut off from the world will need to confront the obvious fact that fully supplemented fictional 'worlds' incorporate a great deal of straightforward information about the real world.

The reality of fictional characters

So far we have not raised any ontological questions about fictional objects, characters, or events. The accounts offered of fictive utterance and the 'In the fiction . . .' idiom are agreeably parsimonious in ontological commitment. To say that a story-teller is referring to, or speaking about, or just describing, fictional objects and states of affairs is to say no more than that a certain kind of propositional content is being presented in the fictive mode, with the implication that the singular terms (or at least *some* singular terms) are not intended to identify actual particulars. Likewise, when a reader makes a report implicitly or explicitly governed by the 'In the fiction . . .' operator putative references to fictional objects are again explicable in terms of predicative content without existential commitment.

But this apparent elimination of ontological matters is perhaps too easy. We appealed earlier to a principle of verisimilitude as a basic guide to the supplementation of fiction; this is the working assumption, for the purpose of licensed inferences, that fictional objects or states of affairs are similar to real objects or states of affairs unless there is indication to the contrary. But how can fictional objects be similar to real objects if there are no such things as fictional objects? Do we after all need to posit a special class of objects or add to our ontology?

The answer to the second question is 'no', or at least not merely on behalf of the principle of verisimilitude. That principle itself involves no special ontological commitments. We can accommodate the principle quite adequately by a kind of 'semantic ascent'. For what we mean by saying that fictional objects are similar to actual objects is that *the very same descriptions (of fictional objects) which appear in fictive utterances or readers' reports could also be used to describe actual objects*. The similarity claim is about descriptive content, not about a special class of objects; and the content itself, as we have seen, bears no undesirable ontological commitments. Perhaps the most fundamentally important—albeit perfectly straightforward—relation between fictional 'worlds' and the real world lies at this descriptive level. Fictional worlds seem 'real' for the simple reason that the descriptions used to characterize them are the very kinds of descriptions commonly used in nonfictional contexts. No doubt some such observation lies behind those speech-act theories which see fictive utterance as a 'representation' of illocutionary acts rather than a performance of the acts themselves. But no speech-act theory is needed to make the point about verisimilitude.

Unfortunately we cannot leave the ontological issue there because there are undoubtedly manners of speaking about fictional characters which are not amenable to treatment either in terms of fictive utterances or in terms of readers' fictional reports. And some of these do seem to engage ontological commitments.

First of all, not all claims about verisimilitude (or similarities) are readily translatable into the 'In the fiction . . .' idiom. Consider

3. Carruthers is just like Jeeves

where the name 'Carruthers' denotes an actual person. Or

4. Bertie Wooster is quite unlike Einstein.

Neither (3) nor (4) can be treated as reports of fictional content because they cannot appropriately be prefixed by 'In the fiction . . .'. The reason why the prefix is not applicable is that neither Carruthers nor Einstein figure in the relevant fictions (novels). The novels are not *about* them and they do not have a role in any authorized supplementation of the fictive content. Nevertheless, (3) and (4) might well be true. The fictional characters, it seems, have been lifted out of their fictional milieu and have entered more worldly discourse in their own right. Does this, then, land us with a commitment after all to fictitious entities?

No. But it does suggest that, in explaining usages like (3) and (4), it is helpful to invoke directly the notion of a *character* as an abstract entity, comparable ontologically to a type, kind, or characteristic. A character in this sense is not a mysterious 'non-existent' entity nor, in Alexius Meinong's phrase, an entity 'beyond being and non-being', nor a possible non-actual object, nor any other ontologically *sui generis* creature. Rather it is a logical derivative of the idea of a *characterizing description*. Even if there were no fictions we would still have a use for the notion of character. It is this commonplace notion from which the idea of a fictional or made-up character is derived. When we speak of a person's character we mean those distinguishing features (usually psychological or behavioural) which 'characterize' the person and which are used for purposes of comparison, moral judgement, and identification. Someone of 'little character' is someone with few special or interesting features while a 'great character' is someone with many.

It is easy enough to describe a character—or, as we also might say, a kind or type of person—without thereby describing any actual person. This is the basis for fiction and already suggests a tentative definition of a *fictional* character:

a fictional character is a set of abstracted human characteristics (or qualities) the original presentation of which is in a work of fiction and which, under the conventions of the fictive stance, involves the make-believe of actual exemplification.

As a first step, then, we can understand (3) and (4) as (5) and (6) respectively:

5. Carruthers is like the Jeeves-character (in the P. G. Wodehouse novels)

6. The Bertie-Wooster-character (in the P. G. Wodehouse novels) is quite unlike Einstein.

The phrase in parenthesis in each case recalls the 'In the fiction . . .' idiom but here its scope is restricted to the character-identifying description; the phrase signals both the fictionality of the character and its root source.

What is meant by the idiom 'the X-character'? For one thing, the context is intensional and should be distinguished from that of 'the character of X' where 'X' occupies a fully extensional position. In the former context a name substituted for 'X' performs a descriptive function; the sense of the name identifies the defining features of the character. The descriptive content of 'the X-character' is given by the sense of the name in the fiction where the name is presented. To understand the comparison in (5) we need to know the defining (or at least salient) characteristics attributed to Jeeves in the relevant fictions. Another way of putting (5) might be

7. Carruthers has Jeeves-like characteristics

which removes even the commitment to characters and becomes purely predicative. This commitment is not so readily removed in (6) where the character occupies subject-position. But (6) means something like

8. The Bertie-Wooster-character does not possess (many) Einstein-characteristics,

which tells us, albeit negatively, something about the defining features of the Wooster-character.

There is a fundamental difference between speaking of characters in fictive utterances or using the 'In the fiction...' idiom and speaking of characters directly, using the 'X-character' idiom. Different kinds of predication are applicable. Consider the following:

9. Jeeves is a gentleman's gentleman

10. Jeeves is one of the great comic creations of the twentieth century

11. Jeeves is a fictional character.

If we take (9) as a reader's fictional report, implicitly prefixed by 'In the fiction...', then there is no commitment to characters. The reader is reporting propositional content in, or derivable from, a work of fiction. Strictly speaking, no property is being ascribed to a *character*; we might say, in Kendall Walton's usage, that make-believedly a property is being ascribed to a *person*. Remember that *in the fiction* Jeeves is not a character but a person. As a claim about a character, (9) must be interpreted as meaning

12. The Jeeves-character contains, or involves, the property of being a gentleman's gentleman.

Unlike (9), (10) and (11) can only be claims about a character; the subject in each case is the Jeeves-character (in the P. G. Wodehouse novels).

A character, then, is constituted by defining characteristics or properties. A *fictional* character, following our earlier suggestion, is a character depicted in a fiction under the conventions of story--telling whereby a reader is invited to make-believe that there is some actual particular who possesses the defining characteristics. The properties that constitute a character are normally those designated by the descriptive sense of the proper name assigned to the character; not always, of course, because some fictional characters do not have names.

In one sense, in spite of its paradoxical appearance, we can say that fictional characters exist. In fact there are many usages which make that assumption explicit. For example:

13. There are fictional characters in twentieth-century fiction which could never have been depicted in the nineteenth century.[19]

Existence claims with regard to fictional characters reveal a surprising multiplicity. Example (11) is not strictly a claim about

[19] For discussion of similar cases, see Peter van Inwagen, 'Creatures of Fiction', *American Philosophical Quarterly*, 14 (1977), 299–304, and 'Fiction and Metaphysics', *Philosophy and Literature*, 7 (1983), 67–77. Also, Currie, 'Fictional Names', 483–4.

existence but about origin or presentation. It does not mean the same as

14. Jeeves does not exist

even though there is one interpretation of (14) by which it is equivalent to (11). But (14) can also mean

15. There is no such person as Jeeves

which in turn can be taken to mean that the Jeeves-characteristics (as depicted by P. G. Wodehouse) are not instantiated in any one (actual) person. But compare (14) with

16. Bunbury does not exist.

Now (16), unlike (14), is an internal claim about the content of *The Importance of Being Earnest* and is true both on a (15)-type reading (about instantiation) and under the 'In the fiction . . .' prefix.

It should now be clear how it is possible to acknowledge the truth of

17. The Jeeves-character exists.

This is compatible with (14) for its truth rests on facts about fictive utterances not on facts about instantiation.

If fictional characters, as identified by the 'X-character' idiom, are constituted by clusters of characterizing properties then there is a problem about the *creation* of characters. An author does not create properties so, strictly speaking, does not create sets of properties. But we need not deny creativity or inventiveness to authors, for authorial creativity lies not in any ontological feat (bringing some *being* into existence) but in a descriptive or linguistic feat. It is the linguistic act of fictive utterance that assembles characters for our attention.[20] And this linguistic act might itself be the product of highly original (inspired, etc.) feats of imagination. Normally readers would never, without the aid of an

---

[20] For other discussions of the non-creationist view of fictional characters, see Wolterstorff, *Works and Worlds of Art*, 144–5; and Arindam Chatrabarti, 'Two Problems in the Ontology of Fictional Discourse', *Journal of Indian Council of Philosophical Research*, 1 (1983), 148–50. Wolterstorff explains an author's creativity in terms of 'the freshness, the imaginativeness, the originality of his selection' (i.e. the selection of 'person-kinds'); Chatrabarti speaks of giving the author 'due credit for choosing the relevant property cluster and for conferring characterhood upon it by pretending for the first time that such a property-set is (or was, etc.) somebody's character when, in fact . . . it is (or was, etc.) nobody's' ('Two Problems', 150).

author's fictive utterances, have the opportunity to make-believe that a person of just *this* kind exists (note that we do not give much credit for creativity to a writer who describes only stereotypical characters).

Once a character has been introduced in a fiction it can become an object of general reflection. Characteristics associated with fictional characters can become paradigms in non-fictional contexts. For example, names of fictional characters, like the names of well-known people, can be turned into general terms. We can speak of someone's being a Raskolnikov or a Falstaff just as we can of someone's being a Quisling or a St Francis. This is a familiar, and rhetorically powerful, device for attributing clusters of properties to a subject. There should be nothing puzzling about this application of the fictional to the real. To say that John is *a Falstaff* (or *the Falstaff* of the group) is not to make an identity claim but a straightforward predication. The properties attributed to John are just those (or some of those) which constitute the Falstaff-character.

Similarly we can make comparisons between characters from different fictions. We can say

18. Jeeves would never have got on with Raskolnikov.

To explain (18) we need the idea of a person's exhibiting or exemplifying an X-character; this entails a person's possessing all (or usually a salient subset) of the constitutive properties of the character. So the sense of (18) is captured by

19. A person exemplifying the Jeeves-character would not get on with a person exemplifying the Raskolnikov-character.

It is not necessary here to give an account of the truth-conditions of counterfactuals like (19); that is no longer a special problem about fiction.

In Chapter 5 we will be looking at problems concerning the identity of characters, sameness, and difference, in relation to a discussion of 'aboutness' in fiction. We must end this chapter, though, by saying a little more about readers' attitudes—cognitive and emotional—towards fictional characters.

Cognitive and affective attitudes towards fictional states of affairs

What counts as *thinking about* a particular fictional character? If Carruthers is really very like Jeeves, what is to distinguish thinking about Carruthers from thinking about Jeeves? The problem concerns generality and particularity. If the Jeeves-character is constituted by a set of properties then it seems that any reflection on that set—which will be a reflection characterizable in entirely general terms—will be a reflection on Jeeves. Now it is possible— in principle—that any number of actual people might exemplify the Jeeves-set-of-properties: perhaps Carruthers does. So wouldn't thinking about such people be indistinguishable from thinking about Jeeves? But that cannot be right. No one is identical with Jeeves simply in virtue of sharing properties with him; cognitive attitudes towards Jeeves must somehow acknowledge his fictional status.

It might seem that the specificity of the Jeeves characterization will get us off the hook. After all, it is highly unlikely, to say the least, that anyone will exemplify *exactly* the properties attributed to Jeeves: it is definitive of the Jeeves-character, for example, that Jeeves attends to Bertie Wooster, foils Gussie Fink-Nottle, sees off Aunt Agatha, and so on, and so on. Certainly the specificity of fictional characters (i.e. the specificity of the descriptions) goes some way towards accounting for their particularity. But not the whole way. It does not meet the point of principle. After all not every fictional character is highly specific.

Part of the answer—concerning how to distinguish thinking about Jeeves from thinking about anyone who happens to instantiate the Jeeves-character—involves the *make-believe* of particularity. Recall that in a fictive response a reader, reflecting on fictive content, entertains sense and make-believes reference. To think about a fictional event is to reflect on the sense of event-descriptions and make-believe that the events actually occurred. So it is with thoughts about fictional characters. The thoughts must have the appropriate content—characterized by descriptions authorized by the fiction of origin—and they must also involve (only) the make-believe of reference and truth. This latter condition requires, in effect, that someone thinking about Jeeves must know that Jeeves is a fictional character. But that is a consequence of a more fundamental point which concerns the manner in which the thought is entertained. Thoughts about fictions are 'unasserted thoughts', they are entertained without the disposition to assert their content; in short their content is *imagined* not *believed*. Someone who believes that Jeeves is an actual person is not strictly thinking *about Jeeves* even in bringing to mind all the Jeeves-characteristics.

Such a person holds inappropriate dispositions (with regard to speech acts, inferences, etc.) and is comparable to the misinformed reader who mistakes the fictional status of a narrative and attempts to make assertions about actual people by recounting parts of the narrative. However, although thoughts about fictions involve imagination (or make-believe) and not belief, there could of course be a disposition to assert the thought-content; but this is a disposition not to assert that p but to assert that *in the fiction* p. Similarly, there could be a belief relating to the thought-content, the belief that *in the fiction* p, not the belief that p *simpliciter*.

We have two conditions so far for thinking about a particular fictional character: that the thought have the required *content* (suitably derived from the propositional content of fictive utterances), and that it have the right *status* (imagined not believed). But these conditions are still not sufficient. We need a third condition, of *origin*. For thoughts to be *about Jeeves* their origin must be traceable, ultimately, to fictive utterances in the appropriate novels by P. G. Wodehouse. This recalls the condition of causal grounding for fictional content introduced in Chapter 2. It does not mean, of course, that someone must have read the novels in order to be able to think about the character; knowledge, and thus thoughts, about characters can be acquired second-hand. What it does mean, though, is that an author's original fictive utterances must play some explanatory role in accounting for the attitudes that readers subsequently acquire about the characters presented in those utterances. This is partly a matter of getting the *right* character but it is also a further way of explaining the *particularity* of fictional characters. Their particularity resides in the fact that they are defined or presented in particular texts. The particularity of origin relates to the particularity of make-believe. Part of what it is for a reader to make-believe that some particular person (or object) is being described in fictive utterances is the make-believe that the story-teller—the teller of *this* story—has in mind particular people and events.[21]

The thoughts that readers form about fictional characters and events can in turn be the cause of affective attitudes that readers take towards fictions. Readers can feel sorrow, anger, joy,

---

[21] Currie has a similar way of accounting for the particularity of characters: see 'Fictional Names', 475.

indignation, sympathy, despair, embarrassment, amazement, and delight in reflecting on fictive content. But can they also *fall in love* with the beautiful princess, *despise* the cruel king, *admire* the brave prince, *pity* the ugly sister, and *fear* the wicked witch? The problem is that these emotions are more than mere feelings, they are also grounded in cognitive states, notably beliefs. Normally, you cannot fear (love, despise, admire, or pity) X without believing, at least, that X exists (and has certain qualities, etc.); but that belief is missing in the fictional case.

There has been extensive discussion of this problem in the philosophical literature but, for our purposes, we do not need to give it detailed treatment. The most promising solution lies in the materials already at hand: thoughts about fictions, make-believe reference, imaginative involvement. Once it is clear what it is for a reader to *have in mind* a particular fictional character it is only a short step to explaining how such a character might be the source of an emotional response. There is no problem in categorizing fictional characters or states of affairs as despicable, admirable, pitiable, or frightening; we need only invoke the similarities between fictional and real situations. Certain *kinds* of situations are frightening, certain *kinds* of characters (real or imagined) are pitiable. However, a reader might recognize that a fictional situation is frightening without being frightened by it. Something more is needed. That surely is an imaginative engagement with the fictional content. Only a thought vividly entertained will evoke an emotional response. Several factors contribute to the vividness of a thought in this context: the fullness and detail of the thought, the connotative richness of its content, the possibilities for imaginative supplementation, and the make-believe of its instantiation. Bringing to mind a character or situation under these conditions is sufficient, often, not just to cause but to justify an emotional reaction.

To explain emotional responses to fiction in terms of thoughts about fictional characters and situations is subject to certain misunderstandings. For example, when a reader fears a fictional monster the claim is not that the reader is frightened *of* a thought but rather is frightened *by* a thought. The idea is that the state of affairs normally described as *being afraid of the monster* is explicable through the notion of *being frightened by the thought of the monster*. We can think of the 'of' locution giving us the

intentional object of the emotion (in the fictional case something
non-existent) and the 'by' locution the real object (in the fictional
case something existent, but psychological).

Another objection to the thought theory of fictional emotion
is that because the thoughts are *general* the particularity of the
objects of our emotions is lost. Here is one version of the objection:

But to say that our response is directed towards the senses of thoughts or
ideas about life is to imply that the object of a fictional emotion is always
general. For example, when we respond to Anna Karenina with sadness,
what we really respond to is not Anna but the general idea that it is
unfortunate and regrettable that a woman should be in such a miserable
condition as described by Tolstoy. This interpretation does not allow the
fictional character to be the focus of attention of our emotional state ... It
diffuses the so-called character into a set of ideas: the character is
reduced to the illustration of the possibility of a certain kind of life. But
this does not seem right.[22]

This objection carries no weight against our own position. We
have been careful to preserve—and explain—the particularity of
fictional characters, through the notions of specificity of description, make-believe instantiation, and rootedness in a source text.
To respond emotionally to Anna Karenina's plight is not the same
as responding to any situation of a similar kind, just as to *think
about* Anna is not equivalent to thinking about anyone who happens to share her properties. A full understanding of emotional
response to fiction must incorporate an account of what it is to
think about a *particular* fictional character. We have provided such
an account.

In this chapter we have explored in detail some of the logical
features of fictive response: what it is to reflect on, or bring to
mind, the content of fictive utterances; how we can talk about that
content, making true judgements, while retaining full cognizance
of its fictionality. We have explored the question of what fictional
characters are, from a logical point of view, and have offered an
analysis of the many different ways of talking about characters.
We have shed light on the various 'gaps' that appear to exist
between fictions and the world. And finally we have looked at
certain cognitive and affective attitudes that readers might take

---

[22] Bijoy H. Boruah, *Fiction and Emotion* (Oxford, 1988), 44.

towards fictional states of affairs. We now have a considerably refined apparatus for raising further questions about the relations that obtain, or can obtain, between works of fiction and the real world. It is time to turn to questions of reference.

5

Reference and 'About'

It is often supposed in debates about literary truth that a great deal hangs on the question of whether, or how, works of fiction can *refer*. There are three clearly discernible views, or clusters of views, on the matter which, in summary, might be labelled pro-reference, non-reference, and anti-reference. Pro-reference views hold that works of literary fiction do, at least can, refer to things in the world, either directly through names and descriptions or indirectly through, for example, allegory, allusion, or *mimesis*; stronger versions hold that reference is not just incidental but inevitable in literary fiction and is the basis for literary value.[1] Non-reference views, in contrast, hold that literary fiction is referentially inert, that there is a 'referential fallacy' in literary criticism[2] or, again in stronger versions, that the search for any kind of word/object or sentence/fact relation is misguided in literature or elsewhere.[3] Sometimes non-reference views make the claim that all reference is self-reference, at least in literature if not more generally.[4] Thirdly, there is an anti-reference view—in some versions similar to, but not identical with, the non-reference view—that dismisses the idea of 'reference' altogether as being 'pointless', 'a philosopher's invention',[5] this view is associated both with the

---

[1] Pro-reference views appear in e.g. Raymond Tallis, *In Defence of Realism* (London, 1988), and Jeremy Hawthorn, *Unlocking the Text* (London, 1987). A forceful defender of a strong pro-reference view is Graham Dunstan Martin: see *Language, Truth and Poetry* (Edinburgh, 1975) and 'A New Look at Fictional Reference', *Philosophy*, 57 (1982), 223–6.

[2] See Michael Riffaterre, 'Interpretation and Descriptive Poetry: A Reading of Wordsworth's "Yew Trees" ', in Robert Young (ed.), *Untying the Text: A Post-Structuralist Reader* (Boston, 1981), 108 ff.

[3] Many non-reference views are motivated by Saussurian linguistics (or at least a conception of Saussure favoured by structuralists and post-structuralists): e.g. Terence Hawkes, *Structuralism and Semiology* (London, 1977); and Catherine Belsey, *Critical Practice* (London, 1980).

[4] The idea that literary works are self-referential was common among structuralists: 'Every work, every novel, tells through the fabric of its events the story of its own creation, its own history.' Tzvetan Todorov, cited in Hawkes, *Structuralism*, 100.

[5] Richard Rorty, 'Is There a Problem about Fictional Discourse?' in *Consequences of Pragmatism. Essays 1972–1980* (Brighton, 1982), 127.

pragmatist's rejection of truth as correspondence and with the conception of language as a 'game' rather than a 'picture' of reality.[6] Pushed further, anti-reference views encourage a weakening of distinctions between kinds of discourse, literary, philosophical, historical, and so forth.

In this chapter we will examine different kinds of referential or quasi-referential relations compatible with fiction (fictive utterance, the fictive stance). While acknowledging that such referential relations do obtain, thereby rejecting non-reference and anti-reference views, we will nevertheless resist the stronger claim that reference is somehow indispensable to literary fiction or is an indicator of literary value. A modest pro-reference position does nothing to support traditional conceptions of 'literary truth'. Of far greater significance for literary fiction than reference is 'aboutness'. To speak of what a work is *about* is not equivalent to speaking of its references. When we come to discuss 'aboutness' in the literary context we will find that what a work is about not only helps to determine its value but is connected with its very status as a work of literature. Before coming to literature, though, we must get a clearer idea of what 'relations with the world' are possible for fiction *per se*.

Referential relations

There are many relations that works of fiction, or fictive utterances, might have to the world (or things in the world) but it would be wrong to conflate them all under the notion of 'reference'. We will begin by considering those relations which are genuine candidates for the title 'referential'.

Speaker's reference

One paradigm of reference, labelled long ago by P. F. Strawson as 'singular identifying reference', consists of a speaker intending to refer to a particular object or person by means of a linguistic device (name, description, indexical, pronoun, etc.) and succeeding in identifying that object or person for some hearer. Sometimes identifying reference is achieved in virtue of the representational

---

[6] Both features are prominent in Prado, *Making Believe*.

content of the linguistic device. Thus a speaker might pick out an individual by means of an identifying description: e.g. 'that tall man in the corner', 'the winner of the game', 'the last person to arrive'. Singular reference in such cases can be accomplished by identifying whoever happens to satisfy the description. Sometimes, though, in what Keith Donnellan calls 'referential' uses of definite descriptions,[7] intention and context can secure identifying reference independently of representational content. Thus a speaker might succeed in picking out a particular person, Jones, by using the description, say, 'the man drinking champagne', even though that description is not in fact true of Jones. The speaker's referential success in these cases relies on contextual features helping to realize the intention.

Donnellan's notion of a 'referential', rather than 'attributive', use of definite descriptions reminds us that identifying reference can be accomplished in many different, sometimes non-conventional, ways. Someone can refer to Ronald Reagan not just by using his name or some attributive description, 'the 40th President of the USA', but also by mime, telling a joke, making up a story, or by tone of voice. Similarly, there is no reason why in fictive utterance a speaker should not have referential intentions. Reference, in fictive utterance, might be secured either through descriptive content or through contextually aided recognition of intention (or of course through both). However, because fictive utterance both disengages conventional commitments of utterance and also blocks certain inferences concerning the author, judgements about speaker's reference must be made with caution. If a story-teller uses the description 'the capital of England' then there is a presumption that he intends to refer to London but if he uses the phrase 'the head of the Civil Service' it cannot be presumed that he is referring to whoever happens to be head of the Civil Service at the time of writing. Story-tellers might use the conventional proper name of an object with the intention of referring to that object but they also might use fictitious names to refer to actual people or places; in the latter cases the intention to refer would have to be divined in other ways. Satirical writing provides a good example of disguised reference. Facts about the historical context

[7] Keith Donnellan, 'Reference and Definite Descriptions', *Philosophical Review*, 75 (1966), 281–304.

of the composition, not to say the specific intentions of the writer, might need to be invoked to determine satirical references. In the *Epistle to Dr. Arbuthnot*, Pope uses the name 'Atticus' (line 214) to refer to Addison and the preceding lines offer a biting portrait of Addison even though no explicit mention is made of him. In Part III of *Gulliver's Travels*, where Gulliver is describing the Grand Academy of Lagado, it is pretty clear (for those in the know) that Swift intends a reference to the Royal Society. Both are cases of speaker's (or writer's) intended reference.

Although explicit appeal is made here to intentions, the point is not meant to beg any questions about the role of intention in literary criticism. For the notion that intention can determine reference in fictive utterance is quite independent of any theory about the nature of literary criticism. This is why we distinguish reference from 'aboutness', such that it might be that an author intends to *refer* to something in a fictive utterance—and succeeds in doing so for an audience—even though the utterance is not *about* that thing in a strictly literary critical sense. We will return to this matter later when we come to 'about'. The main point for the moment is simply this: that there is nothing inherent to fictive utterance or the practice of story-telling that precludes a speaker having referential intentions and also a well-grounded expectation that an audience will recognize those intentions and thereby come to identify an object referred to.

Denotation

A name might denote or 'stand for' an object without there being a speaker on some specific occasion intending to refer to that object. Denotation in this sense is a strictly semantic relation holding between a name and an object, while reference, in the sense of singular identifying reference, is (part of) an intentional act performed by a speaker. It is possible to specify the denotation of a name without specifying any particular referential act in which that name is used. The distinctness of denotation and reference does not entail that at a deeper level of analysis semantic relations might need to be explained in terms of speakers' intentions. All it does entail is that the claim '"a" denotes *a*' does not mean the same as, and is not equivalent to, the claim 'S (intends to) refer(s) to *a* by means of "a"'.

In the context of fictive utterance we might want to say in certain cases that although a name conventionally *denotes* some particular object nevertheless the writer is not on this occasion *referring* to that object. There are two kinds of cases here. One is where a writer uses a name non-standardly, deliberately referring to something other than the name's normal denotation. The other case is where a writer does not strictly *use* the name at all but in some form or other only mentions it. The parallel would be with, say, a grammarian who produces the sentence 'Socrates is wise' for purely illustrative (and thus non-referential) purposes.

We must, however, distinguish this second case from a much stronger position which reasons as follows:

1. Speaker's reference only occurs in the context of fully felicitous illocutionary acts;[8]
2. Fictive utterance involves the disengagement of standard conditions of illocutionary acts;
3. Therefore, speaker's reference never occurs in fictive utterance.

This argument is unsound both because the first premiss places an unjustified restriction on the possible contexts for identifying reference and also because the second premiss does not itself establish that the disengaged conditions include speaker's reference. However, in reminding us of what we earlier called the 'cognitive distance' of fictive utterance, the argument is useful in weakening a general presumption that works of fiction license inferences about reference and denotation as transparently as do standard works of non-fiction. Although both speaker's reference and denotation are compatible with fictive utterance we should be wary of drawing more general conclusions from this about the literary, or literary critical, status of reference.

Allusion

Allusion in literary fiction is, at its simplest, just a special case of speaker's reference in fictive utterance. As with the standard case of singular identifying reference it relies on intention. If, for example, we take the line in *Little Gidding* (line 151) 'And faded on the blowing of the horn' to involve an allusion to the line in *Hamlet* 'It faded on the crowing of the cock' (*Hamlet*, I. ii. 157), then we

---

[8] This view is defended by John Searle in *Speech Acts*.

must suppose that T. S. Eliot intended to refer to the line in *Hamlet* (we might more naturally say he intended to invoke the line or bring it to mind). Allusion in works of fiction is a clear referential relation holding between an author, a fictive utterance, and some parts of the non-fictional world. To deny the possibility of reference in fiction would involve a denial of allusion.

Curiously many of those who hold a non-reference view of fiction are also inclined to defend 'intertextuality', the view that texts refer (only) to other texts. Perhaps they might try to preserve consistency by arguing that allusion (or intertextuality in general) is more like denotation than speaker's reference in that it does not rest on intention. But this will not save the position. It is difficult, if not impossible, to make out a plausible case for a purely non-intentional conception of allusion but even if such a case could be made we are still left with a denotative (or quasi-denotative) function in fictive utterance which weakens the non-reference position.[9] Even on a non-intentional view of allusion, the relation between a section of text and what it alludes to must be understood on the model not of a word's relation to its sense (a non-denotative relation) but of a name's relation to what it stands for (i.e. a denotative relation).

There are many interesting aspects of allusion as a form of reference which we have not discussed. But our purpose for the time being is simply to identify different kinds of referential relations which are compatible with fictive utterance. Allusion is one of the most obvious and familiar.

Quasi-referential relations

Much confusion can be avoided if we restrict the notion of reference *per se* to denotation (as a relation between singular term and object) and identifying reference based on intention, as exemplified by cases of speaker's reference and (in the fictional case) by allusion. These exhaust the genuinely *referential* relations

---

[9] Although intention is almost certainly a necessary condition for allusion, it is probably not sufficient. An intention to make an allusion will fail if the allusion cannot be recognized by a reasonably well-educated audience. Allusion requires 'uptake'. See Stein Haugom Olsen, *The End of Literary Theory* (Cambridge, 1987), 48–9.

possible in fictive utterance. However, there remain a number of quasi-referential relations which are sometimes cited as examples of reference in works of fiction. It is important not to run them together with the paradigms of reference even though they are relations of a linguistic or semantic nature. They would include the following.

Instantiation

We can speak of an object being an instance of a property or general kind, in so far as the object satisfies, in the logical sense, a correlative predicate. If Socrates satisfies the predicate 'is wise' then Socrates instantiates wisdom. The stuff over here is an instance of the kind gold if 'This stuff is gold' is true. We can also speak of the instantiation of natural laws, causal relations, or generalizations. Particular events instantiate laws, and this bird's having wings instantiates (or provides an instance of) the generalization that all birds have wings.

Satisfaction, in the logical sense, is a semantic relation holding between an object and a predicate but is not equivalent to denotation which holds between an object and a name. Likewise, instantiation is not the same as denotation or singular identifying reference. The predicate 'is wise' does not denote (or refer to) Socrates, far less does the property wisdom denote (or stand for) anything at all. Conversely denotation is not a kind of instantiation. Socrates might instantiate wisdom but Socrates is not an instance of the name 'Socrates'. The points are obvious but their application to fiction needs to be fully assimilated.

In so far as works of fiction often depict kinds, there is always the possibility that particular (actual) objects will instantiate those kinds. But fictive utterances do not denote or refer to the objects that happen to instantiate the kinds they depict. If there is reference involved then it will rest on further facts concerning intention, not on instantiation alone. The characterizing properties of fictional objects will no doubt have many instances (individually or in clusters) in the actual world. This might go some way towards explaining the interest readers have in fictional characters or their ability to 'see themselves' or others in the characters. But it has nothing to do with reference. A story-teller does not *ipso facto* refer to those things that happen to instantiate the characterizing qualities, nor does a work necessarily denote or allude to such things.

What if the instantiation should be comprehensive, such that every fictive description turns out to be true of some real object? We have looked at such extreme 'coincidence' cases already in the context of the truth-value of fictive utterances. Should we say there is reference or denotation in these cases? The answer must be no. But the opposite has been argued. Here, for example, is Ryle:

> Now suppose by sheer chance, without the knowledge of Dickens, one person had existed, such that the *Pickwick Papers* were in fact faithful biography. Then we could say that Dickens' propositions were true of somebody.... [W]e should not dream of saying that there were two heroes of the story, one real and one imaginary, and the real one was exactly similar to, though numerically different from, the imaginary one. On the contrary, we should say that while previously we had thought *Pickwick Papers* was only a *pretence* biography, we now find that, by coincidence, it is a real one.[10]

The main response to this is that whether or not something is biography must depend, at least as a necessary condition, on the aims and purposes for which it was written. Curiously, Ryle seems to acknowledge the point in a parenthesis in this very passage: 'Dickens', he writes, 'would not, of course, have been an historian, for he invented his propositions and did not found them on evidence.' This leaves Ryle in the anomalous position of saying that writing a 'real' biography is compatible with not being a historian (or biographer).

One way to salvage Ryle's position might be to distinguish, as does Gale, between two senses of 'refer', such that in one sense (involving intentions) Dickens does not refer to the Pickwick counterpart, and is thus not the author of a history, and in another sense (not requiring intentions) at least *Pickwick Papers* does refer to the counterpart, and thus Dickens turns out to be the author of a biography. Gale speaks of 'locutionary' and 'illocutionary' senses of 'refer', the former determined exclusively by the content of fictive descriptions, the latter determined by a writer's intentions.[11]

However, nothing very useful is added by introducing a 'locutionary' sense of 'refer', for the relevant cases are already adequately explained by the notions of satisfaction or instantiation.

---

[10] Ryle, 'Imaginary Objects', 78–9.
[11] Gale, 'The Fictive Use of Language', 328.

It is simply misleading to run together being 'true of' and 'referring to'.[12]

Although instantiation must be clearly distinguished from reference, that does not imply that instantiation is of no importance in fiction. It is indeed important for at least some genres of fiction that a reader be able to recognize actual instances of characters, kinds, situations, predicaments, and so forth, as they are depicted in the fiction. Certainly much popular fiction (romance, soap opera, university novels, spy stories, etc.) rely on recognizable types, even stereotypes, for their general appeal, including their sense of authenticity or verisimilitude. Certainly too—which is why we have retained the label 'quasi-referential'—there is a colloquial usage whereby we speak of such fictions being *about* the things or people that instantiate their kinds. But we must not draw the wrong conclusions from these observations. There are no grounds for extending the notion of reference to cover instantiation and we need a careful account of 'about' to explain the precise relation behind the colloquial usage.

Extension

The extension of a general term or predicate is the class of objects which satisfy the predicate or of which the general term is true. Once again, it is misleading (at least on our paradigm of reference) to speak of a predicate *referring* to the objects which comprise its extension. However, that usage is not uncommon. Here is a fairly typical example, from a literary theorist: 'if *Howard's End* relies upon its readers' understanding of what a motor-car is, then the novel refers to motor-cars.'[13] The implication seems to be (1) that to understand the general term 'motor-car' is to know its extension, and (2) that if the general term crops up in the novel then the novel makes reference to the items comprising the term's extension. However, while (1) is perfectly acceptable, there seems little justification for (2), which needlessly multiplies references. It is obviously absurd to suggest that just because a character in

---

[12] Gale's notion of 'locutionary reference' covers more than just cases of descriptions *true of* a particular object. E.g. it applies also to first-person narratives, such that the personal pronoun 'I' makes a locutionary reference to the actual author, even though the illocutionary intention of self-reference is suspended. In our own terms we might say that the narrative 'I' strictly speaking *denotes* the author but does not *refer* to the author, nor are sentences containing it *about* the author.

[13] Hawthorn, *Unlocking the Text*, 96.

Howard's End is described as driving a motor-car, then the novel thereby refers to every motor-car there is, or even a subset. It seems more likely that what this theorist means is that the novel refers to the *concept* of a motor-car or to the general *kind* motor-car. But if so talk of reference is inappropriate. The novel, it would be preferable to say, utilizes the concept in characterizing fictional states of affairs; and all that means, put more formally, is that the general term 'motor-car' with its standard sense appears in some sentences, under the fictive mode, in the novel.

The relation between predicates in fictive utterances and their extensions constitutes an important relation between fictions and the world. But it is not in any straightforward sense a referential relation. What is important is that the same terms, with the same extensions, can be used in both fictive and non-fictive contexts. Understanding the one is not different from understanding the other, each calling on the same knowledge (of the term's extension). This, as we saw in Chapter 4, is part of what it is for fictional states of affairs to be similar to actual states of affairs. And also, as with the case of instantiation, it might go some way towards explaining the interest we have in works of fictions.

Non-referential relations

The relations which we have called referential and quasi-referential already make it plain that there is no credence in the idea that somehow fiction *per se* is intrinsically 'non-referential' or 'cut off' from the world. Strictly speaking, the non-reference case collapses here.

But the pro-reference position must avoid multiplying reference beyond necessity. It is important to draw the right conclusions from the possibility of 'reference in fiction'. We have already expressed reservations about the genuine referentiality of both instantiation and extension. We now turn to relations at further removes from reference, though which are sometimes thought to be part of 'fictional reference'.

Origin, genesis, inspiration, etc.

The question of what, in the world, a work of fiction is *based on, drawn from, inspired by* (or whatever) is biographical. It concerns facts about the composition of fiction, including facts about the author's states of mind, conscious and unconscious. There is undoubtedly a relation here, of a causal or genetic nature, between works of fiction and the world but it is not a referential relation. It is never a sufficient condition for a work to refer to, or be about, some object that the object should play a role in the genesis of the work. Other factors must always be involved for determining reference or 'aboutness'. Furthermore, there is no necessity that there be any specific items or events in the world which can be identified as the source of a particular work of fiction. It is possible for a work to be almost entirely the product of a writer's imagination, even though it is no doubt also true, as a piece of a priori psychology, that the imagination must be fed ultimately by 'experience' (for example, something like Locke's basic ingredients of 'sensation and reflection').

Thoughts of a general nature as well as thoughts about actual particulars can provide the genesis of a work. Sometimes both are involved. Here, for example, is John Fowles, in the Prologue to *A Maggot*:

> For some years before its writing a small group of travellers, faceless, without apparent motive, went in my mind towards an event. Evidently in some past, since they rode horses, and in a deserted landscape; but beyond this very primitive image, nothing.

That part of the inspiration is entirely general. But not so all of it.

> However, one day one of the riders gained a face. By chance I acquired a pencil and water-colour drawing of a young woman. There was no indication of artist, simply a little note in ink in one corner, which seemingly says, in Italian, 16 *July* 1683.[14]

If we are to believe Fowles, these events, i.e. the recurring image and the acquisition of the drawing, played a part in the causal process that brought about the fiction. But even though the propositions in the fiction might elaborate on the thoughts comprising its inspiration, they do not refer to, or stand for, either the drawing itself or the young woman in the drawing.

Sometimes the genesis of a fiction plays a more substantial role in the fiction itself. In the Author's Note at the beginning of *Small World*, the author David Lodge tells us that 'Rummidge [the

---

[14] John Fowles, *A Maggot* (London, 1985), 5.

University town in the novel] is not Birmingham, though it owes something to popular prejudices about that city.' He also tells us that 'The MLA Convention of 1979 [an event in the novel] did not take place in New York, though I have drawn on the programme for the 1978 one, which did.' Here, unlike in the Fowles case, it seems less clear what to say about reference. Do not Birmingham and the 1978 MLA Convention figure *in some way* in the descriptions in the novel? Is not the novel *in some sense* about them? Just how such real places and events do figure in fictive descriptions is a topic to be considered in a later section of this chapter. For the moment it is enough to insist only that if there is a referential or denotative relation here it is not based solely on facts about the original inspiration. Genetic factors are never sufficient for determining reference.

The genetic ancestry of a fiction stands to referential relations rather as the etymology of a word stands to its present meaning. Sometimes the etymology is of no relevance to the meaning: the connection with Thor plays no role in the current meaning of 'Thursday'. Sometimes, though, etymology is relevant: 'exit' gets its meaning directly from its Latin root. But etymology is neither necessary nor sufficient for determining current meaning.

Similarities

Fictional objects and events often bear similarities to real objects and events but again this provides no basis for a referential relation. Surprisingly, similarity of fiction and reality has been associated with reference, so the matter requires a little more clarification. Here, for example, is Graham Dunstan Martin:

> there is no Castle, no library of Babel, no Yossarian, and no configuration of events such as is described in *Catch 22*. But there are certainly events in the world that are like them; and these events are the referents of these works of fiction.[15]

Martin's view is based on the notion that fictional creations are 'a collage of familiar bits and pieces'.[16] He views the items in the world from which the creations are drawn, or to which they are similar, as the 'referring components' of the 'fictional concept'.

In Chapter 4 we offered an analysis of judgements concerning

---

[15] Martin, 'A New Look', 233.   [16] Ibid. 225.

similarities between fictional characters and real people. When we speak of such similarities we should be taken to mean only that (some of) the descriptions of a character in a fiction could be truly applied to a person in the real world. In that sense similarity relations are based on relations of satisfaction or instantiation. The major problem with similarities, which undermines their claim to referentiality, is that they can be found anywhere. King Lear is described as an old man, a king, a father, a person who utters 'I prithee, daughter, do not make me mad', and so on. Actual instances of one or other of these properties are easy to find. But it is clear enough that Shakespeare is not *referring* to every old man, king, father, etc. when he offers those descriptions, nor are the descriptions in this use *about* all those people of whom they happen to be true.

Preliminaries on 'about'

We turn now directly to an analysis of 'about' in relation to fiction. We have alluded at several points in the argument to 'aboutness' and we believe that this is a more fundamental relation than that of reference, which can largely be subsumed by it. To say what a fictive description or a work of fiction is about is partly a way of characterizing fictive *content*. Our central question will be 'what can works of fiction, *qua* fiction, be about?' On the face of it the answer is simple: *anything*. But, to parody Quine, there remains room for disagreement over cases. Here then is a case:

Jilly Cooper the best-selling novelist yesterday agreed an undisclosed libel settlement with a Gloucestershire businessman who shared his name and a remarkable number of other features with the central character in her latest book, *Rivals*.

Miss Cooper invented an 'impossibly corrupt' television magnate called Lord Anthony Bullingham, who cheats on his wife and whose dirty double dealings revolve round the fight for an ITV franchise.

The book, published in June last year, was at the top of the best-sellers list for many weeks but infuriated a real-life Mr William Bullingham, aged 46, a director of Cotswold Cable Television and a property company.

Similarities included a large house in the Cotswolds, a taste for BMW cars and Rottweiler dogs, a shareholding in a Cotswold television company, being born in Cheltenham and a wife who is an expert gardener.

But unlike his corrupt fictional counterpart, the real Mr Bullingham is happily married, has four children and is involved in charity work.

In the High Court, Mr Richard Hartley, QC, told Mr Justice Brooke that his client, the real Mr Bullingham, was a well-known local figure and former councillor in his home town, Cheltenham.

Mr Bullingham, who was in court to hear the settlement read, launched the libel action to protect his reputation.

Transworld Publishers have already changed the name Bullingham in the paperback edition and yesterday publicly acknowledged their unreserved regret for any distress and embarrassment caused.

Both sides agreed that the terms of the settlement should remain confidential.[17]

So is, or was, the novel *Rivals* about Mr William Bullingham? No, surely not, either before or after the name change. In fact the change of name makes little difference; all of the similarities mentioned between the real and fictional Bullingham are salient and having the name 'Bullingham' is not of a different order from the rest. Why do we say that the novel is not about Mr Bullingham? After all, it seems to be *true of* him (or largely so) and furthermore it is at least about the *likes* of him, rich television tycoons who drive BMW cars, and so forth. Yet it is not about *him*, we want to say, because Jilly Cooper, let us assume, knew nothing of him. This particular Bullingham played no causal role in the genesis of the novel. But that is not the decisive issue. Suppose Cooper did know Bullingham, suppose she even based the novel on that knowledge. That would still not be sufficient to determine that the novel was about him. Defoe based Robinson Crusoe on the real-life Alexander Selkirk but the novel *Robinson Crusoe* is not about Selkirk. Being 'based on' is not the same as being 'about' any more than is being 'true of' or being 'similar to'.

Perhaps it is referential intentions that settle the matter? Cooper did not intend to refer to Bullingham so the novel is not about Bullingham. Authors often write their disclaimers in terms of intentions: no reference to any living person is intended, and so on. We have already offered an account of referential intentions —and recognized their presence in fictive utterance—but in a general characterization of fictive content (and certainly *literary* content) the notion of speaker's (or writer's) reference plays only a minor role. For one thing not every kind of aboutness in relation

[17] *The Times*, Friday, 28 July 1989, 3.

to fiction involves reference and it would be nice if possible to find a uniform account. For another, talk of intentions in the literary context introduces unnecessary issues of controversy. Narrative or genre conventions can override referential intentions; we saw in the case of allusion that referential intention is not sufficient to establish an allusion in cases where the intention cannot hope to be recognized.

It is more promising to raise something like the following question: do we, or do we not, need to invoke information about Bullingham (the real Bullingham) in order to understand the novel? If we do, then the novel is about Bullingham, if not, then it is not. That just leaves the problem of what it is to understand a novel and what kind of information might be invoked in doing so. And that, quite properly, directs the discussion towards literary criticism where it belongs.

Philosophical bearings

There are two very familiar passages, from the history of debates on fiction, which are helpful in establishing the philosophical bearings of the discussion which follows.

The first is from Aristotle:

The distinction between historian and poet is not in the one writing prose and the other verse—you might put the work of Herodotus into verse, and it would still be a species of history; it consists really in this, that the one describes the thing that has been, and the other a kind of thing that might be. Hence poetry is something more philosophic and of graver import than history, since its statements are of the nature rather of universals, whereas those of history are singulars. By a universal statement I mean one as to what such or such a kind of man will probably or necessarily say or do—which is the aim of poetry, though it affixes proper names to the characters; by a singular statement, one as to what, say, Alcibiades did or had done to him.[18]

The second is from Frege:

In hearing an epic poem . . . apart from the euphony of the language we are only interested in the sense of the sentences and the images and feelings thereby aroused. The question of truth would cause us to abandon

[18] Aristotle, *De Poetica* (1451 *b*, 2–10).

aesthetic delight for the attitude of scientific investigation. Hence it is a matter of no concern to us whether the name 'Odysseus', for instance, has reference, so long as we accept the poem as a work of art.[19]

There are similarities between the two passages: both attempt to characterize some distinctive feature of poetry (i.e. *poesis* or fiction); both contrast poetry with another form of discourse, in Aristotle's case, history, in Frege's, science; both allude to the values of poetry. There are also ways in which they complement each other: Aristotle stresses the 'grave import' of poetry, Frege its 'aesthetic delight'; Aristotle talks of poetic content, Frege of attitudes towards that content; finally Aristotle writes from the point of view of the poet, Frege from the point of view of the reader.

The account that follows will offer a qualified endorsement of the Aristotelian passage, at least in defending this idea: *works of fiction, qua fiction, are (primarily) about kinds rather than particulars, and where they are about particulars these are particulars-under-certain-aspects rather than particulars per se.*

The Fregean passage is more controversial. Some Fregean commentators insist that the passage is an aberration in Fregean semantics, that strictly there can be no sense without reference, no thoughts without truth-values. One reason why these worries do not make us relinquish broadly Fregean sympathies is that the main Fregean insight about fiction—that attention is redirected from reference to sense or 'mode of presentation'—holds *even where there are no non-denoting singular terms* in a work of fiction (for example, in certain historical novels); it is only contingently the case that descriptive fictions use non-denoting or fictional terms. Be that as it may, there are other, non-exegetical, reasons for needing to qualify the Fregean account. Fregean sense is not sufficiently fine-grained to capture all we want from fictional (at least *literary* fictional) content; perhaps Frege anticipated this by alluding also to 'images and feelings'. Furthermore, readers of fiction do not always abandon what Frege calls the 'attitude of scientific investigation'; a concern with truth-values is at least sometimes part of an appropriate response to fiction. But the core Fregean insight must be retained, that the primary response to fiction *qua*

---

[19] Gottlob Frege, 'On Sense and Reference', *Philosophical Writings of Gottlob Frege*, trans. and ed. Peter Geach and Max Black (Oxford, 1970), 63.

fiction is concerned with internal relations of sense rather than external relations of reference.

In linking the Aristotelian insight with the neo-Fregean insight, and adding a few refinements, we hope that we can give an account of fiction and 'about' which can make some small advances on age-old problems: how works of fiction can have value and interest; how they can, in a sense, be about all of us but not about any one of us; how they can depict recognizable human delights and tragedies without depicting actual instances of these; finally, how readers can learn from fiction. We must avoid the trap of aestheticism, which cuts off fiction (or art) from the world, but we must also avoid the indulgent pursuit of special kinds of reference and truth.

There are three kinds of cases where we might speak of what a work of fiction is about: (1) being about some real object (person, place, or event), as when we say that *Bleak House* is about London or *Henry VI* about the Wars of the Roses; (2) being about some fictional object (person, place, or event), as when we say that *Smiley's People* is about Smiley's people and *The Case of the Speckled Band* about . . . well, the case of the speckled band; and (3) being about some theme or conception, as when we say that *Othello* is about jealousy or *Right Ho, Jeeves* about being a wealthy and feckless bachelor playing waggish tricks on his friends.

On the face of it these three applications are very different, not least in virtue of their ontological commitments. Our supposition is that although on an external characterization of a work of fiction (concerning, for example, its genesis or other causal relations) the differences might be significant, from the internal point of view of those adopting the fictive stance, the differences all but disappear. That is, when we adopt the Fregean attitude to fiction, when we engage in imaginative involvement and make-believe, our attention is directed in each case to something more like what Aristotle calls kinds (or universals) than to particulars. What helps to blur the three applications of 'about' is the aspectival nature of fictional content, as introduced in Chapter 4. According to this notion, just as fictional objects and events owe their identity to the multiple aspects, descriptive and evaluative, through which they are presented, so too real objects make their appearance in works of fiction, not through a fully extensional presentation, but only under some set of aspects or other.

About objects: the invocation principle

Under what conditions is a work of fiction F about some actual object *a*? Two conditions seem to be prominent: (1) *a* exists; (2) *a* plays some determinate role in F. But what role? And what signals the relation to *a*? It might seem that the name of *a*—suitably used, not merely mentioned or quoted—in a fictive utterance is sufficient for the utterance to be about *a*, at least to the extent that the name denotes *a*. That assumes of course that we get round the Bullingham problem. The novel *Rivals*, we agreed, is not about the real Mr Bullingham in spite of the coincidence of names. But the names here can be treated as homonyms. No doubt all kinds of factors—referential intention or causal connection or common knowledge—will in practice determine the denotation of a name in fiction. It is clear beyond doubt that the name 'London' in *Bleak House* does not denote London, Ontario.

But there are more subtle issues at hand. In discussing the Bullingham case we introduced a principle—let us call it *the invocation principle*—that sheds light on a fundamental relation between F and *a* (works of fiction and objects). The principle suggested that a significant factor in whether F is about *a* concerns the need to invoke information about *a* in order to understand F. This crucially shifts the emphasis away from the genesis of the work, and causal connections, to the fictive stance, authorized response, and so on. The principle might loosely be formulated as follows:

a work F is about *a* only if a reader must invoke, or bring to mind, *a* for an adequate understanding of F (i.e. in an authorized fictive response to F); or, put in another way, only if information about *a* is a required component in the inferences licensed by an authorized supplementation of F.

This is expressed as a necessary condition. There are doubts about its sufficiency; for example, if a text A makes an allusion to text B then no doubt knowledge of B is needed to understand A but we would not normally say that A was about B. Allusion and reference are not co-extensional with 'about'.

The invocation principle helps to rule out the real Bullingham as an object of reference but does it hold in general? Take another case. Is Shakespeare's *Macbeth* about the real Macbeth? To some it might seem obvious that it is; the genetic, even referential, connections are there. But do we need to invoke information about Macbeth to understand the play? That calls for a literary critical, rather than a semantical, judgement. One problem is that nearly every salient fact that might be produced about the Scottish king is likely to be either contradicted or ignored in the dramatic presentation. For the semanticist that need not affect reference, which could be secured by rigid designation. But rigid designation applies only from an external perspective, in the sense in which it might be true *of* Macbeth that Shakespeare wrote a play about him. With regard to the appropriate fictive response of imagination and make-believe it is at least arguable that information about the real king plays no role in appreciation of the drama. The king himself, it might be said, is as remote from the play as is Dr Joseph Bell from the Sherlock Holmes stories even though Conan Doyle, supposedly, got the inspiration for Holmes from the life of Dr Bell. The matter is arguable because from another critical standpoint it might be essential to view *Macbeth* as a *history* play, in which case facts about the king would have to be invoked in judging the historical treatment; under that reading the aboutness relation would be restored.

The example can be generalized. What it shows is that even the use of a proper name in fiction is not decisive in determining what the fiction is about. It also shows a relativity in aboutness. From the internal perspective—that of the critic or appreciator, say, rather than the biographer—the question of whether a work is about an actual particular is relative to a mode of reading (or understanding) the work. Arthur Miller describes in his autobiography how his play *The Crucible* seems to acquire different meanings according to the place and circumstances of its performance. Thus in 1980 a production in Shanghai 'served as a metaphor for life under Mao and the Cultural Revolution'. In Poland in the 1970s the play became a lesson about Stalinism.[20] Such familiar observations suggest that 'about' from the perspective of the fictive stance is not a fully extensional notion but is irreducibly connected with interpretation. That is a further consequence of the invocation principle and points to a feature which, as we

[20] Arthur Miller, *Timebends: A Life* (New York, 1987), 348.

shall see, helps to bring together the three kinds of 'about' in relation to fiction.

Even where we have established that F is about *a*, in accordance with the invocation principle, not any information that might be invoked about *a* is relevant to an understanding of F. This takes us back to the aspectival nature of fictive content. Normally if sentence S is about *a* then S is about *a* under any description of *a*. So if the sentence S 'Smith is a philosopher' is about Smith and Smith is married to Jones, then S is about someone married to Jones.[21]

But the fiction case lacks this transparency. *The Canterbury Tales* is about a pilgrimage to Canterbury. Now Canterbury, since the 1960s, is a city with a university. But *The Canterbury Tales* is not, from the fictive point of view, about a pilgrimage to a city with a university (or even to a city which would later have a university). Chaucer's fictive presentation does not authorize this perspective on either the city or the pilgrimage. The name 'Canterbury' does not have a fully extensional use in Chaucer's sentences. That is to say that not all co-designative substitutions (for example, 'the county capital of Kent with a university' for 'Canterbury') are permissible *salva fictione*, just as not any imaginings of the city are appropriate when reflecting on Chaucer's narrative. Canterbury appears in the *Tales* only under certain aspects. So it is that when we invoke background information about Canterbury—or any real object depicted in fiction—to aid our imaginings we must select only information suitably connected to or derivable from the aspects under which the object is presented. One constraint, clearly, in this case is to restrict ourselves to aspects of Canterbury contemporaneous with Chaucer's writing but, as we saw in Chapter 4, the principles of supplementation are not bound exclusively to what a reader takes the author's personal knowledge to have been. What a reader is invited to imagine is controlled from several sources, not least literary or genre conventions and such broadly accessible background knowledge as might be needed to make sense of the narrative descriptions.

We can illuminate the aspectival presentation of objects in fiction by looking at parallels with children's games of make-believe (here we are indebted to Kendall Walton). Take a children's game of

---

[21] See Catherine Z. Elgin, *With Reference to Reference* (Indianapolis, 1983), 155.

castles and dungeons. The kitchen door, within the game, has become the door to the dungeon. Now the door is both a real door—*that* door—and a make-believe or fictive door. Some of the properties of the real door—being made of wood, opening outwards, being 7 feet high—are also properties of the fictive door. Other properties of the real door are not (they are not authorized in the game): being made in 1967, being the door to the kitchen, etc. Furthermore, within the game, the door comes to acquire new properties: being the door to the dungeon, having a massive lock, etc. These imaginary aspects conjoin with the real or authorized aspects to produce the required conception. Just as the door is a prop in the game of castles and dungeons so, following Walton's idiom, Canterbury is a prop in the 'game' of *The Canterbury Tales*. Certain features of Canterbury—for example, twentieth-century developments or little-known facts about its history—have no part in the game, they are not authorized for the imagined content. But many real features which are not explicitly mentioned will need to be invoked for a full understanding of that content; and of course some imaginary features as well.

The children's game analogy gives a good idea of the different perspectives we can take to fiction (or make-believe). From an external—parents'—perspective *that* door is part of the game. This external judgement of aboutness is fully *de re*: i.e. the parents are speaking *de re* about the door when they say it figures in the game. But from the internal—children's—perspective only the door-under-certain-descriptions is part of the game. Their judgement about the game and the door is, as it were, *de dicto*: i.e. the children, as participants, speak in the fictive mode only about the door as-a-dungeon-door-with-a-massive-lock or as-a-door-possessing-thus-and-such-properties.

It is important to emphasize, however, that the games analogy here is purely illustrative. On our own account, unlike Walton's, the connection between fiction and games is not essential. Rather than describing *The Canterbury Tales* as a *game*, we prefer to treat it more literally, if prosaically, as a set of sentences the propositional content of which we are invited to respond to with a complex range of attitudes, imaginative and interpretative. The way we imagine—or are intended to imagine—Canterbury in the *Tales* is constrained ultimately by the subtleties of the described content and the conventional responses to that content, both fictive and literary. This determines the aspects under which the narrative, in the fictive mode, is *about Canterbury*. But any such judgement is quite compatible with there also being a purely extensional relation between Chaucer's sentences and the actual city of Canterbury.

Let us consider another example. The notorious *Satanic Verses* is *de re* about the Koran, Islam, and the Prophet Muhammad, but what offence it causes lies in the *de dicto* presentation, the aspects under which the objects are presented. Fictively the novel is not about the Koran *per se* but about the Koran-as-Satanic-verses, not about the Prophet but about the Prophet-as-the-devil, and so on. It is these compound conceptions which have offended, not, or not merely, the fact that under what Frege calls 'the attitude of scientific investigation' the novel contains false or slanderous statements about the Islamic religion. Interestingly, the author himself has claimed that the novel is not really about Islam but about 'migration, metamorphosis, divided selves, love, death, London and Bombay'.[22] But even if this is true as a *de dicto* claim about fictive content, the aspects under which these items are presented invite imaginings which some readers apparently find intolerable. And it is the aspects which constitute the 'world' of the fiction—they are not merely incidental.[23]

So far we have looked only at cases where proper names occur in fiction. But F can be about *a* even where no name of *a* appears in F. How does the invocation principle fare here? *Gulliver's Travels* again provides a good example. There is a passage in part I (chapter 2) where Gulliver is describing the Emperor of Lilliput. Background factors make it plain, amongst the cognoscenti, that Swift intended a satirical reference to King George I. The passage, then, is surely *about* George I even though his name does not appear, nor does any description in the passage literally and accurately apply to him. The determining factor seems to be the author's intention. Does this override the invocation principle? No, it simply shows that in the case of satire an author's intended

[22] Salman Rushdie, 'Salman Rushdie Writes to Rajiv Gandhi', in Lisa Appignanesi and Sara Maitland (eds.), *The Rushdie File* (London, 1989), 44.

[23] Rushdie's use of the defence 'It is only fiction' (or his stronger assertion, it is only 'a fictional dream of a fictional character') is only partially successful against the charge of religious slander. Certainly the fictionality establishes the cognitive distance of the author and perhaps that there are no *claims* being made. But the author is undoubtedly responsible for the aspects under which the fictional content is presented.

reference is a significant constraint in understanding the work: not the only constraint, of course, as genre conventions also help to determine reference. On a satirical reading, then, the passage is about George I because to understand the satire (i.e. draw authorized inferences from it) a reader must invoke contemporary attitudes to the king. Note, however, that on a non-satirical reading, as a children's story for example, no information about George I is needed so the king has no role in the fictive supplementation. The children's *Gulliver's Travels* is not about Georgian England under any aspect.

The invocation principle yields satisfactory results in other cases. First-person fictional narratives are not, on the whole, about their authors. When Defoe writes 'I ... [am] a poor desolate girl' the sentence is not about him but about the fictional Moll Flanders. Defoe has no role in the fiction. (He has of course a role in its creation but that does not make the fiction about him.) Similarly with cases of coincidentally true descriptions, of which Bullingham was an example. Where a description in a fictive utterance just happens to fit an object *a* the description is not about *a* unless information about *a* is required to understand the description.

Readers of fiction sometimes say that a novel is about them. Perhaps they have identified totally with one of the characters or they sense that their own predicament is strikingly similar to that of one of the protagonists. Can a novel be about a reader R in cases where the author had no knowledge of R? We should distinguish a colloquial sense of 'about' from the strict sense we are trying to define. Colloquially, a novel can be said to be 'about' a particular reader just in case the reader satisfies some salient set of descriptions in the novel (or whose life or circumstances instantiate certain significant aspects of the narrative). Such cases, explicable in terms of satisfaction or instantiation, are, we have suggested, at best only quasi-referential. What about the strict sense of 'about'? There do seem to be certain genres of fiction, romantic and fantasy genres mostly, where a condition for understanding a work (getting the point) is for the reader to project him- or herself into the fiction such that the appropriate supplementation of the content will involve (selective) information about the reader. In these cases the fiction can legitimately be said to be *about* the reader. In such cases the content actually changes from reader to reader.

About fictional characters, places, events, etc.

We can turn now to the two remaining cases of 'about', first where we say, for example, that *Smiley's People* is about Smiley's people and, second, where we say that *Othello* is about jealousy. What is interesting here are the parallels with the first kind of 'about' and the way that all three reflect the aspectival nature of fictive content, the notion that fictional worlds are both presented and constituted 'under a description'.

The first case concerns fictional characters, or more generally fictional persons, places and events characterized through fictive utterance. In Chapter 4 we discussed three different idioms for 'talk about' fictional characters: (1) fictive utterance itself, (2) the 'In the fiction . . .' idiom, and (3) the 'X-character' idiom. Only the latter involved ontological commitment to characters as entities of a certain kind, abstract entities. The issue here does not concern ontology, or the logical form of different ways of talking about fictional characters, but the similarities and differences between aboutness claims involving objects and those involving fictions. However, the discussion should provide further reasons in support of the ontological claim that characters are constituted by the qualitative aspects under which they are presented.

Nelson Goodman distinguishes two senses of 'about': as a two-place relational predicate as in 'F is about a' which allows existential generalization and is fully extensional, preserving truth under any designation of a, and as a one-place predicate formulated as 'F is a-about', which is non-relational and does not afford an extensional context for 'a'.[24] 'a-about' is suitable for the case of fictional names. The novel *Rivals* is Lord-Anthony-Bullingham-about, in Goodman's sense, but not strictly about Lord Anthony Bullingham for there is no such person; it is not about Mr William Bullingham for slightly different reasons. We might adopt Goodman's notation for fictional names but for reasons already discussed his strict extensionalist definition of 'about a' does not provide an adequate analysis of extra-fictional names in works of fiction. Under the perspective of the fictive stance a work of fiction's being about a real object is more akin to 'a-about' than 'about a'.

Our underlying hypothesis is this: *that make-believe reflection on*

---

[24] Nelson Goodman, 'About', *Mind*, 70 (1961), 19 ff.

fictional characters (or states of affairs) is not cognitively different from make-believe reflection on real objects (or states of affairs) aspectivally presented in works of fiction. In Chapter 4 we discussed at length what is involved in reflecting on some particular fictional character. The question now is: what are the criteria for determining whether a work is about this rather than that character?

First of all, names alone—as inscription-types—are not sufficient to identify characters; there is no reason why two distinct characters should not share the same name even in the same narrative. There is no need for a character even to have a name. Indeed proper names of characters are not of central importance, from a logical point of view. Being called 'Lord Anthony Bullingham' is as much part of the characterization of the protagonist in *Rivals* as owning a BMW; but it is no more than that. In the old days writers used to pack significance into their characters' names: Everyman, Pilgrim, Mr Allworthy. Jilly Cooper probably just liked the sound of 'Bullingham'. The point is that fictional names have only a characterizing not a referential function. It is only make-believe that the names denote.

Two elements are fundamental in the delineation of character: the descriptive content of fictive utterances and the fictive response. The descriptive content provides the characterizing predicates; the response of make-believe provides the illusion of particularity and reference. The fictional Bullingham is presented under various descriptions (or aspects): liking BMW cars, living in the Cotswolds, being an 'impossibly corrupt' television magnate, and so on. These and other descriptions, yielded by a variety of narrative devices, give the identity of the Bullingham character. But even if an actual person—like the real Bullingham—happens to satisfy the descriptions the novel, as we have argued, is not about that person. This is where the make-believe element comes in. Those adopting the fictive stance make-believe (or imagine) under the prescription of the narrative that there is some unique individual being described.

Character-identity resides not only with the explicit descriptive content but in a fully supplemented content. Authorized supplementation of descriptive content is constrained by the aspects under which the character is presented. P. G. Wodehouse's Jeeves, for example, is presented, with only two exceptions, in a series of

novels where the first-person narrator is Bertie Wooster, the feckless bachelor for whom Jeeves is the butler. Wooster's attitudes
to Jeeves—dependence, admiration, envy, frustration—are integral
to the characterization. The tone and mannerisms of Wooster's
narrative give Jeeves his distinctive identity; they also determine
how readers are to respond to him. It is not just that we happen
to perceive Jeeves through Wooster's eyes, as if this were one
point of view among others, rather his identity as a character is
constituted by that perspective.

How strictly do we want character-identity to be constrained by
these aspectival factors? Does every nuance of description make
a difference to what character is presented? It is helpful to think
of character-identity, more broadly conceived, as interest-relative.
Judgements of whether a fiction is about such-and-such a character
depend on intentional factors, such as interpretation or mode of
reading. The point directly parallels that made earlier with regard
to real objects in fiction.

Think, first, of different treatments of ostensibly the same
character, like Dr Faustus in Christopher Marlowe, Goethe, and
Thomas Mann. On the aspectival view there must be different
characters depicted because the presentations are different, yet
that seems to miss the point. To serve the interests of literary
history we need a more flexible notion of character-type, identified by a core of salient properties. The presentation of that core
in different works is sufficient for the works to be *about* the same
character. Even looser connections are possible. Is not Maria in
West Side Story the same character as Shakespeare's Juliet?[25] The
idea of a core is less helpful here than the idea of interpretation.
It might be illuminating for our understanding of *West Side Story*
to think of Maria as Juliet, to apply Juliet-specific aspects in our
supplementation of Maria; yet on another reading, as contemporary satire perhaps, the assimilation might not be fruitful. The case
is not dissimilar from that of George I and the Emperor of Lilliput.

At the other extreme it is possible for two lexically identical
narratives to be about different characters. Here the salient differences show up not in the explicit content but only in the authorized supplementations. If Borges' Pierre Menard succeeds in

---

[25] The example comes from Joseph L. Camp, 'Why Attributions of Aboutness
Report Soft Facts', *Philosophical Topics*, 16 (1988), 14 f.

producing a replica of *Don Quixote* in the twentieth century his presentation authorizes supplementations of the characters, for example, in terms of Freudian psychology, which are not authorized in the original.[26]

One final problem about characters. Suppose we have a minor character, say, in a whodunit, described merely as a suspicious-looking housemaid with no active causal role in the plot, and a narrative function largely conventional. Could this same character crop up in different whodunits? That might seem odd if the stories are unconnected, yet if a character is constituted by its salient qualities we must accept that consequence. Again we need the notion of a character-type, particularly when describing a genre of fiction. The same type, we want to say, can appear repeatedly in unconnected narratives such that each narrative presents distinct tokens of that type. Yet how is that possible if characters already belong in the ontological category of types? Perhaps the best response is that whereas a character-type is determined solely by clusters of qualities a character-token is individuated both by character-type and by a rootedness in some particular narrative. To determine the identity of a token we need to trace the character presentation back to an original act of story-telling.

About conceptions and themes

The third category of aboutness is where we speak of a work of fiction being about a certain conception or theme. The relevant schema is not 'F is about a' or 'F is a-about' but 'F is about ϕ'. Being 'about ϕ' concerns the descriptive content of fictive utterances and is perhaps the most characteristic form of aboutness claims with regard to fiction. All works of fiction can be said to be 'about ϕ' and our interest in fiction more often than not resides in judgements of this kind, for example an interest in the way particular works present and develop their themes or conceptions.

Claims of the 'a-about' class are strictly speaking a special case of claims of the 'about ϕ' class. Characters dissolve into their constitutive aspects plus the make-believe of instantiation. In fact when we describe the content of a work of fiction we rarely use

---

[26] Currie discusses the case in 'Fictional Names', 486.

the '*a*-about' form (or its colloquial equivalent): we say not that the work is 'about Jack and Jill' but that it is 'about a boy and a girl who . . .'. The make-believe convention determines that this is understood not as subject to existential quantification (i.e. the inference that there exists some boy and some girl who . . .) but as an instance of 'about ϕ'.

'ϕ' in this formulation can be abstract or specific; we can characterize a work as about appearance and reality or about being-a-Moor-of-Venice-cruelly-duped-by-a-scheming-adjutant. For want of a better term, these are universals, though we say this without commitment as to how that might be construed ontologically. Merely in virtue of having descriptive content works of fiction are about universals. But even if Aristotle's thesis about *poesis* is interpreted, which it sometimes is, as a claim about universals in poetry (rather than just about the distinction between universal and singular statements) he presumably wants to go further than our minimal claim. Of more interest to Aristotle, as indeed to us, is how the universals are presented and what special opportunities are afforded by their presentation in literary fiction. In Part 3, and in particular Chapter 16, we explore in detail the central role of such universals in literature and literary appreciation.

What is of interest is not just that fictive utterances involve predication but that the concatenation of predicates in a narrative structure generates and authorizes inferences beyond explicit content, fitting the schema 'F is about ϕ'. Literary interpretation affords the paradigm for inferences of this kind. Interpretation is a process of redescription, generalizing across elements in a work until the maximum number of elements have been subsumed under a higher-order description which articulates the theme of the work. At the thematic level a fiction is about ϕ only relative to an interpretation. Kafka's *The Trial* is about alienation or the inhumanity of industrialized society or neurotic anxiety not because these notions are 'given' in the content itself but only to the extent that it might be fruitful to reflect on the content through these conceptions.

Again we find the same kinds of questions recurring in all three classes of aboutness claims, many related to generalized versions of the invocation principle: what do we need to invoke, what is it illuminating to invoke, in understanding a work of fiction? Sometimes actual objects, or aspects of objects, are needed, sometimes general conceptions, sometimes information of a highly specific nature, both facts and beliefs. We grasp the content of fiction not only by reflecting on propositional content but by an imaginative engagement with it aided by cognitive supplementations. Concern with what a work of fiction is about is a concern with its descriptive content, what it is and how it might be legitimately extended.

Learning from fiction

The principles that legitimate or authorize interpretations of descriptive content are numerous and controversial. We need not pursue them here, in the context of an account of reference and aboutness. Instead we will offer one or two more general remarks about the cognitive implications of the account so far. In what sense, if any, could fiction be a source of learning or instruction?

First of all, it is more interesting to focus on the notion of 'learning about ϕ', in the sense of 'about ϕ' just introduced, than on the simpler notion of 'learning that p'. Certainly there are clearly recognizable instances of 'learning that p' from works of fiction. A reader might pick up incidental facts or come to believe broader generalizations as a result of reading fiction: either because these are explicitly presented in the descriptive content or because they are derivable in obvious ways. In Chapter 13 we will be looking at propositional theories of literary truth which seek more subtle relations between literary works and propositions. Given that fictions can be about actual objects or events and that authors can refer to objects and events through fictive utterances there is no difficulty in principle in admitting that true propositions can be yielded, in some manner or other, by works of fiction.

Not all that can be learned from fiction is propositional.[27] Much of what we know about love, mortality, pride and prejudice we have learned from fiction, not by adopting 'the attitude of scientific investigation', but by an imaginative engagement with fictive content which can be judged to be about these conceptions. It is important to establish a very close link between what can be learned

[27] For an account of learning from fiction in terms of 'strategic and conceptual skills' and 'empathetic beliefs and knowledge', see David Novitz, 'Fiction and the Growth of Knowledge', *Grazer Philosophische Studien*, 19 (1983), 47–68; also *Knowledge, Fiction and Imagination*, ch. 6.

from fiction and the way the fictional content is presented.[28] The aspectival nature of the presentation, embodying attitudinal as well as descriptive content, determines the control that an author has over a reader's assimilation of the content.

'Learning about ϕ' is intimately connected to the constitutive processes of the fictive stance. We reflect on the propositional content, we make-believe that there are actual instances, we import what we know about the world, we supplement imaginatively, we entertain thoughts and hypotheses, we adopt points of view, we assume attitudes and values. So much is familiar. The point is that fiction can provide an occasion for imaginative reflection that perhaps otherwise would not be available to us. Even being in the position of bringing to mind certain imaginary states of affairs can enrich, as we might say, our conceptual repertoire.[29] Through reflecting *on* certain conceptions in works of fiction, we learn to reflect *with* those conceptions in other contexts. Similarly by adopting certain points of view towards imaginary states of affairs, under the direction of a story-teller, we might come to adopt those same points of view in comparable situations elsewhere.

There should be no implication because works of fiction principally depict universals (being about kinds of things or aspects or about conceptions and themes) rather than actual particulars that they must be cut off from the real world. The intuition that fictions are *about* real people (people in love, politicians, parents, university lecturers, and so forth), other than in the somewhat special cases where an author intends directly to refer to named individuals, can be accommodated without invoking any mysterious 'correspondence' relation. By reflecting on fictional content readers can come to see themselves and others under the same aspects that characterize the fictive states of affairs. Nothing as strong as empathetic identification is needed to achieve this. At its simplest

[28] R. W. Beardsmore, in 'Learning From a Novel', *Philosophy and the Arts. Royal Institute of Philosophy Lectures,* vi *(1971–2)* (London, 1973), rightly emphasizes that 'what we learn . . . is essentially bound up with the way in which the writer expresses himself' (45) but he does not develop the idea of fictional 'content'.

[29] A similar point is made by Putnam, giving a gloss on Goodman: 'Consider the experience of reading a novel like *Don Quixote*. One thing that happens to us is that our conceptual and perceptual repertoire becomes enlarged . . . This enlargement of our stock of predicates and of metaphors is *cognitive*; we now possess descriptive resources we did not have before', Hilary Putnam, 'Reflections on Goodman's *Ways of Worldmaking*', *Journal of Philosophy*, 76 (1979), 614–15.

readers just notice that the character-types depicted crop up, more or less, in the world. Mr William Bullingham recognized significant elements of himself in the Bullingham character, so much so that he feared readers might literally take the work to be about him. He won his lawsuit and the name was changed. But the similarities remain and unfriendly readers might suppose that although they do not need to invoke the real Bullingham to understand the fictional Bullingham it might just help to understand the real Bullingham, and people like him, to invoke the fictional Bullingham. This inversion of the invocation principle provides a paradigm of learning from fiction.

6

Aspects, Points of View, and Objectivity

The aspectival nature of fictional content is not an intrinsic feature of a 'language of fiction' but a feature of the conventional response associated with the fictive stance. For it is a consequence of adopting the fictive stance to propositional content, under the conventions of the practice, that the aspects through which that content is characterized acquire special prominence. This account, as we have seen, nicely conjoins the Aristotelian insight that the poet (in contrast to the historian) speaks of 'kinds' or 'universals' and the Fregean insight that the reader of poetry (in contrast to the scientist) attends to the sense of sentences—plus the 'images and feelings' they arouse—rather than their truth and reference. The invocation principle governing judgements of aboutness under the fictive stance also points away from the semantic properties of truth and reference towards considerations of interpretation and understanding. Finally this conception of the fictive stance goes some way towards explaining the nature and origin of fictional objects, episodes, personages, and places; for these are not only presented under, but are also constituted by, the descriptive and evaluative aspects of the content of fictive utterances.

The notion that fictional content is aspectival in this way relates to familiar conceptions of 'point of view' in literary criticism. A central task for the literary critic is to identify the means by which a certain content is presented, and the literary purposes behind such a presentation, usually with the working assumption that the content itself is not clearly independent of the mode of its presentation.[1] Less familiar issues, however, of a more philosophical nature, need to be addressed about 'point of view' with regard to

---

[1] In his essay 'The Heresy of Paraphrase', in *The Well-Wrought Urn*, Cleanth Brooks criticizes Ivor Winters for trying to extract a 'rational meaning' of a poem, apart from the specific connotations of its own phrases. This is another argument for not distinguishing too rigidly between content and mode of presentation.

fiction *per se* before we move to the more strictly literary dimension. What are we to make, for example, of the notion that writers
can take up different points of view on their own fictional creations? Can a writer, as is often supposed, be 'objective' (or non-
objective) in the mode of presenting his creations? And what
kind of attitudes can, or should, a reader adopt to these modes of
presentation?

The idea of objectivity looms large in this discussion for we
need to secure our position on 'point of view'—based on the fictive
stance—against metaphysically motivated arguments that seek to
show that it is not only fictional objects, but in fact *all* objects, that
possess an aspectual nature. According to one well-entrenched
idealist tradition in philosophy the world so-called is nothing more
than a-world-from-a-human-point-of-view: ordinary objects are
'constructs of the mind' and thus have the human perspective built
into their very nature. And in Saussurian linguistics, albeit in a
less metaphysical vein, we find a similar suggestion that *thing* and
point of view are not entirely distinct. Thus Ferdinand Saussure:
'In linguistics we are forbidden ... to speak of "*a* thing" from
different points of view ... because it is the point of view that
MAKES the thing.'[2] Does this not irreparably weaken the distinction
between a real object and a fictional object? What is it, if anything,
that sets apart the aspectival nature of the fictional? What is special about point of view in fiction? The metaphysical challenge will
be taken up in Part 2. For the moment more clarification is needed
on aspects in works of fiction.

Authorial point of view

An obvious fact about any writing is that it is under the conscious
control of a writer, at least in the sense that the writer chose just
those propositions to express.[3] Rhetorical devices manipulate or

---

[2] From the Notes to Saussure's *Course in General Linguistics*: quoted in Ora Avni,
The Resistance of Reference (Baltimore, 1990), 31.
[3] Perhaps strictly speaking we should speak of a writer choosing descriptions
and sentences. The assumption that the writer always has a determinate proposition in mind is probably not justified; for the anti-intentionalist critic it is the
propositions that the sentences *could* express, rather than those *in the writer's mind*,
that are relevant in literary criticism.

direct responses under the fictive stance so that a reader is guided
not only in *what* to imagine but also in *how* to imagine it.

There is an interesting, if complex, relation between (1) what a
fictional character (or incident) is, (2) the point of view from which
the character (or incident) is presented, and (3) the attitudes and
judgements towards that character (or incident) invited of the
reader. When D. H. Lawrence warned the novelist of the immorality of 'put[ting] his thumb in the scale'[4] when presenting characters and when critics praise the objectivity of a writer's attitude
to what he has created,[5] though what they are saying can be
readily understood, nevertheless the presuppositions are puzzling
and call for closer examination. For though we might quite properly find fault with a character it is not so clear, except metaphorically, that we can also, over and above that, find fault with
a writer's treatment of, or attitude towards, a character. For does
not the treatment precisely determine what the character is? Are
the two not inseparable? We know what it would mean to give a
biased account of Ronald Reagan but what would it mean to say
that George Eliot has given a biased account of Mr Casaubon?
Casaubon, unlike Reagan, has no independent existence against
which we can assess the fairness of the account offered. Casaubon
just *is* that complex characterization embodied in George Eliot's
descriptions. Because we cannot prise apart the character and the
descriptions, the descriptions cannot, logically speaking, be a distortion of the character.

Of course the matter is not as simple as that, as the example
of George Eliot makes apparent. For George Eliot is notorious as
an intrusive author, often given to lecturing, certainly one to prompt
and push a reader in his judgements. She would only escape
Lawrence's charge of immorality, if at all, on the grounds that she
is scrupulous in presenting diverse points of view and insisting that
they are all taken into account.

So how does point of view relate to characterization? Take the
case of Mr Casaubon. On the face of it he is an unattractive character, an ageing, somewhat dull clergyman, conventional in manner

---

[4] D. H. Lawrence, 'Morality and the Novel', repr. in David Lodge (ed.), *20th
Century Literary Criticism* (London, 1972), 128.
  [5] A defence of objectivity in literature is a central theme in Iris Murdoch, *The
Sovereignty of Good* (London, 1970); for a useful general discussion see Booth,
The Rhetoric of Fiction, ch. 3.

and opinions, pursuing dry and unending research, and locked in a loveless marriage with the young Dorothea. But George Eliot never allows us to rest with a stock judgement. We are confronted with an enormously varied range of attitudes towards him, shifting constantly and subtly through the novel. Other characters scorn him and at the time we find ourselves agreeing with them: Celia finds him physically repulsive, Mr Brook finds him cold and stand-offish, Mrs Cadwallader is contemptuous of his 'alleged greatness of soul', and of course we watch Dorothea's idealistic dreams turn sour in the marriage. George Eliot, however, insists on eliciting some sympathy from us. She will not rest until all points of view have been aired. Thus, as omniscient narrator, she takes us behind the cold exterior and presents Casaubon's own responses to his impending marriage:

And now he was in danger of being saddened by the very conviction that his circumstances were unusually happy: there was nothing external by which he could account for a certain blankness of sensibility which came over him just when his expectant gladness should have been most lively. . . . Here was a weary experience in which he was as utterly condemned to loneliness as in the despair which sometimes threatened him while toiling in the morass of authorship without seeming nearer to the goal. And his was that worst loneliness which would shrink from sympathy. He could not but wish that Dorothea should think him not less happy than the world would expect her successful suitor to be; and in relation to his authorship he leaned on her young trust and veneration, he liked to draw forth her fresh interest in listening, as a means of encouragement to himself.[6]

And then later on, within the marriage, after Dorothea's disillusion had set in:

One morning, some weeks after her arrival at Lowick, Dorothea—but why always Dorothea? Was her point of view the only possible one with regard to this marriage? I protest against all our interest, all our effort at understanding being given to the young skins that look blooming in spite of trouble; for these too will get faded, and will know the older and more eating griefs which we are helping to neglect. In spite of the blinking eyes and white moles objectionable to Celia, and the want of muscular curve which was morally painful to Sir James, Mr Casaubon had an intense con-sciousness within him and was spiritually a-hungered like the rest of us.[7]

---

[6] George Eliot, *Middlemarch*, Norton Critical Edition (New York, 1977), 57.
[7] Ibid. 192.

These passages are promptings from the author to guide and temper a reader's judgements about the character. Their aim is to stimulate and deepen a reader's reflective attitudes.

We can distinguish two separate elements with respect to narrative points of view on characters, which might be labelled *intrinsic* and *extrinsic*. An intrinsic point of view is that which informs the characterization itself. It is manifest in the descriptive predicates chosen by an author to present the character. Such an intrinsic point of view, to some degree or other, will be manifest in all fictional descriptions. In the passages just quoted the characterization of Casaubon is being deepened and extended. We are offered a network of concepts—'blankness of sensibility', 'expectant gladness', 'weary experience', 'condemned to loneliness', 'shrink from sympathy', 'spiritually a-hungered'—to articulate an attitude of mind which must figure in a rounded understanding of Casaubon and must also temper a reader's imaginative response to him. The predicates themselves embody a point of view; they are not neutral with respect to the response invited. It is not incidental that they elicit that disquieting combination of sympathy and pathos. Competent readers not only respond in this way, they also recognize (at least as literary critics they recognize) that this response is required of them. That is, they notice that it is being controlled and directed by the narrative content. This double process—the response and the recognition that the response is invited—mirrors two facets of the fictive stance, the internal imaginative attitude and the external self-reflective attitude.[8] We will return to this in a moment.

There is also an extrinsic point of view, which does not so much inform the characterization as offer a further, perhaps more distanced, perspective on it. This is the point of view *on* the characterization, not *in* the characterization. George Eliot as an author is particularly prone to an overt kind of intervention: 'I protest against all our interest, all our effort of understanding being given to the young skins.' A reader is being nudged here towards certain attitudes beyond those elicited in the response to the intrinsic descriptions themselves. It is an invitation to stand back and reflect on the very process of acquiring information about characters.

[8] There is a parallel here again with the Gricean account of meaning (see Grice, *Studies in the Ways of Words*); it provides further endorsement of the view developed earlier that the fictive response is *rational*, not just causal.

Extrinsic points of view are developed through authorial comment, narrative tone, attitudes drawn from other characters, and in other ways besides; they foreground the mediated access to fictional objects. No doubt the distinction between intrinsic and extrinsic points of view within a narrative is not always clear-cut but it usefully mirrors, as a literary device, the different sources of information about fictional states of affairs.

We now have a better understanding of what it might mean to commend a writer's 'objectivity' in the treatment of a character. 'Objectivity' here means impartiality or fairness. George Eliot might have created an unattractive character in Mr Casaubon but it would be unreasonable to charge her with showing a lack of objectivity in her presentation of the character. This does not imply that there is some 'object' independent of its characterization towards which different points of view can be adopted. The object itself, being a fiction, remains constitutively 'aspectival'. However, a reader can *imagine* an independent existence for the object. In adopting the fictive stance the reader imagines that there is an object distinct from the characterizing descriptions about which the descriptions can be judged fair or unfair. This imaginative response is made possible only by the depth and subtlety of the characterization itself. The richness of the intrinsic points of view and the diversity of extrinsic points of view determine the extent to which a fictional object can be imagined as 'autonomous'. However, the scope of the imagining remains under the control of the writer, and the narrative. Even the extrinsic points of view are internal to the narrative's descriptive content.

Reader's point of view: internal and external

At several points in the discussion we have alluded to a distinction between 'internal' and 'external' perspectives adopted by readers of fiction. This is not to be confused with the distinction just drawn between intrinsic and extrinsic points of view associated with an author and the presentation of narrative. The former distinction came up, for example, in relation to aboutness claims. From the external perspective of, say, a biographer or a historian it might be truly claimed *de re* of the Scottish king Macbeth that Shakespeare wrote a play about him. But from the internal perspective of the reader adopting the fictive stance to the play it is an open question, to be debated by literary critics, whether *Macbeth* is about the Scottish king; this internal judgement of aboutness is *de dicto*, concerning the sense of the play, how it is to be understood or imagined. The two perspectives came up again, more recently, in terms of modes of response. A reader can have both an ('internal') imaginative involvement with fictive content and an ('external') awareness that the content is under the control of a writer, indeed that it is fictional.

Kendall Walton has emphasized the importance of these two perspectives, though his account relies on the notion of a 'world':

> We, as it were, see Tom Sawyer *both* from inside his world and from outside of it. And we do so simultaneously.... [T]he dual standpoint which appreciators take is ... one of the most fundamental and important features of the human institution of fiction.[9]

Being 'caught up' in fictional worlds and at the same time recognizing their fictionality involves a delicate balance—even a tension—which certainly accounts for much of the pleasure and value of imaginative works of art.

What are these dual perspectives, the internal and the external points of view on fictional content? Although it is helpful heuristically to speak of what goes on inside and outside 'worlds' the two perspectives that we seek to identify do not require the idiom of 'worlds'. They can be captured either as modes of speaking or as modes of responding.

For example, the distinction shows itself systematically in the different kinds of answers we are inclined to give to questions about the content of works of fiction. Who created Frankenstein's monster? One answer, from the internal perspective, is of course: Frankenstein. Only from the external point of view must the reply be: Mary Shelley. The author is not part of what is imagined under the fictive stance. Does Ernest Worthing (in *The Importance of Being Earnest*) exist? Yes he does, internally speaking, inasmuch as he is identical with Jack Worthing who certainly exists. Furthermore, there can be no doubt, again from the internal perspective, that Algernon's friend Bunbury does *not* exist, he is a complete

---

[9] Kendall Walton, 'How Remote are Fictional Worlds from the Real World?', *Journal of Aesthetics and Art Criticism*, 37 (1978–9), 21.

fabrication. Speaking externally, on the other hand, none of them exists, not Ernest, Jack, Algernon, nor Bunbury; they are all fictions. Do you want Cordelia (in *King Lear*) to die? No, surely not, only the most heartless and callous viewer could *will* her death. Yet who but the most philistine would welcome Nahum Tate's rewriting of the play where Cordelia is saved? Internally, we wish her spared; externally, we want the play just as it is. The distinction holds for other media as well. Is that the King and Queen we see in *Las Meninas*? Yes, they are reflected in the mirror on the back wall; they are watching the children in the studio while having their portrait painted. Internally that is what we see, and we see it from the point of view of the King and Queen themselves; externally of course we see only the masterly brushstrokes on Velázquez's canvas.

Sentences uttered, or thoughts entertained, from the internal perspective, are subject not to linguistic constraints but to the conditions of the fictive stance. According to Walton, in adopting this perspective a reader imagines not simply *de dicto* that a (general) state of affairs obtains but also *de se* that he is part of the fictional world observing and describing its contents.[10] Although *de se* imagining might be too strong as a necessary condition for the fictive stance, it rightly emphasizes the idea of a reader's imaginative *involvement* under the internal perspective. In the 'game of make-believe' associated with fiction, readers (and viewers) imaginatively project themselves into the 'world' of the fiction. From the standpoint of this imaginative projection they can reflect on, and form attitudes towards, characters and events in much the same way, or so it seems, as their otherworldly companions can do to one another.

To reflect on characters from the internal perspective is to reflect on them as *persons*, while to identify them from the external perspective is to identify them as *characters*. The external perspective does not require imaginative involvement; it can report content, for example with the 'In the fiction . . .' idiom, without thereby imagining it. No make-believe is involved; its descriptions are of what is the case in the real world, about authorial purposes, literary devices, or fictionality.

This idea of two different perspectives, internal and external,

---

[10] On imagining *de se*, see Walton, *Mimesis as Make-Believe*, 28–35.

on fictive content yields an attractive framework for addressing puzzling questions, some of which we have come across already.

How is it, for example, that fictional characters seem like but also radically unlike real human beings? The beginning of an answer is this: from the internal point of view, they share the same range of properties as real people (being arrogant, wily, hopelessly in love) while from the external point of view their properties belong in a quite different category (being created by an author, being stereotypical, being symbolic of the futility of life).

How can we explain the incompleteness of fictional characters?[11] Internally, the problem is epistemological; there are certain facts that readers just do not know. But that does not disturb their imaginings because ignorance about people is familiar in the actual world. Externally, the issue is ontological; characters as intensional objects are constituted by limited sets of defining characteristics so the fact that characters are 'incomplete' with respect to certain properties is a simple consequence of their ontological status.

What lies behind the 'paradox of tragedy'? How can we explain, as Hume puts it, 'the unaccountable pleasure which the spectators of a well-written tragedy receive from sorrow, terror, anxiety, and other passions that are in themselves disagreeable and uneasy'?[12] There is no simple solution, of course, but a useful starting-point might be to appeal again to internal and external perspectives: while 'caught up' in the imaginary world of the tragedy viewers feel sorrow and terror but when (perhaps even simultaneously) they reflect on the tragedy externally (for example as a work of art) they feel pleasure.[13]

We also find the seeds of an explanation for human interest in works of fiction. On the one hand, adopting the internal perspective indulges the pleasures of make-believe, of projecting ourselves

---

[11] The logical problems relating to the 'incompleteness' of fictional characters are well discussed by Robert Howell, 'Fictional Objects: How They Are and How They Aren't', *Poetics*, 8 (1979), 129–77; Parsons, *Nonexistent Objects*; and Wolterstorff, *Works and Worlds of Art*, pt. 3.

[12] David Hume, 'Of Tragedy', in *Essays: Moral, Political and Literary* (Oxford, 1963), 221.

[13] Susan L. Feagin seeks a solution by distinguishing 'direct responses' to tragic events, which are unpleasant, and 'meta-responses', that is responses to direct responses, which can be pleasurable: see 'The Pleasures of Tragedy', *American Philosophical Quarterly*, 20 (1983), 95–104. Her distinction might be seen as one application of that between internal and external perspectives.

into imaginary surroundings. On the other hand, even on the external perspective where the people of the imaginary worlds become mere representations, we can still make sense of human interest in them. Part of this interest is no doubt formalistic or aesthetic but part will also reflect a deeper and more wide-ranging interest in things abstract, possibilities as well as actualities, kinds as well as particular instances. Such a concern is already fundamental to all knowledge. Here then are further reasons why fictions and real things seem so intimately connected.

The dual perspective on fictive content can also shed light on those problematic passages in works of fiction, which we discussed in Chapter 3 (and will return to again in the context of the propositional theory of literary truth), where an author appears to be offering, *in propria persona*, observations of a general nature not explicitly about any one character or event but seemingly about the world at large. It is worth exploring in a bit more detail how such passages engage the twin perspectives. Consider an example, again from *Middlemarch*. 'Shallow natures', George Eliot writes, 'dream of an easy sway over the emotions of others, trusting implicitly in their own petty magic to turn the deepest streams, and confident, by pretty gestures and remarks, of making the thing that was not as though it were.'[14] This observation occurs in the scene where Rosamund and Will Ladislaw have been caught in intimate, though innocent, conversation by Dorothea, who storms out under the aggrieved misapprehension that she has discovered the man she loves in an affair with another. Rosamund relishes the situation seeing herself at the centre of a little drama and called upon to exercise her calming sympathy with the stunned Ladislaw. She does not anticipate, though, and cannot cope with, the anger which is Ladislaw's deeply felt response.

The generalization about 'shallow natures' invites reflection both from an internal and an external perspective. Internally, the remark provides further concepts to enhance a reader's understanding of Rosamund. She has indeed a 'shallow nature'; her influence over others resides in 'petty magic' grounded in 'pretty gestures and remarks', in other words it is superficial and manipulative. By contrast, reflection on George Eliot's observation from the external point of view involves thinking of 'shallow

[14] Eliot, *Middlemarch*, 536.

natures' in applications beyond that of the immediate fictional circumstances.

The two perspectives nicely interact. For while a reader comes to acquire a deeper understanding of the character in the light of the generalization, he might also come to see an added authority in the generalization in the light of its application to the character. The very ideas of a shallow nature, of an egotistical response, of 'an easy sway over the emotions of others', become more vivid through reflection on the character of Rosamund. It is sometimes supposed that explicit generalizations of this kind, which frequently appear in novels, provide something of a paradigm of 'literary truth'. But the position is more complicated, and interesting. For, as we argued in Chapter 3, such reflections are almost never to be taken at face value, merely as general assertions about the world issued directly by the author. To take them in this way would be to abandon the cognitive distance of the fictive stance. Their interest from the external perspective is conditioned by their role under the internal perspective. But it is their dual function which marks the special status of fiction. They can enhance a characterization by introducing a further framework or point of view for its evaluation and they can themselves acquire subtle colouring, ironic or otherwise, through this application, which in turn might enhance their interest and plausibility in a wider context.

Subjective and objective

To speak of a writer's objectivity in presenting fictional content is, as we have seen, to speak of the writer's *impartiality* with respect to the fictive descriptions, which can be judged by the depth and diversity of the attitudes invited by the narrative content. This notion of objectivity is not to be confused with another notion of objectivity as *independence*, as in the philosophical realist's claim that '[p]hysical entities objectively exist independently of the mental'.[15] Although separate the notions do bear some relation to one another. The fiction-writer's attempted impartiality of presentation can be seen as an attempt to facilitate the imagining of objects independent of their mode of presentation.

[15] Michael Devitt, 'Rorty's Mirrorless World', *Midwest Studies in Philosophy*, 12 (1988), 159.

Thomas Nagel has offered a characterization of what he calls the 'objective viewpoint' on the world, in the sense of independence:

Its essential character ... is externality or detachment. The attempt is made to view the world not from a place within it, or from the vantage point of a special type of life or awareness, but from nowhere in particular and no form of life in particular at all. The object is to discount for the features of our pre-reflective outlook that make things appear to us as they do, and thereby to reach an understanding of things as they really are. We flee the subjective under the pressure of an assumption that everything must be something not to any point of view, but in itself. To grasp this by detaching more and more from our own point of view is the unreachable ideal at which the pursuit of objectivity aims.[16]

As implied in this final sentence, Nagel believes that a totally objective viewpoint, so defined, is impossible. The subjective is ineliminable and thus a purely objective—i.e. independent—view of reality is unattainable.[17]

Nagel's discussion of the subjective and objective is useful in this context for two purposes: first, to reinforce a clear ontological point about the status of fictional objects and 'objectivity', and second to give further insights into the internal and external perspectives on fictional objects. We will come to the second point in the next section.

The first point concerns the relation between *what is represented* and *how it is represented*. Nagel's focus is on actual, not fictional, objects. But it would be wrong to suppose that the difficulties he addresses for the 'objectivity' of actual objects does anything to weaken the distinction between the fictional and the real. Seeing the reasons for this will serve us well in the more metaphysical discussion in Part 3.

The aim to transcend subjective points of view can be seen as the aim to represent things, and thus come to understand them, as they are in themselves and not *for* any type of being. As Nagel puts it, 'the enterprise assumes that what is represented is detachable from the mode of representation ... so that the same laws of physics could be represented by creatures sharing none of our sensory modalities'.[18] He expands on this with an example:

[16] Thomas Nagel, *Mortal Questions* (Cambridge, 1979), 208.
[17] Thomas Nagel, *The View From Nowhere* (Oxford, 1986), ch. 2, sect. 5.
[18] Nagel, *Mortal Questions*, 209.

A Martian scientist with no understanding of visual perception could understand the rainbow, or lightning, or clouds as physical phenomena, though he would never be able to understand the human concepts of rainbow, lightning, or cloud, or the place these things occupy in our phenomenal world. The objective nature of the things picked out by these concepts could be apprehended by him because, although the concepts themselves are connected with a particular point of view and a particular visual phenomenology, the things apprehended from that point of view are not. . . . Lightning has an objective character that is not exhausted by its visual appearance, and this can be investigated by a Martian without vision. To be precise, it has a *more* objective character than is revealed in its visual appearance.[19]

What does it mean to speak of the detachability of *what is represented* from the *mode of representation*? Nagel draws a distinction between (1) the human concept of lightning connected with a particular point of view and a particular visual phenomenology, and (2) lightning itself as a physical phenomenon with an objective character which is not exhausted by the human concept. How closely are these related? On certain empiricist theories of meaning, under the maxim that meaning determines extension, the connection might be described as follows: the phenomenon of lightning just is whatever satisfies the criteria of identification embodied in the concept, such that if these criteria are connected exclusively with, say, a particular visual phenomenology then *lightning itself* will be whatever appears as lightning to human beings. So, for example, it might be constitutive of the concept of lightning that it (lightning) appears as flashes of light in the sky, that it is accompanied by certain characteristic sounds, that it burns whatever it strikes, and that it produces certain other observable effects. These descriptions, derived from the concept, would then provide the means of recognizing and identifying instances of the phenomenon. According to the Verification Principle the cognitive content of a proposition about lightning is exhausted in the means by which the proposition might be verified.

However, as Nagel says, the pursuit of objectivity leads us to believe that there is an objective character of lightning which is not exhausted by these descriptions of appearances. We believe we have a more objective understanding of lightning when we explain it, for example, in terms of electrical discharges, i.e. when

---

[19] Ibid. 173.

we find a place for it in a theory at a further remove from direct observation. In effect what we have done in locating it within such a theory is to provide further means for recognizing and identifying instances of the phenomenon, no longer relying on mere sensory appearances. However, what we have clearly *not* done is provide a 'view from nowhere', a view without a point of view; in effect we have simply provided, as we might say, a further *mode of representation* for lightning. Although the theoretical description might afford a more objective understanding of lightning than the phenomenological description it by no means succeeds in *detaching* the phenomenon represented from a mode of representation. Seen in this light, it is no wonder that a totally 'objective' point of view is unattainable; for inasmuch as a phenomenon is *represented* (or described or characterized) it must be represented *as* something, there must be a *mode* of representation.

It is for this reason that realists, like Michael Devitt, who believe in the genuine independence of physical objects from the human mind (descriptions, categories, representations, etc.), insist on keeping apart questions about *access* to objects and questions about *existence*.[20] The claim that objects exist independently of the mind is itself independent of any claim about how objects are known or represented. The relations that matter between objects and humans are *causal*; any relation between representations and objects must be explained in terms of these more fundamental causal relations.

Devitt-type realism is of course controversial. But what the discussion nicely illustrates are the limits on the kind of 'objectivity' available to fictional objects. On the surface it looks as if there is a disturbing parallel, given Nagel's picture, between the search for an objective point of view on ordinary objects and the range of points of view available to fictional characterizations. This seems to threaten the distinctiveness of the fictional. But on closer inspection the distinction between the fictional and the real remains sharp. For in the fiction case there is no logical space between 'what is represented' and 'the way it is represented' or between questions about access and questions about existence.

We must not be misled by the Casaubon-type cases in which we give sense to the idea of an 'objective' presentation of a fictional

---

[20] This is a central theme in Devitt, *Realism and Truth*.

character; or in general to talk of 'point of view' in fictional representation. For this talk cannot be assimilated to the Nagel–Devitt debate. Objectivity in fiction means either a certain kind of impartiality or a certain kind of imagined content. From the ontological perspective a fictional object is rooted in a mode of representation in a way that no actual object is, *whatever view is taken about realism.* Again we should not be misled by the thought that fictional characters can enter into causal relations with real people. We saw in Chapter 4 how our colloquial ways of speaking of such (apparent) interaction should be interpreted. It is only the mental representation of fictive content, not some mysterious 'fictitious entity', which can enter causal relations.

Relating internal/external and subjective/objective

Nagel uses the terms 'subjective' and 'objective' interchangeably with 'internal' and 'external'. Neither distinction is identical with our own conception of internal and external perspectives but there is sufficient common ground to be able to draw on the one to illuminate the other.

Nagel identifies a common core in a wide range of philosophical problems: 'how to combine the perspective of a particular person inside the world with an objective view of that same world, the person and his viewpoint included.'[21] Take the problem of freedom. From the internal perspective each agent can view himself as confronted with genuine choices, his actions as autonomous; but from an external perspective, where the agent views himself as one among other beings in a web of events, his actions appear to be 'swallowed up' by all the 'conditions and influences' lying behind them.[22] So it is in other areas. The self yields an internal view of 'what it is like to be' that self, but that inner view is threatened, or deemed insignificant, on an external (say, physicalist) account of the world to which the self belongs. In the pursuit of knowledge, as we have seen, we naturally strive for an objective perspective transcending both our individual, and subjective, points of view but also those of our species and world: '[t]he attempt is made to view the world . . . from nowhere in particular.'[23] In ethics there is

---

[21] Nagel, *The View From Nowhere*, 3.
[22] Ibid. 113–14.   [23] Nagel, *Mortal Questions*, 208.

a tension between the internal perspective of the moral agent whose moral decisions are inextricably bound to the particularities of his own life and the external perspective which demands a more impersonal weighing of what is best *sub specie æternitatis*. The perspectives have a bearing also on the meaning of life. From the internal perspective, each person is immersed in his own projects, desires, and achievements, and takes them seriously, but from a more detached, external point of view these petty strivings can come to seem pointless or without justification: '[f]inding my life objectively insignificant, I am nevertheless unable to extricate myself from an unqualified commitment to it ... [t]he sense of the absurd is the result of this juxtaposition.'[24]

At first glance there seems no reason for supposing that a reader's internal perspective on fictive content is inherently subjective in Nagel's sense even though, loosely speaking, we might identify the external perspective with a certain kind of objectivity. On further reflection, however, an interesting complexity shows itself in the juxtaposition.

In adopting the internal perspective of the fictive stance readers project themselves into imaginary 'worlds' and observe them, as it were, subjectively from the point of view of an observer or participant. In doing so they can acquire a sense, in Nagel's usage, of 'what it is like to be' someone in a situation or world of that kind. But likewise they can also get 'out of themselves' in entering imaginary worlds thereby leaving behind many of their own (subjective) concerns. In that sense the internal perspective is also, or can be, an objective view of things, an escape from subjectivity. Correspondingly, the external perspective on fictive content also affords a subjective as well as an objective interpretation. By viewing fictional characters as representations or intensional objects (rather than actual persons in a world) readers distance themselves from imaginative involvement, adopting a detached or objective standpoint. But this very detachment also in a sense returns them to the subjective facts of their own circumstances, as readers of fiction rooted in time and place, not travellers in worlds of the imagination.

The possibilities for identifying subjective and objective aspects within both the internal and external perspectives on fiction certainly complicate the application of Nagel's distinction but does

[24] Nagel, *The View From Nowhere*, 218.

not negate its usefulness. By showing, for example, that even under the fictive stance the subjective/objective distinction applies it invites further reflection on the values of fictive imaginings. It seems safe to say that not all imaginings are of equal value, some (perhaps fantasy, pornography, horror) being dispiriting and destructive, others enhancing, creative, and inspiring. Nagel's internal/external distinction in conjunction with our own can shed some light on this.

What is the value of adopting an internal perspective on a fictional world? One simple thought is this: it allows us to adopt a point of view which is not our own. We can come to see, again in Nagel's terms, 'what it is like to be' a person of a certain kind. But of course there is more to it than that. There is no intrinsic value in adopting different points of view; what value there is must lie in the points of view adopted and in their mode of presentation. Iris Murdoch stresses the importance of *clarity* in the vision of a great work of art:

what we learn from contemplating the characters of Shakespeare or Tolstoy or the paintings of Velasquez or Titian . . . is something about the real quality of human nature, when it is envisaged, in the artist's just and compassionate vision, with a clarity which does not belong to the self-centred rush of ordinary life.[25]

According to Iris Murdoch 'objectivity' in art is to be contrasted with fantasy; and objectivity is one mark of greatness in art.[26] The difference between fantasy and art is that the former is self-centred, literally self-indulgent, while the latter seeks more detachment, a transcending of self-interest. Put in these terms, art might be said to aspire to the objective or external perspective on human affairs, as Nagel describes it. Yet in directly drawing on the imagination, and imaginative involvement, works of art do not seek (as does science) to eliminate the subjective or internal perspective. On the contrary, the subjective perspective, the locating of *oneself* in an imaginary world, is indispensable to artistic appreciation. Nor is there any conflict here. Someone who participates, appropriately, in the imaginary world of a work of art *both* transcends a narrow

[25] Murdoch, *The Sovereignty of Good*, 65.

[26] For a discussion of Iris Murdoch's view of objectivity in art, see Peter Lamarque, 'Truth and Art in Iris Murdoch's *The Black Prince*', *Philosophy and Literature*, 2 (1978), 209–22.

self-centredness or self-interest *and* extends the imaginative re-sources of the self. The imaginary worlds of works of art provide an excellent example of the simultaneous—non-conflicting—occurrence of the subjective and objective points of view.

A further difference between the imaginings of mere fantasy and those associated with art involves the mode of response to fictional events. Here the external perspective on imaginary worlds can be invoked. When we adopt the viewpoint of a participant in an imaginary world we can do so with varying degrees of self-consciousness. But one fundamental difference in modes of imag-ining is this: sometimes we simply *find ourselves* in a certain state of mind, sometimes we adopt a state of mind because we recog-nize *reasons* for doing so. Fantasy belongs with the former, art with the latter. The point once again could be given a Gricean turn. In the case of works of art we respond in a certain way to fictive events (we *locate* ourselves in an imaginary world) at least partly because the recognition of the intention that we should respond in that way acts as a reason for our doing so. In contrast, the imaginings of fantasy are more manipulative; attitudes and responses are the product of *causes*; we adopt a point of view, as we might say, *in spite of ourselves*. Although the difference here is between ways of becoming 'caught up' in fictional worlds, it need not amount to a difference in *beliefs*. A person caught up in a fantasy does not necessarily believe that the events are real, although that might be so in an extreme case. Rather there is only a minimal awareness of the representational modes in which the fantasy is embodied. In short, the internal perspective on the imaginary world overwhelms the external perspective.

In speaking of tragedy, Flint Schier rightly emphasizes the im-portance of the way the tragic events are portrayed in determining the appropriateness of certain kinds of response:

our reaction to fictional characters is not just a reaction to fictional people, it is a reaction to them *as represented* in the text ... Therefore, our re-action is necessarily governed by *how* they are represented, and the kind of emotion that it is appropriate to feel is determined by the quality of the representation.[27]

---

[27] Flint Schier, 'Tragedy and the Community of Sentiment', in Lamarque (ed.), *Philosophy and Fiction*, 85.

The implication is that certain kinds of representations—sensational, sentimental, exploitative kinds, for example—do not merit our emotional involvement. The same point might be put like this: the external perspective, an awareness of modes of representation, dictates the kind of involvement appropriate from the internal perspective. Indeed what Schier's point rightly insists on, once again, is how inextricably connected are the two perspectives. For the attitude we adopt towards fictional characters, whether by manipulation or by reason, is largely determined by the forms of their representation.

On the subject of modes of representation—as viewed from the external perspective—we can again invoke Nagel's distinction between subjective and objective points of view. At a straightforward level, the distinction might be applied to literary devices or narrative styles. Thus, for example, the mode of representation associated with the omniscient narrator suggests a more objective perspective on fictive events than in cases where the narrative voice expresses a point of view from within the fictional world; the former, but not the latter, attempts 'to view the world not from a place within it ... but from nowhere in particular'. But taking a step further back we soon notice that the purported 'objectivity' of the omniscient narrator is as much an internal feature of fictive content—a matter of narrative style—as is the 'subjectivity' of the narrator's persona. In other words the distinction is explicable in terms of what a reader is invited to imagine: a reader imagines, under the fictive stance, that the events described by an omniscient narrator are depicted more 'as they really are' than those portrayed by a narrator who participates in the events and perhaps has a less than impartial view of those events. There is no further objectivity here, in the sense of independence.

Nagel's distinction is even more telling when applied to authors and their works. On one familiar view of art, great art is 'timeless' or 'universal', in the sense that it transcends the circumstances of its production, either personal or historical. (Note that viewing art as timeless is compatible with both 'classical' and 'romantic' conceptions; for even if works of art are considered to be 'expressions' rather than 'imitations', what they express could still be judged as universal.) The parallel with Nagel's view of a striving towards objectivity in knowledge or values is clear enough. But here the moral that Nagel draws, of the ineliminability of the subjective, has a straightforward application. For however the artist strives to cover his tracks, to portray universal truths timelessly, there is no escaping the historical rootedness of art. The very modes of representation that an artist is forced to choose bear the ineliminable traces of tradition and convention on the one hand and the internal perspective of a historical individual on the other.

The fictional creations of the writer or artist are constructs, of course; they have origins and histories, they bear the stamp of their makers and they cannot hide either the mode of their presentation or the method of their construction. To appreciate these constructs we need both an external awareness of their artifice and an internal involvement with their content. Different schools of criticism try to persuade us of the priority of one over the other. Some readers will insist that fictional characters be viewed and judged as real people, while for others characters should be seen for what they are, abstractions, linguistic or ideological constructions. No doubt different genres of writing encourage an emphasis one way or the other. But the simple conclusion must be that the twin perspectives of imaginative involvement and awareness of artifice are both indispensable in an appropriate response to works of fiction.

Perhaps one reason why we accept artistic fictions so readily is that the tension between these two attitudes so closely mirrors that more familiar tension that Nagel notices between our self-absorbed involvement in our own lives and our predisposition to stand back and view ourselves as mere players in a game.

PART 2

The Limits of Fictionality

7

Metaphysics and Fictions

In the next three chapters we turn by way of contrast from the practice of fiction to the practice, or set of practices, concerned with truth-seeking or knowledge-seeking. Our aim is not to develop a theory of truth or knowledge but to show how certain important distinctions can be preserved—fiction/non-fiction, literature/philosophy, the imaginary/the real, what is made/what is discovered, among others—against strong pressures, both philosophical and literary-theoretical, to weaken them or remove them altogether. The whole practice of enquiry, which gives the concepts of truth and knowledge their meaning, is under serious challenge from those who would reduce it to something like the practice of fiction (or story-telling). There are pressures of a metaphysical kind based on the idea that the world itself and its constituents are no more than 'fictions'. But there are also pressures stemming from an anti-metaphysical stance which rejects the whole tradition of philosophizing about truth, knowledge, 'how the world is', etc., suggesting that any broad claims on these topics, be they about literature or philosophy or whatever, are little more than vacuous; a concomitant view is that the discourses of science, philosophy, literature, history, the social sciences, are more or less arbitrarily distinguished and rest on nothing more fundamental than institutional divisions of labour. We will examine in these three chapters both the metaphysical and anti-metaphysical lines of attack, showing how to preserve what might be called the integrity of knowledge and the aim of truth from attacks of this kind.

In this chapter we will begin by addressing pressures of a metaphysical nature, suggesting how they might be resisted sufficiently to retain both the distinctiveness of the practice of story-telling, as we have defined it, and the substance of our later view about literature and its relation to truth. The focus for our discussion will be on certain attempts to extend the idea of fictionality such that not only do all discourses turn out to be fictional but their subject-matters too, the objects and facts of which they speak.

We have already argued at length that an account of fictionality relevant to literary fictions can be given—in terms of modes of utterance, the fictive stance, and so on—which bears no commitment to any particular metaphysical or epistemological view about the world or our knowledge of it and incurs only modest ontological commitments of its own. However, we have not yet done enough to show that fictional discourse, so described, is genuinely distinct from other kinds of discourse or that non-fictional objects are not *au fond* just like fictional objects. We need to establish that there is a genuine aim of truth-seeking and truth-telling, which does not collapse into just another species of fiction-making. Our task is complicated by the fact that there undoubtedly are conceptions of fiction well established in, for example, logic and epistemology which might be thought to undermine the distinctiveness of the fictive stance. It is by no means a wild idea that ordinary objects are in some sense 'fictions', or that the world is essentially 'made' rather than 'found', indeed these views have been held by many reputable philosophers, as we shall see. The trouble is they are not always clearly understood and round them has grown up a more extreme rhetoric, characterizing a widespread trend in modern thought, according to which there is no 'real world', what exists is just what is constructed, truth is an illusion, fiction is everywhere. We must examine such conceptions, asking what they mean, where they originate from, what credibility they possess, and importantly how they bear on the fictive stance.

It was not so long ago that analytical philosophers balked at framing general questions employing such metaphysical concepts as existence, reality, truth, the world, objectivity. Rudolf Carnap, for example, echoing a sentiment of the logical positivists, dismissed as 'pseudo-questions' any enquiry, not relativized to particular 'frameworks', about what exists or is real.[1] J. L. Austin, speaking for 'ordinary language' philosophy, insisted that philosophers in 'sober' discussion consider only the uses of 'true' or 'real' rather than venturing on Truth and Reality.[2] In a not dissimilar vein, though emanating from the pragmatist tradition, Richard Rorty exhorts us even now to abandon our metaphysical ambitions and

---

[1] e.g. Rudolf Carnap, 'Empiricism, Semantics and Ontology', in Leonard Linsky (ed.), *Semantics and the Philosophy of Language* (Urbana, Ill., 1952).

[2] See J. L. Austin, 'Truth', in *Philosophical Papers* (Oxford, 1961), and *Sense and Sensibilia* (Oxford, 1962).

stop thinking that there are deep philosophical questions about reality, truth, the world, and the rest.[3] Yet in spite of these warnings, metaphysical concerns show a remarkable resilience in philosophy and also, in the last decade or so, in literary theory. The pertinence of these concerns is nowhere better revealed than by viewing them through the lens of fictionality.

The sceptical challenge

The simplest way into the issues, for our purposes, is through the challenge of scepticism; and in particular through reflection on the distinction, as Rorty describes it, between what is 'made up' and what is 'out there'. Rorty himself ultimately dismisses the distinction, just as he tries to rid philosophy of what he sees as its sceptical neuroses. But he acknowledges the distinction's tenacious influence on philosophizing both past and present. He sees philosophers as obsessed with the 'anxiety' that maybe what is 'out there' is nothing like what we take it to be, maybe the world is a figment of the imagination, maybe there is nothing 'out there' at all. The sceptical challenge keeps coming back to the same questions:

How would it be different if everything were a dream? How would it be different if it were all *made up*? How would it be different if there were nothing there to be represented? How does having knowledge differ from making poems and telling stories?[4]

The influence of Descartes is strong and his own challenge is a good place to start.

In his *Meditations* Descartes proposed one of the most remarkable thought-experiments in the history of philosophy. He asked us to suppose that all our beliefs about the material world might be false. The hypothesis that we might be dreaming, and therefore mistaken about all 'empirical' beliefs based on input from the senses, had been proposed before. Descartes's suggestion incorporated, but went well beyond, that because he recognized that some beliefs survive the dreaming hypothesis. Beliefs about certain

[3] Richard Rorty, *Philosophy and the Mirror of Nature* (Princeton, NJ, 1979), *Consequences of Pragmatism*, and *Contingency, Irony, and Solidarity*.
[4] Rorty, *Consequences of Pragmatism*, 128.

universal features of the world—space, time, number, extension, configuration, etc.—can remain true even on the supposition that all is a dream. By introducing his *malin génie*, the supreme deceiver, Descartes showed how we might cast into doubt even beliefs of such a universal nature. It is at least conceivable, he thought, that we could be systematically misled in our beliefs, such that there is a radical discrepancy between how the world is and how we take it to be (Descartes in fact envisaged the limiting case of such a discrepancy where there is no world at all, but the weaker hypothesis, that the world is different in every respect from how we conceive it, is sufficient for his sceptical challenge).

It is important to bear in mind Descartes's strategy. He was not of course suggesting that *there is* such a deceiver, nor that all our beliefs about the world *really are* false. He was interested only in whether there is the barest possibility of error on this massive scale. To defeat Descartes's argument it is not enough to show that we have good reason for our beliefs, or that they cohere one with another, but rather that the very conception of massive error is impossible in principle.

Descartes had a polemical purpose in framing his thought-experiment. It was part of an argument towards an equally audacious conclusion, namely, that we are essentially souls not material bodies. That aspect, though, does not concern us so much as the implications and intelligibility of the argument's premiss that all beliefs about the world might be false. Could we have exactly the thoughts we now have if there were no material world at all? There are two sides to this question. One is the hypothesis that the world is radically independent of our thoughts or conceptions. The other is the hypothesis that what we call the world is a pure invention (or fiction). Descartes's solipsistic nightmare is that perhaps all our ideas are *made up* (either on our own accord—albeit unconsciously—or with a little help from a demon), that they are not grounded in an external world but simply originate in the mind. We might note that Descartes's challenge demands more than so-called brains-in-a-vat scepticism; the latter entertains the hypothesis that all our experiences, and hence our beliefs, are instilled into our amputated brains by a wicked or zealous scientist. Descartes's hypothesis purports to show that our beliefs could be independent of the physical world altogether (hence the route to dualism) while the modern hypothesis purports to show only that the truth of a belief is independent of the experiences that normally would cause that belief.[5]

It is possible to characterize the history of epistemology since Descartes as repeated attempts to deal with Descartes's challenge, how to bridge the gulf between ideas and objects. Descartes himself did not help matters by arguing that it is only the goodness of a transcendent God that can give any ultimate guarantee that our beliefs about the world are not mere fictions. He could find nothing in the beliefs themselves, their vividness, the degree of conviction with which they are held, or whatever, that could provide a guarantee of their truth. The need for God's goodness to guarantee conformity between belief and world has seemed to many a *reductio ad absurdum* of the thought-experiment itself. Even Descartes wavered on the seriousness with which we should take the extreme hypothesis: '(w)hat is it to us,' he wrote, 'that someone may make out that the perception whose truth we are so firmly convinced of may appear false to God or an angel, so that it is, absolutely speaking, false? Why should this alleged "absolute falsity" bother us, since we neither believe in it nor have even the smallest suspicion of it?'[6] But once the hypothesis has been raised, it cannot be shrugged off quite so easily.

In spite of this wavering and in spite of being labelled an archsceptic, Descartes sought to defend a position that was in fact resolutely realist. He believed in a mind-independent world, he saw truth as correspondence, he held a causal theory of perception, and he believed that ideas are representations of reality. A far more radical, and sceptical, response emerged within a century of Descartes's death which entailed, in effect, a serious weakening in the idea of an objective world, as Descartes saw it, and a weakening in the idea of truth as correspondence. The growth of idealism in epistemology encouraged the view that ideas are not so much the *route* to the outside world but are somehow constitutive of that world. 'Esse est percipi' encapsulates the retreat from a con-

---

[5] For a good account of the difference, see Mark Sainsbury, *Russell* (2nd edn.; London, 1985), 190.

[6] René Descartes, *Author's Replies to the Second Set of Objections,* in *The Philosophical Writings of Descartes,* ii, trans. J. Cottingham, R. Stoothoff, and D. Murdoch (Cambridge, 1984), 103.

ception of the world as radically independent of thinking subjects (though we should remember that Berkeley's reality was at least not bound to *human* perceptions).

By the time we get to Kant we find something like Descartes's mind-independent things-in-themselves relegated to a shadowy noumenal existence beyond human knowledge. Kant's 'Copernican Revolution' was the first systematic attempt to see the empirical world as to a large extent a product of human intellectual and sensory faculties. Kant showed, or purported to show, how you could be an 'empirical realist' and a 'transcendental idealist' at the same time. From the empirical point of view, ordinary objects are 'out there' and mind-independent, in sharp contrast to illusions and fantasies, but from the transcendental point of view, objects are 'made up' and mind-dependent, not to be confused with unknowable things-in-themselves. From the transcendental viewpoint we have knowledge only of appearances; from the empirical viewpoint, we can readily distinguish how things appear from how they really are. In the twentieth century the 'constructivist' view of knowledge, which had its beginnings in Kant, found full flowering in phenomenalism, the thesis, in its most austere logical form, that material objects are 'logical constructions' out of sense experiences.[7] Such a view stands at the furthest extreme from Descartes's representative realism. Yet perhaps it is not such a big step after all from Descartes's pessimistic thought that what we call the world might be a 'fiction' in the negative sense (made up, not conforming to reality), to the phenomenalist's optimistic thought that what we call the world is a 'construction' in the positive sense (made up, and actually constituting reality).

We do not need to trace the history of its progress to notice the influence of this sceptical scenario on more recent debates in epistemology, philosophy of science, semantics, theory of truth, and philosophical psychology, many of which could be framed round the projected role of a Cartesian-type 'objective world' and the thought-experiment about massive error.

In epistemology, the Cartesian challenge is still in evidence. Recently Barry Stroud has offered a sustained reflection, through the perspective of different theories of knowledge, on Descartes's

---

[7] For a classic account of this view, see John Wisdom, *Logical Constructions* (New York, 1969).

dreaming argument in the First Meditation. Strikingly, he concludes his study with Descartes's hypothesis still intact.

In seeming to find the dream-possibility intelligible even though no one could ever know things about the world I am no doubt revealing my continued attachment to what . . . I called the traditional conception of objectivity or of how it is possible for us to think about the objective world. I think it is very difficult to free oneself from that conception or to see how or why it cannot be correct. On that view, whether I am dreaming or not is simply a question of which state I am in. What matters is only whether the conditions under which it would be true that I am dreaming are fulfilled.[8]

The commitment is still to an objective world 'out there' apart from what humans 'make' or think. Stroud recognizes that that commitment almost inevitably leads back to scepticism but nevertheless sees no clear way to remove it. Even debates in epistemology between foundationalists and coherentists presuppose views about the limits and nature of error.[9] The coherentist who finds justification in the coherence of a set of beliefs might obviate the possibility of massive error in those beliefs but only at the price of legislating a conceptual—rather than a causal—connection between the beliefs and the world.

Cartesian scepticism also appears in debates about realism both in philosophy of science and semantics:

For the realist the truth value of a mistaken but justified assertion does not change when it is shown to be false. It would have been false even had the counterevidence never materialized. The realist extends this concept by analogy first into one of possible error despite the weight of all conceivable evidence and then into that of possible global error, possible falsity of our ultimately corroborated theories. Thus he is committed to the intelligibility of global scepticism, while the nonrealist must deny not only the force, but the sense, of the sceptic's pervasive doubts.[10]

The trouble with the term 'realism' is that it covers so many different theses.[11] Not all realists in philosophy of science are

---

[8] Barry Stroud, *The Significance of Philosophical Scepticism* (Oxford, 1984), 273.

[9] For a useful discussion of the issues, which makes the connection with Descartes, see James van Cleve, 'Foundationalism, Epistemic Principles, and the Cartesian Circle', *Philosophical Review*, 88 (1979), 55–91.

[10] Alan H. Goldman, 'Fanciful Arguments for Realism', *Mind*, 93 (1984), 27.

[11] As is well explained in Haack, 'Realism'.

committed to the intelligibility of global scepticism and even those who are, in principle, might simply shrug off the Cartesian challenge.[12] But this is the ground on which Putnam, for example, chooses to rest his own objections to realism. Putnam's brand of anti-realism, or what he designates 'internal realism', is characterized by a view about truth, namely, that truth is 'idealized justification'.[13] He opposes this view of truth to that of the 'metaphysical realist':

The most important consequence of metaphysical realism is that truth is supposed to be *radically non-epistemic*—we might be 'brains in a vat' and so the theory that is 'ideal' from the point of view of operational utility, inner beauty and elegance, 'plausibility,' simplicity, 'conservatism,' etc., *might be false*. 'Verified' (in any operational sense) does not imply 'true,' on the metaphysical realist picture, even in the ideal limit.[14]

Putnam rejects this position—the idea that 'truth outruns even idealized justification'—as 'incoherent'. Significantly, Putnam appeals to Kant's distinction between metaphysical (or transcendental) and empirical realism to locate his own view; 'internal realism' is a kind of empirical realism. Not only does the correspondence theory of truth get thrown out with metaphysical realism, according to Putnam, but also a certain view of reference:

the idea that the 'non-psychological' fixes reference—i.e., that *nature* itself determines what our words stand for—is totally unintelligible. At bottom, to think that a sign-relation is *built into nature* is to revert to medieval essentialism, to the idea that there are 'self-identifying objects' and 'species' out there. . . . In the context of a twentieth-century world view, by contrast, to say in one's most intimidating tone of voice 'I believe

---

[12] Michael Devitt, for example, brushes aside the Cartesian sceptic, through a version of 'naturalized epistemology': 'From this perspective, scepticism is seen as a consistent position which is, ultimately, unanswerable. Our beliefs are underdetermined by the evidence. We could be wrong about anything. Yet we hold to our beliefs, rejecting other hypotheses against which we have no evidence. We are confident that the sceptic who refuses to follow us in this will have a short life but, in the end, we find ourselves with no argument to convince him. Extreme scepticism is simply *uninteresting*. Instantaneous solipsism, the brain-in-the-vat hypothesis, and other fantasies, are too implausible to take seriously' *(Realism and Truth*, 52).

[13] Hilary Putnam, *Philosophical Papers*, iii: *Realism and Reason* (Cambridge, 1983), p. xvii.

[14] Hilary Putnam, 'Realism and Reason', in *Meaning and the Moral Sciences* (London, 1978); quoted from John Koethe, 'Putnam's Argument Against Realism', *Philosophical Review*, 88 (1979), 92.

that causal connections determine what our words correspond to' is only to say that one believes in a *one-knows-not-what* which solves our problem *one-knows-not-how*.[15]

However, just as it is important not to run together different versions of realism, so we should not assume that questions about knowledge, questions about reference, and questions about the correct theory of truth simply blur into one another. The debate in semantics about realism and anti-realism—roughly the question of whether meaning should be explained in terms of objective truth-conditions or in terms of verification (or assertibility) conditions—need not presuppose a stand on global scepticism. Also, whether truth is 'correspondence' (a semantic question) is independent of whether objects are 'made up' (an epistemological question). An anti-realist rejection of the Cartesian challenge—for example, along Putnam's lines—need not imply a weakening of the distinction between 'made up' and 'out there', nor need it imply a rejection of correspondence truth, nor of causal theories of reference. Davidson, for example, rejects the idea of massive error in human beliefs not through an anti-realist conception of the world as 'mind-dependent' but because of a view of what beliefs are like (and how they are interpreted).[16] Many of these matters will come more sharply into focus through examining exactly what might be meant by saying that 'objects are fictions'. As we will see, shortly, there is a semantic as well as an epistemological version of that notion.

Philosophical psychology is replete with its own thought-experiments for testing intuitions as to how beliefs or other intentional states relate to the world external to the mind. One issue concerns the possibility and desirability of characterizing states like beliefs autonomously (as having 'narrow content'), without reference to the outside world. The issue again recalls Descartes's thought-experiment of whether we could have just the thoughts we do even if there were no world at all. This in turn connects with philosophy of language for the question whether there are 'singular thoughts', i.e. thoughts with objective reference as part of their identity-conditions, exactly parallels the question whether there are propositions which make essential reference to

[15] Putnam, *Philosophical Papers,* iii: p. xii.
[16] See Donald Davidson, *Inquiries into Truth and Interpretation* (Oxford, 1984).

objects.[17] The viability of 'methodological solipsism' in psychology,[18] the idea that psychological explanations require an autonomous characterization of belief, is crucial to the debate about the status of 'folk psychology'. Might our beliefs turn out to be Cartesian fictions? From the standpoint of philosophical psychology the question is less about scepticism and massive error, more about the very nature of beliefs.

The connection with literary theory

Descartes's thought-experiment, which entertains the possibility of a radical split between what is believed and what is the case, connects, as we have seen, with a central core of issues in philosophy. Furthermore, without too much distortion many of these issues can be rephrased using the idea of 'fiction', in the sense of what is 'made up'. But what stake do literary theorists have in all this? We still seem a long way from familiar concerns about literature.

Two closely related topics seem to be involved: the nature of representation and the comparative status of modes of discourse. Literary theorists have long been sceptical of the idea that literary works can 'represent the world'. It is common to find 'realism' so-called in literature viewed not so much as a kind of 'relation' as a kind of writing, a literary convention.[19] The realistic novel, contrary to the claims of its early French proponents, is now widely regarded by literary theorists as having no privileged status in representing the world 'as it really is'. The whole modernist movement in art amounted to a challenge at a fundamental level to the idea of 'representing reality'. The point of modernism, at its best, was to exhibit the plurality of worlds, private and public, in contrast to some single 'objective' world given in experience. Once representation itself had been exposed as a kind of artifice it was natural for artists to highlight the artifice of their own media. In

---

[17] See e.g. Evans, *The Varieties of Reference*; also Blackburn, *Spreading the Word*, ch. 9.

[18] See Jerry Fodor, 'Methodological Solipsism Considered as a Research Strategy in Cognitive Psychology', in *Representations* (Cambridge, Mass., 1981).

[19] The point is made, for example, in Roland Barthes, 'The Reality Effect', in *The Rustle of Language* (Oxford, 1986), ch. 4.

the literary case this manifested itself in an obsession with drawing attention to the fictionality of literary writing. In turn that obsession helped to reinforce the theoretical stance against representation.

Against this background there arose various attempts by literary theorists to generalize the lessons learned from literary fiction. In themselves the generalizations are far from implausible. All writing involves some degree of rhetorical contrivance; there is no pure unmediated representation of extra-linguistic fact; there are other purposes served by words than merely describing how things are in the world. It is a short step, so it seems, from these modest claims to stronger more anti-realist conclusions. Just as the idea of a single objective reality seemed to crumble away in the literary case, perhaps it crumbles away in any case. Perhaps there is a lesson to be learned from literary realism about realism *tout court*. It is no wonder that anti-realist tendencies in philosophy have struck a chord with many literary theorists.

But certain schools of literary theory have wanted to go much further than this. They want a radical reassessment of the comparative status of different kinds of discourse. Drawing on epistemological scepticism (there is no mind-independent world) and semantic anti-realism (words do not picture reality) they seek to show that there cannot be all that much difference between, say, 'works of fiction' and 'works of science'. Deconstructionists, for example, aim to reverse what they see as an age-old prejudice against literature (i.e. *poesis* or fiction) in favour of science and philosophy. Their conclusions are provocative: 'philosophy turns out to be an endless reflection on its own destruction at the hands of literature';[20] 'literary texts are less deluded than the discourse of philosophy',[21] and so on.

What arguments are offered? Not all rest on metaphysical premisses. For example, one weak, largely *ad hominem*, argument, following Derrida, is a reaction to certain remarks by J. L. Austin to the effect that fictional utterances, in poetry or on the stage, are *parasitic* on 'serious' or 'normal' discourse. Deconstructionists have taken this as symptomatic of philosophers' generally derogatory attitudes to poetry (and fiction) and the case against Austin for

---

[20] Paul de Man, *Allegories of Fiction: Figural Language in Rousseau, Nietzsche, Rilke and Proust* (New Haven, Conn., 1979), 115.

[21] Christopher Norris, *Deconstruction: Theory and Practice* (London, 1982), 21.

many years became a set-piece in their war with philosophy.[22] Here is what Austin actually says:

a performative utterance will, for example, be *in a peculiar way* hollow or void if said by an actor on the stage or introduced in a poem, or spoken in a soliloquy.... Language in such circumstances is in special ways— intelligibly—used not seriously, but in ways *parasitic* upon its normal use— ways which fall under the doctrine of the *etiolations* of language.[23]

Deconstructionists, by noticing 'that Austin's own writing is often highly playful and seductive, or that he does not hesitate to undermine the distinctions that he proposes', attempt to 'reverse Austin's opposition between the serious and the parasitic' and to show that 'his so-called "serious" performatives are only a special case of performances'.[24]

Austin might not have offered a correct, or even very sophisticated, theory of fiction but there is nothing in this critique which does much harm to his theory of speech acts. Nor, more importantly, do the points make much headway in the aim of 'deconstructing' the distinction between fact and fiction or philosophy and literature. Behind this argument, however, is an altogether more ambitious programme which seeks to show that there is no 'privileged discourse' with respect to 'speaking the truth'. The central point is that literary devices, like rhetoric, narrative, and metaphor, are so pervasive in discourse that they everywhere undermine simple presumptions of reference and fact-stating. 'The mistake is to imagine—like certain old-fashioned novelists—that there exists some kind of ultimate, self-validating viewpoint from which all the other perspectives would simply fall into place.'[25]

The main pillar of support for this programme lies in the thought that *epistemologically all discourses are on a par with fictional discourse*. Indeed literary (i.e. novelistic) writing is held to be paradigmatic because it draws attention to its fictionality while

[22] The original skirmish between Derrida and Searle (John R. Searle, 'Reiterating the Differences: A Reply to Derrida', *Glyph*, 1 (1977), 198–208; Jacques Derrida, 'Limited Inc.' *Glyph*, 2 (1977), 162–254) is replayed in several of the commentaries, notably Jonathan Culler, *On Deconstruction: Theory and Criticism after Structuralism* (London, 1983), 110–34, and Christopher Norris, *The Deconstructive Turn: Essays in the Rhetoric of Philosophy* (London, 1983).
[23] J. L. Austin, *How To Do Things With Words* (Oxford, 1962), 22.
[24] Culler, *On Deconstruction*, 118, 120.
[25] Christopher Norris, *The Contest of Faculties* (London, 1985), 23.

other—less honest—modes (philosophy, history, even science) try to conceal their fictionality. The reasoning here is sceptical, anti-realist, pragmatist. A composite argument for this line of thought might run as follows.

First of all a more or less familiar stance is set up beginning with a simple idea of fiction, in both its object and description senses. According to this idea a clear divide exists between imaginative literature, defined in terms of fiction-making, and other discourses whose aim is description not creation. Imaginative literature creates imaginary worlds which, though no doubt drawn from aspects of the real world, are nevertheless overtly constructs of the mind. The other, more 'serious', discourses deal not with imaginary entities but with the real thing. They are assessed not in terms of creativity but in terms of truth or correspondence with the facts. Fiction versus fact becomes the crucial characteristic that marks off imaginative literature.

At this point the literary theorist triumphantly proclaims the 'naïvety' of all this. Facts, so the argument runs, are not ready-made items 'out there' in the world waiting to be described; and science is far from purely descriptive in the way presupposed. On a pragmatist conception of truth, even truth itself is man-made. Science 'constructs' entities just as much as imaginative literature does; the whole 'world' that science purportedly describes and explains is a human artifice, 'made' from posits and conceptual frameworks. Literary theorists feel at home with this picture because the lessons are all prefigured in debates over literary realism. It all points, so they believe, to the comfortable conclusion that as far as fiction and fact are concerned, or fiction and truth, there is no significant difference between literature and science (or philosophy).[26] Both are equally 'creative'. Inasmuch as it was precisely in terms of fiction and fact that literature was once given its second-class ranking that ranking must now be rejected or reversed. Fictional and non-fictional discourses are not distinguishable in any fundamental way.

This argument, which represents a line of thought in literary

[26] For a version of this argument, see Ronald Weber, *The Literature of Fact: Literary Nonfiction in American Writing* (Athens, Oh., 1980): 'nonfiction could no more chronicle reality than fiction since all forms of writing offer models or versions of reality rather than actual descriptions of it; consequently nonfiction was as inherently "irrealistic" as fiction' (14).

theory rather than the reasoning of a specific contributor, can be encapsulated in two highly schematic renderings:

A.

(1) The distinction between fictional and fact-stating discourse ultimately depends on a correspondence conception of reference and truth. Fact-stating discourse makes reference to, and corresponds with, what is 'out there' (objects and facts) while fictional discourse concerns only what is 'made up'.

(2) But the correspondence conception of reference and truth is untenable; anti-realist and pragmatist arguments in philosophy of language show this, not to speak of Kantian-type arguments in epistemology.

(3) Therefore, there is no ultimate ground for the distinction between fictional and fact-stating discourse.

B.

(1) Fiction is whatever is 'made up' conceptually or linguistically.

(2) Truth is man-made conceptually or linguistically.

(3) Therefore, truth is just a species of fiction.[27]

In Chapter 8 we will examine the force of the second premiss in each case, in particular the attack by Rorty on truth as 'correspondence', through his defence of truth as 'man-made', and Goodman's 'irrealist' notion of 'worldmaking'. In Chapter 9 we will examine the role of sceptical and anti-realist arguments in attempts to blur different aims of narrative. In the remainder of this chapter, though, we will focus on the first premisses of the two schematic arguments by looking at different conceptions of fiction: the kind of 'making' involved in each (both object-making and description-making), the 'correspondence' relations implied, the commitments, such as they are, to an 'objective world', and the connection with fictions of the make-believe kind. By showing the inadequacy of certain seductive generalizations about fiction, we will refute decisively the suggestion that, because of the presence of 'fictions' in ordinary language and science, the very distinction between what is real and what is fictional must be abandoned. Our account of the practice of fiction in the story-telling context already shows that 'correspondence' (or the lack of it) is not a necessary

---

[27] The conclusion here recalls Nietzsche's famous aphorism: 'truths are illusions of which one has forgotten that they *are* illusions'. See Friedrich Nietzsche, 'On Truth and Falsity in their Ultramoral Sense', *The Complete Works of Friedrich Nietzsche: The First Complete and Authorized Translation*. ii, ed. Oscar Levy (Edinburgh and London, 1909), 180.

feature of fictionality. By examining non-literary conceptions of fiction we hope to establish once and for all that arguments from the nature of fiction—be they epistemological or semantic—will not in themselves serve the literary theorists' programme of 'fiction-alizing' all discourses or even 'fictionalizing' the world itself.

Types of fiction

In addition to the make-believe conception of fiction, explored in Part 1, there are other distinct conceptions, arising in semantics, epistemology, philosophical psychology, and elsewhere, which yield different relations between fiction and the 'objective world'. We will label these: logical fictions, epistemological fictions, notional objects, fictions of convenience, and non-entities.

Logical fictions

Logicians and mathematicians frequently speak of 'fictions' and do not hesitate to maintain that fictions in the relevant sense permeate discourse at all levels. The idea of a logical fiction connects with naming and analysis. If a syntactic naming (or referring) expression can be eliminated by logical paraphrase such that no referent for that expression is required in the final analysis then the apparent entity referred to by the syntactic naming (or referring) expression will be called a logical fiction. In short we can say that a logical fiction is the purported referent of an eliminable syntactic name.

The idea of a logical fiction in this sense probably originated with Jeremy Bentham. Bentham thought that ordinary language was unavoidably committed to 'fictitious entities'. He did not think this mattered, indeed he thought it often advantageous, unless confused inferences were drawn about what exists. Bentham argued, for example, that all of the following were 'fictitious entities', or in our terms logical fictions: motion, relation, faculty, power, quantity, form, matter, as well as, more significantly for his moral and political philosophy, duties, obligations, and rights. It is not fortuitous that all the terms listed are abstract nouns. All abstract entities for Bentham are fictions.

Bentham's rejection of the existence of rights, particularly natural rights, to which his contemporaries were appealing so vigorously in the American and French Revolutions, was a rejection of 'right' as a substantive or a name of an entity. He says this of the word 'right':

in its adjective shape, it is as innocent as a dove; it breathes nothing but morality and peace . . . [but] . . . passing in at the heart, it gets possession of the understanding; it then assumes its substantive shape, and joining itself to a band of suitable associates, plants the banner of insurrection, anarchy, and lawless violence.[28]

'Right' as a name is logically eliminable. It can be paraphrased away, Bentham believed, leaving only innocuous talk about how people ought to treat each other.

Bentham linked fiction with the naming function: 'every noun-substantive not the name of a real entity . . . is the name of a fictitious entity'.[29] He defined a fictitious entity as 'an entity to which, though by the grammatical form of the discourse employed in speaking of it, existence be ascribed, yet in truth and reality existence is not meant to be ascribed'.[30] In spite of what looks like a commitment here to a special type of entity—'fictitious entities'—we should, on a charitable reading, interpret Bentham as meaning that so-called fictitious entities are not entities at all but are only apparently so, given the deceptive use of noun substantives. When he claims that 'every fictitious entity bears some relation to some real entity, and can no [sic] otherwise be understood than in so far as that relation is perceived'[31] he is alluding to a logical, not a causal, relation. This is the connection with paraphrase. The paraphrase explains, and removes, the fictitious (i.e. apparent) reference by rephrasing the proposition in which it occurs such that only references to what is real remain. 'Paraphrasis' is defined as 'that sort of exposition which may be afforded by transmuting into a proposition, having for its subject some real entity, a proposition which has not for its subject any other than a fictitious entity'.[32]

So Bentham's theory of fiction is not, as it might seem, onto-logically extravagant. Rather it consists of two parts: a theory about

---

[28] Quoted in Ross Harrison, *Bentham* (London, 1983), 96.
[29] Jeremy Bentham, *Bentham's Theory of Fictions*, ed. C. K. Ogden (2nd edn.; London, 1951), 12.
[30] Ibid. 12.   [31] Ibid.   [32] Ibid. 86.

what is real and a theory of paraphrase. The first is a thorough-going empiricism: a real entity is an 'object the existence of which is made known to us by one or more of our five senses'.[33] The theory of paraphrase is more interesting, though it of course connects with the theory of the real. It has been hailed, notably by C. K. Ogden[34] (and more recently by Ross Harrison), as a clear forerunner of twentieth-century logical analysis. Bentham's breakthrough was to move from the level of the single term to that of the sentence. Locke had offered a compositional view of complex ideas and mixed modes in terms of the concatenation of simple ideas. Vestiges of the Lockean view remain in Bentham (as they do also in Russell) but the step to the level of sentences allows for a much richer analysis of a concept. For example, Bentham wants to explain rights and duties in terms of liability to punishment under the law; punishment is explained in terms of pain. Bentham is not claiming that rights and duties are somehow constructed out of pains, like Lockean complex ideas. He is rather explaining the conditions under which someone can correctly be said to have a right or a duty. Ross Harrison has argued convincingly that Bentham's paraphrases should be seen primarily as verification conditions, grounded in perceptions, for the sentences para-phrased.[35] By containing names only of real perceptible entities the paraphrase explains how we are to understand the original judgement and also captures what truth there is in the original (Bentham thought that sentences containing names of fictitious entities could not strictly be true).

The connection between logical fictions and paraphrase was taken up later by, for example, Russell and Quine. Russell, in his logical atomist days, believed that ordinary objects, people and places were logical fictions in that they had the logical status of 'series and classes'.[36] Considering the sentence 'Piccadilly is a pleasant street', Russell writes: 'If you analyse a statement of that sort correctly, I believe you will find that the fact corresponding to your statement does not contain any constituent corresponding to the word "Piccadilly".'[37] It is precisely in that sense that Piccadilly

[33] Ibid. 114.
[34] See C. K. Ogden, 'Introduction', *Bentham's Theory of Fictions*.
[35] In Harrison, *Bentham*, 72 ff.
[36] Bertrand Russell, *Logic and Knowledge*, ed. R. C. Marsh (London, 1956), 274, 191.
[37] Ibid. 191.

is a fiction. The paraphrase required would first substitute a definite description for the name 'Piccadilly', i.e. the street at such-and-such a location, and would then analyse the sentence containing the description into an existentially quantified sentence containing only variables and predicates, as specified in the Theory of Descriptions.

Russell's theory, like Bentham's, presupposes a conception of what is real and a mechanism of analysis. It also involves a theory of meaning. Russell conceived of what is real as what we are acquainted with. This idea connects with the theory of meaning, which has two parts: first, a realist view of meaning itself, i.e. the meaning of an expression is the entity for which the expression stands, and second, the principle of acquaintance, i.e. the view that understanding the meaning of an expression involves acquaintance with the entity which is its meaning. The atoms of logical atomism are precisely the entities which, according to the realist view, are meanings and according to the principle of acquaintance are the basis of our understanding. Russell held that only these entities, simple sense-data, for example, are 'genuine entities'; everything else is a 'fiction' or 'construction'. That leaves all material objects, for example, as fictions.

Logical analysis, for Russell, is the process that takes us from ordinary sentences to sentences conforming to the principle of acquaintance, i.e. those that are immediately understandable. Russell also thought it had ontological implications, as we saw in the Piccadilly case. The Theory of Descriptions provides the paradigm of analysis but its connection with what is real and fictional was perhaps originally misunderstood by Russell. Russell seems to have thought that because he could eliminate descriptions by translation into propositional functions this was equivalent to showing that there was nothing real, or no 'genuine entity', answering to the description; he called descriptions 'incomplete symbols', a term which had just that connotation, according to the realist theory of meaning. In fact of course that conclusion requires further premisses from logical atomism. The Theory of Descriptions itself remains neutral as to whether any object is designated by a description. All it shows is that the syntactic form of a sentence containing a definite description does not require the existence of a designated object for it to be meaningful.

Quine followed the lead of Russell's Theory of Descriptions

arguing that all singular terms could be systematically eliminated
from a language in favour of quantifiers and predicates. On this
basis he developed his criterion for testing the ontological commitments of a theory: do not look at the *names* that appear in the
theory (after all these are eliminable), look at the *bound variables*
of the fully paraphrased sentences that the theory asserts.[38] The
values of those variables are the entities to which the theory is
committed. Quine agrees with Bentham in suggesting that 'sometimes [we] choose to speak *as if* certain syncategorematic expressions were names of entities . . . the[se] alleged entities . . . are
convenient *fictions*'; he also speaks of 'fake names'.[39]

An important question for logical fictions is the status of the
paraphrase which removes the apparent reference. Is it just the
possibility of an eliminative paraphrase that determines the fictional
status of a name or is the fictional status only relative to prior
assumptions about what is real? For example, to defend the existence of rights against Bentham's attack is it necessary to show that
his paraphrase is inadequate or only that it is not needed? Bentham,
as we have seen, had clear empiricist, even verificationist, motives
for his eliminative paraphrases. We should distinguish, following
Quine, the question of what exists from the question of what
commitments arise from certain ways of speaking. Logical paraphrase cannot in itself give a direct answer to the question of what
is real; it shows only how we can avoid apparent (syntactically
based) commitments to types of entities. To say that something is
a logical fiction is to say that its existence need not be assumed in
order to make sense of a particular sentence. The fact that material objects for Russell and rights for Bentham turn out to be
logical fictions is a product of other features of their theory.

However, even with these qualifications, it still might seem that
logical fictions offer support for the conclusions of both our schematic arguments: in effect blurring fact and fiction. After all, the
suggestion is that quite ordinary discourse, by means of which we
convey factual beliefs, turns out to be shot through with talk about
fictions. Logical fictions also seem to offer some confirmation of
the first premiss of argument (A), which grounds the distinction

[38] See e.g. Quine, *From a Logical Point of View.*
[39] Quine, 'A Logistical Approach to the Ontological Problem', in *The Ways of
Paradox and Other Essays* (New York, 1966), 66.

between fact and fiction in correspondence. Both Bentham and Russell see meaning itself in referential and correspondence terms.

But on closer inspection there is not much mileage here for proponents of the arguments, at least not for their general ambition of running together different kinds of discourse, imaginative, philosophical, scientific, etc. For one thing, logical fictions belong in the object, not the description, category; they concern reference rather than truth. It is not a sentence or discourse that is fictional in the logical sense, only a kind of name, even though the removal of the fiction takes place at a sentential level.

Furthermore, the dichotomy between what is 'made up' and what is 'out there' is not obviously applicable to logical fictions. For Russell, what is real is not what is 'out there' but what is 'in here', yet there is no confusion between what is real and what is 'made up'. The connotations of construction or imagination are also absent from logical fictions. The focus is on eliminability not creativity. Although Russell often uses 'fiction' and 'construction' interchangeably this is strictly a confusion of logic and epistemology.

Finally, there is a marked difference between logical fictions, defined in terms of elimination by paraphrase, and make-believe fictions, defined in terms of fictive utterance. It is not the semantic eliminability of the names of fictional characters that explains their fictionality, but rather their presentation in the fictive mode and the consequence that how they are described determines what is true of them. There can be no conflating of these conceptions.

Epistemological fictions

If logical fictions are concerned primarily with naming and the possibility of paraphrase, epistemological fictions are concerned with the ways that objects are known. There is clearly a connection, as is evident in the work of Bentham and Russell for whom epistemological criteria helped to determine what counted as a logical fiction. Both philosophers used empiricist criteria, based on what could be perceived by the senses, to define those 'real' entities which were the ultimate referents of genuine names. For Russell these real entities were momentary sense-data, for Bentham they were both perceptible and 'inferential' entities. Nevertheless, it is usually a good idea, if possible, to keep apart questions of logic, ontology, and epistemology. What exists is not co-extensive with what is known to exist or indeed what a particular theory claims to exist.

Epistemological fictions arise from two kinds of constructivist theory: foundationalist and anti-foundationalist. Locke, Kant, and Russell were foundationalists in the sense that they distinguished between a 'given' and a 'construction'; what is constructed in knowledge is constructed out of a given that is not itself constructed. It would be wrong, though, even for foundationalist theories, to associate the given exclusively with the real. Although Locke had reservations about the reality of things corresponding to at least some complex ideas, Kant was in no doubt that the 'synthetic' world of objects was real: that is the point of empirical realism.

Russell, in contrast, did associate the given exclusively with the real. 'All the ordinary objects of daily life', he wrote, 'are extruded from the world of what there is.'[40] And he spoke of 'the unreality of the things we think real'.[41] It is far from clear why Russell could not admit his logical constructions to be real or genuine entities. Part of the answer is that he thought of objects as classes and he held an anti-realist view of classes. Part also rests on the doctrine of logical fictions and the mistaken belief that to eliminate a syntactic name is to eliminate any entity named. For Russell, epistemological fictions are co-extensive with logical fictions. But this need not have been so. The epistemological doctrine that material objects are logical constructions out of sense-data is not equivalent to the logical doctrine that the names for material objects can be eliminated by paraphrase. The atoms of analysis, for example, need not have been sense-data.

Epistemological fictions also appear in anti-foundationalist theories of knowledge. Quine's idea of objects as posits belongs in this category. He offered a famous analogy between physical objects and Homer's gods: 'physical objects are conceptually imported into the situation as convenient intermediaries—not by definition in terms of experience, but simply as irreducible posits comparable, epistemologically, to the gods of Homer.'[42] And elsewhere he says that '(p)hysical objects are postulated entities which round

[40] Russell, *Logic and Knowledge*, 273.   [41] Ibid. 274.
[42] Quine, 'Two Dogmas of Empiricism', in *From a Logical Point of View*, 44.

out and simplify our account of the flux of experience'.[43] This conception of physical objects as posits is a further, more sophisticated, version of the idea of an epistemological fiction. Quine speaks of the 'conceptual scheme of physical objects' as 'a convenient myth'.[44] Of course, in relativizing ontology, he would not hesitate to accept his posits as real. Reality too is relativized. Quine agrees enough with Carnap to reject so-called 'external' questions of existence. There is no contrast for Quine between what is real and what is posited nor ultimately between what is posited and what is given.

Such too is the position of Nelson Goodman, another antifoundationalist. For Goodman we make worlds by making world-versions. There is no single world but a plurality of worlds. And we make a world-version not out of an experiential given but out of other world-versions. We will return to Goodman in Chapter 8.

In the mean time certain general conclusions are already emerging. One is that epistemological fictions, or constructions, in their many forms from Locke to Goodman, provide no sharp line between what is made and what is real. They do not presuppose correspondence relations and they imply that the mind plays an important part in shaping the world that we know. Also, both the object and the description senses of 'fiction' are invoked. Objects and concepts alike are products of human makings, on this view, even though the makings, Lockean complex ideas, Kantian synthesis, Russellian logical construction, Quinean positing, are of different kinds.

Literary theorists might find some comfort in all this inasmuch as they seek to extend the realm of what is 'made up'. But the presence of epistemological fictions will do little to affect the distinction between the literary, say, and the philosophical. For one thing, epistemological makings occur at what Kant and Putnam call the transcendental, rather than the empirical or internal, level. That is, they do not occur at the level at which we distinguish between, say, a real person and a fictional character or a work of philosophy and a work of fiction. Nor do they affect simple semantic relations; it is not as if the constructivist must deny the possibility of reference and truth. Even if the world itself is an

---

[43] Quine, 'On What There Is', in *From a Logical Point of View*, 18.
[44] Ibid. 18.

epistemological construct names can still name objects and there can still be a correspondence relation between a sentence-token and a state of affairs. Even Quine, for example, maintains that he holds a correspondence theory of truth (as did Kant).

Again, epistemological fictions are quite unlike the make-believe fictions of the fictive stance. Both are of course 'constructs' but the latter are of a different kind and serve different ends. They do not presuppose a 'given', nor are they posited as 'real' in anything like the way that the phenomenalist, say, posits physical objects. When a reader responding to fictive utterance is invited to *make-believe* that the objects are real this is explicitly contrasted with attitudes taken towards objects that *are* real or are believed to be real. Make-believe fictions are not assigned roles in any explanatory theory. In Chapter 9 we will consider further the relations between knowledge and fiction by examining the place of imagination and narration in theories of knowledge.

Notional objects

The idea of a notional object, along with that of a notional world, comes from Daniel Dennett[45] but the conception owes much to phenomenology, particularly Brentano's 'intentional objects'. Notional objects are objects of thought: as Dennett says, 'all the objects and events the subject *believes in*'.[46] Notional worlds are relative to individual subjects and the controlling idea is that these worlds can be characterized independently of reference to things outside the subject's mind. In this sense they conform to Descartes's thought-experiment; they concern narrow content only, the characterization given to beliefs apart from their dependence on an external world. The beliefs are characterized *de dicto* not *de re*.

The point can be explained with a simple and familiar example. Suppose that John believes that the man in the brown hat is a spy.[47] He has glimpsed the man on several occasions, always wearing the same hat, and acting in a suspicious manner. Suppose also

[45] Daniel C. Dennett, 'Beyond Belief', in Andrew Woodfield (ed.), *Thought and Object: Essays on Intentionality* (Oxford, 1982); see also Daniel C. Dennett, *The Intentional Stance* (Cambridge, Mass., 1987).

[46] Dennett, 'Beyond Belief', 38.

[47] The example is derived from one given in Quine, 'Quantifying In', in Leonard Linsky (ed.), *Reference and Modality* (Oxford, 1971).

that, unknown to John, the man in the brown hat is *in fact* Smith, the local bank manager, and John's friend. In spite of the real identity of the brown-hatted man it does not seem valid to infer that John believes that Smith, his friend, is a spy. He, John, would strongly reject that suggestion. We can say, then, that the expression 'the man in the brown hat' characterizes a notional object for John; the name 'Smith' and the descriptions 'the local bank manager' and 'my friend' do not characterize the same notional object, though they no doubt characterize other notional objects. There are several notional objects in John's notional world which 'match' with only one real object in the real world.

Dennett introduced the idea of a notional world in response to the challenge to methodological solipsism arising from Putnam's well-known thought-experiment about Twin-Earth.[48] Putnam imagines a planet, Twin-Earth, which is a virtual replica of Earth, including exact atom-for-atom replicas or *doppelgängers* of every person, place, and event. John's *doppelgänger* on Twin-Earth is an exact physical replica of John so we can assume he is an exact psychological replica as well (given the supervenience of the psychological on the physical); they have identical brains. Now suppose, says Putnam, that there is one difference between Earth and Twin-Earth, namely, that the liquid on Twin-Earth that is observationally indistinguishable from water, filling lakes, bathtubs, puddles, and so on, in fact has a different chemical structure from water on Earth; it is not H_2O but 'XYZ'. John's *doppelgänger* and John share all the same theories about water and say all the same things about it. But is John's belief, expressed in the words 'Water is H_2O', the same as his twin's belief, expressed in the same words? No, says Putnam, because John's belief is genuinely *about* water and is *true* but his twin's belief is not about water but only about what he calls 'water', namely XYZ, and is *false*. If Putnam is right that the identity of beliefs is determined not only by inner psychological states but also by *how the world is* external to the mind then this looks like a refutation of Descartes's assumption that we could have exactly the beliefs we do even if there were no world at all.

Dennett's idea of a notional world is designed to capture just

[48] Described in Hilary Putnam, 'The Meaning of "Meaning"', in *Philosophical Papers*, ii: *Mind, Language and Reality* (Cambridge, 1975).

those psychological states that John and his *doppelgänger* share apart from how the world is 'out there'. He says: 'although my *doppelgänger* and I live in different real worlds—Twin-Earth and Earth—we have the *same* notional world. You and I live in the same real world, but have different notional worlds, though there is considerable overlap between them.' 'A notional world', he goes on,

> should be viewed as a sort of *fictional* world devised by a theorist, a third-party observer, in order to characterize the narrow-psychological states of a subject. . . . we will note that some objects in the real world inhabited by a subject 'match' objects in the subject's notional world, but others do not. The real world contains many things and events having no counterparts in any subject's notional world . . . and notional worlds of gullible or confused or ontologically profligate subjects will contain notional objects having no counterparts in the real world.[49]

There are all kinds of difficulties over how to characterize notional worlds. Although the conception is different from both that of a logical fiction and that of an epistemological fiction, there is nevertheless both a semantic and an epistemological aspect in it. For example, at the level of semantics one test for the presence of a notional object is the test of substitutivity for co-referential terms in belief attributions; as we saw, we cannot substitute the name 'Smith' for the expression 'the man in the brown hat' in the above example without altering the truth-value of the belief report. At the level of epistemology, the idea of 'direct access' might be invoked to describe the epistemic status of notional objects. We should, however, be wary about this as an individual's access to his own notional objects is not in any sense 'unmediated'; the access, in Fregean terms, is always embodied in a 'mode of presentation'. Notional objects are identified *under a description*.

This 'aspectival' nature of notional objects recalls that of fictional objects, in the make-believe sense. But although, as Dennett describes it, notional worlds might be thought of as 'fictional worlds', the make-believe conception and the psychological one are distinct. The point must be emphasized because it is commonly supposed that the story-teller's fictions are 'imaginary worlds' in the literal sense that they exist, first and foremost, *in the imagination*. That would make fictional objects *mental* objects somewhat akin to

[49] Dennett, 'Beyond Belief', 38.

notional objects. But on our account of make-believe fictions they are not psychological in any fundamental sense, being defined only in terms of linguistic conventions and social practices. No doubt fictional content is, contingently, a product of imaginative processes but strictly speaking a fictive state of affairs is introduced through a *linguistic* rather than a *psychological* operation. There is no necessity that a writer imagine a fictional character or event before describing it.

Nor is there anything in the concept of a notional world to encourage a blurring of the distinction between the fictional and the real. In fact the concept relies on the contrast between what is 'in the mind' and what is 'outside the mind' or 'in the world', without any implication, in Dennett's account, that this distinction is spurious. Not all objects are notional objects. Notional worlds are introduced to characterize psychological states and to explain behaviour. Dennett's argument that it is possible to characterize beliefs without reference to what is 'outside the mind' is perfectly compatible with a realist conception of truth (the view that there is a mind-independent world to which beliefs can 'correspond'). Finally, the thought that we all live, imaginatively, in notional worlds is tempered by the thought that our individual well-being, not to speak of the survival of the species, depends crucially on the closeness of 'fit' between our notional worlds and the actual world.

Fictions of convenience

The category of 'fictions of convenience' derives substantially from Hans Vaihinger's notion of fiction in *The Philosophy of 'As If'*. The trouble with following Vaihinger too closely is that he tried to subsume every type of fiction within his scheme, therefore blurring important distinctions. However, his basic concept is useful: that of a fiction as a *conscious falsehood introduced for a particular purpose*. He gives examples of legal, mathematical, practical, heuristic, even epistemological fictions.[50] An immortal God, the virgin birth, atoms, the materialistic notion of the world, vital force in biology, and an original social contract are all fictions, according to Vaihinger. The trouble is this throws the net too wide. If we

---

[50] Vaihinger, *The Philosophy of 'As If'*. Vaihinger gives the example of Kantian categories as epistemological fictions (107) and develops the idea in ch. 37, 164 ff.

stick to the basic concept the list will need to be pared down; but the basic concept is worth retaining.

Vaihinger proposed four essential characteristics of his fictions. First, they are either 'in contradiction with immediate reality', i.e. they 'fail to harmonize with facts, laws and phenomena otherwise known' or they are flatly self-contradictory.[51] Second, they disappear either in the course of history or through 'the operation of logic'.[52] In both cases they are only 'used provisionally'. Obviously if a fiction is self-contradictory it will need to be eliminated, perhaps through *reductio ad absurdum*, in sound reasoning. The third feature is the 'express awareness that the fiction is just a fiction, . . . the consciousness of its fictional nature'.[53] Unfortunately, Vaihinger weakens this condition by suggesting that in many cases fictions begin life as hypotheses, aiming at truth, and only later become recognized as fictions.[54] The final feature, which Vaihinger considered to be the 'kernel of [his] position', is the idea of the utility of fiction: 'fictions . . . are *means* to a definite end.'[55] In this they contrast with 'merely subjective fancy'. Vaihinger's fictions are defined, then, in terms of contradiction, logical and historical eliminability, consciousness, and expediency.

If we apply these conditions strictly, taking as the core of 'fictions of convenience' the idea of a deliberate and known falsehood introduced to serve some definite end, we will have to eliminate a great many of Vaihinger's candidate examples. God, the virgin birth, materialism, and the vital force in biology, for example, were almost certainly not introduced as conscious fictions and some of course are still believed to be real or true. Even Vaihinger's epistemological examples—like the Kantian categories or the Thing-in-Itself—seem more like metaphysical hypotheses than deliberate fictions.

However, the concept he has provided is by no means empty. Perhaps the clearest example is that of legal fiction, which Bentham reviled as 'wilful falsehood, having for its object the stealing legislative power'.[56] A legal fiction is a deliberate invention or stipulation in the law, against known facts, for the purpose of simplification or expediency. Vaihinger gives an example from the German Commercial Code whereby if 'goods are not returned to

---

[51] Ibid. 97.   [52] Ibid. 98.   [53] Ibid.   [54] Ibid. 99.   [55] Ibid.
[56] Ogden, 'Introduction', *Bentham's Theory of Fictions*, p. xviii.

the sender within the proper time [they] are to be regarded *as if* the recipient had definitely authorized and accepted them'.[57] The arbitrariness of the time-interval and the stipulative nature of the authorization indicate the fictionality of the transaction.

Fictions of convenience, then, belong in a distinct category of fictions as deliberate departures from known facts for some practical end. The conception does not reduce to other kinds. In particular it is not identical with that of fiction in the make-believe sense.[58] Vaihinger emphasizes truth-values in his definition—fictions as 'conscious falsehoods'—while we have argued that truth and falsity are not definitive of fictive utterance. Also he gives emphasis to correspondence relations—fiction versus fact—rather than to the idea of making. There are other differences too. It would be strange, to say the least, to think of literary fictions as instruments of *expediency*, nor is the idea appropriate that they 'disappear in the course of history'. Needless to say, though, there are some connections. Fictive utterances are purposive and they invite readers to act *as if* they were reading actual reports, while knowing that they are not.

With regard to the metaphysical issues, fictions of convenience bear no special commitments on the nature of facts, the objective world, or theories of truth. They obviously presuppose a distinction between fiction and reality though without any implications for the character of that reality. They rely on the notion of a 'known fact', with the assumption that these themselves are not fictions, but leave it open as to how much 'making' might be involved in knowing.

Non-entities

The central feature of the category of non-entities is that of mistaken belief. Entities believed to exist, and named or described on that basis, but which as a matter of fact do not exist, are non-entities. We borrow the expression from Bentham who

---

[57] Vaihinger, *The Philosophy of 'As If'*, 35.

[58] Frank Kermode uses Vaihinger's 'as if' as a model for literary fictions in *The Sense of an Ending* (Oxford, 1967). Kermode sees fiction primarily in terms of the imposition of structure (particularly temporal structures): 'men need fictive concords with origins and ends, such as give meaning to lives and to poems' (36). But his account relies more on the nature of *narrative* than on fiction. That these are different is emphasized in our Ch. 9.

distinguished a non-entity from what he called a 'fictitious' entity, defined, as we have seen, in terms of eliminable names. Bentham defines a non-entity as the (non-existent) object of a description appearing in a serious assertion.[59] We should supplement this definition by adding that the intended reference is to something real; this captures the idea of mistaken belief and sharpens the distinction with logical fictions (though this is implied in Bentham's account). Bentham gives the example of someone making an assertion about 'a being called the Devil' with 'limbs like a man's, horns like a goat's, wings like a bat's, and a tail like a monkey's'. The assertion is serious but the purported reference absurd.

The category of non-entities, so defined, is once again distinct from the category of make-believe fictions. The term 'empty name' is sometimes applied indiscriminately to the names given by story-tellers to their characters and to the names of non-existent entities rooted in myth or folklore or faulty science. But non-entities, unlike make-believe fictions, have their origins in mistaken beliefs. So, for example, Vulcan, the intra-Mercurial planet, is a non-entity, as is Eldorado, the city paved with gold, and the substance phlogiston, as well as centaurs, unicorns, dragons, fairies, griffins, angels, devils, Homer's gods, and even the redoubtable Pegasus. We assume in each case that its origin lies in mistaken fact rather than deliberate invention; where this is not so the item should be struck from the list. Origins of course are often murky. Why should this distinction matter?

There are several reasons. First of all, when applied to non-entities the term 'fictional' means 'non-existent' yet it has been central to our account of the practice of fiction that the determining factor is not existence or 'correspondence' but mode of utterance. Also, the fictionality (i.e. non-existence) of non-entities is a contingent matter (except where the non-entities are self-contradictory). They are believed to exist but, as a matter of fact, do not exist. The fictionality (i.e. fictive origin) of make-believe fictions is not a contingent matter. Although the constituent aspects of a fictional object might be instantiated in a real individual that has no bearing on the fictional status of the object. A fictional character is an intensional object and for that reason could never be identical with a material object. It takes an empirical enquiry to

---

[59] Bentham, *Bentham's Theory of Fictions*, 16.

establish that phlogiston and Eldorado are non-entities, but no such enquiry is needed, or appropriate, to discover that Dorothea Brooke is fictional.

In this final category of fiction there is no implication that the distinction between real entities and non-entities might become blurred. The non-existence of a non-entity might be hard to discover but it is an objective matter for all that. Ontologically speaking, fact and fiction are here at their sharpest divide.

Retaining the distinctions

Let us assemble some general conclusions about the implications of the supposed widespread fictionality. The presence of fictions or constructions in science and elsewhere encourages the idea that literary fictions are just a species of a more general and ubiquitous creative process. Combine this with different varieties of metaphysical anti-realism—concerning the 'objective world', truth, what is 'made up', what is 'out there'—and we have the makings of a powerful argument, beyond special pleading, for the cognitive rehabilitation of literary fiction, not merely on the 'soft' grounds of literary value but on the 'hard' grounds of epistemological egalitarianism. With fiction and making revealed to be so deeply entrenched in human intellectual processes, the self-conscious artefacts of the artist or story-teller can no longer be dismissed as marginal—indeed they come to appear as paradigmatic. Perhaps, so the argument runs, we should abandon altogether the distinction between fiction-making and truth-telling.

However, the argument is not yet won. Although we give no support to the denigration of literary fiction, and are sceptical of the idea of a 'privileged' discourse, we do not think it serves anyone's interests, far less the literary theorist's, to blur distinctions between different kinds of making or to over-generalize the special features of fiction as manifested in simple story-telling. If we apply our different philosophical conceptions of fiction to the premises in the earlier schematic arguments, and in particular if we apply the conception of fictive utterance, we will find that the polemical conclusions, which seek to undermine the very idea of distinct fictional and factual domains, call for substantial qualification. Even if philosophical anti-realism is true, in epistemology and semantics, even if we accept constructivist theories of knowledge or pragmatist or coherentist theories of truth, we still need to retain some conception of an objective world, some distinction between a fictional invention and a real object, some distinction between different ends of discourse. By reflecting on the different conceptions of fiction and the different kinds of making they involve we see quite strikingly what different meanings can be attached to the thought that all discourses are fundamentally 'fictional' or that all objects are *au fond* 'fictions'. There is simply no unitary notion of fiction which binds together, say, Kant's 'synthesis', Bentham's 'fictitious entities', Russell's 'logical constructions', Quine's 'posits', Dennett's 'notional worlds', Vaihinger's 'as if', ... or the idea of make-believe fiction. This lack of unity exposes as a myth the alleged 'ubiquity of fiction': the myth, on inspection, fragments into different claims set in different contexts about different subject-matter. Even if we accept that *in some sense* facts, objects, events, abstract entities, the mind, persons, etc., are fictions we can draw no general implications for the cognitive status of make-believe, nor for the validity of the fiction/non-fiction distinction as relevant to literary criticism, nor for the standing of literature relative to philosophy. We should not let what we say, philosophically, about the world dictate what we say, as readers of fiction, about the objects and content of those fictions.

8

Truth-Making and World-Making

In the last chapter we offered a critical examination of one aspect—concerning fictionality—of a broad but persistent trend within literary theory to engage metaphysical or epistemological questions. This engagement is a two-way process. On the one hand, it seeks to draw conclusions of a metaphysical nature, about what exists or is real or is 'out there', from observations about literature, in particular relating to fictionality, representation, realism, truth, etc. On the other hand, it seeks to bring to bear considerations of a metaphysical kind—how objects are 'made', the role of the imagination, the mind-dependence of facts—on questions about the nature and status of literary works. Out of this two-way engagement have emerged some striking conclusions, challenging a whole battery of well-entrenched distinctions: fiction/fact, the imaginary/the real, the invented/the discovered, fiction-making/truth-telling, literature/philosophy. Our own enterprise is to try to disengage questions pertaining to literature (and thus literary theory properly so-called) from this metaphysical context and in doing so defend at least versions (those relevant to the literary context) of the distinctions under attack. What we have found so far, looking at conceptions of fiction, is (1) that there is no uniform conception, and (2) that those conceptions which do bear metaphysical implications are distinct in important ways from the 'make-believe' conception grounded in the practice of fictional story-telling. It is no longer possible to claim, in any unqualified way, that 'all is fiction', nor can that claim draw support from observations about literary fictions.

Our argument to locate the relevant conception of fiction within a social practice rather than within a theory about the world, objects, facts, etc., bears certain affinities to the version of 'pragmatism' developed by Richard Rorty. Rorty also believes that metaphysical issues about 'reality' and truth should be kept out of discussions of (literary) fiction. He thinks that philosophers have been led into spurious 'problems about fictional discourse' precisely because of unwarranted metaphysical commitments.[1] But Rorty's view is fundamentally different from ours, not least because he rejects all the substantive distinctions we seek to defend, particularly that between literature and philosophy. Rorty reaches his conclusions about fiction on the strength of a specific (anti-metaphysical) view about truth. His attitude to fiction is a direct consequence of his rejection of the correspondence theory of truth. Our view, in contrast, is that the practice of fiction, as we have described it, is indifferent to theories of truth, be they correspondence, pragmatist, or anything else. Accounting for the status of sentences in novels, or saying what a fictional character is, or explaining how a work of fiction can be 'about' something, does not presuppose a theory of what the world is like, or objects, or facts. Nor does it presuppose, as Rorty thinks, a view that rejects all such theories as spurious.

In this chapter we will give a detailed appraisal of two accounts of truth—propounded by Rorty and Goodman—both of which seek to redraw the bounds of the fictional. The accounts can be taken as exemplary of two marked trends in literary theory: the anti-philosophical and the anti-realist. Rorty's anti-metaphysical stance represents a fairly widespread negative attitude, among literary theorists, towards the 'privileging' of philosophy, while Goodman brings to bear the precision of the analytic philosopher in support of an 'irrealist' view of the world the central points of which are strikingly similar to those found within post-structuralism. On the face of it the rhetoric of 'making truth' and 'making the world', associated with these accounts, seems so to weaken the ideas of 'truth' and the 'world' that the very project of discussing 'pro-truth' versus 'no-truth' conceptions of literature becomes seriously undermined. If these views are right what becomes of the practice of truth-seeking and knowledge-seeking with which we aim to contrast the practice of fiction (and that of literature)?

In fact what we will show is that at the level where it matters the practice of enquiry remains substantially intact in the face of these pressures. Neither the anti-philosophical polemic of Rorty nor the anti-realism of Goodman succeeds in extending the bounds of the fictional in a way that calls for any radical revision in how we

---

[1] Rorty, 'Is there a Problem about Fictional Discourse?' in *Consequences of Pragmatism*.

conceive the relation between works of fiction and works of an overtly truth-seeking kind. But the point has to be argued, it cannot be taken for granted. Furthermore, a close examination of these ideas will afford an important insight into the deep underlying scepticism in much post-structuralist thought.

Truth-making and literature

We saw in the previous chapter that appeal to the pragmatist's notion that 'truth is man-made' might be part of an argument to the conclusion that truth is merely a species of fiction. That argument was severely weakened by the discovery of radically different kinds of making associated with different kinds of fiction. But Rorty, who defends the view that truth is 'made' not 'discovered', wants to hold on to the notion that the truth-seeker is no different in principle from the fiction-maker. What support does he offer for this? What are its implications for the status of literary fictions?

Rorty is insistent that there are implications for literature in what he says about truth. Two general thoughts on the matter run through his recent work: one is that there is no longer much point in trying to distinguish literature from philosophy, the other is that literary criticism has become 'the presiding intellectual discipline'.[2] Unfortunately, though, the only direct support offered for these thoughts seems to lie in changing the meanings of the key terms:

[t]he word 'literature' now covers just about every sort of book which might conceivably have moral relevance—might conceivably alter one's sense of what is possible and important. The application of this term has nothing to do with the presence of 'literary qualities' in a book.[3]

It is no wonder, then, on this definition, that there is not much difference between literary and philosophical works (or presumably historical, scientific, autobiographical ones, as well). As for literary critics, under the proposed new definition of 'literary criticism', they

are not in the business of explaining the real meaning of books, nor of evaluating something called their 'literary merit'. Rather they spend their

---

[2] Both points are made, for example, in Rorty, *Contingency, Irony, and Solidarity*, 83.

[3] Ibid. 82.

time placing books in the context of other books, figures in the context of other figures.[4]

Rorty himself admits that under this description of literary criticism 'there is less and less point in calling it *literary* criticism'.[5]

Clearly this is very weak ground for trying to collapse the distinction between literature and philosophy. For there remains a recognizable, and widely accepted, conception of literature and literary criticism where questions about meaning, evaluation and 'literary merit' are still of central importance. That conception cannot be brushed aside merely by noticing that the term 'literature' is used in some quarters as a catch-all. The question remains what connection the normative conception has with philosophy and, more generally, with truth.

Rorty and the ironist's viewpoint

Rorty's project is to get us to change the way we think about literature and philosophy, with regard to truth, by inviting us to adopt an entirely different viewpoint on the intellectual landscape. He characterizes two kinds of philosophers—later to be dubbed 'metaphysicians' and 'ironists'[6]—in effect those who support the ideal of truth as 'correspondence with the facts' and those who reject that ideal. The first group of philosophers—those who 'have remained faithful to the Enlightenment'—

take science as the paradigmatic human activity, and they insist that natural science discovers truth rather than makes it. They regard 'making truth' as a merely metaphorical, and thoroughly misleading, phrase. They think of politics and art as spheres in which the notion of 'truth' is out of place.[7]

The other group, among whom Rorty would count himself,

realizing that the world as it is described by the physical sciences teaches no moral lesson, offers no spiritual comfort, have concluded that science

---

[4] Ibid. 80.   [5] Ibid. 81.

[6] Ibid., ch. 4; the labels do not appear in the first three chapters.

[7] Ibid. 3. Ch. 1 of *Contingency, Irony, and Solidarity*, from which the quotations in this paragraph are taken, originally appeared as 'The Contingency of Language', *London Review of Books*, 8: 7, 17 Apr. 1986, 3–6.

is no more than the handmaiden of technology. These philosophers have ranged themselves alongside the political utopian and the innovative artist.[8]

He goes on:

[w]hereas the first kind of philosopher contrasts 'hard scientific fact' with the 'subjective' or with 'metaphor', the second kind sees science as one more human activity, rather than the place at which human beings encounter a 'hard', non-human reality.[9]

Expanding on the view that truth is 'made' not 'found', he writes:

[o]n this view, great scientists invent descriptions of the world which are useful for purposes of predicting and controlling what happens, just as poets and political thinkers invent other descriptions of it for other purposes. But there is no sense in which *any* of these descriptions is an accurate representation of the way the world is in itself. These philosophers regard the very idea of such a representation as pointless.[10]

Rorty's characterization of these competing viewpoints reflects many of the issues raised in the previous chapter. The suggestion that the very idea of representing 'the way the world is' is 'pointless' recalls the literary theorist's sceptical stance on 'realism'. Also, the opposition between the view of science as seeking 'hard . . . facts' or a 'non-human reality' and science as 'one more human activity' recalls the debate between metaphysical realists and various kinds of anti-realists. Finally, there is the undercurrent of pragmatism suggesting that scientific descriptions be judged not as 'corresponding to the facts' but as 'useful for purposes of predicting and controlling what happens'.

But Rorty is not entering the debate as one anti-realist among others, meeting his opponents argument for argument. He has no alternative *theory* to offer, so he says, and as an 'ironist' he scorns arguments altogether. Thus:

[o]n the view of philosophy which I am offering, philosophers should not be asked for arguments against, for example, the correspondence theory of truth . . . The trouble with arguments against the use of a familiar and time-honored vocabulary is that they are expected to be phrased in that very vocabulary. . . . Interesting philosophy is rarely an examination of the pros and cons of a thesis. Usually it is, implicitly or explicitly, a contest between an entrenched vocabulary which has become a nuisance and a half-formed new vocabulary which vaguely promises great things.[11]

[8] Ibid. 3–4.   [9] Ibid. 4.   [10] Ibid.   [11] Ibid. 8–9.

Rorty is impressed by Wittgenstein's thought that we become trapped in a particular *picture* and that the way to change the picture is not to seek some fresh answer to the old questions but rather to drop the old questions altogether.

[Wittgenstein] does not say: the tradition has pictured the world with gaps in it [e.g. thought and object, mind and body, etc.], but here is how the world looks with the gaps closed. Instead he just makes fun of the whole idea that there is something here to be explained.[12]

Such is precisely Rorty's attitude to the idea of advancing a theory of truth.

When [pragmatists or ironists] suggest that we do not ask questions about the nature of Truth or Goodness, they do not invoke a theory about the nature of reality or knowledge or man which says that 'there is no such thing' as Truth or Goodness. Nor do they have a 'relativistic' or 'subjectivist' theory of Truth or Goodness. They would simply like to change the subject.[13]

This attitude, needless to say, is not likely to impress anyone who sees the 'old' problems as important. And some commentators have seen clear inconsistencies in Rorty's attitude to his own philosophical pronouncements.[14] Why should we take the Rortyian viewpoint as anything more than a weary despair at the prospect of ever solving difficult problems? If there are no arguments, what points should at least incline us towards 'ironism'?

The case against 'correspondence'

The first point, Rorty thinks, is to recognize a kind of psycho-pathology in certain metaphysical yearnings. Those who hanker after 'correspondence' relations between language and reality are motivated, so Rorty sees it, by various kinds of 'anxiety'. One is the fear that if we rest content, as does the pragmatist, with nothing more than a range of discourses or 'language games', unconstrained by an objective reality, we will 'lose contact' with

---

[12] Rorty, *Consequences of Pragmatism*, 34.
[13] Ibid. p. xiv.
[14] See e.g. Martin Steinmann, 'Rortyism', *Philosophy and Literature*, 12 (1988), 27–47; and Jonathan Rée, 'Timely Meditations', *Radical Philosophy*, 55 (1990), 31–9.

the real. 'This fear', he says, 'is definatory of the Western philosophical tradition.'[15] It is associated, he argues, with an anxiety
arising from epistemological scepticism of precisely the Cartesian
variety: 'How would it be different if it were all *made up*? ... How
does having knowledge differ from making poems and telling stories?'[16] Another fear, related to this, is that of 'the poetic, playful,
arbitrary aspects of language'.[17] If we emphasize, as Rorty recom-
mends, the idea of language as a 'game' in contrast to the idea of
language as a 'picture' (of reality) then the fear arises that we
might lose the very distinction between 'responsible' and 'irresponsible' discourse, 'that need to distinguish sharply between
science and poetry which makes us distinctively Western'.[18]

No doubt Rorty is right that the sceptical tradition in philosophy can give rise to such 'fears'. But the fears, such as they are,
will not be allayed just by poking fun at them. It is more constructive to give an account of the 'games' of fiction and poetry to see
just how they do differ from the 'games' of science and philosophy. The need to distinguish writing a novel and writing a scientific treatise, referring to Sherlock Holmes and referring to George
Bush, being murdered in a play and being murdered, reflecting
on desire in *Thérése Raquin* and reflecting on desire in the
Nicomachean Ethics is not rooted in any anxiety, nor in any disparaging attitude towards the former in each case, but in the simple
quest, to use Bernard Williams's expression, of 'getting it right'.[19]
The dichotomy of either treating imaginative fictions as 'playful',
'arbitrary', and 'irresponsible' or collapsing altogether the distinction between the poet and the scientist is a false dichotomy. It is
possible to take imaginative fictions seriously without supposing
that they are exactly like every other kind of 'serious' discourse.

What other grounds does Rorty have for persuading us to
abandon the vocabulary of 'correspondence' in favour of that of
'making'? One move is to appeal to trends within analytic philosophy which, according to Rorty, threaten the foundations of the
classical 'correspondence' view of truth. These include, for example,
the blurring of 'the positivist distinctions between the semantic
and the pragmatic, the analytic and the synthetic, the linguistic

[15] Rorty, *Consequences of Pragmatism*, 130.
[16] Ibid. 128–9.   [17] Ibid. 130.   [18] Ibid. 132.
[19] Bernard Williams, 'Getting it Right', a review of *Contingency, Irony, and Solidarity*, in *London Review of Books*, 11: 22, 23 Nov. 1989, 3, 5.

and the empirical, theory and observation, . . . the scheme/content distinction'.[20] The main purport of this blurring, as Rorty sees it, is to undermine the idea that 'true sentences divide into an upper and lower division—the sentences which correspond to something and those which are "true" only by courtesy or convention'.[21]

Once again Rorty is surely right that no one sensitive to developments in, say, analytic philosophy of language could simply define truth as 'correspondence with the facts' and leave it at that. But those semanticists who seek to defend versions of realism are less concerned with 'correspondence' relations holding for simple declarative sentences (Tarski's truth theorems are adequate for them) than they are with explaining the meaning and truth-conditions of more complex kinds of propositions, such as moral or mathematical or conditional ones, or propositions about the past or about unobservables. A realist, who believes that there is a 'reality' independent of how we think about it, need not give a realist construal of all these kinds. Nor is such a realist obliged to defend the distinctions in Rorty's list. There is nothing, then, in the appeal to current trends which forces the abandonment of realism or gives special encouragement to the idea that truth is 'made'.

Another move is the repetition of a familiar, and longstanding, objection to correspondence theories: that 'correspond with the facts' is not explanatory. One version of the objection was made, for example, by Strawson: 'statements and facts fit. They were made for each other. If you prize the statements off the world you prize the facts off it too; but the world would be none the poorer.'[22] Here is Rorty: ' "Truth" in the sense of "truth taken apart from any theory" and "world" taken as "what determines such truth" are notions that were . . . made for each other.'[23] Rorty also takes issue with those realists who account ultimately for the success of science by claiming that scientific statements, or some of them at least, 'fit the world'. He compares this to Molière's doctor explaining why opium puts people to sleep in terms of its dormitive power.

[20] Rorty, *Consequences of Pragmatism*, p. xviii.

[21] Ibid., p. xviii.

[22] P. F. Strawson, 'Truth', *Proceedings of the Aristotelian Society*, Suppl. Vol. 24 (1950), 129–56; repr. in Pitcher (ed.), *Truth*, 39, and in Strawson, *Logico-Linguistic Papers*.

[23] Rorty, *Consequences of Pragmatism*, 15.

Clearly there is a serious question here, namely how the ideas of 'correspondence' or 'fact' or 'reality' are to be explained. But we will see in a moment that the kinds of things Rorty himself wants to say about 'facts' and 'the world' would be quite enough to satisfy most correspondence theorists. Furthermore, to say that a theory is trivially true is at least to say it is true.

Nearer the heart of Rorty's proposal is the idea of the 'ubiquity of language': 'there is no way to think about either the world or our purposes except by using language.'[24] This is meant to counter an apparent presupposition of correspondence views that 'there is some way of breaking out of language in order to compare it with something else'. The idea leads Rorty towards two separate, though ultimately related, conclusions: on the one hand, a rejection of foundationalism with a consequent slide towards relativism, on the other, the view that truth is 'made' not 'discovered'.

On the former he writes:

[t]he ubiquity of language is a matter of language moving into the vacancies left by the failure of all the various candidates for the position of 'natural starting-points' of thought, starting-points which are prior to and independent of the way some culture speaks or spoke [e.g. 'clear and distinct ideas, sense-data, categories of the pure understanding, structures of prelinguistic consciousness, and the like'].[25]

Once the ideas of a 'foundation' or a 'given' or a 'privileged discourse' are abandoned, we are left simply with language-games or 'vocabularies' that arise somehow independently of criteria or choice.[26] From this arises the connection with truth: 'the world does not tell us what language-games to play.' Rorty emphasizes the relation between truth and *language* rather than, as in correspondence views, the relation between truth and the *world*. Although the world might be 'out there', truth is not: 'to say that truth is not out there is simply to say that where there are no sentences there is no truth.'[27] So the conclusion that 'truth is made rather than found' amounts to no more than the claim that it is sentences that are true (or false), along with the observation that

---

[24] Ibid., p. xix.   [25] Ibid., p. xx.
[26] 'the notions of criteria and choice (including that of 'arbitrary' choice) are no longer in point when it comes to changes from one language-game to another', Rorty, *Contingency, Irony, and Solidarity*, 6; see also 20.
[27] Ibid. 5.

'sentences are elements of human languages, and . . . human languages are human creations'. Truth is 'made rather than found' because '*languages* are made rather than found, and . . . truth is a property of linguistic entities, of sentences'.[28]

But now the claim that 'truth is man-made' begins to look uninteresting and truistic. Certainly it has no substantive implications for the 'fictionalizing' of discourses. Neither the correspondence theorist nor the realist who defends the idea of an objective mind-independent world need disagree that truth is a property of sentences. But what does it mean to say that 'languages are human creations'? This is innocuous enough if it means only the truism of 'the arbitrariness of the sign'. But 'creation' suggests intention and design and, as is often pointed out. in a priori speculation about the origins of language, such purposive concepts seem to presuppose language. All that Rorty can legitimately derive from this claim is the notion that language belongs in human rather than non-human natural history. A much more crucial concession, from the point of view of the correspondence theorist, is that of the distinction between truth and 'the world' in the first place. Rorty admits that 'the world is out there, that it is not our creation' with the gloss that 'most things in space and time are the effects of causes which do not include mental states'.[29] All that the realist wants is for this world to constrain certain kinds of judgements with regard to truth.

Here Rorty invokes another prompter to try to weaken the idea of 'correspondence'. This is what he calls 'the old pragmatist chestnut' that 'any specification of a referent is going to be in some vocabulary. Thus one is really comparing two descriptions of a thing rather than a description with the thing-in-itself.'[30] But much depends on the interpretation of 'specification'; under one interpretation, where it means 'linguistic representation', the claim is tautological, under another, where it means 'identification', the claim is false. It is a tautology that linguistic representations of objects are representations, i.e. determined by the vocabulary and concepts used; this is comparable to the tautology in epistemology that we cannot experience an object apart from the experiences we have of it. Nothing of course follows from these tautologies

---

[28] Ibid. 7.   [29] Ibid. 5.
[30] Rorty, *Consequences of Pragmatism*, 154.

about the existence or nature of an independent reality. If, on the other hand, a referent (an object) is specified in the sense of 'identified' then this might well be done without any vocabulary; the object could be pointed to or picked up. From a semantic point of view, there are other ways an object can 'enter' discourse, or have a bearing on the truth of a sentence, than through its being represented descriptively. Not every reference is mediated by description. Even where descriptions are involved, we need to hold on to the distinction between the world and the descriptions of it. Rorty consistently plays down the relation between a description and what it is a description *of*, or between a sentence and what items in the world the sentence is *about*. Descriptions are not, of course, always descriptions of other descriptions, nor are sentences always about descriptions.

Rorty encourages us to give attention not so much to single sentences as to whole vocabularies. This is reminiscent of Quine who urged us a generation ago to take 'the whole of science' as 'the unit of empirical significance', not the individual statement.[31] This was part of his own argument towards a 'thorough pragmatism'. Rorty adopts the terminology of Wittgenstein:

When the notion of 'description of the world' is moved from the level of criterion-governed sentences within a language-game to language-games as wholes, games which we do not choose between by reference to criteria, the idea that the world decides which descriptions are true can no longer be given a clear sense.[32]

Like Quine, and perhaps Wittgenstein as well, Rorty gets drawn towards relativism. Is truth always determined 'internally' to a language-game (or a 'theory' or a 'system of belief')? Or does a 'world' external to all such frameworks constrain what is true or false? Curiously Rorty wavers; he never quite rejects a mind-independent world.

Two central questions remain unanswered:

1. What exactly is the status of 'the world' on Rorty's account?
2. What constraints does he provide for distinguishing truth from falsity?

The metaphysician will not be happy to switch to the metaphor of 'making' without answers to these questions.

---

[31] Quine, 'Two Dogmas of Empiricism', *in From a Logical Point of View*, 42.
[32] Rorty, *Contingency, Irony, and Solidarity*, 5.

Rorty's 'world'

On the face of it, Rorty's main target is precisely that independent objective world under threat in Descartes's sceptical thought-experiment. Indeed he explicitly repudiates 'the notion of the world *so* "independent of our knowledge" that it might, for all we know, prove to contain none of the things we always thought we were talking about'.[33] Such a world is a 'world well lost'.

However, the world that remains is still a thing of substance and still retains a good deal of 'independence'. It consists of 'the stars, the people, the tables, and the grass—all those things which nobody except the occasional "scientific realist" philosopher thinks might not exist'.[34] Rorty's objection is not to a world 'out there', apart from what we think of it, but only to a world so remote that its true nature might elude us altogether. Rorty's position is that of the common-sense realist minus the Cartesian fantasy. Although he believes that philosophy took a serious wrong turn from Descartes onwards in its dominant metaphor of the mind as 'mirror of nature', nevertheless the world of which he approves is in no way 'mind-dependent' or 'created'. His claims for it are unexceptionable:

a. [R]eality is indifferent to our descriptions of it.[35]

b. The world may cause us to be justified in believing a sentence true.[36]

c. The world can . . . cause us to hold beliefs.[37]

d. [W]e often let the world decide the competition between alternative sentences (for example, between 'Red wins' and 'Black wins' or between 'The butler did it' and 'The doctor did it').[38]

e. Most of the world is as it is whatever we think about it.[39]

f. [M]ost things in space and time are the effects of causes which do not include human mental states.[40]

Not only does Rorty acknowledge such a world but he even retains vestiges of 'correspondence':

---

[33] Rorty, *Consequences of Pragmatism*, 14.   [34] Ibid. 14.
[35] Rorty, *Contingency, Irony, and Solidarity*, 7.
[36] Ibid. 5.   [37] Ibid. 6.   [38] Ibid. 5.
[39] Rorty, *Consequences of Pragmatism*, p. xxvi.
[40] Rorty, *Contingency, Irony, and Solidarity*, 5.

i. When we rap out routine undeliberated reports like 'This is water,' 'That's red,' 'That's ugly,' 'That's immoral,' our short categorical statements can easily be thought of as pictures . . . Such reports do indeed pair little bits of language with little bits of the world.[41]

ii. There is a 'trivial sense' in which 'truth' is 'correspondence to reality' and 'depends upon a reality independent of our knowledge'; this is the sense 'in which . . . we now know perfectly well what the world is like and could not possibly be wrong about it'.[42]

iii. In the sense of 'the world' in (ii), 'it is the world that determines truth'.[43]

There is nothing in Rorty's conception of the world that encourages the view that the world is 'made up' or a 'fiction'. The common-sense view that the world is 'out there', that we causally interact with it, and that it can make a difference to the truth of some things we say, has not been abandoned by Rorty, in spite of his rejection of the so-called 'picture picture' of language and in spite of his advocacy of so thoroughgoing a pragmatism.

Distinguishing truth and falsity

Turning to the second question, about the constraints on distinguishing truth from falsity, we still find a surprising moderation in Rorty's position. Although he appears to mock the concerns of the traditional philosopher about keeping apart 'responsible' and 'irresponsible' discourse, and about the spread of 'arbitrary' and 'playful' aspects of language, Rorty is by no means suggesting that because truth is 'made not found' it must be unconstrained by how things are in the world. He does not, of course, think that just anything can count as true. So what, for Rorty, does determine whether a sentence is true or false? The answer he rejects is 'correspondence with the facts'. The pragmatic theory he favours consists of two parts, somewhat in tension: a playing-down of the fruitfulness of any *general* account, and a tentative offer of a general account.

Here is the playing-down:

For pragmatists, 'truth' is just the name of a property which all true statements share. It is what is common to 'Bacon did not write Shake-

---

[41] Rorty, *Consequences of Pragmatism*, 162.
[42] Ibid. 14.   [43] Ibid.

speare,' 'It rained yesterday,' 'E equals mc^2,' 'Love is better than hate,' '*The Allegory of Painting* was Vermeer's best work,' '2 plus 2 is 4,' and 'There are nondenumerable infinities.' Pragmatists doubt that there is much to be said about this common feature. . . . The assertion of a given sentence—or the adoption of a disposition to assert the sentence, the conscious acquisition of a belief—is a justifiable, praiseworthy act in certain circumstances. But, *a fortiori*, it is not likely that there is something general and useful to be said . . . about the common feature of all the sentences which one should acquire a disposition to assert.[44]

Elsewhere he says, endorsing a point of William James's, that 'truth is not the sort of thing which *has* an essence'.[45] And he denies the idea that describing truth as 'warranted assertibility' provides an analysis of the meaning of 'true'; this is not the basis of a *criterion* of truth:

the pragmatist, if he is wise, will not succumb to the temptation to fill in the blank in

S is true if and only if S is assertible ——

with 'at the end of enquiry' or 'by the standards of our culture' or with anything else. He will recognize the strength of Putnam's 'naturalistic fallacy' argument: Just as nothing can fill the blank in

A is the best thing to do in circumstances C if and only if ——

so, *a fortiori*, nothing will fill the blank in

Asserting S is the best thing to do in C if and only if ——[46]

Nevertheless, Rorty does recognize the need to give some kind of account of the normative nature of 'true'. Not any sentence can be true. At the very least it is 'a compliment paid to sentences that seem to be paying their way and that fit in with other sentences that are doing so'.[47] The constraints on assertibility, for Rorty, are social or cultural:

there are no constraints on inquiry save conversational ones—no whole-sale constraints derived from the nature of the objects, or of the mind, or of language, but only those retail constraints provided by the remarks of our fellow-inquirers.[48]

Rorty's pragmatism thus faces the charge of both cultural relativism and irrationalism. Rorty recognizes this:

when the pragmatist says 'All that can be done to explicate "truth", "knowledge", "morality", "virtue" is to refer us back to the concrete

---

[44] Ibid., p. xiii.   [45] Ibid. 162.   [46] Ibid., p. xxv.
[47] Ibid.   [48] Ibid. 165.

details of the culture in which these terms grew up and developed,' the
defender of the Enlightenment takes him to be saying 'Truth and virtue
are simply what a community agrees that they are.' When the pragmatist
says 'We have to take truth and virtue as whatever emerges from the
conversation of Europe,' the traditional philosopher wants to know what
is so special about Europe. Isn't the pragmatist saying, like the irration-
alist, that *we* are in a privileged situation simply by being *us*?[49]

To this Rorty can only reaffirm his relativism. The best he can do
is to 'remind his interlocutor of the position they both are in, the
contingent starting points they both share, the floating, ungrounded
conversations of which they are both members'.[50]

By the time the debate gets to this level of generality we have
left far behind the question of how individual statements, or even
sets of statements comprising first-order theories, are assessed for
truth. At this level the warrants for assertibility are little different
for the pragmatist and the correspondence theorist, at least to the
extent that the appeal to evidence, the testing procedures, the
cross-checking, the constraints of consistency and care, and so on,
are common ground. Of course, as Rorty rightly points out, there
are innumerable kinds of sentences inviting different kinds of
warrant. But that does not count against a shared understanding
in most cases—even if with the notable exception of philosophical
cases—about where to look for an answer and what counts as a
good or bad answer. This is to acknowledge that there is indeed
a framework within which 'we' have learnt to make judgements
about what is true; whether it is a framework that exclusively
'emerges from the conversation of Europe' is a matter of historical
research. But that framework is not seriously in question at the
'non-philosophical' levels of enquiry. That is at least part of the
truth in pragmatism. At the level at which we assert 'Black wins'
or 'The butler did it'—and well beyond that level—the idea that
'truth is made not found' gains little purchase. At this level, it is
nonsense to suppose that we 'make it up' rather than 'find it out'.
Rorty is certainly not to be taken as implying in his thesis of truth
as 'made' that we simply jettison the paraphernalia, and the scru-
ples, of 'serious', or at least recognized, enquiry. The thesis proposes no short cut, no change of attitude, no sloppiness in research.
In fact, as far as procedures are concerned, *it leaves everything as*

---

[49] Ibid. 173.   [50] Ibid. 173–4.

it is. Rorty's thesis is simply another 'meta'-thesis, another philosophical theory about truth. Significantly, it does nothing whatever to compromise the basic insight of Aristotle's dictum that to say of what is that it is, and to say of what is not that it is not, is true.

Irrationalism

There is, however, one point at which the idea that truth is 'made' does gain purchase but it is precisely at that point that 'irrationalism' sets in, for it weakens the idea that truths are *deliberately* made or chosen for some pragmatic end. This is the point at which major changes occur, as Rorty would say, in 'vocabulary', uninfluenced by 'how the world is':

Europe did not *decide* to accept the idiom of Romantic poetry, or of socialist politics, or of Galilean mechanics. That sort of shift was no more an act of will than it was a result of argument. Rather, Europe gradually lost the habit of using certain words and gradually acquired the habit of using others.[51]

The suggestion seems to be that at the very point where truth might substantially be 'man-made' it becomes outside the control of man. Paradoxically, it becomes, after all, just the kind of thing that is 'discovered'. There are no *criteria* for changes from one language-game to another; the changes simply occur. But this irrationalism, reminiscent of Thomas Kuhn's view of scientific revolutions, is much less widespread than Rorty might suppose. Changes in 'vocabulary'—including, in one of Rorty's own examples, the metaphor of language as 'game' over language as 'picture'—are often accompanied by *argument* and are adopted, if at all, not just because they are persuasive but because they are reasonable.

However, even if we accept the idea of 'paradigm shifts' occurring through changes in vocabulary, we are still left with only a bare conception of truth as 'man-made'. It turns out that all that is man-made are the sentences (and their vocabularies) with which the truths are expressed. The very cultural relativism that Rorty thought released him from the myths of foundationalism or 'first

---

[51] Rorty, *Contingency, Irony, and Solidarity*, 6.

philosophy' in fact ensures the most severe (and familiar) constraints on what is accepted as true at any given time. Within those culturally imposed constraints the thesis that truth is 'made' loses all of its fictionalizing implications. It should be amply clear by now that no appeal to Rorty's pragmatism or 'ironism' will blur the different kinds of makings associated with the fiction-maker (in the literary sense), the scientist, the philosopher, or other truth-seekers.

The idea that the world is 'man-made'

On the face of it, Nelson Goodman's talk of 'worldmaking' and the 'fabrication of facts'[52]—the thesis that we make rather than find worlds—goes even further than Rorty's idea of truth as man-made. While Rorty's thesis might give encouragement to those who want to weaken the distinction between fiction *in its description sense* and truth, Goodman's seems to encourage a weakening of the distinction between fiction *in its object sense* and reality. 'Of course,' Goodman writes, 'we must distinguish falsehood and fiction from truth and fact.' 'But,' he insists, 'we cannot, I am sure, do it on the ground that fiction is fabricated and fact found.'[53]

It is a notable, if surprising, feature of Goodman's view that his epistemological thesis—worlds are 'made' not 'found'—is quite distinct from his thesis about literary fiction—'[a]ll fiction is literal, literary falsehood'.[54] The only truth he allows to literary, or imaginative, fictions is metaphorical truth. We might epitomize what is wrong with both theses in terms of correspondence and making; in the former correspondence is ignored in favour of making, in the latter making is ignored in favour of correspondence.

As our own view of fiction gives emphasis to making we will concentrate on Goodman's epistemological thesis: examining what his claims about 'worldmaking' amount to and how they are supported, and assessing the possibility of appropriating Goodman in the service of the more general process of 'fictionalization'. If

---

[52] Goodman, *Ways of Worldmaking*, ch. 6.
[53] Ibid. 91.
[54] Goodman, *Of Mind*, 124. We discuss Goodman's conception of literary fiction in Ch. 3.

the world is 'man-made', why should not the makings of the novelist have as much credence as those of the scientist? Is the real world any different from the host of imaginary worlds? How can there be, as Goodman supposes, better and worse makings? Why shouldn't just anything count as true?

Goodman's two primary theses about 'the world' are (1) that we make worlds by making 'world-versions', and (2) that there is no one underlying world independent of our makings. Goodman apparently takes the idea of 'making worlds' literally although he accounts for this in terms of making 'world-versions'. A crucial issue in assessing his theses concerns the relation between worlds and world-versions.

What are world-versions? And how are they made? World-versions are symbolic systems and can take many forms: descriptions, pictures, perceptions, even dance and music. 'We can have words without a world but no world without words or other symbols.'[55] We make a world-version out of these symbols by means of a variety of operations: composition and decomposition, weighting, ordering, deletion and supplementation, deformation. But, importantly, we never start from scratch. 'Worldmaking as we know it always starts from worlds already on hand; the making is a remaking.'[56] A significant consequence of this stipulation is that it allows for quite modest conceptual or pictorial innovation to count as worldmaking. This anticipates the simple objection that worlds are just too vast or comprehensive to be the sorts of things humans can make. Making *parts* of worlds or making *changes* in worlds is more on the human scale, as is the seemingly even more modest endeavour of making adjustments in world-versions already at hand. It also confirms the connection with Otto Neurath, as pointed out by Carl Hempel.[57] Neurath's ship, a central motif in Quine's *Word and Object*, is repaired and rebuilt bit by bit on the open sea without ever putting into land; Neurath saw this as an analogy with the growth and development of human knowledge.

Goodman's claim, then, is that world-versions are tied to symbolic systems and symbolic systems are human creations. In that

[55] Goodman, *Ways of Worldmaking*, 6.
[56] Ibid. 6.
[57] Carl Hempel, 'Comments on Goodman's *Ways of Worldmaking*', *Synthese*, 45 (1980), 193–9.

sense are world-versions made. This recalls Rorty's insistence that languages are 'man-made' and truth a property of language. For Rorty this is all there is to the claim that truth too must be 'man-made'. We have already seen, though, that there is nothing here that the realist and correspondence theorist cannot live with. Is this, then, all there is to Goodman's thesis that the world is 'man-made'?

How can creating a world-version, a symbolic system of some sort, be equivalent to creating a world? Goodman often writes, with a hint of offhandedness, as if world-versions just *are* worlds. '[F]or many purposes, right world-descriptions and world-depictions and world-perceptions, the ways-the-world-is, or just versions, *can be treated* as our worlds.'[58] 'Talk of worlds and talk of right versions are often interchangeable.'[59] Yet on the face of it there is a vast and obvious difference between a version, or representation, of a world, albeit a 'right' version, and a world which it is a version *of*. How does Goodman come to conflate the two?

We can look at his response to Israel Scheffler who presses the objection with the example of the stars. First, here is Scheffler:

the claim that we made the stars is false if anything is . . . Nor is it helpful to say that we made the stars *as* stars—that before the word 'star' existed, stars did not exist *qua* stars. For in the first place, that stars did not exist *qua* stars does not imply that they did not exist, or that we made them. And, in the second place, the existence of stars *qua* stars is just their existence plus their being called 'stars'. No one disputes that before we had the word 'stars', stars weren't called 'stars', but that doesn't mean they didn't exist. It would be altogether misleading on this basis alone to say we *made* them.[60]

Goodman's immediate answer is to challenge Scheffler to describe 'which features of the stars we did not make' and 'to state how these differ from features clearly dependent on discourse'.[61] On the question of how we could make something, like a star, so much older than human beings, Goodman simply retorts that we make 'a space and time that contains those stars'. In short, faced with Scheffler's prima-facie objection, Goodman is unrepentant and insists that we do indeed make the stars, 'not with hands but with

[58] Goodman, *Ways of Worldmaking*, 4 (italics added).
[59] Nelson Goodman, 'On Starmaking', *Synthese*, 45 (1980), 212.
[60] Israel Scheffler, 'The Wonderful Worlds of Goodman', *Synthese*, 45 (1980), 206.
[61] Goodman, 'On Starmaking', 213.

minds, or rather with languages or other symbol systems'.[62] In effect, though, this reply only reiterates the equivalence of versions and worlds. More needs to be said for those, like Scheffler, who want a clear distinction between names and discourse on the one hand and the things to which the names or discourse apply on the other.

Goodman does have more to say about this distinction. He acknowledges the difference between descriptions and things: '[a] version saying that there is a star up there is not itself bright or far off, and the star is not made up of words.'[63] 'A baseball but not a "baseball" can be knocked for a home run.'[64] But he glosses this, in a reminder of the redundancy thesis about truth: 'saying that there is a star up there and saying that the statement "There is a star up there" is true amount, trivially, to much the same thing, even though the one seems to talk about a star and the other to talk about a statement.'[65] While retaining the distinction between name and thing, Goodman internalizes that distinction to versions. Versions determine names and categories but at the same time determine what those names and categories apply to. 'Any notion of a reality consisting of objects and events and kinds established independently of discourse and unaffected by how they are described or otherwise presented must give way to the recognition that these, too, are parts of the story.'[66] Of course not any random description thereby makes a thing: '[o]nly if true does description make things'.[67] It might seem that the mention of truth here gives the game away. If we are constrained in our makings by *truth* then are we not back to the firmest distinction between version and world? We will return a bit later to Goodman's ideas of truth and 'right versions'. In the mean time we must pursue his view that descriptions, or versions, can make things.

---

[62] Ibid. 213. Note the subtly different position of the Rortyian pragmatist: 'It is part of our story about stars and planets that they would indeed exist whether or not anybody ever described them. The pragmatists, unlike some of their idealist predecessors, do not want to change this story. Idealists sometimes said: "if there were no minds there would be no stars." Pragmatists say only: "if there were no minds, there would be no one to use the term 'star'." Opponents like Russell ask: but would it not still be *true* that there were stars? Pragmatists answer that question with another: what is "be true" supposed to mean in a world in which there are no statements to be true nor minds to have true beliefs?' (Richard Rorty, 'Just One More Species Doing its Best', *London Review of Books*, 13: 14, 25 July 1991, 3.)

[63] Goodman, 'On Starmaking', 212.   [64] Goodman, *Of Mind*, 69.
[65] Goodman, 'On Starmaking', 212.   [66] Goodman, *Of Mind*, 67.
[67] Ibid. 35.

Here is one of Goodman's examples of a version creating a thing:

Has a constellation been there as long as the stars that compose it, or did it come into being when selected and designated? In the latter case, the constellation was created by a version. And what could be meant by saying that the constellation was always there, before any version? Does this mean that all configurations of stars whatever are always constellations whether or not picked out and designated as such? I suggest that to say that all configurations are constellations is in effect to say that none are: that a constellation becomes such only through being chosen from among all configurations, much as a class becomes a kind only through being distinguished, according to some principle, from other classes.[68]

An obvious objection to this example as an example of how a version can make a thing is that a constellation is clearly an organization, for human purposes (in this case astronomy), of *antecedently existing objects*, namely stars. Imposing an organization on pre-existing things is not quite like creating things themselves. The question then becomes whether stars stand in the same kind of relation to other more simple objects as constellations do to stars. Goodman suggests something of the sort when he writes: 'we make stars by drawing certain boundaries rather than others.'[69] But when we ask 'boundaries round *what*?' we appear to be on a reductionist slide which is not at all congenial to Goodman's position.

First of all, such a slide has, historically, tended to terminate in things like sense-data or an unconceptualized given or a substratum as the basic building blocks of the empirical world. Yet Goodman is adamant in rejecting any such basic stuff independent of human organization. There is no limit to the man-made world. There are no version-independent features: 'things and worlds and even the stuff they are made of—matter, anti-matter, mind, energy, or whatnot—are fashioned along with the things themselves.'[70] Goodman rejects the idea of a privileged basis, be it phenomenalistic or physicalistic, to which all versions can be reduced. 'Talk of unstructured content or an unconceptualized given or a substratum without properties is self-defeating; for the talk imposes structure, conceptualizes, ascribes properties.'[71] Also rejected is the idea of any kind of a 'neutral *something*', underlying all versions.

[68] Ibid. 36.   [69] Ibid.
[70] Goodman, *Ways of Worldmaking*, 96.   [71] Ibid. 6.

But now the idea of a 'man-made' world is even more problem-atic. If *everything* is man-made how does the making ever get started? Must we postulate a *causa sui* or a creation *ex nihilo*? Of course in practice Goodman sees us always starting with some version or other on which we bring about changes: Neurath's ship is already at sea. Perhaps he might argue that we do indeed have to begin with some version but there is no necessity, logical or empirical, determining what that version is. Goodman is even prepared to concede, behind this original version, 'a world with-out kinds or order or motion or rest or pattern'; this is a world, though, he thinks is 'not worth fighting for or against'.[72] But these concessions do not meet the logical point that it is no easier to comprehend how man could 'make' the world from nothing than it was to solve the old theological crux about how God could create the world *ex nihilo*.

A more promising line comes in Goodman's suggestion that we take one or other of the alternative 'right versions' as basic or as real and 'regard all others as versions of that same world differing from the standard version in accountable ways'.[73] Thus the physicist, the phenomenalist, and the man-in-the-street might take different versions as basic. This at least avoids what Rorty describes as 'Goodman's trope of "many worlds"', in favour of the more modest 'many descriptions of the same world'.[74]

The realist defender of an objective mind-independent world 'out there' rather than 'man-made' need not be committed to Kantian-type noumena nor even to an unconceptualized given. Nor need he dispute the possibility of multiple conceptual schemes or alternative descriptions of the same world. Yet these are the basic ideas, negative and positive, behind the more striking for-mulations of Goodman's thesis.

Devitt, for example, defines and defends what he calls 'Com-mon Sense Realism' as the thesis that: '[t]okens of most current observable common-sense, and scientific, physical types objectively exist independently of the mental.'[75] He insists that the question of the *existence* of these independent objects be kept apart from both the question of the *meaning* of the terms applied to them and the question of *epistemic access* to them. Nothing in Devitt's account

---

[72] Ibid. 20.   [73] Ibid.

[74] Rorty, *Consequences of Pragmatism*, p. xlvii, n. 47.

[75] Devitt, *Realism and Truth*, 22.

implies an unconceptualized given nor anything that precludes different descriptions of the same world. Where does Goodman's so-called 'irrealism'[76] stand in relation to realism of this kind?

The key is in the notion of descriptions 'making things'. For all his nominalist qualms about the idea of meaning, Goodman seems to be committed to a version of what Devitt calls 'a priori essentialism', which ties existence to meaning. Here is an example from Devitt: if we say that 'the word "tiger" . . . means large black-and-yellow-striped feline etc.' then, according to the a priori essentialist, 'tigers wouldn't exist unless there were entities that were large black-and-yellow-striped felines'.[77] In this sense the definition determines what exists. We could 'make' tigers by defining 'tiger' one way and take them 'out of existence' by defining 'tiger' another way. Although this enterprise is trivially possible it hardly looks like 'worldmaking' and it does not tell us anything interesting about tigers. A priori essentialism can be contrasted with 'a posteriori essentialism', described by Devitt as follows:

there are certain essential properties of being a tiger, determined by the genetic structure of tigers, with the result that something would not be a tiger if it did not have those properties. It is the task of science to discover these properties. We do not expect science to show that tigers do not have the properties we commonly believe them to have, but it might show this. If it did it would not have shown that tigers did not exist but simply that we were wrong about them.[78]

Although this account establishes some kind of mind-independence for tigers—and more, apparently, than offered by a priori essentialism—we have not altogether removed the influence of human 'modes of organization' or conceptual schemes. The initial discrimination of tigers from other objects presupposes features of human observation and the subsequent investigation of tiger-properties presupposes a framework of scientific theorizing. All this, though, the realist can grant. His starting-point is not, as we have seen, a neutral 'substratum' or 'unconceptualized given'. He starts, as he must—and this is the truth in Neurath's analogy—with observations and even theories. But he does not let these in

---

[76] See Goodman, *Of Mind*, 29: 'Irrealism does not hold that everything or even anything is irreal, but sees the world melting into versions and versions making worlds, finds ontology evanescent, and enquires into what makes a version right and a world well-built.'

[77] Devitt, *Realism and Truth*, 20.   [78] Ibid. 19.

themselves determine what exists. Rather what exists determines the rightness of the observations and theories.

On the question of access to objects, and the variety of versions, or descriptions, available to us, there is nothing in Goodman's view that gives much substance to the idea that the versions create the objects. Scheffler offers the following reconstruction of Goodman's argument that seeks to establish this conclusion:

Since all our knowledge of objects is . . . embodied in . . . descriptions, our knowledge is, itself . . . shaped by our vocabularies. But what are objects themselves? We have no access to objects aside from our knowledge of them; they are therefore themselves shaped by our vocabularies. It is thus we can say that in making our versions we make their objects.[79]

Scheffler rightly points out that it is only true that we have no access to objects apart from our knowledge of them if by 'access' is meant 'cognitive access' (i.e. through understanding or awareness) but then the claim is trivial, saying that knowledge of objects is possible only through knowledge of objects. Nothing follows from this about the creation of objects by versions.

Goodman on truth

The equation of world-versions with worlds and the claim that there are as many worlds as there are right world-versions has obvious implications for Goodman's views on truth. The most obvious is the rejection of 'correspondence'. 'Truth,' Goodman writes, 'must be otherwise conceived than as correspondence with a ready-made world.'[80] '[T]ruth cannot be defined or tested by agreement with "the world".'[81] Significantly, his target is once again a conception of the world as 'undescribed, undepicted, unperceived'.[82] It is that noumenal world, he thinks, no doubt rightly, that has no explanatory value in an account of truth. So where do we look for truth? 'We must obviously look for truth not in the relation of a version to something outside that it refers to but in characteristics of the version itself and its relationships to other versions.'[83]

---

[79] Scheffler, 'The Wonderful Worlds of Goodman', 207.
[80] Goodman, *Ways of Worldmaking*, 94.   [81] Ibid. 17.
[82] Ibid. 4.   [83] Goodman, *Of Mind*, 37.

What features of versions and relations between versions are constitutive of truth? First of all, not every version is an eligible candidate for truth (or falsity). Truth, for Goodman, is a property only of what is *said* (though he allows metaphorical as well as literal truth). Thus 'for nonverbal versions and even for verbal versions without statements, truth is irrelevant.'[84] Pictures have no truth-value, though they may represent or denote things. A more important consideration for Goodman than truth is the notion of 'rightness'. All versions can be judged for rightness and he suggests that we 'subsume truth . . . under the general notion of rightness of fit.'[85] Before we discuss rightness we should note one or two further observations of Goodman's about truth.

For example, he allows *conflicting truths* and purports to resist all temptations to resolve the conflicts by simple relativization. 'The earth stands still' and 'the earth revolves round the sun' are both true, he thinks, and yet in conflict. To relativize them by adding 'according to the geometric system' or 'according to the heliocentric system' will not help because we want to know not just what version they are true in but what version is true. Goodman prefers to say that conflicting versions can be true and true of different worlds. Indeed this yields a criterion for distinctness of worlds: '[w]orlds are distinguished by the conflict and irreconcilability of their versions.'[86] Of course this manœuvre does not strictly avoid relativization. Truths are relative to versions. It is only under the further, and dubious, equation of versions with worlds that we reach the idea of truth being about different worlds.

Putnam sees the spectre of relativism in Goodman's position:

the whole story Goodman tells about how we build versions from versions, about not starting *ex nihilo*, about precepts and unyielding beliefs, could be told about 'true for me'. . . . Goodman would, no doubt, reply that any superiority of our versions over other versions must be judged and claimed from *within* our collection of versions; there is no neutral place to stand. . . . But what I hope Goodman will say something about in the future is what makes our versions superior to others *by our lights*, not by some inconceivable neutral standard.[87]

This vestigial relativism is common to all theories of truth based on some such idea as 'warranted assertibility'. We have seen it in

[84] Goodman, *Ways of Worldmaking*, 19.
[85] Ibid. 132.   [86] Goodman, *Of Mind*, 31.
[87] Putnam, *Philosophical Papers*, iii. 168.

Rorty. The question always arises as to who supplies the warrant. Goodman never actually defines truth, and rarely speaks of 'warranted assertibility', but he does say this: 'a version is taken to be true when it offends no unyielding beliefs and none of its own precepts.'[88] Of course being 'taken to be true' seems to be crucially weaker than simply being true. It is a near tautology to say that we *take as true* what we believe unyieldingly. Goodman, who seeks to play down the importance of truth, prefers to offer 'tests' for truth rather than a definition: 'the best account of what truth is may be an "operational" one in terms of tests and procedures used in judging it.'[89]

Although he rejects attempts to define truth in terms of utility, credibility, or coherence, he sees merit in each as tests for truth. His remarks about credibility, for example, are interesting with respect to the charge of relativism. He points out that the standard objection to equating truth with credibility is that even 'what is totally and permanently credible might not be true';[90] this is the Cartesian thought-experiment again. His reply is similar to that made by Descartes himself (in the Reply to the Second Objections): 'so long as the belief or credibility is indeed total and permanent, any divergence from the truth could never matter to us at all.' The crucial next step, which Goodman seems prepared to take, is simply to drop the idea of 'truth' altogether and rest content with permanent credibility. However, this step inevitably raises the charge of relativism, through the question 'credible to whom?' There is no legitimate parallel for truth.

One way of rescuing some kind of 'correspondence' in Goodman's view of truth is suggested by Putnam:

we can take some physicalistic description of the environment as 'the world' and analyse perceptual data (as construed) for salient correspondence or lack of salient correspondence to 'the world' (as construed).... Such a comparison is legitimate and important; in his insistence on this Goodman is ... an *empirical* realist ... but comparison of experience with physical theory is not comparison with unconceptualized reality ... All we have is comparison of versions with versions.[91]

The idea of being an 'empirical realist' contrasts with being a 'metaphysical' or 'transcendental' realist. For Putnam, and per-

---

[88] Goodman, *Ways of Worldmaking*, 17.   [89] Ibid. 122.
[90] Ibid. 124.   [91] Putnam, *Philosophical Papers*, iii. 163.

haps for Goodman too, the substantive difference rests with different reactions to Descartes's thought-experiment. The metaphysical realist believes that truth is not an *epistemic* notion, that it transcends what we believe; the empirical realist sees in our systems of belief some kind of internal guarantee of truth. But this is compatible with their believing in the same objects and holding true the same truths. The 'correspondence' demanded by the metaphysical realist is a correspondence with a mind-independent world; but the very items he conceives as existing in that world are perhaps just the items postulated by the empirical realist. The only difference is that the empirical realist, or the Goodmanian 'irrealist', sees these items as ontologically dependent on a 'version' or 'discourse', for example, a 'physicalistic description'. However, *they need not differ in the first-order descriptions they offer*, as in the case of physicalism. We recall that Devitt's realism holds that 'tokens of most . . . common-sense, and scientific, physical types objectively exist'.

Once again we find with Goodman, as with Rorty, that in spite of the startling formulations of their views—talk of inventing truth or making worlds—the constraints they demand on theories or scientific 'discourse' are no less rigorous than those of the strictest realist, indeed at the first-order level they are much the same. When Putnam, and Goodman, speak of comparing versions with versions, as against versions with 'the world', they are not suggesting that any version will do, that, as Goodman puts it, 'tall stories are as good as short ones, that truths are no longer distinguished from falsehoods'.[92] Not all versions are 'right'.

Goodman offers a general characterization of 'rightness' for a version which seems to concede everything a 'correspondence' theorist, or metaphysical realist, might want except of course the metaphysical notion of 'correspondence' itself. He demands deductive validity, inductive validity, and 'rightness of categorization'. In elaboration, he tells us, for example, that 'a right inductive argument must be based not only on true premises but upon all the available genuine evidence'.[93] Furthermore, 'inductive rightness requires that the argument proceed from premises consisting of all such true reports on examined instances as are in terms of

[92] Goodman, *Ways of Worldmaking*, 94.
[93] Ibid. 126.

projectible predicates'.[94] The idea of 'rightness of categorization' is also aimed at the elimination of non-projectible predicates. Significantly, '[c]ategories that are inductively right tend to coincide with categories that are right for science in general'.[95] We might wonder what the ideas of 'genuine evidence' and 'true reports' are doing here. What role can they play in Goodman's account of rightness that they do not play in the realist's? For the realist the genuineness of evidence and the truth of reports are ultimately constrained by how things are in the world. For Goodman they are constrained by how things are *according to a world-version*. Which world-version provides the constraints? The answer must be: the right one (or the right ones). Yet rightness is determined by genuineness of evidence and truth of reports.

The only way out of this circle is to stipulate that science as we have it, with the tests and procedures as they currently are, is a right version, or at least pretty well a right version. This in effect is what Goodman does and perhaps it is the reason why Putnam can call him an empirical realist. He accepts as real the objects the realist accepts and acknowledges as true the theories the realist acknowledges. Rightness of categorization, he says, is 'a matter of fit with practice'.[96] Could not scientific practice be wrong at any given time? This is the realist's worry. Goodman, like Putnam, even allows for that. For it is not merely acceptability at a given time which is sufficient for rightness, but 'ultimate acceptability'.

So in the end Goodman, for all his talk of 'worldmaking' and 'the fabrication of facts', leaves us with a constraint on the rightness of a version—ultimate acceptability—barely less remote than that of the metaphysical realist who, though likewise happy for the time being with the objects and theories we have, allows that things in the long term might turn out to be contrary.

Describing Goodman's position as 'empirical realism' (in contrast to metaphysical realism) obviously recalls Kant, who described himself as an empirical realist and a transcendental idealist. There are two major commitments in Kant's empirical realism: first, to the idea of objects existing in space independently of those who perceive them, and second, to the idea that we can have direct non-inferential knowledge of those objects. Transcendental idealism, in contrast, involves a complex story about the origins

[94] Ibid. 127.   [95] Ibid. 128.   [96] Ibid. 138.

(or 'conditions for the possibility') of the human faculties of sensibility and understanding, such that space itself and the basic categories of existence, causation, objectivity, etc., turn out after all to be 'dependent on us'. Kant's empirical realism seems to give us all we want, not least a distinction in its own terms between what is dependent on us (sensations, hallucinations, etc.) and what is independent (chairs, people, etc.). It offers us everything that we (as scientists or common-sense laymen) demand of the objective world. It distinguishes what is real from what is merely fanciful, what is 'in the mind' from what is 'out there'. Only at the remote transcendental level, the level which invokes the Cartesian thought-experiment that all our beliefs might be false, where we try to speculate how things might be apart from all the conceptions (or 'representations') we have of them, do we fall back into idealism, internalizing the whole apparatus of knowledge.

Although there are fundamental differences between Goodman's view and Kant's (Goodman barely offers a 'theory of knowledge'), there is certainly something akin to transcendental idealism in the idea of 'worldmaking'. For Goodman, how the world is, or how the different worlds are, ultimately 'depends on us'. But at the level of testing an individual version for rightness or truth, all the distinctions the realist requires for a well-grounded science—supported/unsupported by evidence, consistent/inconsistent, 'in the mind'/'out there', fictional/real, subjective/objective—are put to work. Most telling of all, *it cannot be part of a right version that the world is man-made or that it depends on us.* The strictures of 'inductive rightness' at an empirical level preclude the 'fabrication of facts'. Within a right version, we discover the facts by examining the evidence.

There is no possibility of conflating fact and fiction at this level. But even at the 'transcendental' level, Goodman makes a crucial distinction between a version which is overtly fictional (like *Don Quixote*) and a version which is, say, part of science. He refrains, rightly, from making evaluative judgements about the two and he acknowledges the 'cognitive' possibilities of the overtly fictional, but for all that he insists that the fictional is at best only *metaphorically* true. And by this he means only that names of some fictional characters can be applied metaphorically to real people: '"Don Quixote", taken literally, applies to no one, but taken figuratively, applies to many of us—for example, to me in one of my tilts with the windmills of current linguistics.'[97] There is nothing in irrealism, for all its generosity towards worldmaking, that can make Don Quixote literally a real person (Goodman, for example, could never be *identical* to Don Quixote). The kind of 'making up' that issues in Don Quixote can never be *equated* with the 'making', such as it is, of people and stars. But ironically at the end of it all Goodman probably wants too much of a gap between the fictional and the real. There is no need to introduce metaphorical truth to explain how someone might be 'a Don Quixote among philosophers', for all that means is that the person instantiates certain paradigmatic Don Quixote aspects. Those aspects —being chivalric, romantic, wildly out of touch with reality—are not fictions at all but, *pace* the nominalist, perfectly real.

[97] Ibid. 103.

9

Narrative and Imagination

Our third and final chapter on the limits of fictionality moves from metaphysics back to story-telling itself. An important conclusion of the last chapter was that the practice of enquiry, as we have called it, within which truth and knowledge are defined, is able to resist pressures posed by the extreme rhetoric of 'truth-making' and 'worldmaking'. In particular, the simple conception of truth based on the Aristotelian dictum which we invoked in Chapter 1 ('to say of what is that it is, and of what is not that it is not') is not weakened or compromised by theories using this rhetoric. The practice of enquiry which incorporates the everyday work of the biographer, the detective, the archaeologist, or the biochemist, in collecting data, sifting evidence, forming hypotheses, offering explanations, and in a multitude of ways *investigating how things are* can well resist any pressure to dissolve it into something like the practice of fiction. The level at which anti-realism and scepticism seem to leave their mark is not the level at which in these everyday practices we distinguish speaking truly and speaking falsely, undertaking accurate and inaccurate research, finding out the truth and making it up. Yet it is precisely these practices which provide the paradigms of truth-telling and knowledge-seeking in the senses which point up the contrast with the cognitive values of literature.

In Chapter 7 we addressed the question of the supposed 'ubiquity of fiction', based on metaphysical notions of the world and its constituents as 'constructs'. We must now confront two further challenges posed by the alleged 'ubiquity of narrative' and 'ubiquity of imagination'. There are strikingly similar pressures thought to be imposed by narrative and the imagination on the distinction between truth-teller and fiction-maker. Although there need be no direct relation between the two, it has been claimed for both narrative and the imagination: that they are indispensable for human cognition; that they are natural (innate, unlearned) dispositions apparent at the earliest stages of infant development; that their paradigmatic forms are in literary expression; that there is no difference in kind between the way each functions in literary and non-literary applications; and that their fundamental role in all intellectual processes weakens the distinctions between different modes of discourse, historical, philosophical, scientific, and literary.

We will explore some of these claims in this chapter and will defend the view that the functions of both narrative and the imagination in the practice of fiction are distinct in significant ways from their functions in other contexts, for example in history, philosophy, and science. In doing so we will show that the pressures arising from the apparent ubiquity of narration and imagination do not constitute any serious threat to the distinction between fiction and non-fiction as it bears on literature.

Defining narrative

There is a widespread view that narration plays a central, even indispensable, role in cognition. Narrative, we are told, is 'a primary and irreducible form of human comprehension'[1] or 'a primary act of mind transferred to art from life itself',[2] or that humans have 'a fundamental disposition . . . to organize experience narrationally', given that we are 'natural story-tellers long before we are Aristotelian rational beings'.[3] 'Our lives,' it is said, 'are ceaselessly intertwined with narrative, with the stories that we tell, all of which are reworked in that story of our own lives that we narrate to ourselves. . . . We are immersed in narrative.'[4] Indeed, a human being's very identity, so it is claimed, rests on narrative, such that individuals define themselves in terms of a 'life-narrative' which 'lends order and purpose' to their lives.[5]

It is indisputable that narrative or story-telling is deeply rooted in all kinds of descriptive endeavours: in history, biography,

---

[1] Louis O. Mink, quoted in W. J. T. Mitchell (ed.), *On Narrative* (Chicago, 1981), 252.
[2] Barbara Hardy, quoted in Brian Wicker, *The Story-Shaped World, Fiction and Metaphysics: Some Variations on a Theme* (London, 1975), 47.
[3] Prado, *Making Believe*, 136.
[4] Peter Brooks, *Reading for the Plot: Design and Intention in Narrative* (New York, 1985), 3.
[5] Novitz, *Knowledge, Fiction and Imagination*, 228.

journalism, psychoanalysis, and theology, and is common among philosophers, astrophysicists, biologists, lawyers, sports writers, comedians, and children's nannies. How much significance should be attached to the pervasiveness of narrative? And to what extent does this pose a threat to the distinction between, say, what is made up and what is found out or between the fiction-maker and the truth-seeker?

Although the 'primacy', even 'irreducibility', of narrative can be readily granted, on inspection this turns out to be somewhat less exciting than at first it might seem. In fact what makes the claim *seem* so striking turns on an illicit assimilation of narrative and fiction. The idea that fiction should permeate human cognition is indeed remarkable, recalling the metaphysical views discussed in Chapter 7, yet here derived from different premises. But if, as we have argued, fiction, in the description sense, is just one among different kinds of narrative (or story-telling), and narrative is not itself a kind of fiction, then no such remarkable conclusion can be drawn.

The point that narrative and fiction are distinct is not by any means universally accepted. Hayden White, for example, has been especially influential in arguing the opposite, that '*all* stories are fictions': characteristic of his reasoning is the following:

To emplot real events as a story of a specific kind (or as a mixture of stories of a specific kind) is to trope these events. This is because stories are not lived; there is no such thing as a 'real' story. Stories are told or written, not found. And as for the notion of a 'true' *story*, this is virtually a contradiction in terms.[6]

The idea that stories are *told* not *found* reminds us of Rorty's dictum that truth is made not found; but as with Rorty's view no serious implications for literary fictions can be drawn from it. And, *pace* White, there is no reason a priori to suppose that telling is incompatible with telling the truth. We will be looking in detail at White's views of historical narrative in Chapter 12. In the mean time a careful investigation of what narrative is and how it 'relates to the world' will give a better perspective on the supposed ubiquity of narrative. Once it is recognized that narrative and fiction are

---

[6] Hayden White, ' "Figuring the Nature of Times Deceased"; Literary Theory and Historical Writing', quoted in Noël Carroll, 'Interpretation, History, and Narrative', *The Monist*, 73 (1990), 135.

separate concepts, and, most importantly, that narrative *per se* is merely a formal feature of a text without referential or ontological implications, the pervasiveness of narrative comes to seem quite unsurprising. Furthermore, the metaphysical connection is severed when the narrative form is seen to be neutral on questions of truth, reference, and 'correspondence with reality'.

What is narrative? Here is a straightforward working definition from Gerald Prince: 'narrative is the representation of at least two real or fictive events or situations in a time sequence, neither of which presupposes or entails the other.'[7] The 'representation' in a narrative does not have to be linguistic, contrary to a similar definition by Genette.[8] Stories can be told in mime, dance, or pictures. The crucial element is the temporal one; *events*, not merely states of affairs, must be represented and connected in narrative. The temporal location of a single event, for example through a tensed verb, is not sufficient. At least two events are required in a narrative and the connection between them must be temporal not logical, hence the exclusion of a presupposition or entailment relation. 'John loved Mary and Mary was loved by John' does not constitute a narrative because only one event is represented in the two, logically equivalent, sentences.

There is no implication that the events represented in a narrative should be actual, probable, or even possible. Prince's definition speaks neutrally of 'real or fictive events'. Narrative *per se* is indifferent to reference and truth. The appearance of a (syntactic) proper name or a singular descriptive phrase in a narrative does not in itself imply referential intent (the narrative form might be used for purely exemplary purposes). Nor does the appearance of a sentence in a narrative have implications about truth-value, in the sense that narratives can be about real or imaginary objects and their descriptive content can be true or false (or truth-valueless). Narratives are also indifferent to subject-matter and discursive ends. They might amuse or instruct, inform or mislead,

---

[7] Gerald Prince, *Narratology: The Form and Functioning of Narrative* (The Hague, 1982), 4.

[8] Gerard Genette, 'Boundaries of Narrative', *New Literary History*, 8 (1976–7), 1: 'Narrative may be defined simply as the representation of a real or fictional event or series of events by language.' Not only is Genette wrong to restrict narrative to language but he is also wrong, again in contrast to Gerald Prince, to suppose that narrative could be the representation of a single event.

describe a dream, report an experiment, or spin a yarn; they can occur as part of a philosophical argument, a historical analysis, a Victorian melodrama, or a simple piece of gossip.

We can recognize a stretch of discourse as having narrative form from its surface properties alone, with no knowledge of context or purpose. The sorting of sentences into narrative and non-narrative is purely mechanical. Trivial examples make the point: 'John was happy and then John was unhappy' has narrative form (i.e. satisfies the basic definition) while 'John was happy' lacks narrative form.[9] What this shows is that narration *per se* is a formal feature of a text. What the narratives of history, science, philosophy, literature, and sports commentary have in common, *qua* narrative, is the minimal formal quality of being a sequence of tensed sentences, representing (or purporting to represent) two or more logically distinct events temporally ordered.

It is clear that not much has been said, certainly nothing of any ontological or epistemological import, in identifying a piece of discourse, even a thought-process, as being in narrative form. It is only further classifications within narratives that point to matters of interest (and controversy) in epistemology or literary theory. However 'primary' or 'irreducible' narrative might be in our experience of the world nothing follows from that about whether the events represented are *constituted* by the narrative (and thus in some sense 'made up' by the story-telling) or whether the events have an *independent* existence (and thus are simply reported or brought to our attention by the story-telling). Likewise, as already noted, nothing follows about the references or contexts of the narrative, about the truth-value of its sentences, or about any purposes it might serve.

Of course identifying narrative form is usually only a first step towards a more refined classification of different kinds of narrative. We must pursue this classification if we are to understand the special status of fictional narrative. It is helpful to distinguish three dimensions of narrative for purposes of classification and assessment (the distinction is analogous, in some respects, to that between syntax, semantics, and pragmatics). Let us call these *structural*, *referential*, and *genre* dimensions. The structural dimension, concerning formal textual features, determines whether a stretch of

---

[9] The examples come from Prince, *Narratology*, 145.

discourse is a narrative or not. The referential and genre dimensions determine what kind of narrative it is.

The structural dimension of narrative

The structural dimension includes the whole complex typology of narrative 'devices', which form the core of narratology: tense, voice, point of view, narrator identity, implied authors, implied readers, temporal, spatial, and causal structures, presupposition, opposition, pronominal cross-reference, and so on. Here is a not untypical passage showing the subtleties of a structural analysis of a text in narrative form:

By granting one of his characters the privilege of reminiscing from a point in time subsequent to the conclusion of the narrated events, an authorial narrator brings this character close to a first-person narrator. The privileged character regards individual episodes of his experience from a temporal distance corresponding to that of a first-person narrator. Bringing the time of the action up to the narrative present at the conclusion of the narrative also aims in the same direction. Here the narrative tense usually changes from past to present.[10]

The structural characterization of narratives can proceed independently of referential considerations concerning existence, denotation, ontology, allusion, truth-value, author's (as opposed to narrator's) intended reference, and so forth. In other words structural analysis does not invoke 'correspondence' relations with things 'outside' the text. While the identification, for example, of *implied* authors and readers belongs in the structural dimension of narrative, the psychological states (intentions and responses) of real authors and readers do not. It should not of course be inferred from this that questions about authors and readers are irrelevant when discussing narrative; it is just that they belong to a different aspect of narrative.

To a large extent the structural dimension can remain aloof even from subject-matter itself. Structural analyses of the kind illustrated could apply equally well to narratives of different genres, historical, psychoanalytic, biographical, literary, or whatever. Of course it is most common to find such analyses applied to literary

[10] F. K. Stanzel, *A Theory of Narrative* (Cambridge, 1984), 97.

works—indeed they are characteristic of a kind of literary criticism—but that reflects merely contingent factors such as the relative complexity of literary narratives and the special interests of
readers of literary works.

Those who emphasize the role of narrative in, for example, science frequently draw on the structural similarities between scientific and literary discourse. Thus Donald McCloskey in discussing
the role of story-telling in economics shows how attention to reading strategies familiar to literary critics can have an important
bearing on understanding the source of disagreements among
economists. The first thing to note, he suggests, is that 'scientific
prose like literary prose is complicated and allusive, drawing on a
richer rhetoric than mere demonstration';[11] just as it is naïve to
seek a simple 'message' in a poem, so it is mistaken to suppose
that scientific texts are mere 'transparent' conveyors of 'theoretical
results'. He points also to the 'compression' of scientific writing, as
a source of misunderstandings, and to 'an inability of the reader
[sometimes] to assume the point of view demanded by the author'.[12] Scientific texts, he reminds us, involve selectivity of material, the 'sense of an ending', a requirement to 'supply what's not
there', and other such features familiar in literary texts.

All this seems unexceptionable. Attending to the structural or
rhetorical features of scientific writing—for more examples, think
of the use of personal pronouns, the hidden illocutionary forces,
the appeal to authority[13]—can have a salutary effect on understanding how scientists propagate and communicate ideas. But
McCloskey wants to establish a more controversial conclusion,
partly that 'economists . . . are not so very different from poets
and novelists' (a point that could perhaps be granted *at the
structural level*) but, more radically, that 'economics can be shown
to be fictional and poetical'.[14] What is unwarranted, by the evidence adduced, is the attempt to use the structural similarities
between scientific and literary narratives to weaken the distinction

---

[11] Donald N. McCloskey, 'Storytelling in Economics', in Cristopher Nash (ed.),
*Narrative in Culture: The Uses of Storytelling in the Sciences, Philosophy and Lit-
erature* (London, 1990), 11.

[12] Ibid. 12.

[13] For a useful account, see Rom Harré, 'Narrative in Scientific Discourse', in
Nash (ed.), *Narrative in Culture*.

[14] McCloskey, 'Storytelling in Economics', 21.

between fiction and non-fiction. We have seen that this distinction, at least as it bears on literary fiction, is not to be drawn at a structural—syntactic or semantic—level but in terms of non-semantic institutionally based relations between story-tellers and audiences. For all the similarities in 'devices' used, it remains the case that the *practices* of economists and novelists are still fundamentally distinct.

It should be noted that not all attempts to view science in narrative terms focus on the story-telling aspects of scientific research itself (at a first-order level). It has been suggested that research takes place within a kind of meta-narrative:

scientific papers ... do not *tell* stories about how the current research situation came about and where it seems to be heading. They are instead more complicated speech acts, which can only be understood in the *context* of a story.[15]

On this view the work of individual researchers is located in a wider story which helps to explain why they say what they say and when: 'despite the supposed timelessness of scientific knowledge, its canonical form of presentation, the scientific paper, is ruthlessly bound to the interests and conflicts of a local context which is constantly under reconstruction.'[16] It is no doubt true that a similar situation obtains within a developing literary or artistic tradition where it can be argued that works are only fully understood relative to a story (or narrative) which connects them temporally and causally with other works.[17] However fruitful this similarity, though, it goes no way towards weakening the distinction between science and art.

The referential dimension of narrative

To say that there is a referential dimension to narrative (including, in its many senses, what a narrative is 'about') as well as a structural dimension (how the narrative 'works') is not to assign priority to one or the other. In the early days of literary structuralism there was a marked tendency to play down the referential

---

[15] Joseph Rouse, 'The Narrative Reconstruction of Science', *Inquiry*, 33 (1990), 188.
[16] Ibid. 191.　　[17] See Carroll, 'Art, Practice, and Narrative'.

dimension or even to reduce it to the structural. One prominent reason behind this seems to have involved a misapplication of Saussure's linguistics.[18] Saussure believed that the fundamental properties of the linguistic sign resided in the relation between sound and concept, not between concept (or sound) and object. There is no implication, though, in Saussure's thesis that reference to objects does not take place or is irrelevant or impossible. The differential aspect of the meaning of signs—the idea that concepts are defined differentially rather than ostensibly—does not entail that signs cannot be used to characterize and identify objects, through predication and singular reference. The supposition of some such entailment, along with the structuralist assumption that the meaning of narratives is analogous to the meaning of signs, is at least partly responsible for the eclipse of reference in favour of structure in narratology.[19]

From our point of view, it is important to recognize, simply and obviously, that it is always possible to ask of a narrative, however complex or simple its structure, whether the events represented actually took place, what the names stand for, what the narrative is about, what allusions to people or texts are present, and other such 'referential' questions. If some of these questions seem curiously parochial or irrelevant (for example, whether the events actually took place) that is only because we tend to take sophisticated *literary* (fictional) narratives as a paradigm. When we recall the diversity of narratives—from Jones's lying statement to the police, to the historical reconstruction of the First World War—we realize that in some (perhaps most) instances the referential dimension takes precedence over all others and interest in the structural dimension itself comes to seem pedantic and irrelevant. For example, in the narrative of a psychoanalytic patient, reporting a dream, say, or a fantasy, the question of what the descriptions

[18] For a useful account of the misappropriation of Saussure by literary structuralists, see Avni, *The Resistance of Reference*, ch. 2.

[19] Thomas Pavel has called the tendency to play down referentiality 'mythocentrism', whereby narrative structure is 'set in the center of literary studies, and stylistic and rhetorical features, referential force, and social relevance are deemed to be more or less accidental': 'By overemphasizing the logic of plot, mythocentrism helped to create the impression that problems of reference, mimesis, and more generally of relations between literary texts and reality were merely aftereffects of a referential illusion, spontaneously projected by narrative syntax.' (Thomas G. Pavel, *Fictional Worlds* (Cambridge, Mass., 1986), 5–6).

stand for or who is being referred to can be of crucial clinical significance.

While literary structuralism, in its more moderate forms, merely promoted the structural dimension over the referential, post-structuralism, in its most characteristic forms, seeks to remove the referential dimension altogether. Here is a typical example:

the text is so seamlessly interwoven with all utterances—from which what we call reality itself is inseparable—that questions not merely of 'fictionality' versus 'truth' but of referentiality versus non-referentiality dissolve altogether.... [T]here is very little difference indeed between anything we may call 'referential' writing and anything we may call 'pure' writing.[20]

The only support for this purported dissolution of reference comes from highly contentious—and obscure—premisses to the effect that narratives are of necessity self-referential, depicting not worlds but the very words that constitute them:

If narratives are really only made of language, then there is no reason why the events initiating what 'happens' in a narrative may take place not in 'the world' but in the words of its telling.[21]

We will return in a later section to the idea that narratives might in some sense 'create' the facts they represent. But whatever else might be said about that claim, it does not follow from the premiss that narratives are 'only made of language'. There is nothing about narrative per se that raises any special difficulty for reference; again, that mistaken notion only arises from the illicit conflation of narrative and fiction.

However, the distinction between fictive and non-fictive narration is not itself determined by the referential dimension of narrative. It is not the lack of reference that defines fiction. Nevertheless, narratives in the fictive mode (those inviting the fictive stance) are associated, as we saw in Chapter 5, with characteristic ways of establishing narrative reference, particularly what a narrative is 'about'. In other words, once a narrative has been identified as fictional, primarily through genre considerations, certain consequences will follow for how reference is established and what role it plays. That brings us to the third dimension of narrative.

[20] Cristopher Nash, 'Literature's Assault on Narrative', in Nash (ed.), *Narrative in Culture*, 210, 212.
[21] Ibid. 208.

The genre dimension of narrative

The genre (or pragmatic) dimension focuses on the function or point of the narrative, involving the intentions, attitudes, interests, expectations, responses, conventions, and so forth, associated with different kinds of narratives. Historical, philosophical, scientific, psychoanalytical, confessional, and literary fictional narratives belong to different genres. The practices in which they are rooted are different, and so is their function, broadly conceived. The differences do not lie exclusively in subject-matter, style, or structure, although these can often be good indicators of genre.

Of course a whole cluster of features will be involved in drawing these distinctions and we should not expect sharp boundaries between even the broadest genre classifications. What is important is the logical independence of genre questions about narrative from both structural and referential questions. The identification of structural features and referential features is never logically sufficient to determine the point or aim of a narrative.

Genre differences between narratives are settled by the rule-governed practices in which they occur and the intentions, expectations, and procedures of those who engage in the practices. Of course there are pragmatic features that all narratives must share:

the point of [a] narrative is a function of its context. The narrative should be non-obvious and worth telling. It should represent, or illustrate, or explain, something which is unusual and problematic, something which is (made) relevant for and matters to its receiver ... Without desire on the part of the receiver and without the fulfilment of this desire, there can be no point to a narrative.[22]

But between different genres of narrative there will be different desires and different criteria for fulfilling the desires.

We have given a detailed account of the practice of fictive story-telling. As applied to narrative, it is clear from this account that fictional stories belong to a different genre—located in a distinctive practice—from the discursive writings of historians and philosophers. This is not to deny that historians and philosophers might engage the fictive practice for their own (perhaps illustrative)

---

[22] Prince, *Narratology*, 159.

ends; it is to claim only that the fictive mode of utterance is constituted by different conventions from historical or philosophical modes (even when those latter modes use the narrative form). The distinctions do not rest on weighty metaphysical factors, such as truth, correspondence, 'how the world is', nor are they determined by the referential dimension of narrative (denotation, naming, 'aboutness'), but they are adequate none the less to keep a handle on the different purposes people have in telling stories and the different responses they invite.

In the previous chapter we looked at Rorty's 'ironist' viewpoint in the context of discussing the idea of 'making truth'. The ironist holds that genre differences between narratives are spurious and suggests that the only significant differences lie in 'final vocabulary' not in whether the narratives are philosophical, literary, historical, or scientific.

Ironists take the writings of all the people with poetic gifts, all the original minds who had a talent for redescription—Pythagoras, Plato, Milton, Newton, Goethe, Kant, Kierkegaard, Baudelaire, Darwin, Freud—as grist to be put through the same dialectical mill. The metaphysicians, by contrast, want to start by getting straight about which of these people were poets, which philosophers, and which scientists. They think it essential to get the genres right—to order the texts by reference to a previously determined grid, a grid which, whatever else it does, will at least make a clear distinction between knowledge claims and other claims upon our attention.[23]

There are all kinds of ways that writers (and texts) can be compared and classified. Having an 'original mind' or a 'talent for redescription' can bring together writers in the most disparate genres. If we are interested in Romanticism, say, it might be of greater interest that Shelley, Schopenhauer, and Schubert exhibit similar romantic tendencies than that they do so through different media. But none of this weakens the distinctions between the practices—poetry, philosophy, and music—themselves.

Rorty offers no arguments for blurring genre differences though, as we have seen, he endorses a generalized notion of 'literary criticism' which has that consequence. His rejection of argument, reason, and inference as modes of persuasion, in favour of 'redescription', is an integral part of his rejection of the distinction between, say, philosophy and poetry. After all, according to the more orthodox view, one characteristic of the practice of philosophy, which would distinguish it from poetry or fiction, is precisely the use of logical argument assessable through established canons of deductive reasoning. Yet for Rorty, '[t]he ironist's preferred form of argument is dialectical in the sense that she takes the unit of persuasion to be a vocabulary rather than a proposition'.[24]

Rorty's reduction of narratives to *vocabularies* apparently without regard to how the vocabularies are used (for what ends, in what propositions), although it has the consequence he desires of blurring genre distinctions, has little to be said in its favour. For one thing, Rorty's own writing seems to point up the obvious problem, for his *vocabulary* is not in itself very different from that of the metaphysicians he derides: references to 'truth', 'reason', 'inference', 'philosophy' occur throughout his writings, the crucial difference being that he is *rejecting* or *criticizing* the concepts while his metaphysical foes are *endorsing* or *explaining* them. The difference can already be seen to lie in the purposes, or speech acts, involved not just in the words themselves. And even to grant that some discourses have the purpose of persuasion—be it by argument or redescription—is already to acknowledge a genre distinction; it marks off nearly all of philosophy from, for example, the bulk of lyric poetry. Persuading a reader of something or arguing a point of view is not a defining, or even a characteristic, feature of the lyric. Finally, words do not appear in isolation, they occur in sentences, which in turn express propositions; it is at least arguable, following Frege's principle, that a word acquires a meaning only in the context of a proposition. Furthermore, to understand a stretch of discourse we need not only to understand the propositions expressed but also the *point* behind expressing them. All in all, it makes little sense to suppose that readers can ignore propositions in favour of vocabularies. It is an extraordinarily restricted interest in narratives which attends only to their vocabulary—even their 'final vocabulary'—regardless of their aim, their references, the claims they make, their modes of persuasion, and so on.

---

[24] Ibid. 78.

Narrative and the distortion of fact

It might be argued that the distinction between structural, referential, and genre dimensions of narrative is tendentious because
each is indissolubly connected with the other. In particular, it might
be thought, the referential element, such as it is—what a narrative
is about, what events it portrays, etc.—cannot be determined independently of *how* the subject-matter is presented (the structural
dimension) and *for what purpose* (the genre dimension). In the
next section we will look at the extreme version of this argument
which claims that narratives somehow create their own subject-
matter in the telling. In this section we will comment on a more
modest, though more widespread, opinion that narratives inevitably *distort* what they portray and thus, again, that the manner of
presentation is not independent of the matter presented.[25]

Underlying this second thesis is the thought that the structures
of narrative impose some kind of barrier between language and
fact; rather than being directly 'mirrored', the facts, as represented
in narrative, are filtered through layers of linguistic artifice. Various
considerations seem to support this notion. Narratives of necessity
have narrators (real or implied) and narrators occupy some point
of view on what they narrate; they also select the material, assigning
weight to some aspects, playing down others, leaving out some
matters altogether; they structure events in temporal and causal
relations and the order of narration need not reflect the order of
occurrence; they address a particular kind of reader (or audience);
they use a particular kind of vocabulary, often redolent with
connotation, and commonly adopt a stance or attitude towards the
events narrated. All of these factors produce a *prima-facie* case for
narrative distortion.

It is important straightaway to distinguish the *potential* for
distortion in narrative from the *necessity* or *inevitability* of distortion. The point we want to establish is simply this: that there is
nothing in narrative *per se* which entails the distortion of fact or
makes either truth or reference impossible. Let us consider the
issues in more detail.

---

[25] See e.g. Hayden White, 'Historicism, History and the Figurative Imagination',
in Hayden White, *Tropics of Discourse: Essays in Cultural Criticism* (Baltimore,
1978), 111–12.

First of all, to speak of the distortion of fact in narrative already presupposes a conception of undistorted fact. It is not possible both to argue for the unreliability of narrative *and* hold the anti-realist view that narrative creates the facts (or events or objects) it represents. Narrative can only be unreliable with respect to facts that have an existence independent of the narrative itself.[26]

Second, 'distortion' implies lack of objectivity. But we have already seen, in Chapter 6, that 'objective' can mean either 'without bias' or 'independent of the mind'. Applying the latter meaning to 'undistorted fact' brings in epistemological considerations. But we have urged, following Devitt, that epistemology be kept apart from semantics. What epistemic access we have to objects and facts should not affect the reference of singular terms nor the truth-value of sentences. If, on the other hand, we take 'distortion' simply to mean 'biased', then there seems no reason to suppose that narratives are biased of necessity. There are recognized standards of objective reporting, usually defined within the practice of different genres, and these are not compromised by granting that objectivity in this sense is a matter of degree. It is just a fallacy to suppose that there is some ideal narrative, unrealizable in principle, which somehow 'mirrors' the facts without point of view. But only against that presupposition does the notion of a necessary distortion of narrative get off the ground.[27] It is equally fallacious to argue that anything short of that ideal must be 'fictional'.

Third, we should distinguish those features of *language* which might promote distortion of fact from those features of *narrative* that might. For example, predicates can be vague, inaccurate, or ambiguous, they can bear contentious evaluative (or emotive) connotations, or they can be simply false of the subjects they describe. These are features of any descriptive language. Distortions due specifically to narrative would have to result from specifically narrative structures, such as narrative perspective, temporal connectedness, causal relations, or selectivity. No argument about

---

[26] In the case of fictional narrative, where the 'facts' are not independent of the narration, we do nevertheless talk of 'unreliable narrators'. But we could not speak of the *whole* narration being unreliable. The unreliability of a narrator in fiction arises from a dissonance between what the narrator tells and other salient features of the matter told.

[27] Carroll in 'Interpretation, History, and Narrative', 147–8, makes a similar point.

the inherent imprecision, or metaphoricalness, or instability of language will support the view that there is something peculiar about story-telling that distorts events. In fact when it comes to simple narratives, such as the straightforward recounting of observed events, it seems that the only case for distortion could rest on a more general view about the imprecision of language. But that has nothing to do with narrative as such and would require independent support.

A fourth point concerns an important difference between the content of what is said and the saying of it. Narrative involves selection, and selection no doubt involves some kind of value judgement but it does not follow that all narrative content is evaluative (and therefore, perhaps, not wholly objective). The mistake of running together the evaluative nature of the selection of content and the evaluative nature of content itself is made by Terry Eagleton in trying to argue against the fact/value distinction:

[s]tatements of fact are after all *statements*, which presumes a number of questionable judgements: that those statements are worth making, perhaps more worth making than certain others, that I am the sort of person who is entitled to make them and perhaps able to guarantee their truth, that you are the kind of person worth making them to, that something useful is accomplished by making them, and so on.[28]

Eagleton's considerations bear only on the selection of content not on the truth or evaluative status or objectivity of the content itself. The distortions of selection, such as they are, in narrative do not entail a lack of truth.

Finally, what might be called the distortions of narrative are likely to take different forms in different genres of narrative. It is important to establish whether the distortions—in temporal connectedness, point of view, etc.—are deliberate or accidental, whether they are a result of ignorance, deception, or artistic licence, whether they bring about misunderstanding or fresh insight. A novelist who 'distorts' historical events for artistic purposes is clearly judged on different criteria from a historian who distorts events for whatever reason. The practices associated with different genres of narrative will sometimes determine even what counts as distortion; narratives about religious, mythical, or ritualistic

---

[28] Eagleton, *Literary Theory*, 13. Raymond Tallis discusses the passage and comments on the same fallacy in it: *In Defence of Realism*, 26.

events might be deemed to have 'distorted' the events by giving an over-literal account of them. It should be noted though, developing the first point, that whenever we can speak of a narrative— for example, a fictional narrative—distorting historical events there is a presupposition that the narrative has been identified as *about* that event; the reference is not affected.

Narrative and the creation of fact

A far more radical challenge to the referential dimension of narrative is the thought that narrative somehow creates the events it 'represents'. The model here would be precisely that of fiction, as we have described it. Fictional events and objects, so we have argued, have their existence and nature rooted in some original fictive utterance. The utterance *characterizes* the object or event through its predication. But is this the case with all narrative? Is it a feature of narrative itself? The answer must certainly be no.

We have already remarked that the occurrence of narrative form in cognition does not in itself have ontological implications, in the sense that it implies nothing about the nature of events or objects. It has long been recognized by philosophers that temporal connectedness plays a fundamental role in thought processes and that perhaps is unsurprising. But this premiss alone does not have ontological implications even for the status of time. Kant, for example, argued the case for the transcendental ideality of time from the intimate relation between perception and temporal succession but the premiss on its own that experience is temporally ordered is compatible with the alternative thesis of the reality of time. Similarly no ontological conclusion about the reality or otherwise of events follows from this same premiss. The narrative ordering of experience is compatible with both a constructivist and a realist view of events.

The point is that the identification of narrative in the ordering of experience invokes only the structural dimension of narrative and leaves open the referential and genre commitments. While it is quite unexceptionable to claim that 'there is no getting away from the need to tell stories in order to explain ourselves as well as to describe reality'[29] (a claim about the primacy of tense and

---

[29] Wicker, *The Story-Shaped World*, 46–7.

temporal connectedness) it does not follow that 'narratives . . . are not representations at all; . . . they themselves constitute what the world is for someone at a given point'[30] (a claim about the referential status of narratives).

There are many different versions of the ontological or referential claim that narratives 'constitute' or 'create' reality. Here is one version from the psychoanalytic context: 'reality is always mediated by narration. Far from being innocently encountered and discovered, it is created in a regulated fashion.'[31] Already, though, there is an illegitimate slide from 'mediation' to 'creation'. It does not follow from the fact that narrative mediates or gives access to reality that it also creates reality. Here is another version:

> narrative should not be thought of as a scheme imposed from without on an unnarrativized sequence of happenings. Instead . . . the intelligibility of action, and of the things we encounter or use in acting, depends upon their already belonging to a field of possible narratives. . . . [W]e live within various ongoing stories, as a condition for our being able to tell them.[32]

The claim, though, is equivocal. On a weaker interpretation it might mean only that actions and events are already (prior to being described) structured *like* narratives ['belonging to a field of possible narratives'] or it might be making the stronger claim that actions and events just *are* narratives ['we live within . . . stories'].

The paradigm, implicitly or explicitly, lying behind claims that narrative 'creates' reality is that of the writer of fiction creating an imaginary world. The real world is thought to be a creation of narrative processes in much the same way that imaginary worlds are the creation of novelistic fiction. However, now we have identified different dimensions of narrative and have established a clear conceptual distinction between narrative and fiction, the case in favour of this parallel cannot rest merely on premises about the ubiquity of narrative. Narratives are stories told (or thought) by humans for different purposes with different referential commitments and different structural forms. Whether events or actions or reality *per se* are 'created' by narratives is not entailed by anything intrinsic to narrative itself. The 'creation of a world' in fictive narration is explicable only in terms of the practice associated

[30] Prado, *Making Believe*, 119.
[31] Ray Schafer, 'Narration in the Psychoanalytic Dialogue', in Mitchell (ed.), *On Narrative*, 45.
[32] Rouse, 'The Narrative Reconstruction of Science', 181.

with one narrative genre. Nothing follows about the 'creation of a world' in narratives governed by different conventions and bearing different referential commitments. Maybe psychoanalytical narratives (a patient recounting a fantasy, for example) have features in common with the stories of the novelist. But historical narratives take on referential responsibilities and are constrained by genre conventions which are not reducible to those of narrative fiction.

Here is one concise account of the difference between history and fiction:

History is a narrative discourse with different rules than those that govern fiction. The producer of a historical text affirms that the events entextualized did indeed occur prior to the entextualization. Thus it is quite proper to bring extratextual information to bear on those events when interpreting and evaluating a historical narrative. Any important event which is ignored or slighted by a historical narrative may properly be offered as a weakness in that narrative. It is certainly otherwise with fiction, for in fiction the events may be said to be created by and with the text. They have no prior temporal existence, even though they are presented *as if* they did.[33]

We can see how both pragmatic and referential considerations are brought to bear in distinguishing historical from fictional narratives. The pragmatic dimension appeals to 'rules', to what the historian 'affirms', to the constraints on 'interpreting' and 'evaluating'. The referential dimension draws a distinction between events that 'occur prior to entextualization' and events that are 'created by . . . the text'. These simple points capture obvious differences between paradigmatic historical and fictional narratives. Any further claim to the effect that historical narratives also 'create a world' is a second-order consideration (perhaps part of a general epistemological theory) not entailed by the first-order referential and genre conventions governing history. The claim would need to be established independently.

It is not actual truth or falsity which determines the difference between historical and fictional writing; the difference lies in the practice rather than the content, though in obvious ways the practice will constrain the content. A good example is Erich

---

[33] Robert Scholes, 'Language, Narrative, and Anti-Narrative', in Mitchell (ed.), *On Narrative*, 207.

Auerbach's famous comparison of Homer's story of the return of Odysseus and the biblical story of Abraham and Isaac. Ostensibly the stories are equally legendary but the tellings, on Auerbach's account, are governed by quite different constraints. 'The biblical narrator was obliged to write exactly what his belief in the truth of the tradition (or, from the rationalistic standpoint, his interest in the truth of it) demanded of him—in either case his freedom in creative or representative imagination was severely limited.'[34] Homer, on the other hand, knows no such constraints: 'he does not need to base his story on historical reality, his reality is powerful enough in itself; it ensnares us, weaving its web around us, and that suffices him.'[35] Auerbach explores the multiple ways these constraints affect style and structure in the two stories. But from the logical point of view it is the constraints, governing both authors and readers, not style or structure or truth that are the final determinants of narrative genre.

There is no need to deny that non-fictional narratives *can* constitute the events they describe. Historical narrative does so when it clusters events under general classifications: the Hundred Years War, the Renaissance, the Industrial Revolution. There is a sense in which these 'meta-events' are *created* by historians. But again it does not follow from this that there are no events without a narrative to record them or that events themselves are always human constructs. Only a further second-order metaphysical or epistemological theory could establish this stronger thesis: perhaps something like Kant's transcendental idealism. The Kantian process of transcendental synthesis does indeed have certain features in common with narrative structure. According to Kant, it is the human mind, not the intrinsic nature of things-in-themselves, that produces a temporally and causally ordered world of substances and events. Other 'constructivist' accounts of knowledge reach similar conclusions. In all such cases, though, independent arguments are needed for their support. No form of idealism is supported merely by the observation that humans use narrative structures to order their experience.

Even if idealism is accepted this will still not give us reason to

---

[34] Erich Auerbach, 'Odysseus' Scar', in *Mimesis: The Representation of Reality in Western Literature*, trans. Willard R. Trask (Princeton, NJ, 1953), 14.
[35] Ibid. 13.

conflate the concepts of narrative and fiction. For there will still be both referential and genre dimensions by which to distinguish different levels of narrative purpose. The Kantian, for example, is well able to distinguish empirical objects—which are 'made up' transcendentally—from the imaginative constructs of the fiction-maker. And even the most committed Rortyian pragmatist, who rejects 'correspondence' conceptions of language and reference, is at pains to preserve (and explain) the distinction between 'organizational narratives', i.e. those with which we structure our experience, and 'full-blown stories', i.e. those of the novelist: the distinction between 'stories we employ' and 'stories we only enjoy'.[36] There is nothing about the pervasiveness of narrative which undermines the distinction between fictional and non-fictional narratives.

The indispensability of the imagination

Similar pressures on the notion of literary fiction arise in connection with imagination. Just as the concept of fiction is sometimes conflated with that of narrative so the term 'fiction' is sometimes taken to be interchangeable with 'imaginative construction'. No doubt there is a colloquial sense of the term 'fiction' which does have this meaning but it is not the sense that we have identified for literary fiction (nor is it identical with the philosophical senses discussed in Chapter 7). If being an imaginative construction were all there is to being fictional then the bounds of the fictional would be vastly extended. But that, as we have seen, is not so. Nevertheless, the imagination obviously is connected to fiction in the literary sense—indeed it played a role in characterizing the fictive stance—and it is important to get clear on just what differences there are in the ways the imagination is used. Our discussion of imagination will parallel that of narrative in that we will appeal to the different practices in which the imagination has a role in order to investigate the relevant referential and truth-bearing commitments.

Traditionally, imagination is thought of as the creative faculty

[36] Prado, *Making Believe*, 126.

of mind, the faculty, as Hume puts it, of 'compounding, transposing, augmenting, or diminishing the materials afforded us by the senses'.[37] At its best it gives rise to sublime poetry, at its worst to confusion and error. In many epistemological theories, the imagination, like narrative in other theories, is given a fundamental role in the acquisition of knowledge. Kant, for example, connected it with the 'transcendental synthesis' which yields an objective world: 'synthesis . . . is the mere result of the power of the imagination, a blind but indispensable function of the soul, without which we would have no knowledge whatsoever.'[38] But even those without a specific epistemological theory see imagination as ubiquitous: 'one must recognize the universality of the imaginative function both in that it belongs to everyone and in that it is exercised by each over all of his experience.'[39]

If the imagination gives us genuine knowledge and also merely fictitious inventions, how can we distinguish the two? How do we distinguish ideas of real things from ideas that are simply the product of whimsical imaginings? If imagination is the creative faculty, the faculty of 'making', how can we distinguish those makings that are the proper objects of belief and those that are mere 'fancies'?

It is helpful to begin by drawing a distinction between the imagination conceived as an *activity* and as an *attitude*. On one conception, as defined by Hume, imagination is a combinatory activity of the mind; it is creative, it assembles and reassembles ideas. But when conceived as an attitude, imagination need not be creative in this sense; it is reflective, a form of attention, a way of holding something in the mind. One very simple instance of this would be the paradigmatic difference between the poet and the reader. The poet's imagination—an *activity of mind*—creates the images which become the content of the reader's reflective imagining—an *attitude of mind*. The distinction is not hard and fast, of course, because the poet can also adopt a reflective attitude to his imaginings and the reader's creative imagination is likely to be involved in the reflective response. But keeping the distinction in mind will guide us in relating the imagination to fiction.

[37] David Hume, *Enquiry Concerning Human Understanding*, ed. Selby-Bigge (Oxford, 1893), 19.

[38] Immanuel Kant, *Critique of Pure Reason*, trans. Norman Kemp-Smith (London, 1963), A78, B103.

[39] Mary Warnock, *Imagination* (London, 1976), 202.

Imagination in the attitude sense is contrasted with belief. Belief is connected with truth and assertion, such that to believe a proposition is to hold it to be true and to have the disposition to assert it as true should the occasion arise. Imagining on the conception in question is a propositional attitude which involves suspending the connection with truth and assertion. It involves entertaining or holding in mind the proposition without the disposition towards assertion.[40] Imagining is an attitude that can be adopted at will, while belief is not. Also, it is neutral between truth and falsity, in the sense that it is possible to imagine both what is true and what is not true. It is imagining as an attitude that is involved in the fictive stance. When a reader imagines that a story-teller is performing speech acts this is an attitude adopted by convention and is a way of holding in mind the propositional content of the story.

It is imagination in the activity rather than the attitude sense which presents most problems for the fiction/non-fiction distinction because it is the combinatory power of the mind, not the entertaining of unasserted propositions, which is widespread in human cognition. However, strictly speaking this should not put into jeopardy the concept of make-believe fiction we have developed because although this concept invokes the attitude sense of imagination it makes no essential reference to imagination as a combinatory act of mind. As we have frequently emphasized, it is only a contingent fact that the fiction-maker uses the imagination to create works of fiction; the essential combinatory activity is linguistic not psychological. Nevertheless, we do need to find some way of differentiating the activity of the poet from that of the scientist, even granted that both are using their imagination. And it is no good looking only at the structures of imaginative makings, nor, *pace* Hume, at psychological factors ('An idea assented to *feels* different from a fictitious idea'[41]) to locate these differences. It is the context of the makings, their aims, and the practices in which they occur which mark off truth-bearing uses of imagination from fiction-creating uses.

---

[40] This account derives from Roger Scruton, *Art and Imagination: A Study in the Philosophy of Mind* (2nd edn.; London, 1982), 95 ff.

[41] 'An idea assented to *feels* different from a fictitious idea, that the fancy alone presents to us: And this different feeling I endeavour to explain by calling it a superior *force*, or *vivacity*, or *solidity*, or *firmness*, or *steadiness*.' (David Hume, *A Treatise of Human Nature*, ed. Selby-Bigge (Oxford, 1888), 629)

Constructive and fanciful uses of the imagination

In the history of philosophy there has been a marked ambivalence towards the imagination, reflecting something analogous to the positive and negative connotations of 'fiction' that we have already noted. There is no disagreement about the *power* of the imagination to create new conceptions and transcend the immediate data of the senses. Descartes speaks of the ability of the soul 'to imagine something non-existent—as in thinking about an enchanted palace or a chimera'.[42] Thomas Hobbes praises the 'celerity of imagining, that is, swift succession of one thought to another'.[43] Hume comments that 'To form monsters, and join incongruous shapes and appearances, costs the imagination no more trouble than to conceive the most natural and familiar objects.'[44] On the other hand, this creative power is sometimes disparaged as a source of confusion and falsity. Locke, for example, describes the imagination as 'wanton', 'extravagant', and 'chimerical' and contrasts it unfavourably with knowledge for failing to conform to reality.[45] Hume speaks of the 'loose and indolent reveries of a castle builder'.

Hume is not untypical in separating what he views as the useful as against the merely idle aspects of the imagination. He distinguishes a generic notion of imagination, virtually synonymous with mind, or that most general faculty of mind which operates on ideas,[46] from a more specific notion which is contrasted with memory, understanding, and judgement. Broadly speaking, he would associate the scientist and knowledge-seeker with the former, the poet and dreamer with the latter.

On Hume's view, the combinatory power of the mind, incorporating the generic notion of imagination, is indispensable for the formation of beliefs about an objective world. The imagination in this sense even surpasses reason inasmuch as it furnishes that

[42] René Descartes, *The Passions of the Soul* in *The Philosophical Writings of Descartes, Vol. I*, trans. John Cottingham, Robert Stoothoff, and Dugald Murdoch (Cambridge, 1985), 336.
[43] Thomas Hobbes, *Leviathan* (London, 1651), ch. 8.
[44] Hume, *Enquiry Concerning Human Understanding*, 18.
[45] John Locke, *An Essay Concerning Human Understanding* (1690), bk. II, ch. xxxiii, sect. 7; bk. IV, ch. iv, sects. 1–3, 6.
[46] See Hume, *A Treatise of Human Nature*, 20, 28, 33, 107, 198, 204, 208, 220, 338–40, 343.

cohesion, unity, and continuity in our ideas which no principle of reason can supply.

> Reason can never show us the connexion of one object with another ... When the mind, therefore, passes from the idea or impression of one object to the idea or belief of another, it is not determined by reason, but by certain principles, which associate together the ideas of these objects, and unite them in the imagination.[47]

It is the imagination, not reason, which gives us the relation of cause and effect.

> We have no other notion of cause and effect, but that of certain objects, which have been *always conjoin'd* together, and which in all past instances have been found inseparable. We cannot penetrate into the reason of the conjunction. We only observe the thing itself, and always find that from the constant conjunction the objects acquire an union in the imagination.[48]

Not only cause and effect but also '[t]he memory, senses, and understanding are ... all of them founded on the imagination'.[49] Indeed it is also the imagination, according to Hume, which 'convinces us of the continu'd existence of external objects when absent from the senses'.[50] When Hume praises the 'unbounded' power of thought—'while the body is confined to one planet, along which it creeps with pain and difficulty; the thought can in an instant transport us into the most distant regions of the universe'[51]—he is apparently equating thought and imagination. Elsewhere he writes: 'The imagination or understanding, call it which you please.'[52]

Hume distinguishes this generic imagination, as the faculty of the association of ideas, with a more specific imagination—giving rise to reveries and fantasies—which contrasts with judgement and memory. However, it would be wrong to suppose that Hume is postulating different *faculties* here—that which aids belief or understanding and that which produces mere 'fancies'—and probably wrong also to think he is employing different senses of the word 'imagination'. Hume notes only different connotations ascribed to our talk about imagination: as when we mean the 'vivacity of ideas', on the one hand, and on the other the 'whimsies and

[47] Ibid. 92.   [48] Ibid. 93.   [49] Ibid. 265.   [50] Ibid. 266.
[51] Hume, *Enquiry Concerning Human Understanding*, 18.
[52] Hume, *A Treatise of Human Nature*, 440.

prejudices, which are rejected under the opprobrious character of being the offspring of the imagination'.[53]

The crucial distinction, then, is not between different faculties of imagination nor different senses of the term but between different principles that are operative in the imagination: those 'which are permanent, irresistible, and universal; such as the customary transition from causes to effects . . .' and those 'which are changeable, weak, and irregular'. He goes on: 'The former are the foundation of all our thoughts and actions . . . [while] The latter are neither unavoidable to mankind, nor necessary, or so much as useful in the conduct of life.'[54] It is the unconstrained use of the imagination which serves to contrast it with judgement:

The *imagination* of man is naturally sublime, delighted with whatever is remote and extraordinary, and running, without control, into the most distant parts of space and time in order to avoid the objects which custom has rendered too familiar to it. A correct *Judgement* observes a contrary method, and avoiding all distant and high enquiries, confines itself to common life . . . leaving the more sublime topics to the embellishment of poets and orators, or to the arts of priests and politicians.[55]

A double ambivalence towards the imagination runs through Hume's discussion. On the one hand, even while contrasting (unfavourably) fanciful imagination with serious judgement, he shows an undisguised admiration for the freedom of the mind to soar without limit into unknown worlds. On the other hand, he also expresses sceptical reservations about the need to rely on the imagination in knowledge proper. Imagination fills in gaps in our perception and produces a belief in continuity, connectedness, and identity, which is somewhat less than rationally grounded.

The matter of fiction versus reality is complicated in Hume because in speaking even of knowledge-acquiring uses of the imagination, he frequently employs terms like 'feigned' and 'fictitious'.[56] The term 'fiction' itself is common in Hume, but again he uses it to cover different kinds of cases: the concepts of 'chimera', for example, or 'golden age', which are more or less benign 'poetic' inventions, concepts like 'substance' and 'state of nature' which have grown up in a philosophical tradition, and other

[53] Ibid. 117, n. 1.   [54] Ibid. 225.
[55] Hume, *Enquiry Concerning Human Understanding*, 162.
[56] e.g. *A Treatise of Human Nature*, 208.

concepts like 'personal identity', 'self', 'matter', 'cause and effect', 'space', 'time', and 'motion' which are deeply entrenched in ordinary ways of thinking but are 'fictions' none the less. For Hume a fiction is an invention of the mind which does not correspond to any observable reality. But he does not suppose that the world itself is 'made up' by the imagination; his claim is an epistemological one, to the effect that our fragmentary impressions need to be supplemented by the imagination to yield the convictions we have about an objective, mind-independent world. And he relies on a distinction between (useful) epistemological fictions and (dubious) 'poetic' fictions.

Even philosophers more idealistically inclined than Hume, who do think of the imagination as in some sense *creating* the world, characteristically seek to retain a distinction between the epistemological (world-making) creativity and the poetic (make-believe) creativity of the imagination. Thus Schelling, for example, a thoroughgoing idealist, distinguishes what he calls 'productive intuition' and the 'poetic faculty'; the former creates the known world, the latter *re*creates a world from the materials acquired in the former, even though both employ the same power or faculty:

The poetic faculty is what in the first potency is original intuition, and vice versa: the productive intuition which repeats itself in the first power is what we call the poetic faculty. What is active in both is one and the same, the only faculty by which we become capable of thinking and understanding even the contradictory, the imagination.[57]

Coleridge derived his own distinction between 'primary' and 'secondary' imagination from Schelling's distinction:

The primary imagination I hold to be the living power and prime agent of all human perception and as a repetition in the finite mind of the eternal act of creation in the infinite I AM. The secondary I consider as an echo of the former, coexisting with the conscious will, yet still identical with the primary in the *kind* of its agency, and differing only in the *degree* and in the *mode* of its operation. It dissolves, diffuses, dissipates, in order to recreate; or where this process is rendered impossible, yet still at all events it struggles to idealize and unify.[58]

---

[57] *Schelling's Works*, ed. Manfred Schröter (Munich, 1927), iii. 626; cited in Warnock, *Imagination*, 91–2.
[58] Samuel Coleridge, *Biographia Literaria*, ch. 13.

There is much that is obscure in Coleridge's theory of the imagination but this passage captures certain points which seem highly pertinent to the issue at hand: the distinction between two functions of the imagination (corresponding broadly to that between epistemological and 'make-believe', in our terms); the characterization of these functions as different not in kind but in degree and 'mode of . . . operation'; the association of the 'secondary' imagination with 'conscious will' (i.e. with intention and deliberation); and the invocation of 'unity' as one of the aims of the secondary imagination (Coleridge later says of the poet that '[h]e diffuses a tone and spirit of unity'[59]).

It is clear that the distinctions we are seeking to preserve, between fiction and non-fiction, between epistemological and make-believe fictions, between real and imaginary objects, between the use of the imagination in basic cognition and its use in literary or artistic fabulation, are already foreshadowed at the core of radical empiricist, and idealist, philosophy. It is possible to acknowledge a fundamental role for the imagination in the acquisition of knowledge *and* the fact that the very same faculty gives rise to imaginative fictions without supposing that there is no significant difference between either the products or the aims of the imagination in the two cases.

David Novitz has recently mounted a challenge to the Humean—empiricist—view, in effect rejecting the dual function of the imagination, insisting that there is no deep difference between the uses of the imagination in, say, science and poetry.[60] For Novitz it is the poetic or 'fanciful' imagination (the kind apparently disparaged by Hume) that is directly involved in the acquisition of knowledge. But how strong is Novitz's thesis? 'Facts', he says, 'are bred of fancy.'[61] Does he then suppose that the imaginary worlds of the artist are somehow indistinguishable from the real world?

In fact Novitz is a staunch realist, committed to the existence of an objective 'nonlinguistic, nonsemiotic, nonconstructed world'.[62] He rejects the view that the imagination *constitutes* the world or that there is nothing external to human imaginings. Those idealists

---

[59] Ibid., ch. 14.
[60] Novitz, *Knowledge, Fiction and Imagination*. For a fuller discussion see Peter Lamarque, 'Critical Discussion of David Novitz, *Knowledge, Fiction and Imagination*', *Philosophy and Literature*, 13 (1989), 365–74.
[61] Novitz, *Knowledge, Fiction and Imagination*, 33. [62] Ibid. 53.

tempted by such doctrines commit the 'occlusive fallacy', as he calls it, which involves confusing the way we experience a thing with the thing itself.

How then does Novitz distinguish between those 'flights of fancy' which yield genuine knowledge and those that issue in dreams, fantasies, . . . and make-believe fictions? He gives an answer not in terms of use but of usefulness:

Insofar as . . . flights of fancy prove to be useful, they are adopted as being less than fanciful, are eventually relied upon, and so become part of a network of everyday beliefs which we have about the world. Construals or speculations that lead nowhere are quickly dismissed as idle fantasies.[63]

This account, though, cannot be complete. Questions about purpose must be involved in determining different functions of the imagination. Is someone (for example, a scientist) using his imagination to try to solve a problem or frame a hypothesis? Is he just idly daydreaming without any particular aim in mind? Or is he, in an obvious third possibility, trying to create a work of art?

There are correspondingly different constraints on imaginings, governing, for example, what counts as success or failure. Imagining takes place within different practices, involving different ends and different consequences. Knowledge-seeking uses of the imagination (for example, the scientist's Popperian conjectures) are tested and judged against experience in terms of conformity to observed fact. But at the other extreme there are no such pressures on the idle daydream. Novitz tries to merge the two cases by claiming that fancy in both is 'constrained by past experience'.[64] That claim, though, is equivocal. It is true of 'idle fantasies' only in the general (empirical) sense that the mind must draw on the resources in its possession. It is true of the conjectures of the scientist in a much stronger sense, as Novitz admits, whereby 'each successive guess, although fanciful, is modified in the light of past experience'.[65]

It is no part of our argument to defend any sharp separation between *kinds* of imagining, or to suppose that with regard to psychological states there must be some fundamental difference between what goes on in the mind of a poet or novelist and what goes on in the mind of a scientist or historian. It is enough to

---

[63] Ibid. 33.   [64] Ibid. 34.   [65] Ibid.

invoke different practices (including aims, constraints, criteria for success, and so forth). We seek to establish only that the presence of the imagination in the acquisition of knowledge as well as in literary expression does not affect the distinction between fictional literature and non-fictional discourses. Nor does it in itself confer either a truth-seeking status on literature or a fictional status on science.

Imagination *per se*—just like narrative—is indifferent to truth, reference, and existence. Neither the truth nor falsity of p is implied by 'A imagines that p'. Likewise both real and 'purely imaginary' objects can be involved in acts of imagination. Determining an indispensable role for the imagination in cognition is compatible with both idealism (Schelling) and realism (Novitz). The distinction between real and made-up objects as it applies to literary fictions is untouched by epistemological theories about the nature of objects. Even if actual objects are 'constructs of the imagination' it does not follow that they are 'imaginary objects'. Here then is another example where literary theorists are misled in supposing that they need to arrive at a view in epistemology in order to settle questions about literature (or fictionality).

PART 3

Literature and Truth

10

Literary Practice

The concept of literature

So far in our argument we have not distinguished systematically between fiction and literature and the examples used have as often as not been taken from literary works, albeit highlighting their fictional rather than literary features. However, as was pointed out in Chapter 1, it is of central importance to recognize that the *concepts* of 'fiction' and 'literature' are distinct and invite separate analyses. For one thing, they have different extensions. 'Fiction', in the relevant sense, covers a large subclass of all invented stories, which can be realized in a number of media. It covers *Dynasty* as well as *The Tempest*. 'Literature', on the other hand, covers only a small subclass of *linguistic* expressions: the majority of linguistic expressions, even those in the fictive mode, do not fall under the concept 'literature'. Furthermore, even if the concepts of 'fiction' and 'literature' had the same extension, they would still be different concepts with different meanings. For 'fiction' is a descriptive concept while 'literature' is an evaluative concept. This does not mean that works of literature and works of fiction are different *kinds of text*. It has been a main contention of the argument so far that fiction is not a type of text at all but a mode of utterance which can only be identified with reference to the utterer's intention, i.e. the intention to invoke the fictive response, to invite the audience to adopt what we have called the *fictive stance* to the text produced.

In this respect there is a parallel between the concept of fiction and the concept of literature. For it may be argued that the concept of literature too is an institutional concept, a concept that is defined within a practice involving authors (as producers), texts, and readers. There are no syntactic, semantic, or even more loosely 'rhetorical' features of a text that define it as a literary work. A text is identified as a literary work by recognizing the author's intention that the text is produced and meant to be read within the framework of conventions defining the practice (constituting the institution) of literature.[1] With a formulation parallel to that used in our discussion of fiction we can say that this intention is *the intention to invoke the literary response*. In this case, too, we must add the further (Gricean) intention that there be a mutual belief that the response is to be brought about partly at least by means of the recognition of the primary intention. And again with a formulation parallel to that used in our treatment of fiction, we may call this whole complex of attitudes the *literary stance*. Adopting the literary stance towards a text is to identify it as a literary work and apprehend it in accordance with the conventions of the literary practice.[2] The mode of apprehension which the practice defines is one of *appreciation*.[3] The literary stance is defined by the expectation of (and consequently the attempt to identify) a certain type of value, i.e. literary aesthetic value, in the text in question.

An institutional practice, as we understand it, is *constituted* by a set of conventions and concepts which both regulate and *define* the actions and products involved in the practice.[4] We have already introduced the basic conception of a social practice, in Chapter 2, in relation to story-telling. The idea of an institutional practice is an extension of this, the difference being largely one of complexity. An institution, in the relevant sense, is a rule-governed practice which makes possible certain (institutional) actions which are defined by the rules of the practice and which could not exist as such without those rules. Often the actions and objects so defined are characterized by (institutional) concepts which again are given meaning only in terms of the rules governing

[1] The introduction of intention within the characterization of a literary work should not be taken as begging any questions about an 'intentional fallacy' in literary criticism for this characterization has no implications for the author's privileged position with regard to specific meanings assignable to elements in the work.

[2] For an attempt to formulate the conventions defining and structuring the literary stance, see Stein Haugom Olsen, *The Structure of Literary Understanding* (Cambridge, 1978, 1985), chs. 4 and 5.

[3] For a discussion of the concept of literary appreciation see 'Criticism and Appreciation' in Olsen, *The End of Literary Theory*, 121–37.

[4] For further discussion of the distinction between rules that regulate and rules that define a practice, see H. L. A. Hart, *The Concept of Law* (Oxford, 1961), ch. 5; John Rawls in 'Two Concepts of Rules', *Philosophical Review*, 64 (1955), 3–32 and reprinted in Philippa Foot (ed.), *Theories of Ethics* (Oxford, 1967); and Searle, in *Speech Acts*, 33–42.

the practice. One example of an institution in this sense would be the legal system which is constituted both by formal procedures for the administration of the law, on the one hand, and, on the other, by powers invested in individuals through clearly defined offices and roles. Take the simple example of an arrest and detention. The action of arresting and detaining someone, described in purely physical terms, has no inherent features that would set it apart from any other forcible apprehension of an individual, such as, say, kidnapping. The very possibility of a legally sanctioned arrest is dependent on a system that confers powers on individuals to undertake such an action, defining conditions under which such actions may be undertaken, and so on. Apart from such a system the very action of *arresting* someone ceases to exist though the action of forcible apprehension would still remain. The point directly parallels our claim about literary works that they too have no inherent formal features that constitute them as literary works; certain kinds of texts become literary works only by fulfilling a role in, and being subject to the conventions of, an institution.

Literary practice is part of a family of social practices, including that of fictive story-telling, which can be characterized through their constitutive concepts and conventions. The concept of literature itself as well as the literary stance can be characterized and explained only with reference to this framework. The literary stance is an attitude made possible by the defining concepts and conventions of literary practice in the approach to a text. Only by using these concepts and conventions can the reader identify the features of a literary work construed *as a literary work* within the practice. To explore the differences between the concepts of fiction and literature, it is therefore necessary to look at the concepts and conventions which define literary practice.

The concepts of literary practice

Consider the following example:

> A sudden blow: the great wings beating still
> Above the staggering girl, her thighs caressed
> By the dark webs, her nape caught in his bill,
> He holds her helpless breast upon his breast.

*   *   *

How can those terrified vague fingers push
The feathered glory from her loosening thighs?
And how can body, laid in that white rush,
But feel the strange heart beating where it lies?

A shudder in the loins engenders there
The broken wall, the burning roof and tower
And Agamemnon dead.
                    Being so caught up,
So mastered by the brute blood of the air,
Did she put on his knowledge with his power
Before the indifferent beak could let her drop?

(William Butler Yeats, 'Leda and the Swan')

The concepts used to identify the literary features of this poem can be roughly divided into three classes or levels. There is first a descriptive level which to a large extent is technical in nature and whose main, though not only, function is to identify formal structures and formal elements. Identifying this poem as a sonnet, and as an Italian rather than an English sonnet, is identifying the way in which the poem is organized. Knowing that an Italian sonnet normally is organized into an octet and a sestet, and that it conventionally has a turning-point or a *volta* after the octet, makes the immediate identification of the two main stages of *this* poem easy: the octet describes a scene of seduction, the sestet the consequences of that seduction. Equally, knowledge of the convention that the octet of a sonnet divides into two quatrains and the sestet into two tercets opens up the clear recognition of the difference in content and function between the two quatrains of the octet and the difference in content and function between the two tercets of the sestets, as well as the clear recognition of the parallels between the first quatrain and the first tercet, and between the second quatrain and the second tercet. However, none of these conventions is a constitutive convention (individually, they are not essential within the practice). Insight into the structure of the poem is possible without knowing what a sonnet is, but knowledge of the conventions and of the term 'sonnet' eases literary appreciation. This vocabulary of technical concepts can be found in any dictionary of literary terms and it covers all the special needs of description created by literary works. There are concepts characterizing diction and rhetorical features, concepts characterizing structural features, concepts characterizing elements of content, i.e. through such terms as 'plot', 'character', and 'setting', concepts of genres, periods of literary history, etc. This vocabulary is *not by itself* constitutive of the appreciation of a literary work but it is of great help in promoting this appreciation. It is constitutive of appreciation only in conjunction with the other levels of the conceptual scheme of the practice.

The concepts at the second level of the conceptual scheme constitutive of literary practice are unproblematic in the sense that they are wholly taken over from the conceptual scheme any reader would use in everyday life to characterize objects and actions. These concepts are used to characterize what one may call the *subject* of the literary work, its settings and scenes, its characters, the actions of its characters. To a great extent the reader will draw the terms in which to describe the subject from the text of the work itself. In the first quatrain of 'Leda and the Swan' Leda staggers as the great wings of the swan beat above her. However, the reader will supplement these concepts with whatever further concepts he feels are needed to grasp the subject of the work. Thus a reader may say that the first stanza of 'Leda and the Swan' describes how Zeus in the shape of a swan forces himself on Leda sexually. He arrives suddenly and surprisingly. Leda is almost (literally) swept off her feet. He assails her with a mixture of sensual caress and violence that overpowers Leda, who is helpless and terrified. In this description the subject is categorized in such a way that the nature of the events and actions are fixed for the reader.

If the vocabulary used to describe the subject is unproblematic in its nature because it is our everyday vocabulary, it may be problematic in its application since that may require interpretation. This interpretation will not always be controversial, and it may indeed look much like unchallengeable description. But since the function of this part of the interpretative vocabulary is that it should bring the subject of the work under descriptions that clarify it by categorizing it for the reader, alternative descriptions are in principle always possible. For example, the above description of the first stanza of 'Leda and the Swan' stressed the mixture of sensual caress and violence that overpowers Leda. However, a number of critics tend to construe Zeus' action more strongly. The poem, the reader is told by these critics, is 'on the adventures of God as a rapist'.[5] To characterize the action described in the octet

---

[5] Harold Bloom, *Yeats* (New York, 1970), 363.

as a rape would mean that one would emphasize the violence rather than the sensual caress, perhaps pointing out that the caress is presented as passive ('her thighs caressed | By the dark webs') whereas the violence is active. Against this it could be argued that the vocabulary of the second quatrain makes the application of the word 'rape' with its entirely negative connotations problematic; nor is it obvious that so specifically human a concept, rooted in human moral behaviour, is applicable to something un-human like a god or a swan. Even at the level of subject, interpretation is not necessarily unproblematic or uncontroversial.

An apprehension of subject is necessary to the appreciation of a literary work. The work exists for the reader only through the subject and the way in which it is presented. However, an apprehension of 'Leda and the Swan' which did not move beyond an apprehension of subject would be rudimentary and unsatisfactory. It would not capture the qualities that make the poem a valuable work of art. In order to appreciate a literary work, one must attempt to construe the subject under a perspective, and as being in some way the bearer of a theme. The theme is grasped through the application in interpretation of a third level of concepts: *thematic concepts*. These have attained currency in other than literary contexts, and are used to generalize about human concerns and practices. In their literary application they are used to identify the point and purpose of the subject and the way in which the subject is presented.

In the case of this poem the sensual moment is the point in history where God interferes, with momentous consequences. It is the inception of a new social and ethical order parallel to that brought about through the immaculate conception. The octet presents the moment of divine intervention imagined by the speaker in the poem as both familiar in its sensuality and strange in its revelation of an irresistible force. The first tercet presents elliptically the consequences of the intervention: the destruction, through the twin sisters Helen and Clytemnestra, of the old social and moral order based on revenge and relying on blood feud as a social institution, and the inception of a new order which vests the authority to judge and punish in the state. The fall of the old order is symbolized by the destruction of Troy and the subsequent destruction of the Greek fleet on its way home (as a punishment for having violated the holy shrines in Troy); also by the death of

Agamemnon at the hands of his wife as revenge for having sacrificed their daughter Iphigenia to obtain wind for the Greek fleet on its way to Troy. The new social and moral order is symbolized by the establishment of the Areopagite court to judge in cases which previously were seen as calling for blood revenge (the outcome of the *Oresteia* trilogy where Orestes is in the impossible position of being duty bound to kill his mother for having killed his father, Agamemnon, at the same time as being forbidden to commit matricide by the most deep-rooted of Greek moral conventions). Construed like this, the subject as it is presented comes to represent the origin of Western civilization in passion, blood, and violence. It is only when 'Leda and the Swan' is apprehended in some such terms as these, that the poem is appreciated as a literary work.

The conventions of literary practice

The constitutive conventions of literary practice are those that make a work of literature what it is: i.e. a work with aesthetic value. Roughly speaking this value is assumed to reside in two principal dimensions of the literary work: the imaginative and the mimetic. In the remainder of this chapter we will offer some preliminary reflections on these.

First of all, literary works have always been recognized as important products of human imagination, as a manifestation of the ability to create worlds imaginatively. This *creative-imaginative aspect* of literature has always been held to be one of its most central qualities. Even when viewed as pernicious and dangerous, by those stressing the negative side of the imagination, it has been recognized as powerful and ineliminable. '[T]he power which poetry has of harming even the good (and there are very few who are not harmed), is surely an awful thing?' Socrates asks an assenting Glaucon in *The Republic* (i. 605 *c*), when they discuss the poet's ability to move the passions by producing invented imaginings. However, the creative-imaginative aspect of literature has, in general, been recognized as positive, as a quality which makes literature culturally and humanly significant. This creative-imaginative aspect is not a contingent feature, as it is of works of fiction. To recognize something as a literary work is to recognize it as a creative-imaginative effort. That literature should be so is part of the very concept of literature that came into being through the writing and appreciation of the epics, poems, and dramas in ancient Greece in the fifth century and which has been operative in Western culture ever since.

The creative-imaginative aspect manifests itself in two ways. A literary work can give form to a subject or a story which need not itself be invented by the author. Literary works, major and minor, often deal with historical events, or rewrite stories already well known to the audience, as does Milton's *Paradise Lost*, Goethe's *Faust* or, indeed, Yeats's 'Leda and the Swan'. And different literary works can deal with the *same* story. The Greek tragedians rewrote the old mythical stories in their own way over and over again. Aeschylus, Sophocles, and Euripides all deal with the return of Orestes to the waiting Electra and the consequent murder of Clytemnestra. They each give the story a different treatment, but they do not invent the story itself. What they invent is a perspective, a way of seeing the story which endows it with significance, and to define this perspective, they invent dialogue, minor incident, and character. They also modify the form of the drama in the process: Sophocles increases the number of speaking characters from two to three; Euripides changes the role of the chorus. In their case, creative imagination showed itself not in the invention of story or major incident, but in the *conception* of the stories they rewrote and in the 'embellishment' through which they defined this conception. In a wide sense of that vague but much used word, they created the *form* of the story in order to bring out a theme which they believed to be important. Perhaps this is nowhere more obvious than in the kind of highly formalized poem which Yeats uses to make the story of Leda and Zeus the vehicle for his vision.

Secondly, many literary works do, wholly or to some extent, consist of descriptions and stories which are made up or constructed. Literature is *poesis* also in the sense that it is invention rather than report, story rather than history. Authors do not merely retell old stories or provide particular perspectives on historical situations. They invent new stories, new conflicts, new plots and, indeed, if their imagination is sufficiently powerful, new worlds, as do Shakespeare, Dickens, or Scott. In other words, they do not merely create form (a perspective, embellishment) but they also create subject. The distinction between creating form and creating subject is worth insisting on, since most prominent literary theories this century have assumed that the distinction is somehow naïve and theoretically invalid.

The formalist theories of the New Criticism, structuralism, and post-structuralism have had as a central tenet that in creating form, the author creates content. There is one obvious sense in which this is true: the Orestes/Electra story as presented by Aeschylus, Sophocles, and Euripides, are really different narratives with different characters and different visions of the world.[6] However, in another obvious sense it is also false: there is no doubt that the three tragedians and their various audiences (among whom are we ourselves) recognize that they deal with the *same* story. These audiences have also recognized that it is possible to capture the differences between the three plays by seeing them as presenting *different conceptions* of the *same story*. And the point could be made with reference to any author who makes use of an already known story, whether it be history, myth or fiction. Shakespeare deals in his English history plays with the Wars of the Roses; it would be absurd to deny that this same subject was dealt with in Holinshed and has been extensively treated in subsequent historical monographs. And this is true even if the Shakespearian plays, the historical chronicle, and the modern historical monograph give the subject not merely a different form but also present it under different logical constraints which define different types of discourse. There is therefore a sound logical basis for the distinction between form and subject even though the one cannot exist without the other.

There is also a good theoretical reason to insist on this distinction, namely that it is possible to raise as separate questions what contribution subject and what contribution form makes to aesthetic value. For example, Aristotle devotes chapter 13 of the *Poetics* to arguing that 'the finest tragedies are always on the story of some few houses, on that of Alcmeon, Oedipus, Orestes, Meleager, Thyestes, Telephus, or any others that may have been involved, as either agents or sufferers in some deed of horror' (1453 *a*). And though one may disagree with Aristotle on this point, the question

---

[6] The point is well made in John Jones, *On Aristotle and Greek Tragedy* (London, 1962), a large part of which is taken up by showing how these plays differ.

itself whether tragedy is best restricted to known subjects is still intelligible and important.

It is possible to argue that the creation of form (or, on the reader's part, the recognition of form) and thus a conception of a subject, may confer on the subject (invented or not) literary value. Any comparison between Shakespeare's historical plays and his sources will illustrate this point. Here is a passage from Sir Thomas North's *Plutarch's Lives of the Noble Grecians and Romans* (1579) juxtaposed with a passage from *Antony and Cleopatra* with a critical comment pointing out some of the differences between the two passages:

Her ladies and gentlewomen also, the fairest of them were apparelled like the nymphes Nereids (which are the mermaides of the waters) and like the Graces, some stearing the helme, others tending the tackle and ropes of the barge, out of the which there came a wonderfull passing sweete savor of perfumes, that perfumed the wharfes side, pestered with innumerable multitudes of people.[7]

> At the helm
> A seeming mermaid steers: the silken tackle
> Swell with the touches of those flower-soft hands,
> That yarely frame the office. (II. ii. 212)

Leavis points out that the tactual imagery of the second sentence gains its strength from the contrast between the hard and energetic associations of 'tackle' and the sensuous adjective 'silken'—'hands take hold of the cordage, and it seems impossible to dissociate "swell" from the tactual effect'. One could go further than this and say that all the phrases are linked up and indeed subsumed in a sexual metaphor—the 'tackle' is at first limp and silken, but swells under the touch of the 'flower-soft' hands: in little, a recapitulation of what happens to Antony under the enchantment of Cleopatra.

In comparison, North and Plutarch give us facts devoid of meaning—one gentlewoman did this, another did that—with no cohesion among those facts and no organic relationship with the rest of the action.[8]

The creation of form here imposes on the subject a coherence it has not possessed beforehand. And the coherence is defined through a thematic construal: the 'facts' point beyond themselves

---

[7] 'Extracts from North's *Plutarch*', Appendix V, *Antony and Cleopatra, The Arden Shakespeare* (9th edn.; London, 1954), 246.

[8] Philip Hobsbaum, *A Theory of Communication* (London, 1970), 214–15.

and can reasonably be seen as contributing to a general characterization of Cleopatra and her relationship to Antony. The form is 'found' rather than 'invented' by the reader in this sense: the embellishment consists in the invention of extra detail, the swelling of the sails, and the use of the four words 'silken', 'swell', 'flower-soft', 'yarely' which are transferred from other areas of experience to that of sailing a barge. The reader *construes* the swelling of the sails and the application of these words: they do not in themselves hold any theme. But the construal must identify properties which, *under that construal*, can be said to be *of* the passage under interpretation. It is the possibility of this kind of construal which confers on the passage literary value, and it is the assumption that *Antony and Cleopatra* is intended to yield to this kind of construal which constitutes it as a literary work.

Using the distinction between form and subject, we can say that the aesthetic value defined by the creative-imaginative aspect of the concept of literature is constituted by the imposition of form on a subject. Imposing form on a subject is to impose coherence on a complexity of elements: a manifold of elements is in construal both identified and recognized as forming a unity. An *expectation* of a complex and coherent form is thus one central element in the literary stance; and appreciation, the mode of apprehension defined by the literary stance, aims at identifying the complex and coherent form of a literary work of art. Coherence and complexity are not, however, values *sui generis* but acquire value through contributing, with the subject, to the definition of a *humanly interesting content*.

For the creative-imaginative aspect of literature is only one of two basic aspects which define it as an evaluative concept. Let us turn to this second aspect. The concept of literature has always been recognized as having what, for the sake of tradition and convenience, may be called a *mimetic* aspect. The interest which literature has for human beings, it has because it possesses a humanly interesting content, because what literature presents or says concerns readers as human beings. As with the creative-imaginative aspect, the mimetic aspect is both a central and an ineliminable facet of the concept of literature. To recognize something as a literary work is to recognize it as being intended to convey a humanly interesting content. And a humanly interesting content has always been recognized as one of the most important qualities of literature, a quality which gives literature its cultural prominence. Aristotle's claim that 'poetry is something more philosophic and of graver import than history' (*Poetics*, 1451^b), is not only partially definitive of the *nature* of literature, but also places literature between two intellectual practices of recognized importance: history and philosophy. Aristotle uses the point that poetry concerns universals rather than particulars—a point integral to our own account of fiction—as part of his defence of literary value, an attempt to meet the charge that literary fiction is frivolous and a threat to knowledge and truth. An *expectation* of a humanly interesting content is thus the other central element in the literary stance, and the other central aim of appreciation is to identify such a content in a literary work.

Again roughly speaking, it may be said that the mimetic aspect of literature manifests itself in two ways, in the rendering of subject and the presentation of theme. Literary works describe individual objects, places, characters, situations, events, actions, and the interaction between these. One prominent tradition in poetics holds that what creates the humanly interesting content of literature is, in some sense, the *truth* of these descriptions. We shall debate that view fully in Chapter 12. But it is also a characteristic feature of the literary stance that literary works are expected to have a *theme*. Readers assume, in taking up the literary stance, that the descriptions of particular objects, places, characters, situations, events, actions, etc. that one finds in a literary work are there to contribute to the definition and development of theme. From literature at its best it is expected that this descriptive detail will constitute a context for the presentation of universal human concerns, or, in the words of Thomas Nagel, 'mortal questions', 'mortal life: how to understand it and how to live it'.[9] This literary representation is closely linked with the creation of form: form is imposed on subject thereby yielding a representation of general human interest.

However, literary representation raises problems that have nothing to do with form. It raises problems about the cognitive status of literary works, about the relationship between literature and other intellectual and cultural practices such as religion, philosophy, and science, and about *how* literature does

[9] Nagel, *Mortal Questions*, p. ix.

represent 'universal human concerns'. Again there is a tradition in poetics that takes this area of enquiry to be the important element in literary *mimesis*, arguing that it is through its definition and development of theme that literature acquires human interest.

In the following chapters we shall deal with both the subject level and the thematic level of literary *mimesis*, and we shall also deal with some of the arguments used by the different traditions in poetics that focus on the one element or the other as the essential element. However, before we can undertake this discussion we have to clear up some of the confusions that surround the relationship between literature and fiction.

11

Literature and Fiction

The concept of fiction in literary criticism

Since literature for the most part consists of stories that are either invented by the author or are mythical or legendary in character, the unanalysed, non-technical concept of fiction (what is made up, untrue, not conforming to reality) has always had a natural application to literary works. However, the relationship between fiction conceived in this loose sense and literature has always been seen as problematic. For if the subject-matter of literature is 'mere fiction' how can it be taken seriously? The age-old charge against fiction is that there is something at best childish about it, at worst morally reprobate or deceitful. It is therefore common in poetics, going back at least as far as Aristotle, to find apologetics with the aim of defending the serious nature of literature. In the Renaissance in England there appeared a number of 'Defences' of poetry of which Sir Philip Sidney's is but the most famous.

More interesting, from the point of view of our own discussion, is the form the apologetics take when the new genre of the novel finally comes into its own in the eighteenth century. It was common in that period for British novelists to write prefaces to their stories claiming that the accounts they presented were true accounts. One such device was to maintain that they had edited and published papers which they had found or which had been left them by real people, and these papers they asserted to be true and instructive:

The Editor believes the thing to be a just History of Fact; neither is there any Appearance of Fiction in it: And however thinks, because all such things are dispatch'd, that the Improvement of it, as well to the Diversion, as to the Instruction of the Reader, will be the same; and as such, he thinks, without farther Compliment to the World, he does them a great Service in the Publication.[1]

The point of such 'editorial' prefaces is not to fool the reader into believing the story to be true, but rather to underline that these

[1] Daniel Defoe, *Robinson Crusoe* (London, 1719), Preface.

works should be read with the same attitude, with the same attention, and the same *seriousness* as historical accounts and that they deserve this attention for the same reason: they, too, are ultimately true accounts of human life. Explaining to Bishop Warburton why he is reluctant to use the Preface which the bishop had written for *Clarissa*, Samuel Richardson makes the point that it is important to invite a serious attitude to his novel by avoiding any explicit mention of the fact that it is fiction:

Will you, good Sir, allow me to mention, that I could wish that the *Air* of Genuiness had been kept up, tho' I want not the Letters to be *thought* genuine; only so far kept up, I mean, as that they should not prefatically be owned *not* to be genuine: and this for fear of weakening their Influence where any of them are aimed to be exemplary; as well as to avoid hurting that kind of Historical Faith which Fiction itself is generally read with, tho' we know it to be Fiction.

'What Richardson seems to seek for his story', says the critic who quotes this passage from Richardson's letter, 'is an acceptance only a shade different from that of the Middle Ages for the apocryphal tales: they could not be warranted as true, but they might be true, and in any case could be read without danger to the soul, perhaps with profit.'[2] The normal way of defending the seriousness of the novel was, then, to dissociate it from fiction. The fictional nature of so many literary works was an embarrassment and in poetics much energy was spent to explain away this fact.

Towards the end of the last century a use of the concept of fiction as at least partially synonymous with the genre concepts of 'novel' and 'short story' spread rapidly in practical criticism. This use appeared just about the time when the taste for written entertainment of the new mass audience, created by William Forster's Education Act of 1870, was being formed. The 'literary' tastes of this new mass audience were formed and catered for by a new entertainment industry: 'a vast industry which set its own standards, standards which had nothing to do with literary and artistic standards as normally understood.'[3] The serious novel was being pushed to the margins of the market for written entertainment, and it is possible that the spread of the term 'fiction' as a synonym for 'novel' and 'short story' in criticism at this time was due to this

[2] William Nelson, *Fact or Fiction: The Dilemma of the Renaissance Storyteller* (Cambridge, Mass., 1973), 111–12.
[3] Walter Allen, *The English Novel* (Harmondsworth, 1958), 260.

fact. These non-artistic works of written entertainment catering for the new audience had the form of novels and short stories, yet they were not really 'proper' novels and short stories written with an artistic purpose. They did, however, have in common with many literary artistic compositions the fact that they presented an invented subject-matter. The term 'fiction' could thus be used as the lowest common denominator for two modes of discourse that were outwardly similar, but essentially different in purpose.

Whatever the reason for this new use of the term 'fiction', when the modernists came to restate the claim that their art was serious, as serious as history, this new use forced them to formulate their claim as a paradox. They accepted the term 'fiction' as a genre-description of their works, but they insisted that *their* fiction (serious fiction, the fiction of the artist) was as *true* as, and perhaps *truer* than, history. 'The only reason for the existence of a novel', says Henry James in his essay on 'The Art of Fiction', 'is that it does attempt to represent life.' And comparing the novel to a painting, he goes on:

as the picture is reality, so the novel is history. That is the only general description (which does it justice) that we may give of the novel. But history also is allowed to represent life; it is not, any more than painting, expected to apologize. The subject-matter of fiction is stored up likewise in documents and records, and if it will not give itself away, as they say in California, it must speak with assurance, with the tone of a historian. Certain accomplished novelists have a habit of giving themselves away which must often bring tears to the eyes of people who take their fiction seriously. I was lately struck, in reading over many pages of Anthony Trollope, with his want of discretion in this particular. In a digression, a parenthesis or an aside, he concedes to the reader that he and this trusting friend are only 'making believe'. He admits that the events he narrates have not really happened, and that he can give his narrative any turn the reader may like best. Such a betrayal of a sacred office seems to me, I confess, a terrible crime; it is what I mean by the attitude of apology, and it shocks me every whit as much in Trollope as it would have shocked me in Gibbon or Macaulay. It implies that the novelist is less occupied in looking for the truth (the truth, of course I mean, that he assumes, the premises that we must grant him, whatever they may be) than the historian, and in doing so it deprives him at a stroke of all his standing room.[4]

---

[4] Henry James, 'The Art of Fiction', in *'The Art of Fiction' and Other Essays* (New York, 1948), 5–6.

Similarly, that other great modernist, Virginia Woolf, argues, in her essay 'Modern Fiction', that fiction should not be governed by a conception of form but by the standard of life itself. Her charge against realist fiction is that it is conventional rather than true:

> The writer seems constrained, not by his own free will but by some powerful and unscrupulous tyrant who has him in thrall, to provide a plot, to provide comedy, tragedy, love interest, and an air of probability embalming the whole so impeccable that if all his figures were to come to life they would find themselves dressed down to the last button of their coats in the fashion of the hour. The tyrant is obeyed; the novel is done to a turn. But sometimes, more and more often as time goes by, we suspect a momentary doubt, a spasm of rebellion, as the pages fill themselves in the customary way. Is life like this? Must novels be like this?
>
> Look within and life, it seems, is very far from being 'like this'.[5]

And Virginia Woolf launches into that famous description of what life is and what it is not and what the novelist would do if he were not the slave of convention.

By the turn of the century, then, there figure in literary criticism two concepts of fiction. There is the traditional non-technical *strong* concept of fiction which carries the implication that the story or description referred to makes no claim to be true. But there is also the *weak* concept of fiction used by Henry James and Virginia Woolf, which can be used to refer to literary works without embarrassment because it carries no implication that literary works do not make truth-claims. This weak use of the term 'fiction' was simply a theoretically innocent terminological innovation, a straight substitution of the term 'fiction' for the terms 'novel' and 'short story'. When the modernists stake their claim as serious artists, as élites with a message that the audience may not heed, but that they ignore at their peril, they use 'fiction' to refer to what they create, but they emphasize that their task is to tell the *truth*. Today this weak concept of 'fiction' is widely used and well established in practical criticism, and one can find it even in critics with a strong theoretical consciousness. For example, in a collection of essays on the novel published some years ago, called *Essays on Fiction*, Frank Kermode, who always does his best to come to terms with theoretical innovations, comes back again and again to the criterion of 'life', *verity* rather than *verisimilitude*, in his

---

[5] Virginia Woolf, 'Modern Fiction', in *Collected Essays*, ii (London, 1966), 106.

judgements on the novel, though he persists in referring to the novel as 'fiction'.[6] There is no expressed awareness in Kermode's book that the use of 'fiction' to refer to the novel creates a paradox: 'fiction' is simply used as an alternative name of the novel. Its use involves no theoretical assumptions about the fictional status of literary discourse.

Even though this technical identification of fiction with the discursive genres of literature was theoretically innocent, it created a situation where the possibilities for conceptual confusion were greatly increased. 'Fiction' is plausibly applied to the narrative genres of literature only because it is widely recognized that these consist, at least to a large extent, of invented stories and descriptions. When the modern novelists claim that their fiction must represent life, they trade on the strong sense of 'fiction' to create their striking paradox: *in spite of* being fictions their works are true. There is a clear danger in this strategy for the novelist or theorist who wants to establish the point that literature aims at some kind of truth. By introducing the term 'fiction' as an alternative name for the discursive genres of literature there is the risk of promoting exactly the opposite conclusion. For once established in literary criticism as a near synonym for 'novel' and 'short story', the term 'fiction' invites the assumption that it is of the essence of these genres that they make no claim to truth. And given a certain combination of theoretical assumptions, the use of 'fiction' might be construed as expressing a 'profound' intuition about the cognitive status of literature. Such a combination of theoretical assumptions has dominated influential parts of modern literary theory.

Theories of literature from Aristotle onwards have worked with an overt or hidden assumption about the paradigmatic status of some particular genre of literature. For Aristotle it was tragedy. In the New Criticism the object of attention is poetry. The Semantic Definition of Literature, 'a literary work is a discourse in which an important part of the meaning is implicit',[7] applies *par excellence* to poetry, and the emphasis in New Critical practice was on the analysis of poems. Adopting the poem as the paradigm for all literary works, there was no danger that New Critical theory should

---

[6] Frank Kermode, *Essays on Fiction* (London, 1983).
[7] Beardsley, *Aesthetics*, 126.

introduce 'fiction' as an alternative name for 'literature'. There is no critical usage of the term 'fiction' to denote poetry.[8] In New Critical theory the relationship between literature and fiction therefore remained not only controversial but a central theoretical issue. Writing about 'The Problem of Belief', in 1954, Arnold Isenberg could say: '[t]he question, though not excessively clear, has been much debated; and it is possible to speak of "sides".' And he goes on, 'I take one side, holding as I do the extreme view that belief and aesthetic experience are mutually irrelevant.'[9] And the central theoretical work in the New Critical tradition, Monroe Beardsley's *Aesthetics*, published four years later, has one chapter on 'Artistic Truth' (chapter 8) and one on 'Literature and Knowledge' (chapter 9).

However, the literary theories which can be subsumed under the labels 'Structuralism' and 'Post-structuralism', concentrate attention on discursive writing, in particular narrative, and the focus has been on the structure and other properties of narrative. In these theories it is tacitly assumed that the paradigmatic kinds of literature are the novel and the short story. These theories therefore facilitate the identification of fiction and literature in a way that previous theories have not done. In addition, these theories rely on two further assumptions which make it seem natural that literature is fiction in the strong sense of being a description or a story that makes no claim to be true. It is assumed in these types of theory that literary works somehow have 'meaning' and that this is what makes the literary work important.[10] And this assumption is combined with the further, formalist, assumption

---

[8] The use of the term 'fiction' to denote poetry has appeared in certain post-structuralist critics. See e.g. the first ch., 'Understanding Criticism', of Geoffrey Hartman, *Criticism in the Wilderness* (New Haven, Conn., 1980), where Hartman uses 'fiction' consistently to refer to poems and other genres alike. However, the use seems forced and confusing: one is never quite sure what point Hartman is trying to make about *poetry*.

[9] Arnold Isenberg, 'The Problem of Belief', *Journal of Aesthetics and Art Criticism*, 13 (1954–5), 395–407; repr. in Cyril Barrett (ed.), *Collected Papers on Aesthetics* (Oxford, 1965), 125.

[10] Though this is an assumption made by almost all theories of literature produced in this century, it is an assumption which is as problematic as the assumption that the paradigmatic kinds of literature are the novel and the short story. For it is not obvious why the semantic concept of meaning should be suitable as an explanatory concept in literary theory. See Stein Haugom Olsen, 'Text and Meaning' and 'The "Meaning" of a Literary Work' in *The End of Literary Theory*.

that meaning can be explained in purely formalistic, non-semantic, terms based on relationships between signs rather than on referential or truth-bearing relations. If meaning is defined in this way, then a literary work can have meaning without being about anything in the world. Consequently, there is no reason for assuming that a literary work is a kind of discourse which in any way makes true or false statements. And the identification of fiction with literature, which the first assumption encourages, then seems unproblematic.

The three assumptions formulated above do not together *entail* the conclusion that the concept of 'literature' is identical with the concept of 'fiction', nor is there any weaker but logically sound inferential link from these three assumptions to that conclusion. They merely make the identification *seem natural* as long as it is not examined closely. Note what happens in the following passage where the view of literature and language expressed by the two last assumptions is taken for granted:

For the statement about language, that sign and meaning can never coincide, is what is precisely taken for granted in the kind of language we call literary. Literature, unlike everyday language, begins on the far side of this knowledge; it is the only form of language free from the fallacy of unmediated expression. All of us know this, although we know it in the misleading way of a wishful assertion of the opposite. Yet the truth emerges in the foreknowledge we possess of the true nature of literature when we refer to it as *fiction*. All literatures, including the literature of Greece, have always designated themselves as existing in the mode of fiction; in the *Iliad*, when we first encounter Helen, it is as the emblem of the narrator weaving the actual war into the tapestry of a fictional object. Her beauty prefigures the beauty of all future narratives as entities that point to their own fictional nature. The self-reflecting mirror-effect by means of which a work of fiction asserts, by its very existence, its separation from empirical reality, its divergence, as a sign, from a meaning that depends for its existence on the constitutive activity of this sign, characterizes the work of literature in its essence.[11]

This critic turns the theoretically innocent fact that 'we' refer to novels and short stories as 'fiction', into a basic assumption on which a view of literature can be built, by first equating novels and short stories with 'literature'. This is an illicit move. 'We' do not,

[11] Paul de Man, 'Criticism and Crisis', in *Blindness and Insight: Essays in the Rhetoric of Contemporary Criticism* (2nd edn.; London, 1983), 17.

as this critic assumes, refer to 'literature' as 'fiction'; 'we' refer only to the genres of novels and short stories in this way. Second, this critic assumes that this use of 'fiction' is expressive of a profound, shared intuition about the cognitive status of literature, an intuition that literary language is fictional discourse. 'We', Paul de Man assumes, have the foreknowledge that literature is in the mode of fiction. But this is simply wrong. As has just been argued, the use of 'fiction' as an alternative name for the discursive genres of literature, is in this respect, theoretically innocent. That usage does not signal 'foreknowledge' of any kind. In particular, this use of 'fiction' is not an expression of a shared intuition which is prior to and can support a formalist account of literary meaning. Nevertheless, in structuralism and post-structuralism, the identification of literature and fiction is not only a central feature, but it is also beyond argument. Proponents of these views do not argue the point, but assert magisterially, as does de Man in the quoted passage, that literature *is* fiction.[12]

The presence of the concept of fiction in literary criticism and the frequency with which it is used is not, then, expressive of any shared intuition about the cognitive status of literature. Literary works make use of invented stories and descriptions but this does not entail that literary works are works of fiction. Indeed, though in previous chapters we have often analysed passages in literary works that are fictive in the sense defined, it would be wrong to take for granted, without further argument, that any literary work must possess a fictive dimension. It does not seem to be part of the *definition* of literature that it be in the fictive mode or even have a fictional content. A premature and theoretically unsubstantiated identification of literature and fiction will disguise a central problem which the concept of literature raises: the problem of the relationship between the literary work and its representational powers. The relationship between literature and fiction is thus problematic rather than straightforward. It may very well be that the most reasonable position on the issue is to accept as a general presumption that for something to be a literary work it will also be a species of fictive utterance. However, this is no more than a presumption and still leaves us with the problem of literary value.

---

[12] Graff in the first three chs. *Literature against Itself* diagnoses this malady in these areas of modern literary theory in an excellent way.

Literature, unlike fiction, is an evaluative concept and a work is recognized as a literary work partially through the recognition of the intention to present something to the reader that is humanly interesting. This is not a necessary implication of the fictive stance. The highly valued works of the literary canon are recognized as such because they have something to say about the 'human condition'. If literature is closely bound to make-believe, then we have to offer an interpretation of the mimetic aspect of literature which, in spite of its fictive quality, does justice to this central aspect of literary value.

The attack on the concept of literature

When modern literary theory of the structuralist and post-structuralist type so easily assimilates literature to fiction without any further analysis of the process through which the assimilation comes about or any argument about the validity of the moves involved, this is because these types of theory rest on certain further assumptions which undermine the value of rational argument itself. It is instructive to note how in the passage from de Man the substitution of magisterial pronouncement for rational argument affects not only the way in which literature is identified with fiction, but also the way in which the illustration from the *Iliad* is presented. Even if one accepts without further argument that Helen in her first appearance in the third song of the *Iliad* is emblematic of the narrator of the story (she is weaving a cloak on which she pictures the battles fought for her), it is difficult to accept that she creates a 'fictional object'. What she seems to be doing is to picture a reality she sees before her. If she is indeed representative of the narrator, then his claim would seem to be exactly the opposite of that which de Man finds: i.e. that she tells a true story. It may, of course, be possible to interpret the scene in the way de Man does, but there is no *interpretative argument* in de Man's book to support his suggestion. In the quoted passage methodical argument is replaced by authoritarian tone. This substitution of assumed authority for rational argument is typical of de Man's book and indeed of much post-structuralist criticism. It is a natural consequence of a view that construes reason and objectivity as humanist myths which have to be discarded if the critic is to engage with the 'open multisignificance of texts'.

Behind this position lies the more general sceptical and anti-realist stance that we have already examined and criticized. This is the view that it is

impossible any longer to see reality simply as something 'out there', a fixed order of things which language merely reflected. On that assumption, there was a natural bond between word and thing, a given set of correspondences between the two realms. Our language laid bare for us how the world was, and this could not be questioned. This rationalist or empiricist view of language suffered severely at the hands of structuralism: for if, as Saussure had argued, the relation between sign and referent was an arbitrary one, how could any 'correspondence' theory of knowledge stand? Reality was not reflected by language but *produced* by it: it was a particular way of carving up the world which was deeply dependent on the sign-systems we had at our command, or more precisely which had us at theirs.[13]

It is symptomatic of the poor standard of argument in modern literary theory that a well-known literary theorist should present this argument approvingly without showing any awareness of the highly contentious nature of the premisses and reasoning.

In this passage one finds the first of three equivalences which are falsely construed as constituting the 'profound' intuition that literature is identical with fiction. The series of equivalences, if unfolded, would run as follows. The world (reality) is organized through human linguistic systems: there is therefore no independently existing reality to which language refers (*non sequitur*). Since there is no real independently existing world to which language can refer, all uses of language are identical with fictional language (*non sequitur*). Literature being a type of discourse or language use is therefore fiction (*false conclusion*). It does not take much reflection to see that the argument as presented is unsound through and through. First of all, language may organize our reality without thereby creating it. It was a main point in our discussion of Goodman and Rorty that even those philosophers who are most congenial to the post-structuralists supply no adequate arguments for identifying 'the world' with 'language'. Secondly, the distinction between fictional discourse and fact-stating discourse is a distinction between language functions (modes of utterance) and the outcome of the debate between realists, anti-realists, and

[13] Eagleton, *Literary Theory*, 107–8.

pragmatists about whether or not there is an independently existing world would not influence that distinction. We tried to dispel
this confusion with our analysis of different types of fiction. There
is, therefore, no epistemological ground, based on premisses about
knowledge of the world, for identifying literary language with
fictional language. As we have seen, not only are the concepts of
literature and fiction distinct, but there are no formal qualities of
language which serve to define either.

Perhaps in the more extreme post-structuralists' rhetoric of irrationalism these objections will simply be shrugged off as based on
'logocentric' prejudices. But what would be the consequences for
the concept of literature and the activity of criticism if their position were to be accepted? One would be the abandonment of a
central defining feature of the institution of literature: the requirement that literature should have something interesting to say about
human life. Indeed, the whole concept of 'saying something about'
would become otiose. This is not a marginal or unimportant decision for those who are concerned with literature. It is in effect
a decision to reject the very concept of literature that has been in
operation in Western culture since the fifth century BC. Theories
of the structuralist/post-structuralist type aim to replace the concept of a literary work with that of a text, using a value-free notion
of 'text'. The concept of literature is rejected precisely because
it embodies, in its creative-imaginative aspect as well as in its
mimetic aspect, what are taken to be unsupportable and undesirable humanist values.

The substitution of the concept of fiction for the concepts of
novel and short story, the post-structuralists would argue, is
beneficial exactly because it *does not* discriminate between literary
works and other types of invented stories. The emergence of this
use of the concept of fiction at the time when a new mass-culture
was in the making, is indicative, these theorists would argue, of
the challenge to the bourgeois concept of literary art and indeed
of the dramatically diminished importance of this concept. Structuralism and post-structuralism are thus revolutionary theories,
not in the sense that they offer revolutionary new insights, but
rather in the sense that they attempt to revolutionize literary
practice. What they offer is a strong recommendation that literary
research should refocus on different sets of problems along with

revised assumptions about texts (rather than literature) which
define these problems.

In defence of the concept of literature

There are two lines of argument against this 'radical revision', if
it can be called a revision, of the concept of literature. The first
line is to point out that it is difficult to conceive that even the
staunchest deconstructionist would want to accept the full consequences of the rejection of those humanist values embodied in the
concept of literature. Some of the die-hard proponents of structuralism have belatedly woken up to this fact and are now flaunting
their humanist credentials by arguing publicly, as does Tzvetan
Todorov, that 'it is impossible (without being inconsistent) to
defend human rights out of one side of your mouth while
deconstructing the idea of humanity out of the other'.[14] The point
behind Todorov's observation is that the concept of literature as
it is defined by the requirement of the creative use of the imagination and humanly interesting content has a central place in a
scheme of values which defines the very idea of humanity. A radical revision of the concept of literature cannot take place without
a radical revision of the concept of humanity. In particular, if one
gives up all standards of coherence and unity, including such
standards as define rational argument and individual identity, one
also gives up any possibility of arguing and taking a reasoned
stand against repression in all its forms as well as any possibility
of defining and defending the rights of the individual.

The second line of argument is to point out that the concept of
text cannot bear the theoretical weight put on it by structuralism
and post-structuralism. The concept of 'text' is logically secondary
to the concept of 'work' or related concepts which designate types
of text. A text is always a text of something, of a literary work, a
philosophical treatise, a historical chronicle, a historical monograph, a medical article, etc. A text cannot be understood just as
a text. Indeed, considered as a text, a text does not have any

[14] Tzvetan Todorov, 'All against Humanity', review of Robert Scholes, *Textual
Power: Literary Theory and the Teaching of English, Times Literary Supplement*,
4 Oct. 1985, 1094.

determinate textual (rhetorical) features at all. It gets determinate textual (rhetorical) features only when it is construed as a *work*.

Consider an example. In the first act of Shakespeare's *Julius Caesar* the tribunes Marullus and Flavius reproach the festive crowd they meet in the streets for celebrating Caesar's victory over Pompey's sons. Central in the scene is a speech made by Marullus which turns the mood of the crowd from high-spirited rejoicing to guilty shame. The speech is a set rhetorical speech with a pattern of hyperboles and repetitions apparently designed to work on the emotions of the crowd. The character of this episode as a textual (rhetorical) feature cannot be determined until one knows what one is reading. If *Julius Caesar* were read as a piece of reportive or fact-stating discourse, then this episode would be included in the text to establish certain propositions as true in the mind of the reader, to instil the belief that this is how two tribunes by the name of Marullus and Flavius behaved on a day in October of 45 BC in Rome during Caesar's triumph. (Not to complicate this point further, leave out of account that Shakespeare transfers Caesar's victory and celebration to 15 March the following year.) However, if *Julius Caesar* is read as a literary work, this episode must be construed differently and thus becomes a different rhetorical feature altogether. For then the confrontation of the tribunes with the crowd, focused in the set speech by Marullus, can be seen as foreshadowing the forum scene in which first Brutus and then Antony, through their respective speeches, change the mood of the crowd. It is part of a pattern of repetition which establishes, through three parallel scenes, the fickleness of the crowd and its role as an instrument of power which can be controlled through rhetoric. In a more comprehensive analysis of *Julius Caesar* one could show the point of giving the crowd this prominent role in the play, but it is not necessary to do that here. The textual characteristic of the episode described as an element in a pattern of repetition is dependent on the reader construing the text as a literary work just as the textual characteristic of the episode as a true or false account of actual historical events is dependent upon construing the text as fact-stating discourse.

If there is no such thing as a text in general, but only texts of works, then the theoretical basis for rejecting the concept of literature vanishes and the failure to deal with its *mimetic* aspect (which defines literature as an evaluative concept) must be seen as just that: a theoretical failure. It is possible to supplement this line of argument with the simpler but equally weighty argument that a radical revision of the concept of literature is merely a way of ducking the problem or changing the subject without admitting that this is what one is doing. Such a move does not merely amount to theoretical failure but also constitutes a form of intellectual dishonesty.

There are, then, various types of reason for rejecting the post-structuralist attack on the concept of literature. There is the epistemological reason that the premiss on which rests the rhetorical chain supporting the identification of fiction and literature is dubious, even in its best and most qualified philosophical formulation. The degree to which language organizes 'our world' is a controversial issue and it is arguable that anti-realists and constructivists cannot really be said to have provided any clear account of what it might mean that the human mind, through language or in any other way, 'posits' the reality a human being meets. Then there is the logical reason that the argument itself offered in support of the identification of literature and fiction is invalid in each of its steps. Thirdly, there is the evaluative consideration: the values embodied in the concept of literature are so closely connected with broader cultural and human values that it would be inconceivable for even the most committed deconstructionists to reject them. And, finally, there is the conceptual reason: one cannot substitute for the concept of literature a more general concept of text which can be characterized theoretically in an illuminating way.

What literary aesthetics has to deal with is an existing practice of literature within which are embodied the concept of literature and literary values. This practice has been accorded a central place in the culture that traces its roots back to classical Greece. In a broad sense, the values embodied in this practice are humanist values closely linked to the concept of an autonomous human individual possessing interests, goals, and powers of reason. The task for literary aesthetics is to clarify what is involved in the practice and give an explanatory account of the main aspects of those conventions defining literary practice. It is not possible to change the subject and still claim that one is saying something of interest to those who care about literature. That is simply an abdication of critical responsibility.

Fiction and levels of literary description

The relations between literature and fiction and literature and reality must, then, be a central theme in literary theory since these relationships are fundamental in the definition of how literature presents a humanly interesting content. In the formulation and discussion of these relationships it is useful to make three distinctions, which we will present in the following sections.

Literal and thematic levels

The first is between two levels in the literary work itself: the literal level, or subject level, or level of reports, and the thematic level, or symbolic level, or level of reflection. The distinction used to be made as a matter of course in discussions of the cognitive status of literature, but has disappeared almost completely in recent literary theory when the problem of the cognitive status of literature was pushed to the sidelines.[15]

Every literary work contains sentences describing particular events, situations, characters, and places:

The first account that I can Recollect, or could ever learn of myself, was, that I had wandred among a Crew of those People they call *Gypsies*, or *Egyptians*; but I believe it was but a very little while that I had been among them, for I had not had my Skin discolour'd, or blacken'd, as they do very young to all the Children they carry about with them, nor can I tell how I came among them, or how I got from them.

It was at *Colchester* in *Essex*, that those People left me; and I have a Notion in my Head, that I left them there (that is, that I hid myself and wou'd not go any farther with them) but I am not able to be particular in that Account (Daniel Defoe, *Moll Flanders* (London, 1722) ch. 1).

The debate about fiction and the logic of fictional discourse has on the whole been carried out with reference to this type of utterance since it offers the clearest and most perspicuous illustration of problems of reference and truth. It is on this level that it seems unproblematic to say that at least some literary works are fictions: invented stories and not history, inviting make-believe. In this case

[15] For versions of this distinction see standard traditional treatments of the problem such as Beardsley's ch. 9, in *Aesthetics*, or Weitz, 'Truth in Literature'. The distinction was put to use again in Olsen, *The Structure of Literary Understanding*, ch. 3, and Gerald Graff has remarked on the fateful consequences of ignoring it in *Literature Against Itself*, ch. 6.

the lines are written by Daniel Defoe, but are presented as coming from the pen of a character who never existed, Moll Flanders, and the events described never took place. The events, like the character, are made up. It is clear that the intention is that the reader should make-believe, not literally believe, their content.

However, it is not immediately clear at the literal or report level that literary works at that level are *necessarily* to be construed as fictions:

> Five years have passed; five summers, with the length
> Of five long winters! and again I hear
> These waters, rolling from their mountain-springs
> With a soft inland murmur. Once again
> Do I behold these steep and lofty cliffs,
> That on a wild secluded scene impress
> Thoughts of more deep seclusion; and connect
> The landscape with the quiet of the sky.
> The day is come when I again repose
> Here, under this dark sycamore, and view
> These plots of cottage-ground, these orchard-tufts,
> Which at this season, with their unripe fruits,
> Are clad in one green hue, and lose themselves
> 'Mid groves and copses.
>
> (William Wordsworth, 'Lines Composed a
> Few Miles above Tintern Abbey,
> on Revisiting the Banks of the Wye
> during a Tour. July 13, 1798')

It is not at all obvious that these lines and the rest of 'Tintern Abbey' are presented as fiction:

'No poem of mine', [Wordsworth] said, afterwards, 'was composed under circumstances more pleasant for me to remember than this. I began it upon leaving Tintern, after crossing the Wye, and concluded it just as I was entering Bristol in the evening, after a ramble of four or five days, with my sister. Not a line of it was altered, and not any part of it written down till I reached Bristol.' When he did reach Bristol it was written down at once and taken to Cottle, to be included in *Lyrical Ballads*, at the end of the volume. Not a line of it ever was altered, and the *Tintern Abbey* that we know today is identical with that composed on the Wye banks—an unusual occurrence in Wordsworth's poetry.[16]

---

[16] Mary Moorman, *William Wordsworth: A Biography. The Early Years 1770–1803* (Oxford, 1957), 401–2.

'Tintern Abbey' was an outpouring by Wordsworth of descriptions and reflections at a specific time and with reference to specific visits to a specific place. The time and place of the visits are given in the title and in the poem itself. If these lines are nevertheless to be considered as presented in the fictive mode, we must assume that *that* intention, for some reason, can be seen as overriding the intention to describe his personal experience on revisiting the banks of the Wye during a tour, 13 July, 1798. What is theoretically interesting about 'Tintern Abbey' is that it does not present any propositions with which the reader has to agree or disagree. What makes the poem valuable is the presentation of nature and the speaker's reflections on the development of his own view of nature and its restorative power. It does not matter to the literary appreciation of the poem whether it is presented fictively or not. What is important is the theme that grows out of the presentation of subject in the poem. There is a hint here of a possible interpretation of the mimetic aspect of literature which does not conflict with seeing literature as a creative-imaginative effort, but we shall have to leave that aside for the moment.

The problem whether the invitation to take up a literary stance necessarily involves an invitation to take up a fictive stance rears its head on the literal level of literary works in other ways as well. Many literary works not only contain descriptions of historical persons and events but might be based wholly on historical situations. This has led some philosophers, as we saw in Chapter 3, to conclude that literary works are a mixture of the fictional and the non-fictional. '[I]n *War and Peace*', says John Searle, 'the story of Pierre and Natasha is a fictional story about fictional characters, but the Russia of *War and Peace* is the real Russia, and the war against Napoleon is the real war against the real Napoleon.'[17] In discussing such cases, from the point of view of fiction, we proposed that it is helpful to draw on the distinction between content and mode of presentation. Though some propositional content might be factual in nature it might none the less serve a fictive purpose, for example in helping to characterize fictive states of affairs. We suggested at the time that from the literary point of view there was a standing presumption that such passages should

---

[17] Searle, 'The Logical Status of Fictional Discourse', in *Expression and Meaning*, 72.

be treated in this way. Both conventionally, in terms of the literary institution, as well as psychologically, Searle's position that works oscillate between fiction and non-fiction is unsatisfactory, since it means that the reader of a literary work has to be seen as involved in a constant change of perspective, implying a constant change in the premises of the literary appreciation of the work. Note, however, that while it is natural to extend the fictive mode in this way in the *War and Peace* case, where there is at least some undisputed fictional content, it is not obvious that a parallel move is desirable in the 'Tintern Abbey' case which perhaps has no fictional content. A more extreme proposal, which will be discussed later, takes a quite different line; instead of extending the fictive mode in some cases it in effect denies it in all. On this view literary works consist of statements, some of which are true and some false, with the majority being true because they must be construed as saying something about *types of things (events, persons)* in the world.

Though the problems of the relationship between literature and fiction have no obvious solutions even when we deal with the literal or report level of literary works, the problem itself is at least clearly defined in relation to the description of particular characters, situations, events, actions, plots, etc. which constitute this level of a literary work. The problem becomes much less easy to define once one leaves the literal level and moves on to the thematic or symbolic level. We have argued that it is a defining convention of literary practice that the author should produce and the reader search for a humanly interesting content. It is arguable that this content can be formulated in a series of 'reflections' or 'thematic statements', generalizations over the characters, situations, events, actions, plots, etc. which are presented at the literal level of the work. These reflections state the *theme* of the work. 'Shakespeare's *Julius Caesar* presents the futility of opposing the forces of history through individual human action', would be such a thematic statement. But the reader does not always have to interpret the work himself. Sometimes the author generalizes the significance of the situations he presents:

> To each his sufferings; all are men,
> Condemned alike to groan:
> The tender for another's pain,
>   *   *   *

The unfeeling for his own.
Yet, ah! why should they know their fate?
Since sorrow never comes too late,
And happiness too swiftly flies.
Thought would destroy their paradise.
No more: where ignorance is bliss,
'Tis folly to be wise.

This is the final stanza of Thomas Gray's 'Ode on a Distant Prospect of Eton College' where he draws the conclusion from the presentation of the happy boys he sees/remembers there and the host of cares and sufferings which he presents as waiting for them when they grow up.

Theme and subject

The example suggests that it is useful to introduce a second distinction, between *theme* and *subject*. Subject is what the particular descriptions at the literal or report level are *of*: the 'chunks of experience' which the work presents to the reader, the concrete individual fates of the characters, the environment in which they move, the things they say, think, feel, etc. The subject of 'Ode on a Distant Prospect of Eton College' is the happy boys whom the speaker imagines at play and work as he sees the school at a distance, as well as the memory which the speaker has of his youth there (the two are inseparable in the poem). This may seem a slightly artificial notion of subject, for subject, in critical discussion, is often not separated from theme. And subject and theme do overlap, since once one starts talking about the subject of a work at a certain level of generality, thematic concepts have to be employed. However, the distinction between subject and theme can naturally be construed as a distinction between the facts, experiences, etc. described in a work and the interpretation of these phenomena through abstraction and generalization. And it is this contrast which is theoretically interesting in the present discussion.

Now it makes little sense to say that such content, which can be stated as a theme, is fictional. Nor does it make good sense to construe it as being amenable to evaluation as true or false. A theme is not a type of discourse, fictional or fact-stating, but rather a conception (of its subject) which discourse expresses. And different types of discourse define and express theme in different ways. Literature has its own highly characteristic way of doing so. There is, however, one way in which the question of the cognitive status may raise its head at the thematic level. It is a symptom of the poverty of the debate about fiction in recent literary theory that the problem was formulated over thirty years ago, once again by Beardsley, and needs to be rediscovered. Beardsley distinguishes between *theme* and *thesis*:

A theme, then, is something that can be thought about, or dwelt upon, but it is not something that can be called true or false. What I shall mean by the perhaps awkward term 'thesis', however, is precisely something about, or in, the work that *can* be called true or false, if anything can. Critics say, for example, that Shakespeare's *Tempest* embodies a mystical view of life; that Upton Sinclair's *The Jungle* is a protest against the injustices suffered by the poor under a free-wheeling economic system; that there is implicit Platonism in Spenser's 'Epithalamion' and Shelley's 'Epipsychidion'. We speak of the philosophical, religious, ethical, and social ideas in Milton, Shaw, and Sartre. We debate whether Thomas Mann's *Doctor Faustus* is optimistic or pessimistic, how much there is of Schopenhauer and Bergson in Proust. And I take these ideological ingredients to be statable in a form in which we could say, though perhaps only with some hesitation, that they are true or false: even pessimism may be a view of life, not merely a feeling.[18]

While accepting something akin to the distinction between theme and thesis and agreeing that there is a theoretical problem to be formulated by the help of this distinction, one need not accept Beardsley's rather narrow conception of theme. The question which arises in any case is whether it is a convention of literary practice that the reader should expect a literary work to express a thesis, in Beardsley's sense of a bearer of truth, over and above a theme. Again this is a question which will be addressed later.

Saying and showing

The third distinction which is useful in the discussion of the relationship between literature and fiction and between literature and reality is that between saying and showing or stating and presenting. It is sometimes held that even if literary works are

[18] Beardsley, *Aesthetics*, 404.

fictional at the literal level nevertheless the particular situations, events, objects, actions, plots, etc. which a work presents, provide the reader with insight into real life, provide examples of possible modes of experience which the reader can engage. These insights or modes of experience, so the account goes, are not in the form of statable themes or propositions about human life for literature does not deal in propositional knowledge. An interpretation can indicate what the mode of experience or insight is, but it cannot be a substitute for it. In *Julius Caesar* the tragedy of Brutus is that he is crushed by history. He is presented by Shakespeare as a fine man, a loyal friend, a dedicated and considerate husband, a kind master, and a good general. Nevertheless, in the role he is called on to play in the great drama of the transition from the Roman Republic to the Roman Empire, all his excellent human qualities come to nought. His role in this drama is defined by Shakespeare's play, but once the role is adopted, Brutus becomes its prisoner and his admirable human qualities cannot redeem him, nor do they count for anything. Through his presentation of Brutus Shakespeare offers the insight or the experience of what it is to be crushed by history. No interpretation of the play can offer this insight or experience. Only a thoughtful reading of the play can do that. This, some would argue, is what makes literature humanly and culturally important, what makes it a repository of human values.

The aspect of literature here, as with all the others we have glanced at, is clearly recognizable and must be acknowledged. Some literary works undoubtedly have invented content and in that regard can be construed as being fictional. Some works do contain passages that can be firmly tied to the biography of the author, passages that describe historical events, persons, and real places. Works of literature do have themes, and a number also present theses. And works do present readers with modes of experience. The question for the literary theorist is whether any of these aspects of literature define the peculiar value which makes literature culturally and humanly significant and thus provide what the reader demands from a work *as literature*. It is this question we will address in the chapters to follow.

12

The Theory of Novelistic Truth

The traditional version

'Literature' is an evaluative humanistic concept defined, within an institutional practice, by a creative-imaginative aspect and a *mimetic* aspect. The *mimetic* value of a literary work consists in the most general terms in its having a humanly interesting content. The problem for literary theory is how this humanly interesting content is constituted and where it is located. Traditional answers have made use of the concepts of truth and knowledge; literature is held to present some kind of truth, to yield some sort of insight, which makes it cognitively valuable. The 'truth' of literature is located on different levels and explained in different ways by different theoretical traditions.

It was noted in the last chapter that since the very beginning of the novel, novelists have been concerned that their stories should be read with the same seriousness as history because their novels were as instructive as history. This concern is perhaps nowhere more apparent than in Dickens, who insists that his novels are indeed true in their particulars, and his descriptions *true*, not merely probable or lifelike:

It is useless to discuss whether the conduct and character of the girl seems natural or unnatural, probable or improbable, right or wrong. IT IS TRUE. Every man who has watched these melancholy shades of life, must know it to be so. From the first introduction of that poor wretch, to her laying her bloodstained head upon the robber's breast, there is not a word exaggerated or over-wrought. ('Preface' to *Oliver Twist*)

And in cases where he is dealing with actual historical events Dickens is careful to claim that his descriptions are accurate and true of the actual historical particulars:

In the description of the principal outrages [of the Gordon Riots], reference has been had to the best authorities of that time, such as they are;

the account given in this Tale, of all the main features of the Riots, is substantially correct.

Mr. Dennis's allusions to the flourishing condition of his trade in those days, have their foundation in Truth, and not in the Author's fancy. Any file of old Newspapers, or odd volume of the Annual Register, will prove this with terrible ease. ('Preface' to *Barnaby Rudge*)

We saw that this concern developed in modernists like Virginia Woolf and Henry James into a general claim that fiction was as *true as history* and was made true *in the same way* as history, in short, that the novel and history did not really differ:

as the picture is reality, so the novel is history. That is the only general description (which does it justice) that we may give of the novel. But history also is allowed to represent life; it is not, any more than painting, expected to apologize. The subject-matter of fiction is stored up likewise in documents and records, and if it will not give itself away, as they say in California, it must speak with assurance, with the tone of a historian.[1]

The view that the novel is true, true in its particulars, is not, however, a view exclusive to authors. Readers have always had a tendency to identify events, situations, characters, and relationships from novels with events, situations, characters, and relationships in reality which the author can be taken as describing. So strong has this tendency been that there has grown up a convention of prefacing novels with disclaimers, warnings that the novel does not make true statements about what it seems to be making true statements about:

Like *Changing Places*, to which it is a kind of sequel, *Small World* resembles what is sometimes called the real world, without corresponding exactly to it, and it is peopled by figments of the imagination (the name of one of the minor characters has been changed in later editions to avoid misunderstanding on this score). Rummidge is not Birmingham, though it owes something to popular prejudices about that city. There really is an underground chapel at Heathrow and a James Joyce Pub in Zürich, but no universities in Limerick or Darlington; nor, as far as I know, was there ever a British Council representative resident in Genoa. The MLA Convention of 1979 did not take place in New York, though I have drawn on the programme for the 1978 one, which did. And so on.[2]

The necessity of disclaimers like this was demonstrated by the Bullingham case discussed in Chapter 5, and it indicates the strong

[1] James, 'The Art of Fiction' in *'The Art of Fiction' and Other Essays*, 5.
[2] 'Author's Note' to Lodge, *Small World*.

position that the concept of novelistic truth (of the novel as true in its particulars) has among ordinary readers. Indeed, the lesson of the Bullingham case is that the view that the novel is true in its particulars is taken very seriously, not only by unreflective authors and readers, but also by important institutions like the courts.

Such disclaimers also have another interesting function: they present implicitly essentially the same claim that Dickens and older authors present explicitly. Prefacing a work with a disclaimer like this does not merely deny that the novel describes particular historical events, situations, characters, and relationships, etc. It implicitly also makes the claim that the novel, stripped of the names of these particulars, *does* actually describe such events, etc., and that what it says about them is all too true for comfort. Issuing a disclaimer like this the author is thereby making the claim that his work is of a type that naturally can be construed as presenting truths about particular historical events or personages. For the very act of issuing a denial presupposes that there is something that needs to be denied.

The view that the novel is true in its particulars, true *of* certain types of situation, person, etc. in the real world, and that this is what gives it a humanly interesting content, is, then, strong among lay readers as well as among artists. And the view has a certain plausibility. For at least part of the appeal of a novel like *Small World* is that the reader recognizes the portraits of characters like Philip Swallow, the distinguished-looking but undistinguished Professor of English at Rummidge, and Morris Zapp, the over-powering American academic, as portraits of figures familiar in real life. It is debatable whether Lodge makes these characters function as types representing different academic cultures but their interest does not depend on that. It is enough that the reader recognizes that the world has its Philip Swallows and Morris Zapps. Part of the pleasure of reading, as Aristotle pointed out, is to recognize that this is that, to make, that is, an identification.[3]

Formulating the theory

It may perhaps be claiming too much for this view to call it a *theory* of novelistic truth, for the view has not traditionally received

---

[3] Aristotle, *Poetics* (1448^b); *Rhetoric* (1371^b).

much explicit formulation or theoretical backing.[4] However, recently a version of the view has been defended by Graham Dunstan Martin. Fictional entities such as characters, places, events, or actions, he argues, are collages 'of familiar bits and pieces'.[5] A fiction will therefore

> never be entirely fictitious in the sense of there being nothing anywhere that corresponds to it in any way: there will indeed always be things that correspond to its every detail, somewhere, in some way. In short, all its constituent parts will be drawn from reality. It is their non-occurrence together, in that combination, that constitutes the fiction.[6]

What Martin calls 'fictional concepts' have 'referring components';[7] the various partial descriptions that constitute the description of a fictional entity refer to entities, qualities, and relations that exist in the real world, and they are true or false of these entities, qualities, and relations. As a rule, Martin argues, the description of each single part or some combination of parts of the fictional entity is true. A composite description becomes fictional and thus also false only when qualities and relations are attributed to a character, place, or event which does not exist *in toto*.

Evelyn Waugh's *The Ordeal of Gilbert Pinfold*, for example, describes a series of actions which are attributed to a fictional character, Gilbert Pinfold. However, the described actions and behaviour can be observed in various individuals in real life ('we have the author Evelyn Waugh's testimony that some of these events really happened to him', says Martin[8]), so, according to this version of the theory, Waugh's various descriptions of Pinfold refer to the behaviour and actions of Waugh himself and his associates and say something true about them. Furthermore, an important point, it is the fact that a literary work says something about real

---

[4] Part of the reason for this might have been that the rise of literary theory as an academic discipline took place after Russell's analysis of descriptive sentences had been called into question by Strawson in 'On Referring'. This, and Austin's work, opened the possibility of seeing 'stating' as just one of many uses to which sentences could be put. Literary uses of language were immediately identified as 'etiolated' or 'non-serious' uses. For many, this seemed the obvious answer to the long tradition of suspicion within philosophy of literature as a type of lying or falsity. Strawson's conclusions were immediately applied to story-telling by H. L. A. Hart in the article 'A Logician's Fairy-Tale', *Philosophical Review*, 60 (1951), 198–212.

[5] Martin, 'A New Look', 225.   [6] Ibid. 229.

[7] Ibid. 225.   [8] Ibid. 231.

behaviour, real actions, real situations, and real events, which gives the literary work its value and makes it interesting to the reader. For, Martin says in another discussion of the problem, 'if poetry is supposed to be a form of discourse which does not, in any way, even indirectly refer to the world, what interest would there be in it?'[9]

In its strongest formulation, then, as represented perhaps by Martin, the Theory of Novelistic Truth rejects the analysis of the literary work as fiction in the sense we have developed. Literature is instead construed and assessed as a species of fact-stating discourse with many of the concomitant commitments. Even on the literal level the literary work is subject to judgements about the truth or falsity of its statements and descriptions, and these judgements are of exactly the same kind as judgements about the truth or falsity of other types of fact-stating discourse.

There are, however, serious weaknesses in the theory as outlined. First, it runs together the question of reference and the question of truth. As we argued in Chapter 5, fiction *per se* is compatible with reference. When in *Brighton Rock* Graham Greene begins the book with the sentence, 'Hale knew, before he had been in Brighton three hours, that they meant to murder him', Greene no doubt intends to refer to Brighton. We also argued, though, that the Brighton of *Brighton Rock* still in a sense remains a fictional city, for when the reader invokes information about the real Brighton, in an imaginative supplementation of the novel, he must select only such information as is authorized by the rest of the work, i.e., such information as is suitably connected to the aspects under which Brighton is presented in *Brighton Rock*. And as long as *Brighton Rock* is construed as a work of fiction, there will be imaginative Brighton-aspects in the novel which do not hold true of the real Brighton of the 1930s.

The mistake of the Theory of Novelistic Truth is to assume that reference is sufficient to define a piece of discourse as fact-stating:

There is thus no problem of fiction. It can be analysed into true and false referring components. 'Yossarian' is a fictional instance, whose referring components refer to a large number of war-time situations and events.[10]

Referring components, however, are neither true nor false. They yield truths and falsehoods only when incorporated into

---

[9] Martin, *Language, Truth and Poetry*, 84.
[10] Martin, 'A New Look', 233.

propositions or assertions. Even if we grant that literary fictions (sometimes) aim to refer to actual things or events it does not follow that they have the further aim of stating facts about those referents.

Moreover, the Theory of Novelistic Truth confuses the relation of reference with other relations between the literary work and the world. In particular it assumes that life-likeness is sufficient to secure reference and therefore truth. Henry James talks about 'the *illusion* of life' and 'the *air* of reality' as the 'supreme virtue of a novel'.[11] Virginia Woolf, when she attacks H. G. Wells, Arnold Bennett, and John Galsworthy for a lack of truth ('life escapes [them], and perhaps without life nothing else is worthwhile'[12]), also uses the criterion of resemblance: 'Look within, and life, it seems, is very far from being "like this".' Again, though, as we argued in Chapter 5, similarity is not a referential relation. It is undoubtedly true, as Martin would also argue,[13] that there are people in the real world who are in many respects similar to Philip Swallow and Morris Zapp in *Small World*. There may even be professors of English in the academic jet-set who resemble these characters in *all* respects. But similarity, or even complete matching, does not entail reference or denotation, far less the aim to state truths.

Nor does the Theory of Novelistic Truth distinguish between reference and genesis. 'We have the author Evelyn Waugh's testimony that some of these events really happened to him', says Martin (quoted above). This testimony concerns the genesis of the work, what inspired the author to write the work, or which events he kept his eye on when writing it. But genesis, as we have also argued, does not add up to reference. There is little doubt that *Small World* originated in David Lodge's experience of the conference-mania of the international academic scene of which he himself is a part, and that he kept his eyes on events he had experienced as a conferee when he wrote the novel. The fact that these events inspired the novel, that Lodge must have had these events in mind when he wrote, is, however, again neither necessary nor sufficient for establishing that the novel *refers* to these events or makes true claims about them.

Finally, there is the distinction between reference and

---

[11] James, 'The Art of Fiction' in *'The Art of Fiction' and Other Essays*, 12.

[12] 'Modern Fiction' in *Collected Essays*, 105.

[13] See the comments made on Graham Dunstan Martin in Ch. 5.

instantiation. Actual objects might well instantiate some of the descriptions constitutive of fictional entities. However, fictive utterances do not denote or refer to such objects. This, though, is apparently a crucial premiss in the theory: fictional entities are collages of familiar bits and pieces, i.e. those things which instantiate fictive descriptions, and *therefore* those descriptions can be construed as making truth claims *about* those bits and pieces.

The paradigm of reference rests on a speaker's intention to identify an object, usually for the purpose of saying something about it. In the literary case, an author can refer in this sense as long as the intention is realizable. However, although reference might be *facilitated* by the use of 'connotations' or 'referring components', in Martin's sense, it is not *constituted* by them. There are different ways an intention to refer could be recognized. The Theory of Novelistic Truth not only fails to clarify the role of reference in literary works but also, because of that, fails to establish that literary works must be construed as aiming to state truths about particulars. Above all it fails to establish that it is an essential property of a literary work that it should refer to actual particulars.

Proponents of the theory can, at this stage, make a defensive move. The distinctions made above between reference and truth, reference and similarity, reference and instantiation, and reference and genesis, may be admitted to be valid and illuminating. But, it could be argued, these distinctions do not by themselves establish that the sentences at the report level in a literary work do not refer and do not make truth-claims. Even if it is admitted that traditional formulations of the theory confuse the question of reference with the question of truth and confuse similarity and reference, and also admitted that reference is constituted by speaker's intention, while similarity only involves a relation between two objects being compared, it may still be argued that the Theory of Novelistic Truth can easily shift its ground and be restated in intentionalist terms. The theory may be reformulated as saying simply that in choosing to write a literary work, the author intends to refer and to make truth-claims about the referents. Writing a literary work, so the argument might run, logically entails making truth-claims about those persons, events, actions, and so on in the real world which the characters, events, actions in a work most closely 'fit'. This argument does not say that a reader must ascertain in each single case whether or not the author intends to refer and make truth-claims. It makes the point rather that it is a convention of literary practice (a feature of the logic of the institution of literature) that literary works are understood as expressing these intentions.

If the theory is restated in intentionalist terms, then it has to be defended with reference to the logic and conventions of literary practice. For the theory to be acceptable there would have to be features of this practice which would make it reasonable to assume that to write a literary work is to make truth-claims about the particulars to which the literary work refers. There are two aspects of literary practice of which the Theory of Novelistic Truth could possibly be taken to provide an explanation.

First of all it might be construed as an explanation of how a literary work is understood. However, in Chapters 3 and 5, we saw that there is nothing in fiction *per se* which implies that the intelligibility of fictional discourse relies on its referential status. Fiction is intelligible because fictional descriptions are made up of predicative expressions which also have a recognizable non-fictive use: or, put in the material mode, because fictional entities are comparable to entities in the real world. It is not a precondition for the intelligibility of fictional descriptions that they should refer or make truth-claims. Consequently there is nothing in the way in which *fiction* is understood which could be a reason for accepting the Theory of Novelistic Truth as valid for *literature*. Secondly, it might be maintained that the theory offers an explanation of one of the basic assumptions of literary practice referred to earlier, namely that it is a function of a literary work, in some way, to express ideas about human nature, and that a work is valuable in so far as it serves this function and thus presents a humanly interesting content. If truth is a precondition of a humanly interesting content, then the theory can be offered as an explanation of an important evaluative assumption which defines literary practice. However, there is nothing in the arguments so far advanced on behalf of the Theory of Novelistic Truth which establishes a connection between reference (and consequently truth) and *value*. Nor are there any general logical considerations which force us to suppose that interest in literary works must reside in their truth-claims at the level of particulars. Obviously, in a study of this kind, much more needs to be said about the relation between truth and literary value. However, in the mean time it is worth noting that since most literary works, according to the theory itself, would contain a number of false statements, this should, if there were a simple correlation between truth and value, influence our appreciation of a work in a way it clearly does not. It is no part of the literary stance to test the work for a percentage of false statements. Indeed, the skill with which an author moulds and changes historical facts to suit artistic purpose is an object of praise not of censure. When Shakespeare in *Julius Caesar* moves Caesar's victory over Pompey's sons to 45 BC this is no ground for artistic criticism.

Truth and literary appreciation

We can perhaps best illustrate the point that questions of truth and reference do not enter into literary appreciation at the report level, and therefore do not influence value judgements about literary works, by offering an extended example which actually engages literary practice.

In Ibsen's *Rosmersholm* Rebecca West reacts with horror to the suggestion that there is a possibility that she may be Dr West's real daughter rather than his adopted foster daughter. The reaction seems in excess of the fact, and Headmaster Kroll is led to ask why she reacts so strongly. Rebecca answers that it is simply the discovery of her illegitimacy that makes her react with such horror. Kroll accepts this explanation 'for the nonce' (Act III). But some modern critics have not done so. Instead they connect this over-reaction to the news of her illegitimacy with her refusal to become Rosmer's second wife in spite of her final admission in Act IV of her overwhelming passion for Rosmer. Admitting this passion to Rosmer, she gives as one reason why she cannot become his wife that she has a past which comes between them and prevents her from giving herself to him. This 'past', some modern critics maintain, is the fact that she has had a sexual relationship with Dr West, and her reaction of horror to the news that she may be his daughter is exactly what may be expected in connection with a discovery that she has been the partner in an incestuous relationship.

This interpretation of Rebecca's reaction sees it as precisely in line with—or true to—such behaviour as could be attributed to real people who, in similar circumstances, have discovered that they have been partners in an incestuous relationship. In as much as the interpretation holds that it is one aim of the play to make a truth-claim about such behaviour then it conforms with the Theory of Novelistic Truth. However, the interpretation does not explain how Rebecca's behaviour contributes to the aesthetic value of the play. At most the critic can commend Ibsen for having displayed a sharp insight into the sort of behaviour which a recognition of an incestuous relationship would cause. Since those critics who do interpret Rebecca's behaviour in this way tend to defend their interpretation with reference to some type of psychoanalytic theory, Ibsen is praised for having anticipated Freud.

The appreciation of the *aesthetic* value of this 'piece' of Rebecca's behaviour, on the other hand, must be grounded in an appreciation of the function which the reaction has in the play as a whole: through an appreciation, that is, of its artistic purpose. It is with reference to this function that the question whether there is an incest motif in the play has to be settled. And there are other, more plausible, explanations of Rebecca's over-reaction than seeing it as due to the fact that she has had an incestuous relationship with Dr West. The pronounced over-reaction by Rebecca to the news that she may be Dr West's daughter may simply be introduced by Ibsen to make the point that Rebecca's liberation is much more a surface phenomenon than she herself recognizes, to make the point that liberation from the ideas of the past is not merely or even mainly an intellectual matter. This explanation would place her reaction in a pattern defining her as a traditional rather than a liberated woman: the fact that she lies about her age, that the basis for her relationship to Rosmer, an overwhelming passion, is the same as Beate's, that she enters into the traditional role of the intriguing and deceiving woman in her attempt to get rid of Beate. If the reader accepts an incestuous relationship to Dr West in Rebecca's past this will weaken this pattern, since one does not have to be a slave to convention and the ideas of the past, nor particularly prejudiced, to react against that type of relationship. This simple explanation of her reaction also ties in with another characteristic of Rebecca which disappears if one accepts the presence of an incest motif: Rebecca is a thoroughly unreliable woman who constantly changes her explanation of her motives and goals. The admission that she has a past which prevents her from giving herself to Rosmer is just the last revelation in a series where the reader does not know what is true and what is false. The final scene of the play, when Rebecca and Rosmer together go the way of Beate and jump from the bridge, is motivated by the doubt that Rebecca's deviousness has raised in the breast of Rosmer. When she assures him that he has ennobled her soul through the quiet love that he has inspired in her (which she tries to make him believe just after she has said she has a 'past' which prevents her from becoming his wife) Rosmer says:

Oh Rebecca,—how can I trust you fully? You who have concealed so much!—And now you bring out this new thing. Is there some hidden motivation behind this,—then tell me straight out. Do you wish to achieve something through this? I want to do everything I can for you.

It is to end this doubt that they jump into the river. The reader who chooses the explanation that Rebecca's past consists in an incestuous relationship with Dr West must accept that Rebecca is suddenly, on this occasion, to be trusted when she says she has a past that comes between her and Rosmer. However, there is no indication in the play that Rebecca is to be taken as more reliable on this occasion than on other occasions. Rosmer's accusation of unreliability comes only a few lines after she has admitted to having a past (though it comes in connection with another issue). And the play does seem to give a point to Rebecca's unreliability which is weakened if she is suddenly believed to tell the truth. For Rebecca is Rosmer's opposite. He is identified with Rosmersholm; he *is* Rosmersholm with its generations of officers and clergymen, the leading family, the cornerstone of the district. Rebecca is indeterminate; the mystery around her birth leaves her without any social or generic definition; the constant shifts in her explanations leave her without any personal definition. This makes her a personification of what has come to Rosmersholm: a dissolution of all tradition without any well-defined new set of values to take its place.

We shall not argue this interpretative point further, though other arguments could be given to reject the presence of an incest motif in *Rosmersholm*. However, the point relevant in the present discussion is this: the decision whether such a motif can be found in the play depends on whether or not it can be given an artistic function in the characterization of Rebecca and in the definition of the theme of the play. In the appreciation of the play as a literary work, the question whether Rebecca West's behaviour and the information she gives us are indications of an incestuous relationship between her and Dr West is decided primarily with reference to artistic function. There must, of course, if an incest motif is to be identified, also be the possibility that her behaviour and the information she gives could be interpreted as indicating an incestuous relationship. That is, Ibsen must rely on a certain degree of *verisimilitude* to get his point across. But appreciation involves no evaluative judgement concerning 'how true' Rebecca's behaviour is to the actual reaction patterns of women who have been involved in similar relationships. Such a judgement may or may not be passed by the reader but it does not make up any part of a literary appreciation of the play.

If this argument is accepted, then the Theory of Novelistic Truth cannot be defended on the grounds that it offers an explanation of the evaluative assumptions on which literary practice rests: for example, that literature is valuable in so far as it possesses a humanly interesting content.

The traditional version of the Theory of Novelistic Truth tries to explain the unknown (the concept of 'literary truth') by assimilating it to what is familiar and well known (the truth of certain types of fact-stating discourse). Its argument relies on a paradigmatic conception of truth-seeking enquiry, for example, straightforward historical narrative with its own constraints on truth and accuracy (we have characterized this conception in Chapter 9). It then highlights all the features of fictional narrative—reference, verisimilitude, and so forth—which appear similar to that paradigm and attributes a truth-seeking function to literature on the basis of those. Given this notion of history, the argument against identifying literature as a kind of history is easy to formulate, simply by pointing to other features of the practices where they clearly diverge.

There is, however, another view of history and its relationship to fiction which makes the identification of history and literature 'natural' in a way it is not in the traditional Theory of Novelistic Truth.

The post-modernist version

In George Orwell's *Nineteen Eighty-Four* there is a Ministry of Truth which, among other things, is concerned with the continuous reconstruction of the past. This reconstruction is undertaken from the vantage point of the present and brings the past into line with the present so that it can always be seen as justifying present policies and actions by Big Brother and as confirming his wisdom and foresight. The reconstruction of the past is the task of a number of officials who carry out their work in accordance with certain rhetorical conventions which are not articulated or written down anywhere but which are part of their craft. The way they do their job is not unlike the way in which a hack-writer turns out cheap novels, but the role they fill also gives them the opportunity for something like artistic creation. Here is how Winston Smith, the central character of *Nineteen Eighty-Four*, goes about changing a piece of the past:

Winston read through the offending article. Big Brother's Order for the Day, it seemed, had been chiefly devoted to praising the work of an organization known as the FFCC, which supplied cigarettes and other comforts to the sailors in the Floating Fortresses. A certain Comrade Withers, a prominent member of the Inner Party, had been singled out for special mention and awarded a decoration, the Order of Conspicuous Merit, Second Class.

Three months later FFCC had suddenly been dissolved with no reasons given. One could assume that Withers and his associates were now in disgrace, but there had been no report of the matter in the Press or on the telescreen. That was to be expected, since it was unusual for political offenders to be put on trial or even publicly denounced....

Winston decided that it would not be enough simply to reverse the tendency of Big Brother's speech. It was better to make it deal with something totally unconnected with its original subject.

He might turn the speech into the usual denunciation of traitors and thought-criminals, but that was a little too obvious; while to invent a victory at the front, or some triumph of over-production in the Ninth Three-Year Plan, might complicate the records too much. What was needed was a piece of pure fantasy. Suddenly there sprang into his mind, ready made as it were, the image of a certain Comrade Ogilvy, who had recently died in battle, in heroic circumstances. (chapter 4)

And Winston goes on to write a story about this Ogilvy and his heroic deed.

The distinction between a true account of the past and a pure fantasy is clear in Winston Smith's consciousness. And Orwell takes it for granted that his audience will share Winston Smith's acceptance of this distinction. Orwell's description of the activity that goes on in The Ministry of Truth relies for its effectiveness on such a shared distinction and a shared assumption that to change the true account of the past to suit the needs of the moment, is forgery of the worst possible sort. And it is so because it puts the very concept of historical truth at risk:

The frightening thing, he reflected for the ten thousandth time as he forced his shoulders painfully backward (with hands on hips, they were gyrating their bodies from the waist, an exercise that was supposed to be good for the back muscles)—the frightening thing was that it might all be true. If the Party could thrust its hand into the past and say of this or that event, *it never happened*,—that, surely, was more terrifying than mere torture and death?

The Party said that Oceania had never been in alliance with Eurasia. He, Winston Smith, knew that Oceania had been in alliance with Eurasia as short a time as four years ago. But where did that knowledge exist? Only in his own consciousness, which in any case must soon be annihilated. And if all others accepted the lie which the party imposed—if all records told the same tale—then the lie passed into history and became truth. 'Who controls the past', ran the Party slogan, 'controls the future: who controls the present controls the past'. (chapter 3)

The loss of the true past is a threat worse than torture and death and the distinction between historical truth and mere fiction is thus invested with the very highest importance, an importance beyond that of personal annihilation and suffering—a view we can all understand and which most of us will share.[14]

[14] Not all. Those who tend to support a version of the post-modernist position do not find this standard interpretation of *Nineteen Eighty-Four* at all palatable. This is what Rorty, for example, finds to be the essential message of the book: 'How does this passage [from an Orwell column] mesh with the passage from Winston's diary I quoted earlier, the one which concludes, "Freedom is the freedom to say that two plus two equals four. If that is granted, all else follows"? I suggest that the two passages can both be seen as saying that it does not matter whether "two plus two equals four" is true, much less whether this truth is "subjective" or "corresponds to reality". All that matters is that if you do believe it, you can say it without getting hurt. In other words, what matters is your ability to talk to other people about what seems to you true, not what is in fact true. If we take care of freedom, truth can take care of itself.' ('The Last Intellectual in Europe: Orwell on Cruelty' in *Contingency, Irony, and Solidarity*, p. 176.) Yet it seems impossible to reconcile so indifferent an attitude to 'what is in fact true' with Winston

What frightens Winston Smith is that Big Brother's attitude to history has a certain logic which subverts the very distinction between fiction and historical truth. The historical truth of which Winston Smith is aware exists only in his own consciousness. It is subjective because the only authority behind this knowledge is his individual memory. To transcend this individual, subjective memory, to establish a description as historically true, some other authority is needed. But since the past, as a series of events, is forever gone, all that exists are descriptions of the past. That means that the one thing needed to establish a description as historically true is to make others share it. One makes others share one's descriptions of the past through *persuasion*. Persuasion is a rhetorical art which does not discriminate between fair and foul means and where success is measured in terms of conversion and not truth. But if there is no distinction between what descriptions of the past are *accepted* and what descriptions of the past are *true*, then truth collapses into acceptance and proof (or verification) into persuasion. This need not mean, however, that all accounts of the past will be accepted as equally good. For persuasion always has a further purpose: one wants someone to accept a description of the past for some specific reason. In the case of Big Brother the purpose is social control, of both society and the individual. An account of the past can, if one wants to use the subverted notion of truth, be said to be *pragmatically true* when it serves this purpose well. Big Brother's reconstruction of the past is pragmatically true in that it serves well the purpose of confirming his own authority, foresight, and wisdom. And if we use this subverted notion of truth we can also say that Big Brother's reconstruction of the past is an imaginative truth, an account of how the past ought to have been, constructed by the human mind, by help of imagination and intelligence.

One might see Winston Smith and Big Brother as representatives of two different views of history. Winston Smith represents the traditional view of historical truth on which the traditional Theory of Novelistic Truth is based. Big Brother, on the other hand, can be seen as representing in its ultimate consequence what

Smith's own attitude to truth, e.g. in the passages we have quoted. Nor does Rorty tackle the question how we can 'take care' of freedom if there are no objective grounds for viewing freedom as an ultimate value. His interpretation of *Nineteen Eighty-Four*, though clever, is in the end not very plausible.

one may call the post-modernist view of history, the view that all history is construction and that history explains only by telling a good story, or if you are Big Brother, the *right* story (but not the true story, as there is no such thing). This view takes as its point of departure what is alleged to be the irreducibly rhetorical character of historical discourse which, it is held, has not so far been taken seriously by either philosophers or historians:

there is one problem that neither philosophers nor historians have looked at very seriously and to which literary theorists have given only passing attention. This question has to do with the status of the historical narrative, considered purely as a verbal artifact purporting to be a model of structures and processes long past and therefore not subject to either experimental or observational controls. . . . [I]n general there has been a reluctance to consider historical narratives as what they most manifestly are: verbal fictions, the contents of which are as much *invented* as *found* and the forms of which have more in common with their counterparts in literature than they have with those in the sciences.[15]

According to this view, the fictional quality of historical accounts manifests itself in several ways. First of all, any historical account involves suppression, subordination, and the highlighting or foregrounding of certain elements of the story. Some elements are given special attention, some are simply not mentioned at all. This, of course, is obvious enough. Since any historical account must have a limited scope, and since the class of facts that can be identified within a certain period of time, even within a limited geographical area, is an open class which can be added to indefinitely, a selection has to be made. The point is perhaps most easily recognized in the history of art or philosophy or literature which are histories of canonical texts, where what to include depends on what one takes to have been important in forming the canon. But even a book-length account of such a limited, if complex, event as the Battle of Waterloo would involve selection and foregrounding.

Secondly, according to this view, a historical account explains by *emplotting* the events that have not been suppressed, in a traditional type of story which is recognized in the culture as conferring meaning on those events:

[15] Hayden White, 'The Historical Text as Literary Artefact', in *Tropics of Discourse*, 82. Originally in *Clio*, 14 (1975).

The historian shares with his audience *general notions* of the *forms* that significant human situations *must* take by virtue of his participation in the specific processes of sense-making which identify him as a member of one cultural endowment rather than another. In the process of studying a given complex of events, he begins to perceive the *possible* story form that such events *may* figure. In his narrative account of how this set of events took on the shape which he perceives to inhere within it, he emplots his account as a story of a particular kind. The reader, in the process of following the historian's account of those events, gradually comes to realize that the story he is reading is of one kind rather than another: romance, tragedy, comedy, satire, epic, or what have you. And when he has perceived the class or type to which the story that he is reading belongs, he experiences the effect of having the events in the story explained to him. He has at this point not only successfully *followed* the story; he has grasped the point of it, *understood* it, as well. The original strangeness, mystery, or exoticism of the events is dispelled, and they take on a familiar aspect, not in their details, but in their functions as elements of a familiar kind of configuration.[16]

The emplotment of the events is not logically independent of their selection. Selection is a function of emplotment, for it is the purpose, perspective, and format of the story that defines what sort of events are needed to fill the frame.

So far, however, we have a view of history that still lacks an essential ingredient to be found in a genuine Big Brother view of history. We are still left with a distinction between fact and fiction on the level of events. So far the question of the reality of the events emplotted has not been addressed. However, the postmodernist view of history does not leave the distinction between fact and fiction standing even at this level. For all facts have to be represented in language and language generalizes and interprets; a linguistic presentation itself represents a point of view, a perspective which is defined through the use of tropes or figures which the historian uses to *identify* and *characterize* the facts. This means

that the *shape* of the *relationships* which will appear to be inherent in the objects inhabiting the field will in reality have been imposed on the field by the investigator in the very *act of identifying and describing* the objects that he finds there. The implication is that historians *constitute* their subjects as possible objects of narrative representation by the very language they use to *describe* them. And if this is the case, it means that the

[16] Ibid. 86.

different kinds of historical interpretations that we have of the same set of events, such as the French Revolution as interpreted by Michelet, Tocqueville, Taine, and others, are little more than projections of the linguistic protocols that these historians used to *pre*-figure that set of events prior to writing their narratives of it.[17]

This view has not been widely popular with historians who see it as their task to tell the *true* story. And it has received little attention in the philosophy of history. It is, however, strongly represented in modern literary theory. Literary theorists may not have paid much attention to actual historical writing but the general strategy, discussed in Chapter 11, of dispensing with the notion of *work* and replacing it by the general notion of *text* encourages the identification of literature and history. Historical accounts, like literary works, are texts and, like all other texts, are in crucial respects fictions since they '*constitute* their subjects as possible objects of narrative representation by the very language they use to *describe* them'. If historical accounts are true at all, they are true in the same way as literary works are true. They are then not true *of* the world, but have some kind of *imaginative truth*, a truth *made* by human imaginative construction.

The way in which the post-modernist version of the Theory of Novelistic Truth attempts to assimilate history and literature introduces a problem peculiar to this version of the theory. The traditional Theory of Novelistic Truth explains by assimilating the notion of novelistic truth to the notion of historical truth (the truth of fact-stating discourse) which is assumed to be better understood. That is, it explains by assimilating the less clear notion to what is assumed to be a clearer notion. The post-modernist version does exactly the opposite. It assimilates the notion of historical truth to the problematic notion of imaginative or literary truth (*obscurum per obscurius*). But this latter notion is exactly what *needs* explanation. So the assimilation of history to literature in the post-modernist version is theoretically unilluminating.

There are also profound confusions in the post-modernist view of history which make it an unattractive foundation for the Theory of Novelistic Truth. First, the question about the cognitive status of facts in historical accounts is not solved in the post-modernist view simply by declaring—somewhat in the manner of Goodman

---

[17] Ibid. 95.

—that there is no distinction between what is given and what is made up at the level of events. For the theorists who suggest that this distinction is invalid tend to make constant use of it themselves. Thus it is not clear from the quoted passage, or indeed from any other of the writings of Hayden White from whom the passage is taken, exactly what the status of facts is, or how facts constrain the descriptions that can be given of them. Can one ever talk about the *same facts* if facts are *constituted* as objects of explanation by the 'linguistic protocols' used (the problem becomes analogous to that of the identity of fictive states of affairs across narratives)? White writes much of the time as if there are facts to be interpreted, facts which are identifiable as the same facts from one historical account to another. And this is true even when his message is that 'It is not the case that a fact is one thing and its interpretation another.'[18] The two concepts of 'what is given' and 'what is made up' do not at any time *merge* in his conceptual scheme, and he even admits a relationship of correspondence between historical accounts and an 'extra-textual domain of occurrence or happening'.[19] This is not an accidental slippage in terminology, but a symptom of a problem of principle: the post-modernist view of history cannot be stated without presupposing the distinction that it denies.[20]

History as description and history as fact

To diagnose the problem of the post-modernist view of history, it is useful to draw a distinction parallel to that made in Chapter 1 between the object sense and the description sense of fiction. An analogous distinction appears in handbooks on historical method as a distinction between history and historiography, where 'history' is used about the past and 'historiography' about accounts of the past. However, the word 'history' itself is standardly used with both an object sense and a description sense. Sometimes we talk

[18] Hayden White, 'Historicism, History and the Figurative Imagination', in *Tropics of Discourse*, 107.
[19] Hayden White, 'The Fictions of Factual Representation', in *Tropics of Discourse*, 122.
[20] For a broadly based attack that develops further points against the theory here, see Carroll, 'Interpretation, History and Narrative'.

about history as what has happened in the past—the Battle of Waterloo, the introduction of Forster's Education Act, the 1979 election—and sometimes we talk about history as accounts— Hume's *History of England*, Gibbon's history of the Roman Empire—that is, history as written accounts about the past. To say about an event that it is history, is to place it in the past; to say about a description that it is history, is to place it as a certain *type* of account.

History in the description sense is constructed, a product of human intelligence and imagination. It is the privilege of the historian to be an authority on this type of construction. History in this sense involves the use of literary techniques and is subject to aesthetic requirements of both style and structure. These techniques and requirements play a part in defining this genre of writing, though the emphasis on literary and aesthetic requirements will vary from one account to another depending upon consid- erations of target audience, the purpose the writer has in writing, etc. This does not mean that historical accounts become literary works, though some works of history survive as literature rather than history. Nor does it mean that literature can be identified with history, though some works may survive because of their value as historical sources rather than because of their value as literary works. Above all, the fact that historical accounts neces- sarily make use of literary stylistic and structural devices cannot be used as a basis for concluding anything about the cognitive value of historical discourse, i.e. cannot be used to conclude that history is fiction or carries 'imaginative truth'.

The post-modernist attempt to identify history with fiction gains whatever plausibility it has from a confusion of the distinction between history in the description sense and history in the object sense. Note how in the last but one passage quoted the distinction between description and event is blurred. The confusion between the object sense and description sense of history is focused there in such expressions as 'the events in the story'. Events do not as such figure in a story, only descriptions of events do that. It is not events but descriptions of events that function 'as elements of a familiar kind of configuration', etc. As long as one talks about *fiction*, this confusion between the object sense and the description sense of the word does not matter: the events are invented, im- agined, constructed, and they come into existence (or such existence

as they have) through the construction of the verbal expressions
that make up the story in which they occur. An author of a fiction
constructs not only a fictional account but also fictional entities
like Jeeves, 221B Baker Street, and the death of Little Nell. When
one uses the word 'history', on the other hand, a confusion between the two senses of this word is fatal; such a confusion would
mean that one talked about history in the object sense as if that
could be constructed too. In other words, the confusion would
legitimize a conclusion that in constructing an account of the past
one was also constructing the past. But this is exactly where the
analogy between the concept of fiction and the concept of history
breaks down. For saying about an event that it is fiction is to deny
that it is historical. History in the object sense is constituted not
by a series of descriptions but by a series of past events, which are
not the kind of thing that one can *construct*, though the author of
a historical account will of course *reconstruct* a sequence of events.
Fictional events, on the other hand, are constructed and not re-
constructed by the author. If past events were constructed, they
would no longer be the past but simply fictional events. It therefore
makes no sense at all to say that in constructing an account of the
Battle of Waterloo, one also constructs the Battle of Waterloo, if
one does not use this as a metaphor or metonymy for saying that
one constructs an account of it. This is a purely conceptual point
and has no ontological implications for the nature of what exists.
But it does signal a difference between the practice of constructing
historical accounts and the practice of constructing fictional accounts. The two practices are subjected to different logical constraints. Historical accounts are challengeable in a way that fictional
accounts are not.

History in the description sense can meaningfully be seen as a
product of human constructive ability, intelligence, and imagination. In this respect and in respect of a number of rhetorical and
structural features it is similar to fictional stories. It therefore also
makes good sense to compare a historical account of the Battle of
Waterloo with fictional accounts of various types, to bring out the
way in which it uses rhetorical features, including perspective
and even plot. But the similarity between fictional and historical
accounts does not extend to the way in which they are *about*
the phenomena they deal with. In Chapter 5 we gave a detailed
account of what it means for a work of fiction to be about

something; the account would have to be quite different for historical writing. There are what Goodman calls 'right versions' of historical accounts while there are no 'right versions' of fictional accounts. The logical constraints on historical accounts are manmade and conventional, but they are constraints that define our notion of *true* accounts of the past. It is these logical constraints that define the different practices of the artist and the historian. The artist does not only create an expression but also an imaginary world. The historian does not create the past but only a verbal expression, an account of the past. Both activities make demands on the human imagination and intelligence. But while fiction is construction, history is reconstruction.

One may, of course, note that past events, like present events, can only be construed under a description and that the type of description will be determined by the purpose it is intended to serve, and one can raise the epistemological question concerning how and how far it is possible to give a true account of past events. But the answer to such questions will not affect the difference in logic between the two types of discourse constituting the different practices of history and imaginative literature.

The problem of the post-modernist view of history is that it is without a conception of the past. It is not a view which can see the past as explained by creative fiction, as the Greeks explained their past through myth, for the ultimate consequence of the post-modernist assimilation of history and fiction is that there is no past to explain. According to the post-modernist view belief in the past is belief in a fiction and it therefore undermines all constraints concerning what can be said about this past. As a view of history this is uninteresting, for a view of history without a concept of the past abdicates responsibility for explaining what it sets out to explain. As a view of the cognitive status of literature, the attempt to collapse the distinction between history and literature is both confusing and theoretically unilluminating.

Literary realism and reality

There exists in literary criticism a tradition which presents an argument that is in some ways similar to that developed by the traditional version of the Theory of Novelistic Truth. Realist writers and a number of critics writing on realism have made the claim for realist literary works that these are true *to* reality in a way previous literature had not been. The claim is made on the very first recorded application of the word with a literary as distinct from a philosophical application:

cette doctrine littéraire qui gagne tous les jours du terrain et qui conduirait à une fidèle imitation non pas des chefs-d'œuvre de l'art mais des originaux que nous offre la nature, pourrait fort bien s'appeler le réalisme: ce serait suivant quelques apparences, la littérature dominante du XIXe siècle, la littérature du vrai.[21]

Literary realism has been seen by many critics as closely connected to philosophical realism and to the ordinary, common-sense concept of realism. 'What unites the two areas of meaning—the real-life and the literary meanings [of the term "realism"]—' says J. P. Stern,

is their representational quality, is the fact that they both designate a 'standing-for-something', and a process of selection: they designate not a content but a condition, or at least an outlook, *and* a form. They refer to a way of thinking (in the one case) and to a way of writing (in the other), each of which is positively related to the real world.[22]

What secures this 'positive relation' to the 'real world' is a certain mode of writing, a set of literary techniques:

Realism in literature connotes a way of depicting, describing a situation in a faithful, accurate, 'life-like' manner; or richly, abundantly, colourfully; or again mechanically, photographically, imitatively.[23]

There is no complete agreement on the criteria for what is to count as a realist mode of writing, nor on the application of these criteria.[24] However, broadly speaking three features are prominent: a certain kind of *aim*, namely truth-telling or 'faithfulness' to the facts; a certain kind of *content*, the representation of social reality in its particulars; and a certain kind of *form*, involving simplicity rather than ornateness, mirroring that of documentary

---

[21] *Le Mercure français du XIXe siècle* (1826). Quoted from Lars-Olof Åhlberg, *Realismbegrepp i litteratur och konst: En idéhistorisk och konstfilosofisk studie.* Acta Universitatis Upsaliensis: Aesthetica Upsaliensia, 4 (Uppsala, 1988), 21. Åhlberg traces in great detail the various uses of the concept of realism in art criticism.

[22] J. P. Stern, *On Realism* (London, 1973), 42.

[23] Ibid. 40.   [24] As Åhlberg clearly demonstrates.

history. Ian Watt, in *The Rise of the Novel*, attempts to bring these features together by appeal to 'narrative procedures'. These involve, first of all, the rejection of literary convention and traditional plots and an emphasis on inventing new plots and on creating the impression of fidelity to life. Secondly, the emphasis on fidelity to life leads to the introduction of individual characters acting against a particular and particularized real-life background rather than literary types acting against a background determined by the appropriate literary convention. This particularization of character also manifests itself in the rejection of type-names and the adoption of real-life names that do not place the character in a category. Thirdly, there is the emphasis on the importance of time which manifests itself in the creation of a causal chain working itself out in the plot, in the creation of characters that develop through time, and in the attention given to the historical process. As a correlative to this emphasis on time, there is a particularized description of place. The novel as a realistic genre, Watt argues, not only has a consistent time scheme, but also a consistent geography and fully realized exteriors and interiors. Finally, realism uses the language of concrete particularity and avoids ornate and poetic language.[25]

However, a list of narrative procedures constituting realism as a mode of writing does not yet clarify the 'positive relationship' to reality that this technique is supposed to establish. A mode of writing cannot by itself *constitute* a positive relationship to something outside the work. The existence and nature of this relationship have to be established by an independent argument. Stern's suggestion is that this relationship is constituted by the *representational* nature of the description, and most critics who write on realism make use of the concept of representation in their definition or description of it. Realism, says René Wellek, is 'the objective representation of contemporary social reality',[26] and central to Watt's account is the purpose of creating 'what purports to be an authentic account of the actual experiences of individuals'.[27] Stern further suggests that representation is constituted

---

[25] Ian Watt, *The Rise of the Novel: Studies in Defoe, Richardson and Fielding* (London, 1967), ch. 1.

[26] René Wellek, 'Realism in Literary Scholarship', in *Concepts of Criticism* (New Haven, Conn., 1963), 240.

[27] Watt, *The Rise of the Novel*, 27.

through the relation 'standing-for-something', that representation is representation *of* something, i.e. social reality.

If one accepts at face value the claim that realism is 'la littérature du vrai', it would seem that the obvious interpretation of the relation of 'standing-for-something' which constitutes representation would be denotation or reference. Inasmuch as this might explain how representation involves 'correspondence' with reality, it might in turn clear the way to the claim that realist literature is the 'literature of the true' (of truth). However, if the argument given in the discussion of the Theory of Novelistic Truth is correct, namely that the referential properties of literary works, such as they are, are an insufficient basis for assimilating literature to fact-stating discourse, then much more needs to be said about the representational nature of realism to make the case for literary realism as a kind of truth-telling.

It is possible to distinguish at least two kinds of representation. In one familiar sense, representation is closely related to reference.[28] A description of a general represents Napoleon if it is used to refer to Napoleon, otherwise not. However, there is a different, but equally familiar, concept of representation, the core of which is the idea that a description or picture represents *kinds* rather than particulars. *War and Peace* can be said to give a representation of Napoleon, the invasion of Russia, etc., but it can also be construed as giving a representation of war, heroism, nationalism, love, etc. The former are concrete particulars, the latter universals or kinds. The former type of representation is relational (the description (D) is a representation *of* an individual object or event (O)), the latter non-relational (D is a representation of an-F; or alternatively D is an F-representation).[29] The distinction recalls that between relational and non-relational senses of 'about' (about *a*, *a*-about, and about ϕ), which we discussed in Chapter 5. Thus a picture can be a portrait of an individual (the Queen) or it can be a representation of an old man, a dancing girl, etc. without there being any actual individual depicted. The former is a genuine

---

[28] See Nelson Goodman, *The Languages of Art* (London, 1969): 'A picture that represents—like a passage that describes—an object refers to and, more particularly, *denotes* it. Denotation is the core of representation and is independent of resemblance' (5).

[29] See Goodman, *The Languages of Art*, 21 ff; though Goodman, being a nominalist, would not be happy about a description representing 'kinds or universals'.

relation between the picture and a person (a representation *of* O), the latter is non-relational (an F-representation). Of course, a picture of the Queen can also be an old-woman-representation. But even if the Queen *is* an old woman, the picture may be a-young-woman-representation. An F-representation is determined by the qualities depicted, a representation of O is normally determined by referential intentions or denotative conventions.

Consider this passage from Arnold Bennett's *Anna of the Five Towns*:

In the slip-house begins the long manipulation which transforms raw porous, friable clay into the moulded, decorated, and glazed vessel. The large whitewashed place was occupied by ungainly machines and receptacles through which the four sorts of clay used in the common 'body'—ball clay, China clay, flint clay, and stone clay—were compelled to pass before they became a white putty-like mixture meet for shaping by human hands. The blunger crushed the clay, the sifter extracted the iron from it by means of a magnet, the press expelled the water, and the pug-mill expelled the air. From the last reluctant mouth slowly emerged a solid stream nearly a foot in diameter, like a huge white snake. Already the clay had acquired the uniformity characteristic of a manufactured product. (From chapter 8, 'On the Bank')

The chapter from which the passage comes presents to the reader a complete description of a pottery factory with all the production processes that take place in the factory. It is not untypical, in its concern for detail, of a characteristic kind of realist narrative. Though the reader has no reason to doubt that it is a correct description of how a slip-house in such a factory would look, the description is not a description *of* a real slip-house. It is a slip-house-representation rather than a representation of a slip-house. It represents to the reader a kind of entity that also exists outside the work of literature, but it does not represent it *as existing*. No doubt the author drew on his knowledge of some particular slip-house(s) for his description but it does not follow, as we have seen, that he is thereby *referring* to such particulars or that the passage is *about* them.

Both relational and non-relational representation can be realistic. A slip-house-description which does not describe any particular slip-house can be as realistic as a description of Napoleon as a general (which is intended to refer to him as a general and to inform the reader of a range of facts about him). It soon becomes clear, then, that it cannot be an essential or defining feature of literary realism that it be a kind of *relational* representation, explained either in terms of reference or truth. Nor is representation, of any kind, a sufficient condition for realism: both relational and non-relational representation can be *non-realistic* as well as realistic. Realistic representation is *just one type of representation*. There are other types as well. There are probably, for example, more pastoral than realistic representations of country life in English literature, and realistic representation is a relatively late arrival on the literary scene. Inasmuch as realist works of literature are representations, then, they can be defined only as one species of non-relational representation. In this connection it is important not to confuse 'non-realistic' with 'unrealistic'. An unrealistic description is one which fails to be realistic. A non-realistic description is a description in some other mode of writing than a realistic one.

The conclusion that literary realism will not support a truth-telling conception of literature or literary value is important and fits into our general strategy of argument. It brings together both the thesis of Chapter 5 that fictions *qua* fictions are primarily about kinds (or universals or aspects of things) rather than particulars and our conclusion earlier in this chapter that it is no part of the conception of literature to suppose that authors of literary works are making truth-claims about those objects which happen to satisfy its descriptions or which share similarities with its fictional characterizations. Literary realism is a 'mode of presentation', to use our earlier Fregean vocabulary, not a kind of 'correspondence' relation. Any special 'positive relationship' which the realist novel is supposed to hold to something outside literature ('social reality') is better accounted for in non-referential terms, perhaps similarity or verisimilitude.

Literature and probability

But could literary realism be reformulated within these terms and still retain a place for truth? Consider the following claim made by Balzac in the preface to *La Comédie humaine*. 'French Society', says Balzac, was to be the historian, I had only to be the secretary. I would draw up the inventory of the vices and virtues, collect the main effects of the passions, portray characters, select the principal events of Society, and compose types by combining the traits of several homogeneous characters; and I might thus succeed in writing that history forgotten by so many historians, the history of manners and morals. . . . [B]ut if I was to deserve the praises which any artist must aspire to, I must needs study the *causes or central cause* of these social facts, and discover the meaning hidden in that immense assembly of events.[30]

One way of interpreting Balzac here would be as aiming to report *truths about kinds*, informed by the facts and constrained, perhaps in the manner prescribed by Aristotle, by probabilities. He can be construed as seeing his task as subtly different from that of the historian who writes about particular political and social events. Balzac, it may be argued, does not here express referential intentions, but only an intention to produce an account that is lifelike, authentic, and has a high degree of verisimilitude, because it presents a scene that has a high degree of probability. The 'positive relationship' between the realist literary work and external reality then becomes comparable to that between a hypothesis and the facts about which it hypothesizes. This would be a claim about a non-relational representation, a claim that his novels are to be read as an account of a range of types of fact (a range-of-facts-account), morals, and manners, which might have occurred, though as a matter of fact have not done so, in the world outside the work.

This interpretation of the realist claim has the advantage that it permits an explanation of how the 'positive relationship' to the world can dictate a mode of writing. A probable account has certain features which, if they do not constitute, at least contribute to, its probability. Probability is enhanced by the 'introduction of individual characters acting against a particular and particularized real-life background', by 'the rejection of type-names and the adoption of real-life names that do not place the character in a category', by 'the creation of a causal chain working itself out in the plot, and the creation of characters that develop through time', and by the use of 'the language of concrete particularity' and the avoidance

[30] Honoré de Balzac, 'Preface' to *La Comédie humaine*, trans. in Arnold Kettle (ed.), *The Nineteenth-Century Novel: Critical Essays and Documents* (London, 1972), 143–4.

of 'ornate and poetic language'. And circumstantial detail has the function that it provides fact-representations that mutually support the probability of each other at the same time as they provide a basis for the probability of action- and event-descriptions by representing conditions under which such actions and events take place in the real world. When Balzac says that he 'must needs study the *causes or central cause* of these social facts', he can naturally be interpreted as saying that he wants to give action- and event-descriptions that are probable in the light of a set of fact-representations which he provides as a backdrop. Indeed, the strategy of defending the probability of a representation of actions and events in a literary work by pointing to the background of conditions for these actions and events which the work also represents is a familiar one.[31] And it is this feature of the realist work that provides the basis for the slogan 'letting the facts speak for themselves' and for the view of the realist novel as a 'laboratory' for 'testing' human reactions to find their true causes.

However, the interpretation of the realist claim as a claim about the probability of realist literary works does not avoid problems similar in kind to those that arose in connection with the traditional version of the Theory of Novelistic Truth. For one thing there are problems about fiction and probability. Probability, at least in its modern sense,[32] is dependent upon evidence, and it is logically anomalous to ask about evidence for a made-up event-description:

Probability statements about the characters or plots in imaginative literature logically belong to a different space than do statements about the real world, and there is something fundamentally strange—or absurd—about discussions of the probability of Mr. Pickwick, say. Why should there ever be a question about the 'probability' of people and events that are known certainly never to have existed or occurred? This logical strangeness is in fact the distinguishing feature of questions about what is

[31] For a discussion of the concept of probability that such an argument takes for granted see Robert Newsom, *A Likely Story: Probability and Play in Fiction* (London, 1988), 85 ff. and 92–5. Newsom also gives a detailed example of such an argument from a correspondence between a Swiss scientist, Albrecht von Haller, and Samuel Richardson.

[32] The theory that there is a distinctive 'modern' concept of probability is presented by Ian Hacking, *The Emergence of Probability* (Cambridge, 1975). Robert Newsom in his analysis of literary probability in *A Likely Story* argues for seeing the new concept as essentially an extension of the classical concept as found in Aristotle.

probable in literature and therefore important enough to be marked by its own name. I call it the antinomy of fictional probability.[33]

The logical strangeness arises because to claim probability for works of literary fiction involves a category mistake in Gilbert Ryle's sense. Literary works *qua* literary works are neither probable nor improbable just as they are not modes of fact-stating. It is not part of the literary stance to construe literary works in terms of their probability. Although readers do sometimes use the vocabulary of probability in their critical judgements (such-and-such an incident being 'highly improbable', and so forth) this talk is not strictly of probability in the mathematical sense and, to be intelligible at all, must be reducible to other terms, perhaps verisimilitude or credibility. Inasmuch as the point rests on modes of literary appreciation it could be supported with some such example as that from *Rosmersholm* where the literary stance dictated that questions of artistic function override judgements (in that case about the presence of an incest motif) solely based on 'comparisons with reality'.

It is interesting to note that realism as an aesthetic doctrine declined in France at the end of the last century just as the new social sciences came into their own. And it has been argued that realism declined *because* it became obvious that the social sciences performed so much better the descriptive and explanatory tasks which the realist authors tended to see themselves as performing.[34] If this is really the case, it could be interpreted as disillusion on the part of realist writers and their audience as they discovered their category mistake. However, the decline of realism *as an aesthetic doctrine* making a cognitive claim for literature led neither to the disappearance of the *realist mode of writing*, though for a while it was eclipsed by other, modernist, modes of writing, nor to a lasting devaluation of works written in the realist mode.

The decline of the doctrine of realism and the growth of theoretical views that do not leave any room for a concept of literary probability did not remove appeals to literary probability from criticism. This fact and the fact that there was widespread use of the concept of literary probability in the eighteenth and nineteenth

[33] Newsom, *A Likely Story*, 96.

[34] For a summary of this argument see F. W. J. Hemmings, 'Conclusion: The Decline of Realism', in Hemmings (ed.), *The Age of Realism*. The Pelican Guide to European Literature (Harmondsworth, 1974), 361 ff.

centuries, poses the problem of *how* a reader can meaningfully talk about the probability of a work of literature when, on closer inspection, such talk is logically absurd. It has been suggested by Robert Newsom that such talk rests on the reader's ability to entertain multiple frames of reference at the same time:

What the commonness of expressions such as 'improbable but true' suggests is that under some circumstances people ordinarily do not have trouble weighing multiple frames of reference simultaneously. Because it is concise to the point of being elliptical, what looks to the philosopher like the sign of solecism and confusion may more positively look to us like the sign of an ability or faculty. This is because all of the references to literary probability we have discussed are the logical equivalents of expressions like 'improbable but true' (or 'improbable but false' or 'probable though false' and so on): they all make ascriptions of probability in spite of certain knowledge. Either we can resign ourselves to the ill-expressedness of literary discourse or try to see if in this case, to borrow from Wittgenstein, ordinary language is not all right after all. If indeed there is an acceptable way beyond the antinomy of literary probability, it will be via the assumption of multiple frames of reference and the reader's ability to maintain such multiple perspectives—in effect simultaneously.[35]

It is part of the convention of realist writing, this critic argues, that it is read *as if* it were an account of real life. The reader *pretends* to believe in the realist literary work at the same time as he *knows* that it is fiction. This may well be right but now it ceases to be an account of realism as such but is assimilable into a more general account of the fictive stance. Also we should recognize the logic of the matter. In Kendall Walton's terms we can say that it is fictional (or make-believe) that a reader is making probability judgements about what actually happens. But that does not entail that the reader *is* making probability judgements. The simultaneously adopted frames of reference are just like the internal and external perspectives we have identified in fiction. Only from the internal perspective—of someone engaging imaginatively with the fictional world—do judgements of probability make sense. Our own suggestion is that from the external perspective the reader is most likely making a judgement of verisimilitude, not a failed judgement of probability.

However, it is not necessary for, or an aim of, the present

---

[35] Newsom, *A Likely Story*, 104.

account to have an explanation of the concept of literary probability. It is worth noting that an explanation of how one can meaningfully talk about literary probability, such as the one provided by this critic, does not have to endorse any epistemological claim (concerning truth, for example) for the realist literary work. The explanation offered does not question that it is a category mistake to claim probability for literary works. It is actually based on that assumption.

13

The Propositional Theory of Literary Truth

The new realists

Neither the traditional nor the post-modernist version of the Theory of Novelistic Truth, nor the doctrine of literary realism, has yet provided a satisfactory account of the mimetic aspect of a literary work. They have not succeeded in establishing that it is a constitutive aim of literature to state truths in any sense comparable to that in which history, for example, aims to state truths. In spite of the claims of Richardson, and James, and Woolf, and Balzac, the novelist is not a kind of historian; nor, *pace* Hayden White, is the historian a kind of novelist.

The traditional alternative to such theories has been what we may call the Propositional Theory of Literary Truth. Proponents of this theory admit the reasonableness of the view that literature at the 'literal level' is for the most part fictive, i.e. that characteristically its content is fictional and its mode of presentation is not that of fact-stating. But they claim that at a different level literary works do, perhaps must, imply or suggest general propositions about human life which have to be assessed as true or false, and that these propositions are what makes literature valuable. This Propositional Theory of Literary Truth has recently been represented by theorists who have reacted against post-modernist claims about the lack of meaning in literature. These critics have spent considerable intellectual energy arguing (successfully) against the basic assumptions of the post-modernist position.[1] Unfortunately,

---

[1] See e.g. Graff, *Literature Against Itself*; Nuttall, *A New Mimesis*; Laurence Lerner (ed.), *Reconstructing Literature* (Oxford, 1983); Tallis, *Not Saussure. A Critique of Post-Saussurean Literary Theory* (London, 1988) and *In Defence of Realism*. The arguments of these books are in the main negative. It is symptomatic that Gerald Graff's book has two chapters with the titles 'How not to Talk about Fictions' and 'How not to Save the Humanities' but no chapter on *how to talk* about fictions or *how to save* the humanities.

they have had little new to contribute to the formulation of the Propositional Theory, and they have tended to ignore some useful distinctions, such as Beardsley's distinction between *theme* and *thesis*,[2] the distinction between asserted and unasserted propositions, between trivial and non-trivial truths, between the claim that an interpretative statement is true of a literary work and the claim that the interpretative statement is true also of the world.

In a chapter on 'How not to Talk about Fictions' in *Literature against Itself* Gerald Graff argues that the question which post-modernist criticism has apparently laid dead, the question whether literature makes a claim to knowledge, a claim to be true, needs to be 'reopened'. He gives as his very simple reason for this that literary works do not merely contain sentences dealing with particulars:

Obviously it makes a good deal of difference what kind of utterance you choose as your paradigm of literary language. If you choose sentences like 'Call me Ishmael' or 'Slowly wading through the meadows of brit, the Pequod still held on her way north-eastward towards the island of Java', you will end up deciding that literary propositions are merely fictive imitations of genuine statements. But *Moby Dick* also includes sentences like this: 'For as this appalling ocean surrounds the verdant land, so in the soul of man there lies one insular Tahiti, full of peace and joy, but encompassed by all the horrors of the half-known life'. If you take this kind of example into your reckoning, you may have to reopen the question.[3]

Unfortunately, when Graff 'reopens' this question, because he fails to distinguish between themes and theses, he takes the post-modernist view of the cognitive status of literature as paradigmatic for no-truth views. The post-modernist view is that a literary work has no consistent meaning or theme that can be expressed through a proposition or set of propositions. What in post-modernist criticism is held to be a non-naïve analysis (that is a deconstructive analysis) of any work of literature, will show that the propositions it apparently puts forward, directly or by implication, in fact contradict each other, and that what any literary work will do is to draw attention in this way to its lack of coherent meaning.

However, this view is very different from a no-truth view of

---

[2] See above, Ch. 11.   [3] Graff, *Literature Against Itself*, 154–5.

literature which holds that a literary work does indeed have themes or meanings which can be stated as propositions, but which holds that these propositions have a unique role in literary appreciation, which is not reducible to the role they might have in philosophy, religious discourse, or the social sciences. Yet Graff, in the chapter 'How not to Talk about Fictions',[4] does not distinguish the two views and apparently thinks that to refute the former, he also has to refute the latter. Much more serious, however, is the fact that Graff fails to give any coherent account of how propositions in literature *should be* construed, of what their logic is in the context in which they appear.

Commenting on Culler's reading of Flaubert's *L'Education sentimentale*, he does say that

Culler writes as if he *takes seriously* the view [developed in *L'Education sentimentale*] that we learn little or nothing from our experience, that egregious failure brings no compensatory understanding, and he writes as if the novel itself demands such a response from any reader [as according to Graff it does indeed do].[5]

Graff uses Culler's comments on *L'Education sentimentale* to show that his theory is pragmatically self-refuting. However, he says nothing about what it is for a reader to 'take seriously' a 'view of life' set out in a work of literature. Nor does he explain other concepts, such as 'plausible', which he uses to characterize whatever thematic statements literary works might express or entail.

This example illustrates a common weakness of these theorists: the analytical tools they use are simply not sharp enough or accurate enough when it comes to discussing the role of propositions in literature. It is perhaps in such authors as Graff, Nuttall, and Raymond Tallis more than anywhere else that one can see how post-modernist theory has set back by decades the discussion in literary theory of this central issue. Post-modernist theory leads these authors to focus on the rejection of what are after all not

---

[4] Graff may, of course, be right in thinking that a no-truth view of literature is unsustainable, but his attack on this view forms no natural or necessary part of his attack on post-modernist criticism, and the general absence of analytical distinctions in his discussion makes his attack confused. It is symptomatic that he singles out Jonathan Culler for attack as the representative of the no-truth view. Even in *Structuralist Poetics* (London, 1975) (which Graff discusses) Culler was closer to a post-modernist view of fiction than, say, to our own no-truth view.

[5] Graff, *Literature Against Itself*, 160.

particularly appealing or sophisticated views instead of developing new ways of dealing with the problem of literature and truth.

A Propositional Theory of Literary Truth

A coherent and strong formulation of the Propositional Theory of Literary Truth cannot therefore be sought in these theorists who apparently are its most recent representatives. We shall try, therefore, to work out our own formulation of the theory. As a point of departure, it is useful to go back to the rough distinction made at the beginning of Chapter 10 between the two levels of the conceptual scheme which structures a reader's literary appreciation: the subject level and the thematic level. Propositions which describe or mention particular situations and events, characters, and places in a literary work may be labelled *subject descriptions*. Propositions which express generalizations or judgements based on or referring to these described situations, events, characters, and places may be labelled *thematic statements*.[6]

Thematic statements may be of two types, *explicit* and *implicit*. Explicit thematic statements occur in the literary work itself: 'When a tender affection has been storing itself in us through many of our years, the idea that we could accept any exchange for it seems to be a cheapening of our lives. And we can set a watch over our affections and our constancy as we can over other treasures.' (*Middlemarch*, chapter 57). In such cases (instances of which we have discussed before, in the context of the practice of fiction (Chapter 3)) the author seems to be directly addressing the reader much like a moralist or a philosopher in an essay or treatise, and the proposition often has the appearance of a conclusion or a 'topic sentence' which the descriptions it generalizes illustrate or underpin. But thematic statements need not occur in the literary work itself. They can be extracted from the work by the reader in interpretation. Thus the Lydgate story in *Middlemarch* can be

---

[6] This distinction is reminiscent of, but not identical with, Beardsley's and Weitz's thirty-year-old distinction between *reports* and *reflections*. See Beardsley, *Aesthetics*, 409–26; Morris Weitz, *Philosophy of the Arts* (Cambridge, Mass., 1950), 134–47, and 'Truth in Literature'. The distinction between *reports* and *reflections* was used in Olsen, *The Structure of Literary Understanding*, 62–72. Mary Sirridge also uses this distinction in her attack on the theory in 'Truth from Fiction?'.

understood as having the theme that 'the best human hopes and aspirations are always thwarted by forces beyond human control'. In this case we have an implied thematic statement.

A Propositional Theory of Literary Truth could then be formulated as follows: *the literary work contains or implies general thematic statements about the world which the reader as part of an appreciation of the work has to assess as true or false.* The theory presents two claims. First, a literary work implies propositions which can be construed as general propositions about the world. Second, these propositions are to be construed as involved in true or false claims about the world. In the terminology of *theme* and *thesis* the theory would be that a literary work develops not only a theme but also a thesis and that part of the appreciation of a literary work as a work of art is an assessment of the truth-value of this thesis. It might even be held that such a Propositional Theory of Literary Truth is a plausible interpretation of Aristotle's doctrine, which we have appealed to on several occasions, that 'poetry is something more philosophic and of graver import than history, since its statements are of the nature rather of universals, whereas those of history are singulars',[7] thus placing it in a venerable tradition.

The view has a number of attractive consequences. It can accommodate the fictive aspects of literary works by identifying two levels of description, the subject level and the thematic level, thus taking care of the basic convention that the substantive content of literary works is made up or invented. What is invented are the descriptions of events, situations, characters, etc.: the subject descriptions which make up the body of the work. This still leaves room for a higher, cognitive level. It also provides a possible solution to the problem of why literature is held in high esteem in the culture, and through this solution links this high esteem with the absolute value of the single literary work and the comparative value of different literary works. If literary works present interpretations of general statements about human life, then, in so far as these statements are true and important, literature is valuable. Bad literary works state trivial truths, falsehoods, or do not imply any statements about the 'human situation' at all. And because literature as a body of works has this truth-telling function, it is,

---

[7] Aristotle, *Poetics* (1451[b]).

as are activities like philosophy and science, held in high regard. Furthermore, the Propositional Theory of Literary Truth also permits the theorist to assign a well-defined function and logic to interpretation. The goal of interpretation can be seen as that of eliciting implied thematic statements, i.e. general statements about the human situation. And the structure of interpretation will then be an argument aimed at establishing in what way a literary work implies these statements. A successful interpretation is that which establishes with good arguments that a literary work expresses important insights into the human situation. The theory would, in other words, have many advantageous *consequences*. The question is whether the theory itself will stand up to closer examination.

The problem of implication

The first claim of the theory needs some comment. The general statements about the world to which the theory refers cannot be just any general statement which a work can be said to imply. It is implied in *Middlemarch* that people walk on the ground and do not fly when they move from place to place. It is implied that people live in houses and not in caves, etc. These statements are undoubtedly true, but they are trivial and of no interest to the reader except in so far they constitute part of a network of assumptions which the reader makes about the fictional world of the work. The implied statements which the theory can reasonably be taken to refer to are such statements as have general interest because they in some way concern the human situation. They must be thematic statements in the full sense that they formulate propositions about human existence that are substantive and interesting; statements of the type 'the best human hopes and aspirations are always thwarted by forces beyond human control', which, as was suggested above, is implied by the Lydgate story in *Middlemarch*. It is this type of thematic statement that an interpretation of a literary work attempts to establish and support.

The first claim of the Propositional Theory is also problematic because it makes use of an unanalysed concept of implication. It seems obvious that 'imply' cannot be analysed merely as the logicians' material implication or even logical entailment. To get the results it requires the theory must rest on a looser conception of implication. Clearly an account is needed of the way in which literary works imply general propositions. It has, however, been argued that there are good reasons to believe that all such accounts must fail.[8] The argument goes like this. All the loose conceptions of implication—like 'suggests', for example—are much too vague to give the theory any substance. The only plausible substantive version of the theory is one that holds that language as used in a literary work has a special 'poetic' meaning and that whatever propositions are implicit in the work, are implicit in it by virtue of its poetic meanings. If the poetic meaning is to be seen as residing in the literary work then we must assume a code for translating the literal content of the work, the content constituted by the ordinary meanings of its sentences, into 'symbolic paraphrase', which gives us the poetic meaning. However, according to the argument in question, this view is itself unsustainable. One objection is 'simply that novels are not allegories', another that 'it is unclear how much of the literal content of the work should be assigned a figurative counterpart'.[9] We will see in Chapter 14 how similar problems beset accounts of figurative truth.

But it is not clear that we must abandon all attempts to find a relevant sense for 'imply'. The most obvious place to look is the literary institution itself. For without getting too caught up in terminological matters the notion being sought must involve in some way the practice of interpretation and appreciation through which any general proposition regarding literary works is *elicited* and *supported*. A literary work 'implies' general propositions only in the sense that the practice of literary appreciation makes use of such propositions to organize into an intelligible pattern the events and situations described literally in a work.

The following remarks on Euripides' *Hecuba* offer the reader a perspective which subsumes the actions and the development of the various characters in the play under a complex general description which assigns a significance to these actions and to the development:

I have said that this tragedy shows us a case of solid character and shows us that, under certain circumstances, even this cannot escape defilement. It also has shown us that even the good character who has not suffered

---

[8] By Mary Sirridge, 'Truth from Fiction?', 459 ff.   [9] Ibid. 468.

any actual damage or betrayal lives always with the risk of these events: for it is in the nature of political structures to change, and in the nature of personal friendship that the confidence man should be indistinguishable from the trustworthy man—sometimes even to himself. In this sense, nothing human is ever *worthy* of my trust: there are no guarantees at all, short of revenge or death.[10]

And this critic goes on to expand these generalizations of the play further and apply them to other characters and other actions and events in the play. These general propositions, stated as a thesis about what the play 'shows us', are about the play itself, and they are supported by lengthy descriptions at various levels of generality of the actions, events, and characters of the play. The Propositional Theory need mean no more than this by the term 'imply'. There may be a problem about the nature and objectivity of interpretation, there may be a problem about what role general propositions of the type we have exemplified play in interpretation and appreciation (this is a problem which will be discussed later), but all the Propositional Theory has to assume is that this kind of interpretation (appreciation) is possible. The problem of how general propositions are implied by or associated with literary works is the problem of interpretation itself, if such a problem can be distinguished from the various problems of clarifying the practice of appreciation.

Propositions and truth

It is with the second claim, i.e. that the truth-value of the general propositions has to be assessed as part of the literary appreciation of the literary work, that the Propositional Theory gets into real trouble. To clarify this claim, it is useful first to make a point parallel to one made in Chapter 12, that the subject descriptions of a literary work, construed fictively, can be understood and assigned significance without any requirement that they be referential or involved in truth-claims. The parallel is that thematic statements, explicit as well as implicit, can be assigned significance and thus be understood without being construed as *asserted*. To understand the proposition 'The best human hopes and aspirations

---

[10] Nussbaum, *The Fragility of Goodness*, 419.

are always thwarted by forces beyond human control', which can be abstracted through interpretation from the Lydgate story in *Middlemarch*, one does not have to construe it as an assertion, either of the author or the work. There is consequently nothing in the way that a reader assigns significance to thematic statements, implicit or explicit, which in itself could be a reason for accepting the Propositional Theory. The question of truth is separate from the question of intelligibility. Although a reader might need to know the truth-*conditions* of the proposition to assign significance to a thematic statement this does not imply assessing its truth-*value* and requires at most some knowledge of how the propositional content might figure in contexts outside literary practice.

It might be thought that any playing-down of truth-assessment —for example, by pulling apart thematic content from asserted content—involves seeing the formulation of thematic statements, either in the literary work itself or in literary interpretation, as a derived use of language. That is, it might involve accepting that the use of general propositions to characterize and give coherence to the situations and events in a literary work is logically secondary to other truth-affirming modes of expression outside literary interpretation. But this is a logical point which does not really offend against any basic intuitions one might have about the nature of literary language or the way in which one talks about the worlds of literature in interpretation. As long as there exists a special practice of writing and reading of the type identified under the label 'literature', the derived nature of the literary use of language and of the interpretative vocabulary is difficult to deny. So this consequence of a no-truth view of literature cannot, in its turn, be used as a negative argument for accepting the Propositional Theory of Literary Truth.

The distinction between the content and mode of expression of a proposition can be used to make a further point. As we have seen, what makes the Propositional Theory attractive is not that it attempts to establish that literary works state truths about human life, but that they state *interesting* rather than *trivial* truths. Judgements about interest are made with regard to content and are independent of judgements concerning truth. What gives the Lydgate story in *Middlemarch* depth is not so much that it implies a true proposition, but that it can be interpreted as about humanly interesting concerns—for example, the nature and consequences of noble human desires. The thematic statement that noble human desires and aspirations are thwarted by forces beyond an individual's control gives focus to the treatment in the novel. No doubt a different artistic treatment could present a theme of equal interest albeit formulated in a proposition which is the precise negation of this one. It is the *content* of the proposition, what it is about, not its truth as such, that confers interest on the Lydgate story.

So far no reasons have been given for rejecting the Propositional Theory of Literary Truth. All that has been done is to remove some spurious reasons for accepting it. There is also a psychological factor involved: once judgements concerning interest and importance, or whatever one chooses to call this, are separated from judgements about truth, it is less *tempting* to insist that thematic statements are propositions that are asserted as truths about the world, commanding belief. And it is easier to focus on the real issue of whether there are aspects of literary practice which make it reasonable to say that thematic statements are subject to judgements about truth or falsity in relation to the world. The argument of the Propositional Theory is that there *must* be if literature is to be taken seriously, but presentations of this theory give no positive account of literary practice which demonstrates that the general propositions used to identify a significant pattern among the events, actions, and characters of a literary work must be construed as true or false assertions.

Before an attempt is made to say something about this, yet another distinction should be brought into play. The temptation to construe thematic statements as assertions about the world relates not merely to the failure to separate judgements about content from judgements about truth, but also to the distinction so central to this book between fact-stating and fictional discourse, i.e. between modes of utterance aimed at belief and modes of utterance aimed at imaginative reflection. It seems natural to admit that report-sentences in literary works are fictional (that is, characteristically, if not of necessity). That involves no stretching of the concept of fiction. However, to say that general propositions about human life and the 'human predicament' are fictional in their literary application is on the face of it more problematic. These propositions, particularly those derived from a literary work rather than those explicit in the work, are often held to be something 'more' than fiction. Again of course we must bear in mind the difference between the role of such propositions in assertions *about the work* and their role in assertions *tout court*. There is no need to deny the assertive function of the former, where questions of truth and falsity do legitimately arise (in connection to the validity or otherwise of the interpretation). The issue is only whether the propositions should be taken as assertions *about the world*; certainly it is not obvious that they should be construed *fictively*. Even in the case of those propositions contained explicitly in a work, like the one quoted from *Middlemarch*—'When a tender affection has been storing itself in us through many of our years, the idea that we could accept any exchange for it seems to be a cheapening of our lives'—we have argued that the *content* at least should be viewed as world-directed even if the mode of utterance is best viewed as fictive. However, again, this offers no positive support for the conclusion that such general propositions make truth-claims demanding belief—indeed the fictive mode points away from belief towards a different kind of response. It may, though, be a reason for suggesting that a discussion of the cognitive status of thematic statements needs a less rigid distinction than the one between fiction and non-fiction.

The role of general propositions in literature and criticism

It is time to tackle head-on the question whether there are in fact any reasons for maintaining the view that the general propositions elicited and supported through interpretation of a literary work are to be construed as true or false statements about human life. This question is not a question whether the general propositions used to organize the events, characters, and situations of a work into a significant and meaningful pattern have any application in contexts outside literature. Clearly they do and many have been so used. The question is whether assessment of their truth enters into the reader's appreciation of a literary work as a literary work.

Notice that there is one way of answering this question which is not open if one accepts that literature is defined and constituted within an institutional practice involving readers and authors. If literature is this type of practice, then the question about the cognitive status of the general statements implied by literary works must be answered with reference to the conventions of the practice and not with reference to the declared intentions of the single individual practitioner.

Perhaps the first feature to notice concerning the discourse about literature which one finds in criticism and conversation is that it does not contain much *debate* about the truth-value of these propositions. There is an absence of argument about whether or not a particular proposition or set of propositions implied in a literary work is true or false. Indeed, critical work is ended when it has been demonstrated how such a general proposition or set of propositions organizes the various features of a work into a meaningful pattern. Though the works of critics may contain statements to the effect that a literary work represents a certain view of life, and though it may be intimated that this view is shared or endorsed by the critic, critical treatments of literary works almost never present arguments in support of the view, or against the view in those cases where the critic intimates disagreement with it. Literary criticism is not defined by a series of speculative issues (of a psychological, sociological, philosophical, or historical nature) which are debated with reference to canonical standards of truth and correctness. Nor is there a part of criticism which deals with the truth or falsity of works, as there are parts which deal with, for example, narrative technique, themes and motifs, genres, and so forth. The issues of literary criticism concern aspects of literary works, and among these issues will be their handling of certain types of themes and concepts, but there is no accepted place for debate about the truth or falsity of general statements about human life or the human condition.

One might suggest that the reason for this is that such propositions are immediately recognized as true or false by every reader with a certain experience of life and the world. The ability to recognize the truth or falsity of the implied propositions, it might be argued, is what distinguishes the mature reader from the immature or adolescent reader. We all have the experience that the literature of our youth fades in importance as we come to see that it distorts certain facts about life and living. There is no debate about truth in literary criticism, so the argument might run, because every mature reader is in possession of such reasons as would lead to broad agreement with other readers on the acceptance or rejection of the explicit and implicit thematic statements of a literary work.

This, however, is a weak argument. First, it again confuses the question concerning the interest or importance of the implied general proposition with the question of its truth. The literature of our youth is defined by the prominence it gives to adolescent concerns and these are concerns that become less important to the mature reader. Secondly, it is untrue that mature readers agree on the acceptance or rejection of the explicit and implicit thematic statements of a literary work. As a general claim about human life the statement that 'The best human hopes and aspirations are always thwarted by forces beyond human control' would not be accepted by everyone but only by people with a certain view of life and a certain kind of temperament, as would the statement that 'Nothing human is ever *worthy* of my trust: there are no guarantees at all, short of revenge or death.' These statements are controversial and are formulations of philosophical views that have been the subject of centuries of philosophical debate.

The lack of debate in literary criticism and critical discourse in general about the truth of such general propositions must therefore be understood as a feature of the literary practice itself. In this respect literary practice is quite different from, say, philosophy where interpretation of the masters is subordinated to the question of where they failed and where they succeeded in achieving real insight. This feature of the logic of the literary practice can be illustrated by the different ways in which the word 'show' is used, on the one hand, in the passage on Euripides' *Hecuba* quoted on pp. 327-8 and, on the other hand, in the following passage:

In his meditations *Eperons* (*Spurs*), Jacques Derrida has shown how a text can be taken to have any number of contexts. Inscribing a specific context for a text does not *close* or *fix* the meaning of that text once and for all: there is always the possibility of reinscribing it within other contexts, a possibility that is indeed in principle boundless, and that is *structural* to any piece of language.[11]

Both these passages expound the views expressed in a specific text, maintaining that the author in that text has shown the reader something. However, the contexts in which the passages occur are different. The latter passage occurs as a part of a rhetorical project to convince the reader of the necessity and importance of the field

[11] Toril Moi, *Sexual/Textual Politics: Feminist Literary Theory* (London, 1985), 155.

of a 'new' discipline, 'textual theory'. The reference to Derrida is
an appeal to authority aimed at imposing a view of reality on the
reader which will make him more likely to accept the 'new' discipline. 'Show' is here used in what we may call a strong sense. The
use of 'show' invites the reader to disagree or agree with a view
of reality. And one would only agree that Derrida had shown
'how a text can be taken to have any number of contexts', if one
accepted his view and recognized how his arguments supported
that view. The use of 'show' in the passage on *Hecuba*, on the other
hand, is a *weak* use. The context in which that passage occurs is
that of a full-length interpretation of the play, and the rhetorical
aim of the passage is to convince the reader that *this is how the
work is to be interpreted*. The use of 'show' in that passage invites
the reader to agree or disagree with the critic about what that play
shows us, and we could agree that the play shows that 'nothing
human is ever *worthy* of my trust: there are no guarantees at all,
short of revenge or death', without accepting that this is true.

Debate about the truth or falsity of the propositions implied by
a literary work is absent from literary criticism since it does not
enter into *the appreciation of the work as a literary work*. Consider, for example, that central moment in Lydgate's story when
the trap closes gently over his head:

He touched her ear and little bit of neck under it with his lips, and they
sat quite still for many minutes which flowed by them like a small gur-
gling brook with the kisses of the sun upon it. Rosamond thought that no
one could be more in love than she was; and Lydgate thought that after
all his wild mistakes and absurd credulity, he had found perfect woman-
hood—felt as if already breathed upon by exquisite wedded affection
such as would be bestowed by an accomplished creature who venerated
his high musings and momentous labours and would never interfere with
them; who would create order in the home and accounts with still magic,
yet keep her fingers ready to touch the lute and transform life into romance at any moment; who was instructed to the true womanly limit and
not a hair's-breadth beyond—docile, therefore, and ready to carry out
behests which came from beyond that limit. It was plainer now than ever
that his notion of remaining much longer a bachelor had been a mistake:
marriage would not be an obstruction but a furtherance. And happening
the next day to accompany a patient to Brassing, he saw a dinner-service
there which struck him as so exactly the right thing that he bought it at
once. It saved time to do these things just when you thought of them, and
Lydgate hated ugly crockery. The dinner-service in question was expensive,

but that might be in the nature of dinner-services. Furnishing was necessarily expensive; but then it had to be done only once. (*Middlemarch*, chapter 36)

In this passage Lydgate is shown as falling victim to what George Eliot earlier in the novel had described as his 'commonness'. He falls for the lures of Middlemarch in the shape of Rosamond Vincy because of his prejudices about women and about familial and social life generally:

Lydgate's spots of commonness lay in the complexion of his prejudices, which, in spite of noble intention and sympathy, were half of them such as are found in ordinary men of the world: that distinction of mind which belonged to his intellectual ardour, did not penetrate his feeling and judgement about furniture, or women, or the desirability of its being known (without his telling) that he was better born than other country surgeons. He did not mean to think of furniture at present; but whenever he did so, it was to be feared that neither biology nor schemes of reform would lift him above the vulgarity of feeling that there would be an incompatibility in his furniture not being of the best. (*Middlemarch*, chapter 15)

'Middlemarch', George Eliot tells us in this chapter where she introduces Lydgate, 'in fact, counted on swallowing Lydgate and assimilating him very comfortably.' What makes the passage describing Lydgate's surrender crucial, what gives it what may be called depth and interest, is its imaginative realization of how Lydgate, because of the weakness of his character, is unable to resist the limiting and corrupting influences of Middlemarch society. The passage moves from registering the quality of the feeling of the romantic moment when Lydgate's fate is sealed (rendered in vulgar romantic cliché), to his thoughts about Rosamond as a woman and as a wife (again formulated in terms of romantic and adolescent clichés), to his false conclusion that it had been a mistake to think of remaining a bachelor, and to his consequent action of buying the dinner-service he can ill-afford because of the 'vulgarity of feeling' that things like dinner-services 'must be of the best'. The ironic tone of the passage also underlines that Lydgate's weaknesses and the influence of Middlemarch society are not only forces beyond the control of Lydgate himself but are also beyond the limits of his intellectual grasp. They can therefore destroy him all the more effectively. It is only when grasping the passage in some such way that the reader appreciates it properly as an aesthetic element in the work. However, this appreciation does not involve the reader asking further questions about the truth of the proposition 'The best human hopes and aspirations are always thwarted by forces beyond human control' (as a proposition about 'human life'). A debate about the substance of this thematic statement will be a debate about the possibility of free will and this is central in philosophy. The critic is free to join this debate, of course, but when he does he has moved on from literary appreciation of *Middlemarch*.

The conclusion to this argument must therefore be that the Propositional Theory of Literary Truth fails to give a plausible account of what we have called the mimetic aspect of literature. There is, however, one further move which the proponent of this theory can make. He can take up a more modest position and argue that literary appreciation does involve judgements about the truth and falsity of general propositions about reality, but only as a preliminary to or as a step in aesthetic appreciation:

an assertion about ideas in a work is not a reason for an aesthetic evaluation unless it assesses how well or badly ideas in the work are expressed. . . . But part of an assessment of how well ideas in a work are expressed is sometimes an assessment of the truth or falsehood, in certain respects, of ideas in the work . . . Since assessment of the truth of ideas in a work is not, however, in itself, assessment of the adequacy with which ideas in the work are expressed, truth-assessment is, at most, a part of expression-assessment, and, hence . . . provides at most a part of a reason for an aesthetic evaluation of a work.[12]

For example,

Suppose I say, '*As the World Turns* is inane. It constantly conveys the idea that suffering always results from malice, i.e., is either the intended result or the fated punishment of malicious action. But it shows no awareness of how paradoxical this conception of suffering is, in a world where most suffering seems to be neither the outcome of malice nor the punishment for it.' As I intend it, this criticism includes the assertion that the 'world of the work' wildly diverges from the real world. But my remarks are also a condemnation of the way the serial expresses its idea that suffering always results from malice. I condemn it for expressing this idea with appalling naïveté, without any attempt to acknowledge and cope

[12] Richard W. Miller, 'Truth in Beauty', *American Philosophical Quarterly*, 16 (1979), 324.

with the actual contrast between its conception of suffering and the apparent sources of suffering in the real world.[13]

However, this argument does not introduce anything new and, like some of the other arguments that have been discussed, is plausible only as long as one is willing to overlook a number of distinctions. For the reasons already given against seeing thematic statements as *asserted* statements, it is difficult to accept that this criticism of *As the World Turns* can be construed as a step in an aesthetic appraisal. If it is construed in that way, aesthetic appraisal would, in this case, lead straight into a discussion about the nature of suffering. For it is not obvious that the conception of suffering underlying the criticism of *As the World Turns* as 'inane' is correct or true. But, as was argued above, *this* type of discussion has no place in literary practice but forms part of other discursive practices.

The present example derives its appeal from two facts. First, it is true that in order to understand a fictional rendering of suffering, a reader would have to have some conception of suffering. This conception would at some point rest on knowledge about the world. In general, a reader always has to make assumptions about what beliefs an author has about the world, about what physical and social facts the author takes for granted and which he assumes the reader to recognize.[14] Any interpretative statement will therefore provide a basis for concluding that the reader is drawing on certain beliefs about the world. However, the reader's conceptions of the world would not have to be identical with those of the author, which merely have to be intelligible to him. One can, of course, criticize a work because it does not conform sufficiently well with one's own conception of the world, but this would not be aesthetic criticism.

The second fact which encourages the idea that such non-aesthetic criticism may appear to support aesthetic appraisal, is that there is a type of aesthetic appraisal that is concerned with *quality of thought* in a literary work. What we have been referring to as the human interest or importance of a literary work, or its

[13] Ibid. 323.

[14] This presupposed knowledge is often quite complex and detailed. For a discussion of this issue see Stein Haugom Olsen, 'Biography in Criticism' and 'History in Criticism' both in *Critical Instruments and Critical Concepts* (forthcoming). See also *The End of Literary Theory*, 64–5 and 174–5.

depth, is dependent upon two factors, the type of theme or idea presented and the development of that theme or idea in the work. The theme has to be of a type that is recognized as relevant to a 'central human concern'. Human suffering would be such a theme. Failure to identify such a theme in a literary work would lead to negative aesthetic appraisal. Then there is the question, not of how the theme is expressed, but about how it is developed. The analysis of the quotation from the Lydgate story in *Middlemarch* shows one step in the development of the theme that 'the best human hopes and aspirations are always thwarted by forces beyond human control'. The passage renders the inner workings of Lydgate's mind in such a way as to make the reader see how Lydgate is trapped by the combination of his own weaknesses of personality and the limitations of Middlemarch society as represented by Rosamond Vincy. This imaginative realization of the theme is complex and nuanced and other parts of the Lydgate story add to this complexity and these nuances. The analysis of the quoted passage is an attempt to appreciate the way in which the passage develops the theme. It provides an explanation of why this was not a naïve or simplistic way of dealing with the theme. In isolation, the thematic statement that 'The best human hopes and aspirations are always thwarted by forces beyond human control' is relatively empty of content. Until it is connected to a literary work through an interpretation which shows how the work develops the theme, we are not in a position to say anything about the quality of the theme.

The critical remarks on *As the World Turns* presented in the above example, can, in other words, be construed in two different ways. They can be construed as a criticism of the notion of suffering discoverable in *As the World Turns* because this notion does not conform to the notion of suffering which this critic, on the basis of his own experiences, believes to be adequate or true. In this case, as has been pointed out, there is no reason for maintaining that the criticism constitutes a step in aesthetic appreciation. Or it can be construed as a criticism of the way in which *As the World Turns* develops the theme of human suffering. This would be a step in the aesthetic appreciation of the work, but it would not involve attributing to the work any truth-claim about suffering itself. So even this modest version of the Propositional Theory is unacceptable.

14

Metaphorical Truth

Metaphorical truth and literary truth

One of the issues to emerge from the discussion of the Propositional Theory of Literary Truth concerned whether or how general propositions about human life might be thought of as *contained in* a literary work. Obviously those propositions which are explicitly expressed by sentences within the work are part of the work's *content* but even they pose problems as to how they should be construed. Do they serve a fictive, characterizing function? Do they define a literary theme? Are they authorial pronouncements asserted *in propria persona* about the extra-literary world? In general, what difference does their truth-value make, if any, to how the work is understood and appreciated? The propositions which are merely implied—and extracted in interpretation—bear a highly complex relation to the explicit sentential content yet we have seen that they are constrained by rather similar factors regarding their mode of construal.

Many commentators have supposed that at least for the implied general truths in literature the best model to explain the relevant kind of 'containment' is that of metaphor or figurative language. Although literary works are not *literally* true, so it is argued, they are none the less *metaphorically* true. The truths are contained in them in just the way that truths are contained in metaphors. We have seen that Goodman holds some such view of fiction and that Hayden White, who collapses the distinction between history and fiction, holds it of history.

Certainly the idea of metaphorical truth is comparable in many respects to that of literary truth. This is not because it is in any way essential to literary works that they use metaphorical language—some do, some do not—nor is the fictive the same as the figurative. Many narrative fictions only incidentally contain metaphors. But one striking similarity relates to appraisal. Metaphors, like literary works, are often praised for their ability to convey a special kind of truth, a truth not accessible by other means. Metaphors and literary works alike, so it is said, have a unique cognitive function. Their indirect presentation of truths perfectly complements the more direct means of literal and scientific language. The trouble is it is notoriously difficult to sustain these claims with any precision, for although low-key truth-values (those of simple assertions) are easily associated with many individual metaphors, the idea of some *special* cognitive potential of metaphor has proved just as elusive as the supposed truth-telling powers of literature. This, as we shall see, makes metaphor an uncomfortable model for explaining literary truth. In spite of this, however, we hope to show how a satisfactory and sustainable account of the powers of metaphor can turn out to be highly illuminating in understanding the powers of literature, just as the intuition that metaphors are potential bearers of truth closely parallels the intuition that literary works convey truths.

Metaphor gets into trouble right from the start because the expectations are so high. Aristotle, for example, praised metaphor as 'a sign of genius',[1] the Romantic poets saw poetic metaphors as 'the first and last of all knowledge',[2] and even a hard-headed analytic philosopher explains metaphorical truth as 'a transfer of a schema, a migration of concepts, an alienation of categories'.[3] Why should metaphors be thought to have such powers? The underlying idea is simple enough: that the unfamiliar juxtapositions effected by metaphor can, on a modest view, reveal previously unnoticed aspects of the world[4] or, on more radical views, even create new realities.[5] But that does not solve the truth problem. The question remains whether 'truth' is the right way to assess such achievements.

There is still a live debate among theorists of metaphor between those who reject the relevance of truth altogether and those who

---

[1] On the grounds that 'a good metaphor implies an intuitive perception of similarity in dissimilars', Aristotle, *Poetics* (1459ᵃ).

[2] William Wordsworth, Preface to the *Lyrical Ballads* (1800).

[3] Nelson Goodman, *The Languages of Art*, 73.

[4] e.g. Percy Bysshe Shelley: '[metaphorical language] ... marks the before unapprehended relations of things and perpetuates their apprehension', *A Defence of Poetry*, ed. Albert S. Cook (Boston, 1890), 4.

[5] e.g. Ina Loewenberg: 'a novel metaphor has created something in the world, has changed the world', has brought about a 'creative reconstruction of the world', in 'Creativity and Correspondence in Fiction and in Metaphors', *Journal of Aesthetics and Art Criticism*, 36 (1977–8), 348.

continue to try to find some precise role for it. And the kinds of reasons offered for rejecting the truth-assessment of metaphors are just like those familiar in the literary context. Here, for example, is a recent 'anti-truth' theorist:

We possess a battery of terms of appraisal. Many of these—'rich', 'insightful', 'imaginative', 'inspiring', 'provoking', 'deep', 'mind-stretching'— are perfectly at home in the appraisal of metaphor along 'cognitive' lines. We do not need, I believe, to add 'true' to this list. And if we do, we lose more than we gain in understanding why we produce metaphors and why we are concerned to appraise them.[6]

Even those who support the notion of a special metaphorical truth are likely to acknowledge a certain unease about using truth as a primary form of appraisal for metaphors and will often either extend the idea of truth itself or supplement it with other 'cognitive' terms.[7] Part of the unease comes from a sense that truth-assessment does not always seem appropriate (particularly in the case of complex poetic metaphors), part from a genuine uncertainty in individual cases about how to make the assessment.[8] A similar sense of unease underlies the resistance to truth-assessment in the literary case.

Also the traditional, empiricist, hostility to figurative usage is comparable to the hostility found towards literary fiction and poetry. In both cases it has been thought that truth itself is compromised. Here is Locke's famous onslaught:

if we would speak of Things as they are, we must allow, that all the Art of Rhetoric, besides Order and Clearness, all the artificial and figurative application of Words Eloquence hath invented, are for nothing else but to insinuate wrong *Ideas*, move the Passions, and thereby mislead the

---

[6] David Cooper, *Metaphor* (Oxford, 1986), 251.

[7] e.g. Eva Feder Kittay, while developing a new version of an 'interaction' account of metaphor which accommodates the idea of 'metaphorical truth', emphasizes 'cognitive force' and 'epistemic access' more than truth *per se*: 'The cognitive force of metaphor comes, not from providing new information about the world, rather from a (re)conceptualization of information that is already available to us', *Metaphor* (Oxford, 1987), 39.

[8] Monroe Beardsley, whose view we will be examining, acknowledges the point, in spite of being a strong defender of metaphorical truth. He admits that we often have to resort to appraisals like 'largely true' or 'apt', even in the case of non-poetic metaphors: 'The Nixon administration ... was the high-water mark of the imperial presidency', he says is 'apt' but 'contains some untruth', 'Metaphorical Senses', *Nous*, 12 (1978), 15.

Judgement; and so indeed are perfect cheat: And, therefore, however laudable or allowable Oratory may render them in Harangues and popular Addresses, they are certainly, in all Discourses that pretend to inform or instruct, wholly to be avoided; and where Truth and Knowledge are concerned, cannot but be thought a great fault, either of the Language or Person that makes use of them.[9]

Note that Locke is not strictly criticizing the art of rhetoric, including metaphor, as such, only its use in certain contexts. The distinction between the nature of metaphor *per se* and the uses to which metaphors can be put ('moving the passions', embellishment, obfuscation, poetry) will be central to what follows.

We will argue that it is no more a constitutive aim of metaphor to convey truth than it is of literature. But in certain contexts, and contingently, metaphorical utterances can yield truths—and be intended to do so—just as can fictive utterances and literary works. We will not offer a fully worked-out theory of metaphor but will show that the kind of approach we have proposed for fictive utterance can be fruitfully applied also to figurative utterance, with similar implications for truth-assessment.

The diversity of metaphor

One problem for any theory of metaphor is accounting for the remarkable diversity of the phenomenon. Metaphorical utterances vary enormously in quality, purpose, and context and it is perhaps a forlorn hope, if not actually a misguided one, to suppose that any substantive uniform account could be given. Take the question of quality. Metaphors are often spoken of as either 'dead' or 'live' but this is a gradation not a polarity. The more a metaphor is used the less 'life' or 'freshness' it possesses; metaphors are in a constant process of 'dying' through use and familiarity. When they are finally 'dead' they cease to be metaphors as such altogether and acquire a new, perhaps idiomatic, sense subject to standard literal truth-conditions. 'Pass the buck', 'pull someone's leg', 'the star of the show' are no longer metaphors strictly speaking (or, to say the same, they are thoroughly 'dead'). But there is

[9] John Locke, *An Essay Concerning Human Understanding* (1690), bk. III, ch. x, sect. 34.

a continuum up through moribund figures, having one's 'back to the wall' or 'being caught out' in an argument; to fresh and interesting one-off metaphors, like Wittgenstein's remark 'a cloud of philosophy condensed into a drop of grammar'; right up to developed poetic metaphors, such as Shakespeare's 'Then let not winter's ragged hand deface | In thee thy summer, ere thou be distill'd' (Sonnet VI). This diversity of quality, though obvious enough in itself, is important in a discussion of truth. For broadly speaking the less 'life' there is in a metaphor the easier it is to assign a truth-value, yet it is only in the 'lively' metaphors that truth, of the alleged 'special' nature, seems to be of interest.

A similar point could be made in connection with the diversity of purpose. Sometimes the occurrence of a metaphor in an assertion is incidental to the intended content—the information conveyed—and thus has no direct impact on truth-assessment. In a context where factual information is of primary importance one could assert that one's enemy had gone into hiding by saying, for example, 'the fox has gone to ground' without raising any particular problem about truth. In such a context the truth or falsity of the metaphorical assertion is no more problematic than that of its literal counterpart.[10] But the metaphor is of low quality so the intended sense is clearly recognizable. Sometimes a metaphor is incidental to the truth-conditions of a sentence, not because it has a stock meaning, but because it figures in the presuppositional rather than informational content of the sentence. 'That crafty weasel has passed the exam' is true if and only if the person identified in the subject-term has passed the exam. The informational content, that a particular person has passed an exam, is both literal and determinate, thus again presenting no problem of truth-assignment.[11]

---

[10] Timothy Binkley makes a related point: '"Richard is a fox" ... is no more vague and ill-defined, no less connected with definite criteria, than "Richard is a good husband" or "Richard is a scoundrel"': 'On the Truth and Probity of Metaphor', *Journal of Aesthetics and Art Criticism*, 33 (1974), 174. However, a lot depends on the purpose of the assertion; if the purpose is just to make a simple claim or judgement about Richard, in the context of an exchange of information or opinion, then Binkley's point is right. But if the purpose is to elicit a full appreciation of the metaphor, then the 'criteria' might be somewhat less 'definite'.

[11] Such cases recall Strawson's discussion of the truth-evaluation of sentences containing non-referring names; whether or not these have a determinate truth-value, he argued, will depend on whether the 'offending' expressions occur as part of the 'topic' or the information content. See 'Identifying Reference and Truth-Value'.

In general the occurrence of a metaphorical expression in a sentence does not *of itself* create a problem for either truth or reference. What matters is the role or status of the metaphor. In cases where it is clear *what is being conveyed* by a sentence there is no special problem arising for truth or reference even if the sentence contains a metaphor. But that of course takes us to the central issue. For it is precisely in the cases of 'lively' or poetic metaphors—where, to use different terminology, the metaphor is 'foregrounded'—that there is no simple identification of 'what is being conveyed' or of 'content'. And it is for that reason we have difficulty assigning a truth-value. The question of truth cannot be separated from that of content or meaning. For sentences (including those containing metaphors) are not just true, they are true under an interpretation (or an assignment of meaning). What is true is relative to what is meant. No theory of metaphorical truth can be advanced independently of a theory of metaphorical meaning.

Metaphorical meaning

Needless to say, there is as much disagreement about the kind of meaning that metaphors have as there is about metaphorical truth. It is worth remarking that this is principally a disagreement of theory, about the nature of metaphorical meaning, rather than a practical disagreement about how to interpret individual metaphors. With a little prompting and coaxing most of us can come to agree, more or less, on how to 'take' a particular metaphor, even of the most 'lively' kind. We 'bring to mind' the same kinds of considerations and we agree about the appropriateness of certain (ranges of) responses. That does not mean that we can always supply an accurate literal paraphrase but then paraphrase is a problem for both literal and metaphorical language. Paraphrasing and understanding are different skills and the latter does not presuppose the former.

Theoretical interest in recent years has focused on where to 'locate' those thoughts, ideas, images, and so forth, that a good metaphor 'brings to mind'. That is where the parallel with literature, and literary understanding, arises again, particularly in debates about the status (objectivity, etc.) of interpretation. Some theories, inspired by earlier attempts within analytic philosophy to explain the meaning-generativity of metaphor, identify these derived thoughts and ideas as essentially linguistic in origin, rooted in the senses or connotations of words.[12] Others, under the influence of Davidson, have sought to give a non-linguistic (or non-semantic) account of the understanding of metaphors, locating the 'content' in the minds of respondents, as psychological effects, rather than in the meanings of words.[13] We will be looking in detail at examples of both these approaches, for they have radically different implications for metaphorical truth. If, as Davidson believes, there is no fixed 'content' of a ('lively') metaphor other than the strictly literal meaning of its constituent terms, then there seems to be nothing *in the metaphor* which could be a bearer of truth. Truth would have to reside, if anywhere, only with the thoughts or beliefs that the metaphor 'brings to mind'.

Content versus no-content

The search for metaphorical meaning, and thus truth, has to confront the idea of metaphorical 'content', or what might be called the location problem. If metaphors express truths, how are those truths 'contained in' the terms comprising the metaphor? A similar question confounded the Propositional Theory of Literary Truth. To help bring the issues into focus we will look at two paradigmatic accounts: Davidson's 'no content' theory and Beardsley's 'conversion' theory which, in contrast, proposes a clearly defined notion of metaphorical content.[14] Although we do

[12] Particularly influential here was the work of Max Black (e.g. 'Metaphor', *Proceedings of the Aristotelian Society*, 55 (1954), 273–94, repr. in *Models and Metaphors: Studies in Language and Philosophy* (Ithaca, NY, 1962)), Goodman (e.g. *The Languages of Art*), and Beardsley (e.g. *Aesthetics*, ch. 3). More recently, Kittay in her book *Metaphor* has offered a refinement of Black's interaction theory; Robert Fogelin, in *Figuratively Speaking* (New Haven, Conn., 1988) has developed a new version of the 'comparativist' view; and Novitz, in *Knowledge, Fiction and Imagination*, has applied truth-conditional semantics to metaphorical meaning.

[13] Donald Davidson, 'What Metaphors Mean', *Critical Inquiry*, 5 (1978), 31–47, repr. in *Inquiries into Truth and Interpretation*. Davidson's position is developed and defended in Cooper, *Metaphor*. A similar view can be found in Richard Rorty, 'Unfamiliar Noises: Hesse and Davidson on Metaphor', *Proceedings of the Aristotelian Society*, Suppl. Vol. 61 (1987), 283–96.

[14] Citations from Davidson and Beardsley (with page references in parenthesis) will be from: Davidson, 'What Metaphors Mean', and Beardsley, 'Metaphorical Senses'.

not endorse either theory *tout court* each has important elements which need to be retained. What must be rejected is the very framework set up by the location problem.

Beardsley's influential attempts, in a series of discussions,[15] to define metaphorical meaning are of special interest because of their connection with his conception of literary criticism. For Beardsley 'the explication of metaphor is the model of all explication'[16] so he holds that the process involved in understanding a poem (or other literary work) is just a special case of that involved in grasping the content of a metaphor. His strenuous attempts to keep psychology out of criticism and to identify a 'textual meaning' independently of authorial intent and affective response are closely mirrored in his account of metaphorical meaning. Although he is right to see parallels between the two kinds of interpretation—literary and metaphorical—he is wrong, so we argue, to explain the common element in terms of the meanings of 'texts'.

On the face of it the disagreement between Davidson and Beardsley is substantial, the former rejecting the notion of metaphorical meaning, the latter proposing it. Davidson argues for two negative theses: first, against the idea that 'a metaphor has, in addition to its literal sense or meaning, another sense or meaning', and, second, against the idea that 'associated with metaphor is a cognitive content that its author wishes to convey and that the interpreter must grasp if he is to get the message'. Likewise there are two positive theses: first, that 'metaphors mean what the words, in their most literal interpretation mean, and nothing more' (32), second, that 'a metaphor makes us see one thing as another by making some literal statement that inspires or prompts the insight' (47).

Beardsley's theory, in contrast, is a version of what Fogelin has called a 'meaning-shift' theory.[17] The central idea, common to all theories of this kind, including those of Henle,[18] Black, Goodman, Kittay, Novitz, and others, is that metaphors generate new

[15] Beardsley, *Aesthetics*, ch. 3; 'The Metaphorical Twist', *Philosophy and Phenomenological Research*, 22 (1962), 293–307; 'Metaphor', in Paul Edwards (ed.), *Encyclopedia of Philosophy* (London, 1967); 'Metaphor and Falsity', *Journal of Aesthetics and Art Criticism*, 35 (1976), 218–22.

[16] Beardsley, *Aesthetics*, 144.

[17] Fogelin, *Figuratively Speaking*, 69 ff.

[18] Paul Henle, 'Metaphor', in Paul Henle (ed.), *Language, Thought and Culture* (Ann Arbor, Mich., 1965).

meanings, that a shift of meaning takes place within the terms comprising the metaphor. Beardsley puts it like this: 'when an expression becomes a metaphorical segment it acquires a sense different from any of its standard senses' (5).

Beardsley's theory has two parts. The first gives the conditions for the identification of a 'metaphorical segment' (i.e. expression):

(A) An expression E is a metaphorical segment of sequence S iff
   (i) E is a proper part of S and is a predicate or modifier of part or all of the (literal) remainder of S ($S\bar{E}$) (note that this allows for metaphors within metaphors);
   (ii) the combination of E with $S\bar{E}$ is barred by a rule;
   (iii) some credence-properties of the extension of E (in one of its standard senses) are such that it is possible for them to be properties of members of the extension of (part or all of) $S\bar{E}$ (in one of its standard senses).

The second offers a characterization of the metaphorical sense or intension that the metaphorical segment acquires:

(B) The intension of E in S consists of the set of all the credence-properties of the extension of E (in the relevant standard sense) that are not denied of members of the extension of $S\bar{E}$ (in the relevant standard sense) by the context, verbal or situational, of S.

The key term is 'credence-property'. This is a property 'commonly believed to belong to most or to normal members of the extension' of a general term (8):

The properties that count in metaphor are not the actual properties denoted by the metaphorical term, but believed properties. The metaphorical uses of 'lion' depend on what people tend to think lions are like. (8)

The idea is similar to that of Max Black's 'system of associated commonplaces' (or, in a later version, 'implication-complex'[19]).

In spite of radical disagreement on the question of whether or not a metaphorical expression has a sense over and above the literal sense of its component terms, there remain significant points of agreement between Beardsley and Davidson.

1. They agree on the capacity of metaphor to convey insights, novel ideas, or new ways of looking at things; they disagree only

---

[19] Max Black, 'More about Metaphor', in Andrew Ortony (ed.), *Metaphor and Thought* (Cambridge, 1979), 29.

on how this is done. There is no reason to think that they would disagree on what insights or ideas are conveyed by any given metaphor.

2. They agree that a complete literal description of all that a metaphor conveys is not always (readily) available. Although Beardsley's Principle (B) specifies what constitutes the meaning of any metaphor, namely a set of credence-properties, he concedes that '[m]etaphor is inherently expansive' (12) and that a 'speaker/ writer on a particular occasion will probably be unaware of many of these properties' (12). For Davidson, what a metaphor conveys might be neither 'finite in scope nor propositional in character' (46).

3. They agree that interpretation or 'explication' of metaphor is often needed and that this is a skill going beyond mere linguistic competence; knowledge of (literal) meanings is not enough. For Davidson, interpreting a metaphor involves attempting in some other way 'to evoke what the metaphor brings to our attention' (46); '[t]he legitimate function of so-called paraphrase is to make the lazy or ignorant reader have a vision like that of the skilled critic' (47). For Beardsley, interpretation 'requires empirical knowledge of relevant applicable credence-properties' (8).

4. They agree on the assumption of some notion of the 'standard' or literal sense of an expression. Both their accounts rely on such a notion. For Beardsley, the 'standard sense' of an expression when it becomes a 'metaphorical segment' gives way to a new metaphorical sense. He describes a 'standard sense of an expression' as 'a sense that remains invariant through some range of verbal or situational contexts that are of the same kind, though varied' (5). For Davidson, the standard or literal sense of an expression used metaphorically, a sense defined by the truth-conditions of the sentence in which it appears, is the only sense it possesses.

5. Finally, they agree on a criterion for 'cognitive content': that it be propositional in form and assessable as true or false. Part of Davidson's argument against cognitive content in metaphors is that much of what is brought to mind by a metaphor is 'not propositional in character' (46). Beardsley indicates that he takes the issue of the 'cognitive status of metaphors' to be the question 'whether metaphorical sentences can properly be called true or false' (3).

Davidson says this of his agreement and disagreement with theorists such as Beardsley: 'I don't disagree with [them] . . . in their accounts of what metaphor accomplishes except that I think it accomplishes more and that what is additional is different in kind. My disagreement is with the explanation of how metaphor works its wonders' (33). For Davidson, the prime mechanism is *causal*. What a metaphor accomplishes, i.e. what it conveys or 'brings to mind', is to be located in the *effects* or *consequences* of attending to the metaphor. For Beardsley, who need not deny any of the effects that Davidson identifies, a significant portion of what a metaphor accomplishes or brings to mind is to be located in the *intension* or *sense* of the metaphorical segment itself. Is there any way of deciding this issue of location?

Consider this metaphor from a leader in *The Times*:

Reticence usually descends on the Northern Ireland Office when it has an initiative in the oven. This time it is more like a cookery class. The ingredients are laid out, their properties discussed, the mixture tasted. The only reason for some uncertainty remaining about the dish is that the cooks are making up the recipe as they go along.

There is little problem grasping what is being said and that can be done without labouring to produce a detailed paraphrase. The bare factual information is easily recognized. A further response, though, is to call to mind other metaphors or idioms associated with cooking or kitchens. A powerful association, for example, is that of something's being 'cooked up', which has come to mean doing something in an *ad hoc* or even unprincipled or dishonest fashion. This association with the *ad hoc* is confirmed in the claim that 'the cooks are making up the recipe as they go along'. Other kitchen idioms or sayings are triggered as well: 'too many cooks spoil the broth', things are 'heating up' or being 'brought to the boil'; something is 'in the melting pot' or in the mixing bowl. But there is more to the metaphor than that. It is also a strikingly *homely* figure; the suggestion is that there is nothing too dangerous, alarming or even serious going on. The tone of the passage is light-hearted.

The example helps establish several preliminary points about the understanding of metaphors: straightforward factual information can be conveyed through metaphors; comprehending a metaphor often involves invoking other metaphors; metaphors can set a tone which affects attitudes or response; lively metaphors initiate a thought-process—a 'working out'—which is not normally involved in grasping a literal sense; much of the pleasure of a metaphor comes from following through its associations and suggestions.

But where does that leave metaphorical meaning and content? Is the process of 'working out' we have described merely, as Davidson would have it, an imaginative reaction to the stimulus of a piece of literal nonsense ('an initiative in the oven', etc.) or is it, following Beardsley and the 'meaning-shift' theorists, a matter of recovering a new metaphorical sense acquired in the context by the sentences and phrases?

Neither view seems quite right. First of all, what are we to make of Davidson's rejection of the thesis that 'associated with a metaphor is a cognitive content that its author wishes to convey and that the interpreter must grasp if he is to get the message' (46)? If he is claiming there is never some such content or message he must be wrong; our example clearly shows otherwise in its unequivocal assertion that the Northern Ireland Office is planning a new initiative. The passage would have to be judged false (contrary to fact) or inaccurate if this proposition were false. But Davidson is not denying that some such (true or false) thoughts might be conveyed; he admits that some of what is 'brought to mind' by a metaphor might be propositional. What he denies is that these propositions are part of the *content* of the metaphor. 'The common error', he writes, 'is to fasten on the contents of the thoughts a metaphor provokes and to read these contents into the metaphor itself' (45). Presumably he would think that Beardsley's theory commits just such an error.

We are now confronted with the dichotomy between what is 'brought to mind' by and what is 'contained' in the sample passage. The matter goes to the heart of the wider problem of interpretation. But there are no clear guidelines for settling the issue precisely because 'containment' itself is a metaphor subject to different interpretations. There are 'rich' and 'austere' accounts of meaning 'content'. Beardsley's is rich: it includes all the credence-properties associated with the constituent terms. Others prefer a more 'modest' account, for example distinguishing a core, truth-conditional, meaning and other 'affective' dimensions (Novitz is one such[20]). Others again distinguish between the content of what a speaker means and that of what the sentence means.[21] Davidson's view is the most 'austere', recognizing no content other than that of literal meaning.

The rejection of 'content'

We are better doing without the idea of 'content' altogether.

Talk of 'containment' is pervasive in discussions of language as part of a wider network of metaphors that dominate our conception of meaning: we 'discover', 'uncover', or 'dig out' meanings; meanings can be 'hidden', 'disguised', or 'brought to the surface', and so on.[22] The idea of content has kept alive a central, longstanding debate in aesthetics (including literary criticism) about how to distinguish those properties thought genuinely to be *possessed* by, or *contained* in, a work of art and those *imposed* on it by perhaps over-zealous interpreters. Is the critic merely describing properties discovered in a work or imputing properties to a work arising from an interpretation of it? In literary criticism the issue often centres on the containment of *meaning*.

However, the validity of these questions—particularly as applied to literary interpretation—can be called into doubt. The idea that aesthetically relevant properties of literary works have an objective existence 'within' words and sentences embodies a misconception of the nature of literary works.[23] For the 'content' that is identified or characterized by literary interpretation is dependent on the very same institutional rules that define a work as 'literary'. Certainly there are textual features of a literary work, including 'meanings', that are independent of the literary institution. But literary interpretation identifies aesthetic as well as merely

[20] Novitz, *Knowledge, Fiction and Imagination*, 182–3.

[21] Searle's theory is the clearest example. See the chapter 'Metaphor' in *Expression and Meaning*.

[22] Michael Reddy has characterized this pervasive metaphor about ideas and meanings as the 'conduit metaphor' and has identified 141 examples of idiomatic uses in English which relate to this metaphorical system. He goes on to argue that this 'conduit metaphor' has an insidious effect on our understanding of human communication and that what is needed is a 'frame restructuring'. See Michael Reddy, 'The Conduit Metaphor', in Ortony (ed.), *Metaphor and Thought*.

[23] See Olsen, *The End of Literary Theory, passim.*

textual features and to speak of the 'content' of a literary work—
its themes, what it is about—is to speak of its aesthetic properties,
those that explain its purpose and interest. The dichotomy between
discovering properties and imposing them through an interpretation
gets lost if we introduce such institutionally dependent properties.
The validity of interpretations is subject to constraints, of course,
but these are not illuminated by appeal to 'content'; in fact quite
the reverse, for the idea of 'content' in this context gets its sense
from the institutionally determined constraints governing interpretation.

Much can be learned from these observations about literary
practice when applied to the understanding of metaphors. Indeed
the debate about what a metaphor 'contains' in contrast to what
it 'brings to mind'—like the debate about what a literary work
'contains'—is also misconceived. We will be arguing, in the case of
metaphor, for a radical shift away from the notion of meaning as
content. But to see precisely how the idea of 'content' unravels we
must return to the theories under consideration.

Why not apply to metaphor the idea of 'content' familiar in
componential semantics where the model is *analytic* containment
such that, for example, the components MALE and UNMARRIED could
be said to be part of the semantic content of 'bachelor'? One
problem with this model, at least for a theory like Beardsley's, is
that more than merely semantic facts are involved in metaphors.
To put it in epistemological terms, knowledge of the meanings of
words is not sufficient for understanding a metaphor. Beliefs about
the world (about objects, about other people's beliefs) are required
as well. Beardsley's theory, we have seen, relies on the distinction
between those characteristics *designated* by a word, comprising its
standard sense, and those *connoted* by the word, which he calls
credence-properties. For Beardsley, in certain linguistic contexts,
where semantic combinations are 'barred by a rule', the standard
senses (involving analytic containment) are suppressed, and
credence-properties thereby released and selected to form the new
metaphorical senses. The credence-properties, based on non-
semantic beliefs and triggered by the specific metaphorical combination, are not attached to the terms *independently of any context*;
they become semantic features of the sentence, temporarily, in
context.

One reason why the issue between Davidson and Beardsley on

the location problem might seem insubstantial, resting on a tenuous notion of 'content', is that the semantic content that Beardsley identifies is (1) acquired only in context, and (2) is extra-linguistic in origin, involving facts (and beliefs) about the world rather than facts about language. This very loose connection between what metaphors 'bring to mind' and standard literal meanings is the core of Davidson's theory. In effect Beardsley, while appealing to semantic content, compromises with the paradigm offered by analytic containment.

However, another theorist, L. J. Cohen, does not compromise with that paradigm and offers a more purely semantic account of metaphor; his theory brings out sharply one way in which metaphorical meaning might be said to be *contained* in or a property of linguistic expressions.[24] It is helpful bringing this theory into the debate because its emphasis on linguistic meaning as a source for all metaphorical meaning has certain parallels with textualist accounts of literary meaning, i.e. accounts which see texts themselves as generators of meaning. Indeed it is instructive to run through the difficulties we identify for the semantic theory in application to textualist theories in literary criticism. The difficulties substantiate our earlier rejection of 'texts' in favour of 'works'.

For Cohen there is no distinction, except as a matter of degree, between what Beardsley calls a standard sense and what he calls a credence-property. Cohen believes that all belong among semantic features; they should figure in the ideal lexicon. 'The metaphorical meanings of a word or phrase in a natural language are all contained, as it were, within its literal meaning or meanings.'[25] Indeed, he 'regard[s] a feature's lending itself ... to the construction of metaphor as evidence that it has in fact passed into the language'.

According to Cohen, metaphorical combinations acquire their meaning through the cancellation of semantic features (rather as the feature + ANIMATE is cancelled in the expression 'stone lion'). The main difference between this theory and Beardsley's is that for Beardsley when an expression becomes, in context, a

[24] L. J. Cohen, 'The Semantics of Metaphor', in Ortony (ed.), *Metaphor and Thought*.

[25] L. J. Cohen and A. Margalit, 'The Role of Inductive Reasoning in the Interpretation of Metaphor', in Donald Davidson and Gilbert Harman (eds.), *Semantics of Natural Language* (Dordrecht, 1972), 735.

metaphorical segment it acquires a new sense with semantic components that it does not possess apart from that context, while for Cohen the context serves merely to *select* a sense whose components are already present. Where both theorists agree is in the view that, whether through cancellation or multiplication, the resultant metaphorical sense is a linguistic (semantic) property of an expression.

However, neither theory is satisfactory and the reasons for their failure are also reasons why the understanding of metaphor cannot be explained through the idea of discovering the meaning content of a linguistic expression.

Let us address Cohen's theory first. Many objections could be raised, not least against the supposition that metaphorical meanings are already semantic in origin, that metaphor is part of *langue*, as he says, not *parole*.[26] But the most serious objection, from the point of view of literary criticism, is that the theory denies the possibility of a metaphor's creating new associations, going beyond those already contained as part of the meanings of the expressions used. For Cohen the contextual selection of a metaphorical reading is not different in principle from the process of disambiguation. However, it seems clear that, unlike disambiguation, in the case of lively metaphors, context can do more than merely select between antecedently present alternatives. The contexts can *create* associations; the frame of reference within which the connections are formed is not so much given as made. It seems likely that any substantive cognitive theory of metaphor would have to rely on such an assumption.

Literary metaphors provide the clearest illustration of the way that contexts can create, as well as merely select, associations. To establish the point convincingly would require the detailed exploration of particular literary examples.[27] However, literary critics probably need little persuasion; the complex development of a metaphor through a poem, for example, is stock in trade. Here is

[26] David Cooper produces powerful objections; see *Metaphor*, 63–6. See also Peter Lamarque, 'Metaphor and Reported Speech: In Defence of a Pragmatic Theory', *Journal of Literary Semantics*, 11 (1982), 14–18.

[27] The point is well illustrated by examples from Novitz and Olsen: see Novitz, *Knowledge, Fiction and Imagination*, 185 ff.; and Stein Haugom Olsen, 'Understanding Literary Metaphors', in David S. Miall (ed.), *Metaphor: Problems and Perspectives* (Brighton, 1982), 39 ff.

Cleanth Brooks pursuing the metaphor of the sun (and light) in Wordsworth's 'Intimations of Immortality':

the implied comparison of the child to the sun or the moon is still active here [Stanza v] ... If the sun, at his glorious birth, lights up a world with the glory and freshness of a dream, with a light which persists even after he has begun to ascend the sky, yet [sic] the sun gradually becomes the destroyer of his earlier world and becomes his own prisoner. Indeed it is very easy to read the whole stanza as based on a submerged metaphor of the sun's progress: the soul is like our life's star, the sun, which has had elsewhere its setting. It rises upon its world, not in utter nakedness. The trailing clouds of glory suggest the sunrise. The youth is like the sun, which, as it travels farther from the east, leaves the glory more and more behind it, and approaches prosaic daylight. But it is the sun itself which projects the prosaic daylight, just as the man projects the common day which surrounds him and upon which he now looks without joy.

[In the final stanza] ... the hint that it is the child who confers the 'gleam' upon the world becomes explicit. The clouds take their sober colouring from the eye. Even if we make 'eye' refer to the sun as the eye of day, we have but brought the basic metaphors into closer relationship. If the sun, the eye of heaven, after it has watched over mortality, is sobered, so is the eye of man who has kept the same watch. The parallel between the sun and the developing child which we noticed in Stanza v is completed.[28]

In drawing out the connections in the poem between the sun and the growing boy, Brooks himself relies heavily on Wordsworth's own metaphors, 'glorious birth', 'clouds of glory', and so on. He is not so much explicating as connecting, filling out the frame of reference for the poem's recurring images. But what he shows, among other things, is that the poem both uses and extends the standard metaphorical associations of the sun: life, growth, nurture, time, light, etc. Of course the interest lies not simply in what new associations the poem manages to conjure from an otherwise familiar metaphorical frame rather in the way the metaphor contributes to, and helps to develop, the more general themes of the poem. In the case of a literary work the relevant context that serves to create as well as select metaphorical meanings is not just semantic in nature but also thematic. Only relative to an overall thematic interpretation is it possible to identify the function of the metaphor and thus its 'meaning'. A semantic theory such

[28] Brooks, *The Well-Wrought Urn*, 106-7.

as Cohen's, which limits metaphorical meanings to antecedently predictable semantic features, is ill-equipped to explain this interconnectedness of metaphor and theme within a literary context. More precisely the method of cancellation cannot explain the way the semantic features supposedly brought to light in a metaphor are themselves affected, perhaps acquiring further metaphorical accretions ('life', 'growth', 'birth' all have at least extended senses in the 'Ode'), by their role in the development of a thematic conception.

Although the case of literary metaphors well illustrates the generativity of context, much simpler artificial examples can establish the principle. Consider the effects of this stretch of discourse on the metaphors that follow it:

Jane prefers lobsters to crabs. Lobsters are more exotic, albeit expensive and not readily obtained; their meat is sweet and delicate and they are fine looking with their rich red colour and their massive claws. It is also easy to crack open their shells. Crabs, on the other hand, are fiddly to eat, have hard shells, and leave little spikes in the mouth; and they don't even provide a substantial meal.

For Jane, while Richard is a lobster, John is a crab.

There are several points to note about this example. First of all, the metaphorical attributions that the predicates 'crab' and 'lobster' invite in this context, deriving from the preceding descriptions, cannot reasonably be said to be antecedently present among the semantic features of the two terms. 'Lobster' acquires the association of being sexually attractive if elusive, while 'crab' suggests something unappealing and difficult. These are not semantic in origin. Such counter-examples to Cohen's cancellation thesis could be generated at will.

Second, it is doubtful whether even on Beardsley's conversion theory the attributions could be said to belong among the credence-properties of the extensions of 'crab' and 'lobster'. This suggests that Beardsley's Principle (B) fails to capture the *ad hoc* character of many metaphorical connotations.

One reason why this example poses difficulties for both Cohen and Beardsley is that without reference to a specific context the sentences 'Richard is a lobster' and 'John is a crab' seem to lack even the potential for successful interpretation. Without contextual guidance it is difficult to think of any relevant properties of crabs and lobsters that can be transferred to people. It is not even clear that failing such guidance it is even correct to identify the sentences as metaphorical. According to Cohen's theory, being metaphorical is a property of sentences in *langue*; our own view, to which we will return, is that it is rather a property of utterances in context. Not just any semantic anomaly can count as a metaphor; it is important, for example, to distinguish making a metaphor and making a mistake.

However, it should not be thought that the need to refer to contexts in metaphorical interpretation is sufficient to count against semantic treatments of metaphor. Both Cohen and Beardsley rightly stress the importance of context; and context-relativity—ambiguity, indexicality, and so forth—is well accommodated in semantic theory. The weakness of their accounts lies in the assumption that contexts can generate in a more or less mechanical, or at least predictable, manner the appropriate interpretations, either through the cancellation of semantic features or through the selection of credence-properties. What the theories crucially lack is not reference to contexts but references to *the purposes of speaking metaphorically* and to the imaginative processes involved in the understanding of metaphors.

Returning to Beardsley's theory, we can soon see the consequences of this omission. For one thing, the application of Beardsley's Principle (B), which identifies the new metaphorical sense with the set of credence-properties not denied by the context, leaves it a complete mystery why any new sense should emerge. Why should the terms lose their literal senses and acquire a new sense solely in virtue of their juxtaposition in a sentence? Also there can be no purely mechanical way by which the relevant set of credence-properties is selected, even given, *per impossibile*, an exhaustive list of such properties. Worse still there is the problem that for most metaphors the transference of credence-properties from one set of objects to another cannot be carried through except metaphorically. We saw this in the case of the *Times* metaphor; what came to mind in interpreting the metaphor of having an 'initiative in the oven' were not properties which could be literally attributed to both initiatives and ovens but rather a cluster of other metaphors, like being cooked up, heated up or brought to the boil. There is a severe limit to the credence-properties satisfying condition (A) (iii), i.e. those that *can* belong to both sets of objects.

This difficulty for transference theories is widely acknowledged but it has serious implications for the idea of metaphorical content and ultimately for metaphorical truth. It also points towards a quite different approach to understanding the purpose of metaphor. Take Beardsley's own example of 'iron will'. What we know the expression to mean (and our confidence might indicate that this has become idiomatic rather than metaphorical) is, as Beardsley puts it, 'firmness of resolution' or 'stubborn persistence'. But it is not clear that these properties can be derived from credence-properties of pieces of iron. Iron might be firm, but not in the sense in which resolutions can be; and it cannot in any literal sense be either stubborn or persistent. Beardsley recognizes the problem and offers two comments:

First, in all such cases there is in fact a transferred property, generally several, at some level of abstraction (here, for example, *difficulty of changing*, which can both be a property of iron and part of a metaphorical sense of 'iron'). But second, we have to allow for (and take much more account of) a two-way movement in metaphorical interpretation. After we read 'iron will' (partly) as *will that is difficult to change once set*, we will be invited in the metaphorical word-game to consider what sort of will it is that is difficult to change, and to cash in the highly abstract predicate for more concrete predicates suited to psychological traits alone: the 'firmness of resolution', etc. that I have alluded to. (13)

This passage introduces two new, and absolutely crucial, notions: that of being 'invited in the metaphorical word-game to consider' something and the need to 'cash in' one predicate for another. They introduce elements of *intention* and *endeavour* into the explanation of how metaphorical senses are arrived at that are quite absent from the formalist account offered in Principle (B). Yet these elements are integral to any satisfactory account of metaphor. To get from the hardness and inflexibility of iron to the stubbornness and single-mindedness of a person requires an imaginative leap and an analogical construction quite unlike any straightforward transference of properties. Here is clear intimation that understanding a metaphor involves something more than merely grasping a predetermined content and involves a more constructive, imaginative, exercise on the part of a hearer.

Davidson's theory acknowledges the imaginative nature of the response called for by metaphor but attempts to explain it in merely causal terms. The patent falsity or perhaps trivial truth of a metaphor inclines us to disregard the literal meaning and causes us to notice similarities, analogies, or whatever. However, Davidson's theory errs in the opposite direction from Cohen's and Beardsley's; he eliminates nearly all the controls on how the final meaning is arrived at. By accounting for metaphor as just a *stimulus* to thought, Davidson fails to give due weight either to the purposive and communicative function of speaking metaphorically or to the rule-governed nature of the interpretation of metaphor.

Metaphor and meaning-intentions

Someone uttering a sentence intending it to be taken metaphorically has meaning-intentions in the sense described by Grice.[29] He intends the utterance to produce a response. In this way the very same framework that was applied to both fictive utterance and literary works is applicable also to metaphorical utterance. In the language of speech acts, the user of a metaphor intends to produce not just perlocutionary effects, as Davidson's theory implies, but illocutionary effects as well; i.e. the mechanism for bringing about the required response is rational and rule-governed, not simply causal. It is rational in the sense that Grice's 'non-natural meaning' is rational, namely, that the utterer of a metaphor intends there to be a reason for the required response such that the utterance brings about the response for that reason. The primary reason is the recognition of the speaker's intention to speak metaphorically. Furthermore, to establish it as a genuine act of communication, there must be a shared belief between the speaker and hearer that the speaker intends the response to be achieved for that reason.

The very possibility of speaking metaphorically, forming and recognizing the requisite intentions, is bound by convention; it is helpful, as in the other two cases, to invoke the idea of a *practice* to explain the conventionality of metaphorical speech. The complex interplay of intention and response presupposes an established practice of speaking metaphorically, known (and known to be known) by each of the participants. To paraphrase Wittgenstein, it is not possible for one person alone to utter a metaphor.

The first stage in characterizing the practice is to determine the

---

[29] Grice, 'Utterer's Meaning and Intentions'.

nature of the response which is the constitutive element in meta-phorical utterance. Here we need to distinguish two separate communication-intentions, or classes of such, in speaking meta-phorically. Let us call these *constitutive* and *context-specific* aims. The constitutive aim, definitive of metaphorical utterance *per se*, is simply this: *to invite or encourage a hearer to think of, conceive of, reflect on, or imagine one thing (state of affairs, idea, etc.) in terms associated with some other thing (state of affairs, etc.) often of a quite different logical type.* This is, as it were, a minimalist account of metaphor; it says nothing of how such an aim is exhi-bited or how it might be carried out yet it captures a core feature of metaphor common to virtually all theories. The theoretical ap-paratus of 'interaction', transference of properties, cancellation of semantic features, comparisons, perspectives, semantic fields, and so on, is evoked to help explain the task that a competent hearer must undertake in coming to understand a metaphor. But in describing the constitutive aim of metaphorical utterance—in a minimalist theory—we need go no further than outlining the general character of this task. Indeed the key notion is precisely that of a task or process invited and undertaken.[30]

Suppose we call the complex task just outlined the 'metaphori-cal process'; then we can say that the constitutive aim of meta-phorical utterance is for a hearer to undertake the metaphorical process. It is some such aim that Davidson probably has in mind when he denies that there is any 'cognitive content' or 'message' conveyed in a metaphor. For the intention to invoke the meta-phorical process is not in itself an intention to say or state *that something is the case* but rather an intention *that someone is to do something*.

The metaphorical process, conceived as an imaginative as well as a conceptual task, is not restricted to finding predicates com-patible with tenor and vehicle so it is not subject to the difficulties we noted with Beardsley's 'conversion' theory. Nor does the minimalist theory presuppose that there must always be a specific

---

[30] Interestingly, Robert Fogelin who defends what might be called an old-fashioned 'comparativist' account of metaphor (the idea that metaphors are com-parisons or elliptical similes) highlights the idea of a 'task': 'figurative meaning derives its force by including the respondent in a mutually recognized task of *making sense* out of what is said': see Fogelin, *Figuratively Speaking*, 112 (see also 89).

propositional content in, or derivable from, a metaphorical utterance which a speaker intends to convey. Indeed the idea of a metaphorical process or task moves away from the paradigm of understanding associated with grasp of content or truth-conditions. Even Searle's theory, which utilizes the idea of speaker's meaning, is too determinate in this respect.[31] On Searle's view, to speak metaphorically is to say one thing (S is P) and mean something different (S is R). The bulk of the theory involves specifying the principles of inference by which a hearer recovers a speaker's intended meaning. Although Searle's principles undoubtedly figure in the metaphorical process it is wrong to suppose that their essential purpose (i.e. in every case) is to identify a content, with truth-conditions, that a speaker intends to convey.

This brings us to context-specific aims of metaphors. For as well as the constitutive aim of metaphorical utterance (initiating the metaphorical process) there are always context-specific aims associated with any single metaphorical utterance. A speaker does not just issue a metaphor but will do so in the context of some further communicative purpose.[32] One such aim, prominent but by no means universal, is that of conveying, *via* the metaphor, a particular belief or thought. Davidson accepts that some of what is brought to mind by a metaphor might be propositional in nature but seems reluctant to accept that this might be a deliberate communicative intention on the part of the speaker. Beardsley and Searle, on the other hand, suggest that the conveying of propositional content is integral to metaphor.

Assertion has as its constitutive aim the conveying of a belief held true by the speaker (lying is a form of infelicitous assertion). A metaphorical assertion might indeed aim to convey a belief but that is in virtue of being an assertion not in virtue of being metaphorical. The use of a metaphorical expression can occur in speech acts of all kinds, not only that of assertion. And even within different speech acts a metaphor might be fulfilling different purposes. Some metaphors are purely decorative or 'rhetorical',

---

[31] Searle, 'Metaphor', in *Expression and Meaning*.

[32] A parallel might be Searle's treatment of 'propositional acts' (reference and predication) in relation to illocutionary acts. According to Searle, it is not possible to perform a propositional act except in the context of an illocutionary act but that does not mean that the rules governing illocutionary acts also govern propositional acts (see Searle, *Speech Acts*). However, the parallel is not exact because the context-specific aims of metaphorical utterances need not be illocutionary acts.

merely embellishing a speech act, not contributing to its purpose or content. Others have a summarizing effect, distilling into epigrammatic form something already stated or established.[33] Sometimes a speaker will invite the metaphorical process of exploring analogies and similarities for the sake of getting a better understanding of one of the terms, rather than intending to formulate a specific content. Some of Richard Boyd's 'theory-constitutive metaphors' in science are of this kind.[34] Boyd considers 'the metaphorical claim that men are computers and that thought is information processing' and argues that 'part of the function of this metaphor as a theoretical statement is to suggest strategies for future research by asserting that, as investigations of men and machines progress, additional, or, perhaps, entirely different important respects of similarity and analogy will be discovered'. Here the metaphorical process takes on the proportions of a research project. Similar context-specific aims occur in philosophical metaphors: mind as *tabula rasa*, the veil of perception, language as a game, and so on. What counts in the understanding of these metaphors is not, or not only, the identification of a specific intended content but the exploration of analogies. *Contra* Searle, new analogies might come to light which the originator of the metaphor had never envisaged, so could not have been part of that person's meaning-intention.

Constitutive and context-specific aims can have a determining effect one on the other. Where, for example, a hearer recognizes a simple information-imparting aim for a metaphorical utterance he will probably not devote much effort to the metaphorical interpretative process. On the other hand, in the context of a poem, say, that process of exploring connections will assume central importance, albeit constrained by the more general aim of finding thematic unity and interest in the poem as a whole.

This balance between constitutive and context-specific aims suggests a criterion for distinguishing live from dead metaphors. Broadly speaking, where context-specific aims overwhelm the constitutive aim of a metaphor that metaphor will lie at the 'dying' end of the live–dead scale, but where the constitutive aim remains

---

[33] On 'summarizing' and 'ornamental' metaphors, see Olsen, 'Understanding Literary Metaphors'.

[34] See Richard Boyd, 'Metaphor and Theory Change: What is "Metaphor" a Metaphor For?', in Ortony (ed.), *Metaphor and Thought*.

foremost the metaphor will still have 'life' in it. Thus a speaker who uses semi-idiomatic expressions like 'coughing up money', 'being in a different ball-game', 'dodging the question', and so forth, is unlikely to want, or expect, a hearer to spend much time exploring 'tensions' within the metaphorical terms. But when Wittgenstein writes of a 'cloud of philosophy condensed into a drop of grammar' he presumably intends his philosophical (context-specific) point to be enhanced and enlivened by getting a reader actively to imagine or visualize the connections in the metaphor.

Metaphor and truth

So where does this leave content? And truth? The principal point is this: the conveying of a determinate propositional content might be a context-specific aim of a metaphor but it is not part of the constitutive aim of speaking metaphorically. This inevitably distances metaphor from truth-telling. Conveying truths might be a contingent feature of metaphorical utterance but it is not an integral feature or aim. Furthermore, as a context-specific aim it is likely to be low-key truth—the imparting of fact or information—that is involved rather than some special kind of cognition. If we are looking for special cognitive powers of metaphor it is better to focus on the constitutive aim rather than on the context-specific aims. But then it ceases to be *truth* as such that is at issue. For the constitutive aim involves a process of thought not a grasp of content.

Truth, as a mode of appraisal or a constitutive aim, is not integral to the practice of metaphorical utterance any more than it is integral to the institution of literature. Speaking metaphorically, engaging in the practice, involves utterance governed by constitutive rules. These rules make no reference to truth. They merely specify that a speaker has the Gricean-style meaning-intention that a hearer should undertake a certain kind of thought-process (thinking of one thing in terms of another, etc.) without making this explicit either as a direct instruction or as a statement of comparison.[35] A hearer must first recognize that a speaker has this

---

[35] These further qualifications are needed because a speaker is not deemed to have spoken metaphorically either in making the instruction explicit (e.g. 'Think of time as a tyrant') or in offering an explicit simile (e.g. 'Time is like a tyrant').

meaning-intention[36]—i.e. intends the utterance to be taken metaphorically—and then must engage this thought-process under the constraints of whatever further context-specific aims give point to the utterance.[37]

Can we not rescue metaphorical truth even if we give a secondary role to metaphorical content? A metaphor is true, we might say, either if it succeeds in the context-specific aim of conveying a truth, or if some of what is brought to mind (i.e. propositions, beliefs, etc.) in fulfilling the constitutive aim is true. Neither condition, though, is likely to satisfy those who seek special truth-telling powers in metaphor. The former, as we have seen, is likely to be associated either with low-key truth or with low-quality metaphors. The latter is problematic in other ways.

Davidson admits that we might be led to acquire true beliefs as a result of attending to a metaphor but insists that this is merely a contingent, causal, consequence, not part of the metaphor's content. David Cooper has called the truth of these beliefs 'vicarious truth'.[38] The connectedness of the beliefs with the metaphor is problematic. For one thing, not any, or anyone's, true beliefs prompted by a metaphor could be sufficient to make the metaphor itself true. Wildly idiosyncratic response should be ruled out and perhaps only beliefs associated with an 'authorized' response admitted. But that might soon slide back into 'content' and context-specific intention. Also, which, and how many, of the 'authorized' beliefs should count towards truth-appraisal? A majority? A weighted subset? The whole approach seems misguided. For it gives unwarranted emphasis to the acquisition of beliefs among the responses to metaphor. As it is, the metaphorical process, as we have called it, involves a much wider range of cognitive states—imagining, 'seeing as', conceptualizing, comparing,

[36] There will be many different kinds of contextual cues for this, usually centred on an oddity in the utterance if taken literally: patent falsity or trivial truth, semantic or categorial 'deviance', inappropriateness, and so forth. An advantage of our 'minimalist' view of metaphor is that it does not place any semantic conditions on metaphorical utterance. There is a parallel here, of course, with the accounts of fiction and literature.

[37] Note that Davidson's causal account of metaphorical response does not do justice either to the rule-governed nature of speaking metaphorically or to the constraints on 'interpreting' metaphors associated with the context-specific aims. Davidson leaves little room for talk of 'correct' and 'incorrect' interpretations of metaphors.

[38] Cooper, *Metaphor*, 200 ff.

and so on. To highlight belief—and thus truth as a mode of appraisal—is to distort the aims that are constitutive of metaphor. Just the same point of course is central to our argument about literature where acquiring and assessing beliefs are again remote from constitutive aims.

None of this is to deny the 'cognitive potential' of metaphor, or its creativity, its powers of 'insight', or its interest. Indeed once we have recognized that truth is only a subsidiary and contingent achievement of metaphor we have cleared the way for broader styles of appraisal. Here the minimalist can be hospitable to the considerable variety of detailed claims in other theories on the special contribution of metaphor. Interaction, interanimation, tension, transference, credence-properties, similarities, comparisons, analogies, substitutions, and so on, are all involved *in some way* with metaphors and it would be surprising if they did not yield a capacity of metaphor to advance knowledge or extend understanding. The crucial theoretical issue is not the relevance of these matters but their *location*. In arguing for a shift from 'content'-centred theories to a 'response'-based theory we have left it open that the thought-processes constitutive of an appropriate response to metaphor might indeed promote improved understanding of a subject, new ideas, new perspectives, and so on. We can learn from metaphors, just as we can learn from fiction, and not merely factual truths but new ways of thinking; a good metaphor, like one of Boyd's 'theory-constitutive' metaphors, can change our conceptual resources. Cognitive usefulness clearly extends much wider than grasp of propositional content. Appraising a metaphor for its truth is either faint praise—some determinate content has been conveyed—or itself a metaphor for a deeper kind of achievement, perhaps the bringing into being of valued cognitive states of mind.

The account of metaphor we have offered has many parallels with the account of fiction and literature. Understanding a literary work is not the same as grasping a propositional content or meaning. As with metaphor, it involves the *exploration* rather than *translation* of meaning. A literary interpretation of a work cannot be 'read off' from textual features alone; there is no 'calculus' of meaning which yields thematic concepts. Interpretation takes place, is made possible, only within the constraints of an institution or practice which determines a specific mode of appreciation. The idea of a practice, which figures so large in the account of fiction and literature, is also important in explaining metaphor. There are several reasons for this.

First, being metaphorical is not a property of sentences (or sentence parts or texts) *per se* but of utterances in context (utterance-tokens). Strictly speaking, there are no metaphors in a *language* (just as there are no fictions or literary works), only sentences or expressions with a greater or less potential to be used as such. No purely formal linguistic features are sufficient for being a metaphor. The presence of semantic anomaly, for example, as normally associated with metaphor, is neither necessary nor sufficient for metaphorical utterance. Some sentences used metaphorically—'The fox has gone to ground'—contain no intrinsic categorial anomaly, while other sentences, as used say by children, contain anomaly—'The car has hurt itself'—without being metaphorical. Something similar is true of fiction. It is utterances that are fictional, not sentences *per se*. To identify fiction (in the literary sense) is to identify a certain kind of context, not a kind of content.

Also both fictive and metaphorical utterances, as well as literary works, are characterized, within a practice, in terms of intention and response. In all three cases there is a communicative-intention of a Gricean kind, but not to affect belief, or to verify propositional content, so much as to undertake an imaginative thought-process. Appeal to a practice is needed because the appropriate response, in all the cases, is not merely *caused* (as Davidson supposes for metaphor) but engaged in deliberately. Recognition that the rules of the practice are being invoked is a necessary condition for an understanding of fiction, literature, and metaphor.

There are parallels too with regard to truth. Truth (or falsity) is not part of the definition of either fiction, literature, or metaphor. Yet truth (and falsity) can arise in connection with all three, in unproblematic ways. The *sentences* used in fictive utterances and which appear in literary works, like those in metaphorical utterances, can have truth-values. More interestingly, there can also be truth-values associated with the *utterances* apart from that of the sentences. There might be a further intention behind a fictive utterance to convey some belief or truth (a 'moral' of the tale, for example), just as there might be a context-specific intention in a metaphorical use to state something to be the case. Perhaps these further beliefs are 'brought to mind' as a result of the imaginative response, perhaps they are recognized as conversational implicatures, or whatever; there is no special difficulty in explaining how a speaker can convey a belief through fiction or metaphor that marks them off from other cases of indirect speech acts—hints, insinuations, suggestions, and so forth.

Defenders of literary truth and metaphorical truth are usually seeking something over and above the contingent, context-dependent, conveying of beliefs. Our response is the same in both cases. 'Truth' is not the right mode of appraisal. The 'special' achievement of literary fiction and metaphor must be consonant with their constitutive aims. Literary works and metaphors invite an imaginative task, that of the former far more complex than that of the latter but both concerned in essence with pursuing connections, be they among concepts, perceptions, images, themes, or whatever. The *appreciation* of metaphor, like that of literary fiction, is a process of mind and should be valued as such.

15

Literature as Philosophy

The view from somewhere

Let us recall the argument in Chapter 13 against the Propositional Theory of Literary Truth. It went roughly like this: if literary works are construed as having the constitutive aim of advancing truths about human concerns by means of general propositions implicitly or explicitly contained in them, then one should expect some kind of supporting argument, the more so since the purported truths are mostly controversial. However, there are no such arguments or debate either in the literary work itself, or in literary criticism. Literary works cannot therefore be construed simply as one among other discourses with the primary intention of advancing truths. This argument, along with the argument against the Theory of Novelistic Truth, is based on a conception of truth and truth-telling which is located within a nexus of activities such as making judgements, reasoning, providing evidence, questioning, debating, falsifying, and so forth: within a practice, as we have called it, of enquiry. There is clearly a conceptual link between this notion of truth and that of knowledge. What is known is true, and what is not true does not constitute knowledge but mere opinion. Knowledge is achieved by marshalling evidence supporting whatever truth-claim is being made. These conceptions of knowledge and truth are basic to the concept of science and they guarantee what may be called the *cognitive value* of the insights achieved in science. This is so not merely in the natural sciences, but also in the social sciences and in history. The doubts that have been raised about the scientific status of these latter disciplines concern just the applicability in these disciplines of these notions of truth and knowledge. And what has been established so far in this discussion is that they cannot simply be presumed to explain the cognitive status of literature.

There are two possible ways out of this *impasse*. One is to redefine the concepts of knowledge and truth-seeking, at least loosening the connection with supportive evidence and argument. The other is a more radical redefinition of the whole notion of cognitive value, severing any necessary connection with the concepts of knowledge and truth. Supporters of the first alternative would attempt to retain the direct link between literature and truth and would insist that literary works yielded insights complementary to, yet as equally valid (in the same sense of 'valid') as, the knowledge yielded by sciences of all descriptions. Supporters of the second alternative would be ready to abandon the notion that literature has a direct truth-seeking link with the world and instead settle for a different form of insight which lent itself to appraisal in terms other than those of knowledge and truth. We shall produce further arguments in favour of the second alternative in Chapter 16. Here we shall deal with the first.

As a point of departure for the discussion of the first alternative, it is useful to return to Thomas Nagel's distinction, which we invoked in Chapter 6, between the external or objective and the internal or subjective point of view. We recall that Nagel identified in the sciences, and all knowledge-seeking enquiry, a striving for a kind of objectivity which

allows us to transcend our particular viewpoint and develop an expanded consciousness that takes in the world more fully. All this applies to values and attitudes as well as to beliefs and theories.[1]

An ideal objectivity would provide what Nagel dubs a *view from nowhere*. Yet, he argues, such a view is unobtainable because each individual also has his own subjective nature which is

an irreducible feature of reality—without which we couldn't do physics or anything else—and it must occupy as fundamental a place in any credible world view as matter, energy, space, time, and numbers.[2]

This subjective point of view is not only ineliminable, but 'there are things about the world and life and ourselves that cannot be adequately understood from a maximally objective standpoint'.[3]

Developing Nagel's notion of a subjective point of view, one might say that it has two aspects. There is what may be called the *experiential aspect*: everyone has mental experiences which are peculiarly their own. The character of these experiences 'can be

---

[1] Nagel, *The View from Nowhere*, 5.   [2] Ibid. 7–8.   [3] Ibid. 7.

understood only from within or by subjective imagination'.[4] There is also what may be called the *perspectival aspect*: the world is seen from a particular point of view, at a particular time and place, and under the influence of particular circumstances. The subjective point of view thus not only affords a unique quality of experience but also a unique location for the experience. It is the distinctive view of the world from somewhere in particular.

Those who want to argue that the cognitive value of literature can be identified with the help of redefined concepts of knowledge and truth could be taken as proposing a change in focus from the external, objective point of view from which generalizations of universal validity can be made, to an internal, subjective point of view. The particular experience and particular situation are seen by the supporters of the first alternative as embodying a special kind of knowledge. One can come to share this knowledge through an act of 'subjective imagination' in which one occupies in imagination the point of view of another self. Literature, according to this theory, is particularly suited to effecting this imaginative participation, by means of which practical wisdom is increased and moral knowledge expanded. On this view, although a literary work is held to yield the knowledge it does because of its distinctive literary features, nevertheless genuine knowledge and genuine truth are at stake and literature is seen to keep the same company with philosophy and even the sciences. Indeed inasmuch as one task of philosophy is to seek a better understanding of moral matters in its own terms, so literature, with a similar task, becomes a companion to philosophy or even a branch of philosophy.

Literature as a source of subjective knowledge

Depending on whether the experiential or the perspectival aspect of the subjective point of view is taken as a point of departure, different theories of the cognitive value of literature result. The principal type of theory that makes the *subjective experience* central is that which presents a traditional humanistic view of literature as an instrument for training and extending our sympathetic

[4] Ibid. 26.

understanding of other people. This type of theory might be
labelled the Subjective Knowledge Theory of Cognitive Value. It
faces three principal problems. First, it must justify the claim that
'anything that might assist us to an imaginative participation can
properly be said to extend the range of our humanistic understanding';[5] i.e. the claim that the subjective experience which a
literary work induces represents a kind of *knowledge*. Second, it
must give some sort of account of the difference between genuine
and merely putative knowledge of this kind, including some means
of distinguishing between the true and the false. And, finally, it
must establish that literature *in virtue of being literature* promotes
imaginative participation of the type that yields this kind of
knowledge.

Drawing on Gilbert Ryle's distinction between 'knowing how'
and 'knowing that' proponents of the Subjective Knowledge Theory
argue that this distinction needs to be supplemented with a third
type of knowledge, 'knowing what it is like'. 'Knowing what it is
like'

is not the acquisition of information, or the inferential knowledge about
something, as I might know that the cat is in the house on the basis of
acquaintance with the cat-in-house situation, it is knowing in the sense of
realizing by living through.[6]

Full recognition of the facts is compatible with failing to know
what it is like to live through the situation made up of these facts:

Recognizing that such and such is so with reference to some kind of
human experience is not the same thing as *realizing* what this might
be like as lived experience. Confession of failure to understand, in the
sense of realize, is perfectly compatible with absence of doubt concerning
matter-of-fact. For example, 'I do not doubt that certain persons enjoy
situations of physical danger and even seek them out, but I don't understand it.' What the speaker does not understand is the lure, the fascina-
tion, of danger.[7]

Knowledge of the kind associated with 'living through' is not
amenable to evidential support (or any kind of reasons, or even

[5] Walsh, *Literature and Knowledge*, 104. For another subtle and compelling
account of the values of subjectivity in art, see Ronald W. Hepburn, 'Art, Truth
and the Education of Subjectivity', *Journal of Philosophy of Education*, 24 (1990),
185–98.
[6] Walsh, *Literature and Knowledge*, 101.   [7] Ibid. 104.

proof). It is accepted on the authority of the person whom one knows to have lived through a situation. It attains its character of knowledge rather than mere awareness through being not just experience but an experience that one is self-consciously aware of having lived through, that is, by being 'self-consciously recognized by the experiencer as his'.[8] Knowledge of what it is like, for example, to fall suddenly in love, to lose a child to death, or undergo religious conversion, can only be attained and therefore shared by living through the experience personally or, derivatively, by reading an evocative description of the situation and the experience of living through it. Such a description would constitute an imaginative evocation of the experience.

Literature, so it is argued, is the mode of writing above all that can provide this type of evocative description for it presents to its readers a piece of 'virtual experience, embodied, objectified, expressed, in the literary presentation'.[9] This virtual experience embodied in the literary presentation 'has a kind of "public presence" and a kind of "permanent presence" not possible in any case of actual experience'.[10] Through the presentation of an evocative description of this virtual experience literature offers the reader the opportunity of living through situations that he has never encountered in life. Moreover, since virtual experience can be elaborated and controlled by the artist, it is purer, focused on essentials in a way that everyday experience cannot be because of the contingencies of everyday life. 'The importance of literary art, from the strictly cognitive point of view, is that it provides an enormous extension and elaboration of this kind of knowledge',[11] i.e. the knowledge of subjective experience.

A claim to have experienced what it is like to live through a certain kind of situation is normally accepted even though the one making the claim may not be able to convey his knowledge of it:

Knowing beyond saying is acceptable in such a case, not because saying is impossible, but because the only kind of saying that would be relevant is a saying that requires some degree of literary talent.[12]

This means that the question of truth arises only in connection with evocative descriptions. However, according to this theory,

---

[8] Ibid. 137. [9] Ibid. 91. [10] Ibid. 91.
[11] Ibid. 137. [12] Ibid. 104.

such a description is not true or false in an ordinary 'correspondence' sense of true, but is instead authentic or inauthentic. The inauthentic evocation is 'banal' or 'pretentious',[13] the authentic evocation a powerful 'imaginative enstatement'.[14] Literary works therefore have to be true in the sense of being authentic in order to attain to the cognitive merit that the Subjective Knowledge Theory ascribes to them.

The Subjective Knowledge Theory has at its core experiential and psychological phenomena which are perfectly familiar to nearly all readers of literary as well as non-literary fictions. It is no part of our argument to deny that such responses are real or indeed that they are valuable and a source of much of the pleasure afforded by works of fiction. In Chapter 6 we offered an extended discussion of the potential values of imaginative involvement with fictive content. However, it is the further claims (1) that such involvement amounts to a kind of knowledge (and thus truth), and (2) that it lies at the heart of the cognitive values of literature, that we feel are not well substantiated. Our objections do not rely on the relatively trivial point that the terms 'true' and 'false' are used in an extended sense when equivalent to 'authentic' and 'inauthentic', though it is at least not obvious that authenticity as a mode of description is a cognitive value.

A more important issue is the cognitive status of an *experience*; it seems a much less acceptable extension of terminology to say that an experience as such can be a kind of knowledge (albeit 'subjective' knowledge or 'knowledge what it is like'). It is more plausible to suppose, not that the experience *is* the knowledge, but that knowledge arises as a *result* of the experience; the experience gives rise to the knowledge. In the literary case, we might say that as a result of reading the novel—and imaginatively engaging with its content—we now know better what it is like to be in a situation of a particular kind. This is not different in principle, though, from the knowledge we might gain about the town or country or culture where the novel is set, except that in the former case perhaps our knowledge rests more on imaginative involvement. It has been no part of the thesis of this book that knowledge of this kind is not derivable from reading works of fiction or literature. But as we saw in the case of metaphor what is prompted or stimulated or

[13] Ibid. 121.   [14] Ibid. 123.

brought to mind by an imaginative turn of phrase is not necessarily to be projected back into the 'cognitive content' of the phrase, nor grounds for assessing it as 'true'. Similarly in the literary context we cannot just take it for granted that any knowledge derived from an imaginative involvement with a work must be attributed to the artistic purpose of the work and serve as a yardstick for the value of the work.

This brings us to the principal objection to the Subjective Knowledge Theory which concerns its connection to literature *per se*. Can the idea of subjective knowledge illuminate what makes works of literature valuable within a culture? How does it relate to the kind of responses which are distinctive of a literary attention, or, as we have called it, the literary stance? One obvious problem is that many literary works simply do not provide the relevant kind of experience of 'knowing what it is like' to live through a certain situation. It may make sense to say that Thomas Hardy's short lyrical poem 'The Darkling Thrush' gives knowledge of what it is like to feel exhausted and burnt out yet nevertheless, inexplicably, to feel hope rise again for the future. It may even make sense to say that *Hamlet* gives knowledge of what it is like to be Hamlet or a person of that kind.

But let us consider a more sustained example, which we will develop through the remainder of this chapter, to see how engagement with the literary dimension of a work is something more than, and different from, subjective experience.

[*Within the room, Bolette is sitting on the sofa by the table, left, busy embroidering. Lyngstrand is sitting on a chair at the top end of the table. Down in the garden, Ballested is sitting painting. Hilde stands by him watching.*]

LYNGSTRAND [*his arms on the table, sits silently for a moment watching Bolette working*]. It must be awfully difficult to work a border like that, Miss Wangel.
BOLETTE. Oh, no! It isn't so difficult. As long as you remember to count.
LYNGSTRAND. Count? Do you have to count?
BOLETTE. Yes, the stitches. Look.
LYNGSTRAND. So you do! Fancy that! Why, it's almost like a form of art. Do you also design it?
BOLETTE. Yes, if I have a pattern.
LYNGSTRAND. Not otherwise?
BOLETTE. No, not otherwise.

LYNGSTRAND. Then it isn't really proper art after all.
BOLETTE. No, it's mostly what you might call ... handicraft.[15]
[Henrik Ibsen, *The Lady from the Sea*, Act v]

The scene from which this passage comes has all the subtlety of
late Ibsen. Lyngstrand is the aspiring artist. His declared desire
and aim is to become a sculptor, a profession for which he is
singularly unsuited. He has a chest complaint which will ultimately
kill him (though he does not know that himself), he has none of
the physical strength that is needed to handle heavy materials, nor
does he have any practical knowledge of the art. In this scene he
is given the part of the spectator. He, like Hilde who watches
Ballested painting, is the ignorant looker-on. Though he is the
self-declared artist, the artist's role is in this scene given to Bolette
and Ballested. Ballested, we know from the first act, like Bolette,
needs a pattern or model. 'What I am working on', he says to
Lyngstrand at the beginning of Act i, 'is that bit of the fjord over
there between the islands.' And he cannot finish his painting
because 'There isn't a model anywhere in town' for the figure he
wants in the foreground. So, like Bolette, what he is producing
will not, according to Lyngstrand, be really 'proper art'. And in
the play he is not an artist, but a jack-of-all-trades who has acclimatized himself (to use his own word and one of the key concepts
in the play) to the little coastal town where he was left behind
when the theatre troupe to which he belonged broke up, seven-
teen or eighteen years before. However, the concept of 'proper
art' introduced here by Lyngstrand, is not one that Ibsen endorses.
It is Bolette, whose handicraft requires an exactitude that demands
that she counts, who does the creative work here.

Lyngstrand is in fact almost a parody of a class of characters in
Ibsen's later plays (from *The Wild Duck* onwards) who in some
way represent aesthetic as opposed to moral values, the values of
'art' against the values of 'life'. It is a common feature of these
characters that they are supremely egotistic and even vulgarly and
pettily selfish. The scene round the quoted passage continues with
a conversation between Lyngstrand and Bolette where Lyngstrand
advances the view that marriage is 'a kind of miracle' because of
'the way a woman gradually comes to be more and more like her

---

[15] Henrik Ibsen, *The Lady from the Sea*. All the translations are from *The Oxford Ibsen*.

husband'. To Bolette's suggestion that a man may also grow like his wife, Lyngstrand reacts with what today would be called male chauvinism, 'A man? No, I never thought that.' Lyngstrand, it turns out, is not talking about *men* in general either, but of the artist. The artist has a vocation which makes him superior to any woman. However, the artist, Lyngstrand maintains, needs a woman's attention as inspiration, and he proceeds to ask Bolette if, when he goes away 'to become a famous sculptor', she will give her word that she will be faithful to him in her thoughts, will stay where she is, and think only of him, because this will help him in his art. Though Bolette gives Lyngstrand no indication that she takes his suggestion as anything but a further indication of his conceit, Lyngstrand firmly believes, as he reveals to Bolette's sister Hilde in Act v, that she has given him such a promise and that she will not accept the proposal of her former teacher, headmaster Arnholm, for that reason. As he admits to Hilde, he does not want to marry Bolette:

LYNGSTRAND. No, that wouldn't really work. I daren't think about anything like that for several years. And when I reach the point where I can, she'll be a bit too old for me then, I think.
HILDE. And yet you've asked her to think about you?
LYNGSTRAND. Yes, that can be of great assistance to me. As an artist, I mean. And it's something she can do very easily, since she hasn't any real vocation of her own. All the same, it's very nice of her.
HILDE. You think you'll be able to get on quicker with your sculpture if you know that Bolette is here thinking of you?
LYNGSTRAND. Yes, I think so. To know that somewhere in the world there is a lovely young woman sitting and silently dreaming about you . . . I think it must be so . . . so . . . Well, I don't really know what to call it.
HILDE. Perhaps you mean . . . exciting?
LYNGSTRAND. Exciting? Yes! Exciting is what I do mean. Or something like that. [*Looks at her for a moment.*] You are very clever, Miss Hilde. Really very clever indeed. When I come home again, you'll be about the same age as your sister is now. Perhaps you'll even look like her. You might even be of the same mind as she is now. As though you were both yourself and her . . . in one, so to speak.

[Act v]

Lyngstrand proposes to do what Hedda Gabler, Solness, Borkman, and Rubek actually do: feed on human life like a vampire to sustain their own aesthetic values. And when that life is used, he simply turns to another.

The theme of the egocentric artist who feeds on and destroys the values of life and love is a subsidiary but nevertheless important theme in *The Lady from the Sea* which links up obliquely with the main theme. However, the recognition and appreciation of this theme cannot really be described as going through an experience of what it is like to be such an artist or his victim. The reader or the audience notes the contrast between the ordinary, homely characters of Bolette and Ballested, who have acclimatized themselves to the backwater of the small, provincial, coastal town and who represent its values, and Lyngstrand who represents the destructive values of art. And the reader will note how they are evaluated through the way in which Ibsen presents them. This in itself, of course, constitutes an experience, but it is not at all of the same type as the experience of 'falling suddenly in love, losing a child to death, or undergoing religious conversion', which the Subjective Knowledge Theory uses as its main examples. It may, perhaps, be described as the experience of what the characters of Bolette, Ballested, and Lyngstrand are like, but this is the experience of the spectator observing the interaction and behaviour of these characters. It would be to stretch the concept of 'knowing what it is like' beyond any useful limit to insist that it could be applied to this experience.

An attempt has been made to strengthen the Subjective Knowledge Theory so as to take care of these objections; we shall look at this strong version in a moment and return to our example. However, the theory also runs into a more intractable problem relating to the nature of literature. It assumes that knowledge of what it is like can be acquired only by going through an experience oneself or by reading and being receptive to an evocative description, which is essentially a literary description. The problem arises because of the uniqueness and specificity of each individual literary work. Even literary works that deal with the same story present different visions of that story. As was pointed out in Chapter 10 the Orestes/Electra stories as presented by Aeschylus, Sophocles, and Euripides, are really different stories with different characters and different visions of the world. Equally, works dealing with the same themes, as perhaps do, say, Euripides' *Hippolytus* and Kingsley Amis's *Lucky Jim*,[16] define these themes

[16] For a discussion of the way in which they present the same theme, see Ch. 16.

in totally different ways. Thus each literary work defines its own unique subjective experience *sui generis*. Moreover, although individual aspects, characters, or incidents abstracted from a work might yield an empathetic response in a reader it is most unlikely that literary works taken as a whole—as *works*—will present situations that could provide a coherent and unified experience describable as 'knowing what it is like'. A Hamlet-situation, for example, is far too complex and specific to give rise to any single and sustained experience of this kind, certainly not one that will be relevant to a reader's daily life. This does not mean that literature does not deal with 'central human concerns', but it does imply that situations used to define these concerns and the manner of dealing with them are specific to literature, and consequently that the virtual experience offered by literature is specifically literary as well as unique. The view that 'The importance of literary art, from the cognitive point of view, is that it provides an enormous extension and elaboration of this kind of knowledge [knowing what it is like]' thus seems to reduce to the near tautology that reading literature extends our knowledge of the kind of subjective experience offered by literary works.

Subjective knowledge and conceptual enrichment

A stronger version of the theory defines a wider, more ambitious concept of subjective knowledge, and provides for this subjective knowledge affecting the reader's intellectual and moral life in a significant and positive way. This strong version of the theory emphasizes the capability of the subjective virtual experience offered by a literary work to enrich and modify the reader's concepts and conceptual scheme in such a way that his perception of, and his perspective on, his own life is changed. A literary work provides no new information, brings no new facts to light, but makes the reader perceive the facts he already recognizes 'in a different light'. Reading a literary work brings about 'a modification of a person's concepts, which is in turn capable of altering his thought or conduct'.[17] An example would be John Stuart Mill who was brought out of a near suicidal depression by reading

[17] Catherine Wilson, 'Literature and Knowledge', *Philosophy* 58 (1983), 495.

Wordsworth. Through his reading of Wordsworth he came to see that what he felt before, that 'life, to all who possess the good things of it, must necessarily be a vapid, uninteresting thing',[18] was untrue, and he had gained a new perspective on life which conferred meaning where there was none before. Another example, used by proponents of the theory, is Wittgenstein suggesting to Norman Malcolm that he should read Tolstoy's *Hadshi Murat* in order to realize that war was not after all 'boredom':

Malcolm might have found a new idea of how it is possible to think and speak of war and of its relationship to a host of other things, to love, to power, to fear, and to life and death. In this way, Malcolm's concept of war would have been enriched and extended, so that there would be new things which he would say about it, and things which he would no longer say—like perhaps that it was all boredom.[19]

This modification of a person's concepts implies that the reader

(a) recognizes the conception [of a situation] presented in the novel as superior to his own [conception of the same type of situation] and (b) adopts it, in recognition of its superiority, so that it comes to serve as a kind of standard by which he reviews his own conduct and that of others.[20]

For example, Edith Wharton's *The Age of Innocence* can be read in such a way that if the reader adopts this reading, he can no longer

believe, as the reasonable man does, in the unity of reason. Fundamental changes in moral perspectives need no longer be seen as the rejection and replacing of hypotheses or policies within a single framework within which moral beliefs must be determined. Old values do die, and new ones take their place. What separates Archer and his son is not a matter of different tentative beliefs within a common notion of reason but, rather, different ways of looking at the world, different conceptions of what is important in life.[21]

---

[18] John Stuart Mill, *Autobiography* (Oxford, 1924), 124.
[19] R. W. Beardsmore, *Art and Morality* (London, 1971), 74.
[20] Wilson, 'Literature and Knowledge', 495.
[21] D. Z. Phillips, 'Allegiance and Change in Morality: A Study in Contrasts' in *Through a Darkening Glass: Philosophy, Literature, and Cultural Change* (Oxford, 1982), 25. Originally in *Philosophy and the Arts*. Royal Institute of Philosophy Lectures, vi (1971–2) (London, 1973), 47–64.

These philosophical consequences are not brought about through any normal argument, but by *'waiting on* the novel or story',[22] i.e. by being sensitive to what the literary work presents, by exploring the experience which the work offers. The philosophical consequence is logically tied to the literary work: 'I have taken a good deal of time over the discussion of Tolstoy's story. There is no other way, I believe, of grasping the nature of the understanding Ivan attained on his deathbed.'[23] Or put in general terms:

> though we may speak of a novel or a poem's bringing a man to see what is possible for him, we can no longer conceive of these possibilities existing independently of the way in which he was brought to recognize them. If asked what he has learned from the novel or poem, the man may tell me to read it more carefully. Or he may read it himself, emphasizing what he takes to be the correct expression. But if this is unsuccessful, then he will not offer an alternative statement of the work. For what it has to tell us is internally related to the work itself.[24]

The strong version of the Subjective Knowledge Theory of the cognitive value of literature thus provides a strong justification for the claim that subjective experience represents knowledge. It also makes the relationship between the literary work and the imaginative participation in the subjective experience a logical one and thus ensures that the knowledge yielded by a literary work is specific to it as literature. What it does not provide, though, is an alternative account of the distinction between genuine and merely putative knowledge.[25] Both authentic and inauthentic literary works would seem to have the same capacity in principle to bring about 'seeing things in a new light'. Furthermore, although we acknowledged in discussing the fictive stance that entertaining propositions in works of fiction and engaging imaginatively with them might help to extend conceptual resources—thinking *of* things previously unthought in ways previously untried—there is not much beyond this that the distinctively literary qualities of a work can add; in other words there is no specific aesthetic contribution to

---

[22] In his analysis of Edith Wharton's *The Age of Innocence* as well as in an analysis of Tolstoy's 'The Death of Ivan Ilych' ('Philosophizing and Reading a Story', *in Through a Darkening Glass*, 64–81) Phillips has a section 'Waiting on the Novel' ('Waiting on the Story' in the case of Tolstoy) followed by a section entitled 'Philosophical Consequences of Waiting on the Novel (Story)'.

[23] Ibid. 79.   [24] Beardsmore, 'Learning from a Novel', 31.

[25] Ibid. 34 ff.

the idea of conceptual enrichment which is not already present in any activity where new situations are brought to mind. Yet the Subjective Knowledge Theory claims some privileged cognitive value along these lines for works of literature. Otherwise, it is in the nature of the theory that such an account must proceed along the lines laid down by the weak version, albeit differing in detail, and therefore the same range of problems will also recur.

There are, moreover, two decisive objections against the strong version of the Subjective Knowledge Theory. First of all, the ambitious concept of subjective knowledge that includes philosophical consequences is incompatible with the view of the relationship between this subjective knowledge and the literary work as an internal or logical one. If one employs a concept of subjective knowledge that involves a modification of certain concepts which the reader has, i.e. a concept of subjective knowledge that entails consequences for the way in which the reader sees reality, then this new perspective on reality cannot *only* be available through one specific literary work. For even the modified or enriched conceptual scheme must, if it is applicable to the world, be *independent* of the work which modifies it. One can come to realize that war is not boredom in other ways than by reading *Hadshi Murat*, or that life after all must not necessarily be 'a vapid, uninteresting thing' in other ways than by reading Wordsworth. To see exactly how this objection affects the strong version of the Subjective Knowledge Theory, it is illuminating to develop the example introduced earlier, bringing in references to other works by Ibsen.

In *The Lady from the Sea* a contrast is presented between Lyngstrand, the egocentric artist who feeds on and destroys the values of life and love, and the more homely characters of Bolette, Ballested, Arnholm, and Dr Wangel himself who represent these other values. However, in that play Lyngstrand is a subsidiary character and the values he represents die with him. In *When We Dead Awaken* when Arnold Rubek comes home 'as a famous sculptor, prosperous and in good health', as Lyngstrand says *he* will do (*The Lady from the Sea*, Act IV), Rubek has created his masterwork and sucked the soul out of the woman who loved him. ('I gave you my young living soul', Irene says to him. 'Then I was left standing there, all empty within. Soul-less. [*Looks fixedly at him.*] That's what I died of, Arnold' (Act I)). He let her remain his model and his inspiration but never touched her as a woman thus denying his own love for her and her love for him. 'I was an artist, Irene', Rubek says when after many years they meet again at the beginning of Act I, 'Above all else an artist.' And to this explanation she responds, '[*with a hint of scorn*] The work of art first . . . the human being second.' Irene is then slowly recovering from a period of madness, walking around as a living dead, constantly watched over by a nun in black, an ominous figure who never speaks but whose presence oppresses Irene all through the play until the last act. Irene herself is also a powerful dramatic presence with her stiff bearing and her floor-length creamy white dress: a ghost out of the past that is to lead Rubek to his death among the snow and ice at the top of the mountain.

Rubek pays for his art with his and Irene's life and happiness. Art usurps life. Rubek's artist's role is incompatible with his life as a man. An artist lives in a house but does not have a *home. Home* and the values associated with it, love, companionship, loyalty, compassion, are values which the artist cannot realize in his life for himself or others. 'Think', says Maja, Rubek's wife,

how happy and comfortable we could be down there in our nice new house . . .

RUBEK [*smiles indulgently*]. Shouldn't one rather say 'our nice new home'?
MAJA [*curtly*]. I prefer to say 'house'. Let us keep it at that.

[Act I]

The point is made even more strongly in *The Master Builder* where Solness has built his whole career on the fire that destroyed his wife Aline's ancestral home and his own possibility of ever having one:

To be able to build homes for other people, I have had to renounce . . . for ever renounce . . . any hope of having a home of my own. I mean a home with children. Or even with a father and mother.

[Act II]

Everything I've managed to achieve, everything I've built and created . . . all the beauty and security, the comfort and the good cheer . . . all the magnificence, even . . . [*Clenches his hands*] Oh, the very thought of it is terrible . . . !

[Act III]

All this I somehow have to make up for. Pay for. Not in money. But in human happiness. And not with my own happiness alone. But also with

others'. Don't you see that, Hilde! That's the price my status as an artist
has cost me—and others. And every single day I have to stand by and
watch this price being paid for me anew. Over and over again—endlessly!

[Act II]

Aline Solness in *The Master Builder* is, like Irene, a living dead.
For Solness to be able to build, her talent for 'building children's
souls' and 'So building their souls that they might grow straight
and fine, nobly and beautifully formed' (Act II) had to be wasted.
And if we go to Ibsen's second-last play, *John Gabriel Borkman*,
there is Borkman with his single-minded pursuit of his vision to
build, who lays not only his own life waste but also those of the
twin sisters Ella and Gunhild. 'You are guilty of a double murder',
Ella Rentheim says to him, 'The murder of your own soul and of
mine' (Act II).

In *The Master Builder* the price paid for 'the status of an
artist' is defined almost exclusively in negative terms. Solness has
crushed everyone in his egotism and there is no alternative to the
Solness ethos. However, this price is also positively defined in
various ways in Ibsen's later plays. In *The Lady from the Sea*, the
values of life and home are given content by Dr Wangel and
Arnholm and what they have to offer the women. In *Hedda Gabler*
the Tesman family provides a set of moral and homely values
which are beyond Hedda's recognition.[26] In *John Gabriel Borkman*
the marriage of the divorcée Mrs Wilton and student Borkman
provides an alternative, though an ill-defined and thin one, to the
death and destruction Borkman has brought over himself and his
home. And in *When We Dead Awaken* Maja and Squire Ulfheim
provide the contrast of the full-blooded couple to the now blood-
less Rubek and Irene.

With the exception of *John Gabriel Borkman* it is characteristic
of these late plays that the values of life and home are presented
forcefully. They are well defined and come to life on stage. Even
where they are ironically treated, as they are in *Hedda Gabler*, and
even where their limitations are clearly brought out, as in *The Lady
from the Sea*, they appear attractive. Art, on the other hand, becomes a prison of the soul, a threat to the homely values, a road

---

[26] For a discussion of the conflict between aesthetic and moral values in *Hedda
Gabler*, see Stein Haugom Olsen, 'Why Does Hedda Gabler Marry Jörgen Tesman?',
Modern Drama, 28 (1985), 591–610.

to death or death-in-life. One does wonder whether the repetition of Maja's song which stands at the very end of everything Ibsen wrote, is not also his own song:

I am free! I am free! I am free!
No longer this prison for me!
I'm free as a bird! I am free!
[*The sound of Maja's song is heard still further down the mountain.*]

All of Ibsen's plays after *The Wild Duck* arguably present a situation where art and the artist are conceived as destructive and this is contrasted with the values of life and love. If one retained the idiom of 'enriching or modifying the reader's concepts', one could say that each of the plays enriched or modified the reader's concepts of art and the artist in the *same way*. Each of them presents Ibsen's mature view of his own vocation and in the light of the parallels between the plays developed above, it would be unreasonable to insist that this view was unique and idiosyncratic in each of the plays. One might argue that each of the late plays offered a different *interpretation* of the view, but that would not imply that one learnt something different or that the reader's concepts were differently enriched or modified by each of the plays. The *same* modification or enrichment of a reader's concepts can consequently be brought about by *different* literary works. Furthermore, there is nothing in the modification or enrichment of these concepts which attaches it logically to reading a literary work and excludes other possible ways in which a reader could be brought to revise his concepts of art and the artist.

The second objection is that the strong version of the Subjective Knowledge Theory fails to make a distinction important in any theory that assumes cognitive consequences, i.e. between recognizing a conception of a situation and adopting that conception. A reader is not constrained to adopt a conception of reality which a literary work realizes for him through a subjective experience. The idiom of 'enriching and modifying the reader's concepts' tends to obscure this distinction. What the reader learns from Ibsen's late plays is *Ibsen's* view of art (or at least that developed in his plays) and to the extent that he comes to see what Ibsen's concepts were, we might say that the reader's concepts have been modified or enriched. However, they are not enriched in the sense that he necessarily adopts the view of art and the artist developed by Ibsen. Moreover, the same logical constraint applies here as to the Propositional Theory. Reading a literary work a reader does not construe the work as *requiring* or *inviting* him to modify his concepts. These plays may bring some readers to adopt the conception of art and the artist which Ibsen, on the proposed interpretation, presents. But this is not something a reader will expect the plays, as literary works, to bring about. They are not read as treatises on art. The reader will work through interpretation to recognize the concepts the author uses to organize the presented situations, but there is no demand that he should accept or reject the authorial perspective. As will have become clear, there is a strong parallel between the philosophical consequences of 'waiting on a story', i.e. the modification or enrichment of the concepts through which a reader understands a type of situation, which the strong version of the Subjective Knowledge Theory introduces, and the propositions of the Propositional Theory of Literary Truth; and most of the arguments against the Propositional Theory apply equally to the strong version of the Subjective Knowledge Theory.

The problem is that once one takes the step from the weak to the strong version of this theory, literature ceases to be a source of insight into the subjective sphere of human existence *paralleling* philosophy as a source of insight into the external aspects, and becomes *subordinated* to philosophy. The strong version of the Subjective Knowledge Theory is not a theory of the cognitive value of literature at all, but represents a view of how to do philosophy, ultimately deriving from Wittgenstein. According to this view philosophy should shun general theories and concentrate on the particular situation. Literature is then naturally seen as a source of descriptions of particular situations which can be used to illuminate a philosophical problem. Literature is 'a source of reminders (not examples) from which philosophy can benefit in wrestling with issues concerning the firm or slackening hold of various perspectives in human life'.[27] Ignoring such particularity and detail as literature has to offer can not only 'lead to an obscuring generality in philosophical theories about morality, but . . . it can also lead to blindness with regard to certain perspectives on human life'.[28] Trying to turn this view of a possible use of literature into

[27] Phillips, 'Introduction', in *Through a Darkening Glass*, 1.
[28] Ibid. 4.

a theory of the mimetic aspect of literature is necessarily problematic since this use is neither a *constitutive* nor even a *characteristic* function of literature. Literary works can be used as eyeopeners or as reminders in philosophy, and it is possible to discuss the effectiveness of literary works in these uses. But that discussion is not about the cognitive value of literature that defines or explains the high cultural value accorded to literature.

Literature as moral philosophy

Those theorists who are impressed by the perspectival aspect of the subjective point of view develop a different theory of the cognitive value of literature from those emphasizing the subjective experience. These theorists argue that the cognitive value of literature consists in the contribution it makes to moral reasoning. Literature presents to the reader various attempts to work through prominent alternative views of an ethical problem,[29] it aids him in the imaginative re-creation of moral problems,[30] presents 'the mystery, conflict, and riskiness of the lived deliberative situation',[31] and is therefore a part of or a necessary adjunct to 'moral reasoning':

A novel, just because it is not our life, places us in a moral position that is favorable for perception and it shows us what it would be like to take up that position in life. We find here love without possessiveness, attention without bias, involvement without panic. Our moral abilities must be developed to a certain degree, certainly, before we can approach this novel at all and see anything in it. But it does not seem far-fetched to claim that most of us can read James better than we can read ourselves.[32]

Literature does not, or does not often, depict *solutions*. What especially the novel does is aid us in the imaginative re-creation of moral perplexities,

[29] Nussbaum, *The Fragility of Goodness*, 12.

[30] Hilary Putnam, 'Literature, Science, and Reflection', *New Literary History*, 7 (1975–6), 483–92, repr. in *Meaning and the Moral Sciences*.

[31] Martha C. Nussbaum, 'Flawed Crystals: James's *The Golden Bowl* and Literature as Moral Philosophy', in *Love's Knowledge: Essays on Philosophy and Literature* (Oxford, 1990), 142. Originally in *New Literary History*, 15 (1983–4).

[32] Martha C. Nussbaum, '"Finely Aware and Richly Responsible": Literature and the Moral Imagination', in *Love's Knowledge*, 162. Originally in Anthony J. Cascardi (ed.), *Literature and the Question of Philosophy* (Baltimore, 1989).

in the widest sense. (I don't contend that this is what is aesthetically valuable about novels; indeed I shall not deal with questions of aesthetic value at all. But I contend that this is an important fact about the novel as it has developed in the last few centuries.) Sometimes it is said that literature describes 'the human predicament', which is perhaps a way of referring to this. But the pomposity of the phrase obscures the point. The important point is not that there is some *one* predicament which is *the* human predicament, and which literature sometimes describes; the point is that for *many* reasons it seems increasingly difficult to imagine *any* way of life which is both at all ideal and feasible; and literature often puts before us both extremely vividly and in extremely rich emotional detail why and how this seems to be so in different societies, in different times, and from different perspectives. I want to suggest that if moral reasoning, at the reflective level, is the conscious criticism of ways of life, then the sensitive appreciation in the imagination of predicaments and perplexities must be essential to sensitive moral reasoning. Novels and plays do not set moral knowledge before us, that is true. But they do (frequently) do something for us that must be done for us if we are to gain any moral knowledge.[33]

What literature supplies in moral reasoning is the working-out of a moral choice from a subjective point of view. This is important, according to these theorists, since a significant proportion of moral choices do not consist in the application of general rules, but in the exercise of moral judgement in given circumstances. Many moral judgements cannot, in other words, be made if one adopts the 'view from nowhere' because they need to take into account the individual, subjective perspective on a situation.

In order to see exactly what this argument amounts to, and to assess it, it is useful to make a number of distinctions. First, a distinction needs to be made between the traditional humanist view that literature is valuable because it educates the reader's moral awareness by presenting situations of moral conflict and choice in all their complexity and with all their emotional implications, and the claim that literature because it presents such situations is an integral part of or necessary adjunct to *moral reasoning* and therefore to *moral philosophy*. Both Nussbaum and Putnam tend to run these two claims together: literature becomes an integral part of *moral argument* because it involves the reader in a process of discrimination and perception which develops his

---

[33] Putnam, 'Literature, Science, and Reflection', 86–7.

moral awareness, something which ordinary philosophical texts
fail to do:

For this novel [Henry James's *The Golden Bowl*] calls upon and also
develops our ability to confront mystery with the cognitive engagement
both of thought and feeling. To work through these sentences and these
chapters is to become involved in an activity of exploration and unravel-
ling that uses abilities, especially abilities of emotion and imagination,
rarely tapped by philosophical texts.[34]

What I am suggesting is that if we want to reason rationally about feminism, communism, liberalism, or just about life in the twentieth century,
then what Doris Lessing does for our sensibility [in *The Golden Note-
book*] is enormously important.[35]

The view that literature is an integral part of or necessary adjunct
to moral argument and therefore to moral philosophy is, however,
logically independent of the view that literature is educative of the
reader's moral awareness. The former does not entail the latter in
any way, and there is nothing contradictory in holding the latter
while denying the former. This, indeed, was the position taken up
by F. R. Leavis who spent considerable energy and space defending both the moral importance of literature and the independence
of both literature and criticism from philosophy.[36]
   A further distinction has to be made between a strong and a
weak thesis about the relationship between moral philosophy and
literature. The strong thesis would be universal and essentialist,
analogous to the claim that 'All literature aspires to the condition
of music'. That is, it would claim that all literary works aspire to
be part of or a necessary adjunct to moral philosophy and that it
is in so far as they succeed in fulfilling this aspiration that they
become good or great literary works. This thesis is implausible for

---

[34] Nussbaum, 'Flawed Crystals' in *Love's Knowledge*, 143.

[35] Putnam, 'Literature, Science, and Reflection', 91.

[36] His most systematic development of this view is perhaps to be found in the
first part of *The Living Principle: English as a Discipline of Thought* (London, 1975).
It is remarkable how similar in style and tone Nussbaum's interpretation of *The
Golden Bowl* is to F. R. Leavis's analyses of various novels and short stories. In
particular they both tend to write, when they interpret a literary work, as if they
were making moral assertions. See e.g. F. R. Leavis's interpretation of Conrad's
The Secret Sharer in 'The Secret Sharer', included in *Anna Karenina and Other Essays*
(London, 1967), which Leavis himself uses as an example in *The Living Principle*.
For the sort of confusion this leads to, see the comment on F. R. Leavis in Olsen,
The Structure of Literary Understanding, 68–9.

two important reasons, one concerning its universalist, the other its essentialist aspect. First, there is the same objection as against the Subjective Knowledge Theory that it fails to account for all types of literary works: not all literary works present situations of moral conflict and choice. Indeed, there are major genres of literature, such as the lyric poem, that cannot very well be said to be occupied with 'the sensitive appreciation in the imagination of predicaments and perplexities . . . essential to sensitive moral reasoning'.[37] And there are particular literary works that would not fall under the thesis, such as the Ibsen plays discussed earlier which, on the interpretation given there, concern themselves with the role of art and aesthetic value.

Secondly, it is a consequence of the strong thesis that a reader must ascribe value to a literary work on the basis of a judgement about the truth of the moral position involved. Moral reasoning is concerned with truth, with 'getting it right', whether the nature of moral reasoning is thought of as the application of general rules or as discriminating between conflicting moral claims in a complex situation and balancing them against each other. However, as was argued at length in connection with the Propositional Theory, appreciation of a literary work can proceed independently of judgements about the truth of the work (or its content). In the case of Ibsen's plays as conceived under the interpretation given, it is arguable that the situation presented in the later plays (where the values of life are separated from the values of art and, even where ironically treated, represent a preferred alternative to the values of art) is 'truer to life' and also more complex than the situation presented in the early plays (where the values of art and life are identical, but where 'daily life' appears as conventional and constricting). However, to conclude on the basis of this that, for example, *The Lady from the Sea* is a better play than *Peer Gynt*, would be eccentric indeed, placing the highly competent above the truly excellent.

The thesis may also be given a weak form: some literary works incidentally have the feature that they contribute to moral reasoning. In this case, the fact that these were literary works would be of no special significance. There would be little reason to object to such a thesis, but it would be uninteresting from the point of view

---

[37] Putnam, *Literature, Science, and Reflection*, 447.

of literary aesthetics since it makes no claims about any systematic relationship between literature and philosophy. Again the philosophers who insist on a close relationship between moral philosophy and literature do not distinguish between the strong and the weak thesis. Nussbaum implies that her thesis will have consequences for 'our conventional distinction between philosophy and literature', but she explicitly makes her claim with reference to one novel in particular, James's *The Golden Bowl*, adding that the claim holds good for 'other related novels' and 'tragic drama',[38] and elsewhere she makes it with particular reference to Greek tragic drama.[39] Putnam makes his claims with reference 'especially' to the novel.[40] With regard to the *nature* of the relationship between philosophy and literature Putnam explicitly avoids making the claim that the contribution of the literary work to moral reasoning is part of its aesthetic value though he apparently believes that it is a property in particular of *good* novels. Nussbaum, on her part, insists that this contribution is made by virtue of the fact that the literary work is the sort of work that it is:

But it is, in fact, not possible to speak about the moral view revealed within this text without speaking at the same time of the created text, which exemplifies and expresses the responses of an imagination that means to care for and to put itself there for us.... I claim that the views uncovered in this text derive their power from the way in which they emerge as the ruminations of such a high and fine mind concerning the tangled mysteries of these imaginary lives. And we could hardly begin to see whether such views were or were not exemplary for us if this mind simply stated its conclusions flatly, if it did not unfold before us the richness of its reflection, allowing us to follow and to share its adventures.[41]

But Nussbaum too avoids the question whether the moral value of this novel is (in part) *constitutive* of its aesthetic value. What appears then, is the following mixed thesis: *Some literary works make a contribution to moral reasoning and must therefore be considered as an integral part of or necessary adjunct to moral philosophy. The features of these works that make them valuable as moral philosophy are identical in part with those features that make them valuable as imaginative creations, i.e. as literary works. The*

---

[38] Nussbaum, 'Flawed Crystals' in *Love's Knowledge*, 138.

[39] Nussbaum, *The Fragility of Goodness*, 13.

[40] Putnam, *Literature, Science, and Reflection*, 447.

[41] Nussbaum, 'Flawed Crystals' in *Love's Knowledge*, 140–1.

function they serve in moral philosophy could not therefore be served by any other kind of text. The question whether their moral value is part of, or integral to, their aesthetic value is simply not raised or not considered.

One final distinction, useful in the evaluation of this thesis, may be made between two types of relationship between philosophy and literature, philosophy *through* literature and philosophy *in* literature.[42] Philosophy *in* literature is the sort of relationship brought out in the above analysis of Ibsen's plays: a theme that is also the object of philosophical deliberation is given literary interpretation in terms of an imaginative world artistically constructed. However, this imaginative working-out of the theme is incommensurable with philosophical deliberation on the theme: one cannot transfer insights from one sphere to another though it is quite possible that an insight in one field should *inspire* the development of an insight in the other. Philosophy *in* literature is a relation where philosophy is subordinated to the purpose and function of literature, and consequently the aspect identified as philosophical in a literary work can only be identified as an integral part of, or as partially constitutive of, aesthetic value. Philosophy *through* literature, on the other hand, refers to 'the use of imaginative literary forms as devices of exposition, for the more effective communication of philosophical conceptions that have already been fully worked out'.[43] In this relation literary works are subordinated to the function and purpose of philosophical argument, and the focus of interest is consequently on the way in which an imaginatively realized fictive situation can throw light on a moral problem and not on the way in which a literary work redefines and develops these conceptions in a fundamentally

---

[42] The distinction is borrowed from Anthony Quinton's lecture, *The Divergence of the Twain: Poet's Philosophy and Philosopher's Philosophy*, A Lecture to Mark the Official Opening of the Centre for Research in Philosophy and Literature, University of Warwick, 8 October 1985 (Centre for Research in Philosophy and Literature, University of Warwick, 1985), 1. Quinton actually makes a threefold distinction between philosophy *as* literature, philosophy *through* literature, and philosophy *in* literature. 'Philosophy as literature' is of no concern to us here as it names a relationship where philosophical texts are subsumed under the category of literature. It must not, however, be confused with 'literature as philosophy' which names the opposite relationship, i.e. when literary works are subsumed under the category of philosophy. The distinction between philosophy *through* literature and philosophy *in* literature is not used here exactly as Quinton uses it.

[43] Quinton, *The Divergence of the Twain*, 1.

different *literary* way. The focus is on the features that make the situation representative rather than the features that make it unique. Philosophy *in* literature refers to an essential relationship between philosophy and literature. Philosophy *through* literature names a contingent relationship: it is incidental to their philosophical function that the texts used also have a function as literary works. This would be so even if it were true that those features that made these texts valuable in moral argument coincided with the features that made them valuable literary works.

Typical examples of works where it is easy to identify the relation philosophy *through* literature are Pope's *An Essay on Man* which presents, Quinton maintains,[44] the philosophy of Bolingbroke, and *An Essay on Criticism* which presents neo-classical poetic doctrine. However, works of literature are rarely expository in the way that Pope is, and more interesting examples would be Dante's *Divinia Commedia* or Milton's *Paradise Lost*. Whether James's *The Golden Bowl* can be construed in such a way that an independent philosophical view can be identified in it, is a question to which there is no immediately obvious answer. What is clear is that philosophy *through* literature, just like philosophy *in* literature, is a relationship that has to be identified through an interpretation, though the logic of the interpretative argument in the two cases will not be the same.

The relationship which Putnam and Nussbaum assert to hold between a limited range of literary works and moral philosophy must be characterized as philosophy *through* literature. The thesis formulated above is nothing more than a special version of the weak thesis. It asserts neither a universal nor an essential link between literary works (*qua* literature) and philosophy. Consequently it does not say anything that is theoretically interesting about the way in which philosophy either as discourse or as a provider of concepts and themes enters into the reader's appreciation of literature. The thesis is in fact a thesis about the role of literary works in moral philosophy. The focus of interest for both Nussbaum and Putnam is the nature of moral argument and moral philosophy. They are both concerned to extend the notion of moral argument to involve 'not just the logical faculties, in the narrow sense, but our full capacity to imagine and feel, in short, our full

---

[44] Ibid. 4.

sensibility'.[45] And the capacity to imagine and feel is necessary in moral philosophy because moral reasoning is concerned with practical situations which must be fully realized. However, when they are presented in literature, these situations are always, as Nussbaum herself puts it in the quoted passage, 'exemplary'. Literary representations provide particularized illustrations that fall under general descriptions and judgements.

It may still be argued that if it is true that certain literary works make a significant contribution to moral argument, this is a value of these literary works which necessarily must influence the reader's total (as opposed to his merely aesthetic) evaluation of these works. Their contribution to moral reasoning is an additional reason for reading these works and recommending others to read them. It is of little importance that this merit is not aesthetic merit. However, this argument fails because there is no such *total* evaluation of a literary work. A work is read for a purpose. If it is read as literature, it is read in a special way, with a special type of attention, the sort of attention given to Ibsen's *The Lady from the Sea* in the first sections of this chapter. The grouping of characters set up at the beginning of Act IV, with Bolette embroidering and Lyngstrand looking on, Ballested painting and Hilde looking on, is construed as full of meaning, as setting up a contrast between Lyngstrand and Ballested and Lyngstrand and Bolette. And from this point of departure was developed a whole network of characterizations of Lyngstrand and his relationship to the other characters in the play. *The Lady from the Sea* might have been read in other ways, for example as an attempt to present a picture of a small Norwegian coastal town in the late nineteenth century. In that case all the attention to the artistic significance of details would have been wasted. Reading is purposeful, directed towards a goal, towards seeing the work from a perspective, and evaluation is always evaluation in relation to this perspective.

If a work is read as a piece of moral reasoning, one does not take up the literary stance towards it and the standards for evaluation will be different, even if the features of the literary

---

[45] Putnam, 'Literature, Science, and Reflection', 86. Putnam is not willing, as is Nussbaum, to accept that this makes literature *part of* moral philosophy (see Hilary Putnam, 'Taking Rules Seriously: A Response to Martha Nussbaum', *New Literary History*, 15 (1983–4) 193–200), but in 'Literature, Science, and Reflection' he does look upon good literary works as a necessary adjunct to moral philosophy.

works that make it valuable as moral reasoning are in part identical with those that make it valuable as a literary work of art. One such standard that operates when a work is judged as moral reasoning is the standard of 'truth'. Céline's novel *Journey to the End of the Night* comes in for criticism from Putnam because he presents the reader with 'a "mere" possibility'[46] rather than with a presentation that would cohere better with the reader's actual experience. Henry James receives praise from Nussbaum because 'there are candidates for moral truth which the plainness of traditional moral philosophy lacks the power to express, and which *The Golden Bowl* expresses wonderfully'.[47] But moral or philosophical truth is not a standard governing literary appreciation. One may find Ibsen's vision of the artist and aesthetic value unconvincing though this may not prevent one from recognizing the power of his vision.

Literature in moral philosophy

The final question, then, is whether the thesis formulated above about philosophy *through* literature says something that is true and important about the role of literature in moral philosophy. There is no problem with the modest part of the thesis that says that 'Some literary works make a contribution to moral reasoning.' Indeed, it would be strange if some works did not make such a contribution in a branch of reasoning that depends to such an extent on the use of examples. However, problems do arise in connection with the claim that 'The features of these works which make them valuable contributions to moral reasoning are identical in part with those features that make them valuable literary works.' The features identified in literary appreciation are features that contribute to the uniqueness of the literary work of art. The statement of a philosophical theme that organizes the identified poetic vision, is, in and for itself, without much significant content. Only by relating the thematic statement back to the literary work does it become anything but empty words. But when the thematic statement is related to the work, it also receives a unique

---

[46] Putnam, 'Literature, Science, and Reflection', 90.

[47] Nussbaum, 'Flawed Crystals' in *Love's Knowledge*, 142. Similar remarks can be found elsewhere in the article and in '"Finely Aware and Richly Responsible"' in *Love's Knowledge*, 148–9.

interpretation. The situation represented in a literary work is created through a series of rhetorical and structural means that is the fingerprint of that work. The situation presented by a literary work is therefore unrepeatable. The Ballested/Lyngstrand/Bolette constellation in *The Lady from the Sea* and the relationships into which each of these characters enter with other characters in the play define the play as such. And this is not merely a contingent fact. A literary work is always a representation where the mode and means of presentation constitute the nature of the situation represented. A real-life situation that was similar to that which the reader meets in *The Lady from the Sea* would not strictly be even the same type of situation. And if the real-life situation were presented in exactly the same way as the play-situation, then the presentation would itself most likely invite a literary response and the content would then be characterizable in literary thematic terms.

Any attempt to construe a literary work as part of a moral argument would identify the features of the work that contributed to making the situation in that work 'exemplary', 'paradigmatic', 'patterns for public life', i.e. the features that would define the situation as *repeatable*. Nussbaum indeed admits that the role of the literary work is not as a literary work but as an example:

The tremendous development of 'applied ethics' and the increasing concern of most major (Anglo-American) ethical writers with concrete and complex examples is a welcome development. I do not believe that these examples eliminate the need to turn to works of literature ... As examples become increasingly complex, however, we can expect to find not a sharp contrast between example and literary text, but, instead, a continuum.[48]

The consequence of this admission would have to be the further admission that what she says about *The Golden Bowl* has absolutely no consequences for 'our conventional distinction between philosophy and literature'.[49]

In the light of this, the further and more ambitious claim that some literary works are 'major or irreplaceable works of moral

[48] Nussbaum, *The Fragility of Goodness*, 32 n.

[49] Nussbaum leaves 'to the reader the job of exploring the wider consequences of what I shall say for our conventional distinction between philosophy and literature', the implication apparently being that the distinction will have to be modified or abolished; 'Flawed Crystals' in *Love's Knowledge*, 138.

philosophy'[50] becomes difficult to sustain. If literary works function as examples, if they are 'exemplary', 'paradigmatic', 'patterns for public life', then they are in need of a generalizing commentary to elicit their exemplary value. A literary work is apprehended and appreciated through an interpretation which is in its very nature challengeable. An interpretation of Ibsen's late plays that made them into moral allegories would be open to challenge from the kind of interpretation which we developed above. Nussbaum's ethical interpretations of James are in the same position. The claims that she and Putnam make for some novels thus seem to be claims for these novels *under an ethical interpretation*. If there is anything that might be construed as a work of moral philosophy in this, it would have to be the specific novel together with a specific ethical interpretation attached, for example James's *The Golden Bowl* with Nussbaum's article attached to it. Whether this extended text is actually labelled 'a work of moral philosophy' seems of limited importance as long as one is aware of the difference between this type of text and the major works, ancient and modern, in moral philosophy. We can only register here our impression that Nussbaum's discussions of James and of classical tragedy seem more illuminating as pieces of literary criticism, than as contributions to a moral debate.

Philosophy through literature, then, is identified through a special type of construal different from the sort of construal that constitutes literary appreciation. Moreover, this type of construal is not limited to literary works but is a mode of apprehension which is also applied to non-literary examples in moral philosophy. The claim made by Nussbaum and Putnam that literature is an integral part of or a necessary adjunct to moral philosophy therefore seems much too strong. It might be right that moral philosophy would do well to make more extensive use of examples from literature because these are more fully conceived than anything a poor philosopher can invent on the spur of the moment,

---

[50] Ibid. Nussbaum also makes the claim that Henry James's later novels are 'moral achievements on behalf of our community' ('"Finely Aware and Richly Responsible"' in *Love's Knowledge*, 165). It is difficult to see what basis she has for this claim. It is logically independent of the claim that these works are works of moral philosophy. Works of moral philosophy are rarely construed as 'moral achievements'. And the conclusion that a work is a moral achievement cannot be drawn merely on the basis of an analysis of the form and content of a work even if one believes that the analysis reveals 'patterns for public life'.

but this does not make literary works, as such, a necessary part of moral argument. D. Z. Phillips's remark, that literature can provide 'reminders' for philosophy, here seems a much more reasonable characterization of the sort of function literature can have in philosophy.

Both the Subjective Knowledge Theory and the Theory of Literature as Moral Philosophy are philosophers' theories of literature. They are ultimately theories about the nature of philosophy and not about the nature of literature. These theories insist on a role for literature in philosophy, and they see this role as guaranteeing its cognitive value. However, they are not concerned with literature as a separate and independent practice defined by its own logic and its own constraints and conventions. They are therefore not concerned with providing an account of the mimetic aspect of literature as such, but limit themselves to such genres or works of literature as they think provide examples (or reminders) for philosophy. In their discussion they do touch on central problems in connection with the mimetic aspect of literature, but the solutions they offer are motivated by their desire to clarify the role and function of philosophy rather than the role and function of literature.

16

The Mimetic Aspect of Literature

Thematic concepts and thematic statements

In Euripides' *Hippolytus*, Phaedra, wife of Theseus, King of
Athens, falls in love with the unsuspecting Hippolytus, Theseus'
son by the Amazon Antiope. Phaedra's passion is the work of the
goddess Aphrodite, who wants to revenge herself on Hippolytus
because he has rejected her and devoted himself to the chaste
Artemis. Through Phaedra's nurse Hippolytus is made aware of
her love and invited to her bed. He emphatically rejects her offer
and violently abuses Phaedra and her nurse. To save her honour
Phaedra commits suicide and leaves a note accusing Hippolytus of
raping her. Theseus, confronted on his return from an expedition
with the suicide and the note, banishes Hippolytus and prays to
his father, the seagod Poseidon, to fulfil one of the three wishes he
has granted him and kill Hippolytus. Leaving Troezen, Hippolytus
is killed when his horses are frightened by a monster thrown on
shore by Poseidon from a giant wave. Theseus is brought to realize his mistake by the goddess Artemis who appears to him and
reveals the truth. The play ends with the reconciliation of Theseus
and the dying Hippolytus. This, in bare outline, is what happens
in the play. It is what in Chapter 10 was called its subject.

The play is framed by a prologue and an epilogue spoken by
two different goddesses: Aphrodite speaks the prologue and
Artemis the epilogue. These goddesses represent supernatural
forces beyond human control and influence and Aphrodite determines the outcome of the action. At the beginning of the play she
initiates a sequence of actions which will destroy Hippolytus, her
reason being that he has sinned against her. Being a goddess, she
knows that her initial action is sufficient to ensure that Hippolytus
is destroyed and she displays her knowledge about the future to
the audience by giving a brief summary of what will happen in the
play. Noticing this deterministic framework it would be reasonable to suggest that the play raises the problems of free will and

responsibility. The play cannot, however, be construed as present-ing a simple and crude form of determinism. For each of the main characters has weaknesses which are necessary for the tragic out-come of the action. If the characters had not displayed these weaknesses, Aphrodite's initial action would not have led to tragedy.

Phaedra's weakness is one of will. She fails to control her natu-rally amorous disposition:

> We know the good, we apprehend it clearly.
> But we can't bring it to achievement. Some
> are betrayed by their own laziness, and others
> value some other pleasure above virtue,

Phaedra says (II. 380–3),[1] and it soon becomes clear that Phaedra values some other pleasure above virtue. For though her passion for Hippolytus is the work of Aphrodite, she not only fails when she tries to resist it, but the very form of the attempted resistance is a kind of indulgence. In his first speech to Artemis, Hippolytus draws a distinction between 'those who by instruction have profited I to learn' and those 'in whose very soul the seed I of Chastity toward all things alike I nature has deeply rooted' (II. 79–82), and as the audience becomes acquainted with Phaedra it becomes clear that her virtue is a result of instruction, of nurture rather than nature. She is born amorous rather than virtuous and she be-moans this inheritance: 'Mine is an inherited curse. It is not new' (I. 343). Her mother, Pasiphaë, conceived an unholy passion for Poseidon's white bull and gave birth to the Minotaur; and her sister Ariadne was Theseus' helpmate when he entered the laby-rinth to kill the Minotaur, and later his mistress before he left her on the island of Naxos where she became the bride of Dionysus.

Hippolytus and Theseus have weaknesses which complement that of Phaedra's and which promote to an equal degree the tragic outcome. Hippolytus is one of those 'in whose very soul the seed I of Chastity toward all things alike I nature has deeply rooted', but his total devotion to Artemis and chastity excludes him from society. Socially he is an outsider: Theseus' bastard son with the Amazon Antiope. He has been sent to Troezen, to his grandfather Pittheus, in order not to compete with Theseus' legitimate children

---

[1] Trans. David Grene in *Euripides: The Complete Greek Tragedies*, ed. David Grene and Richmond Lattimore (Chicago, 1955). All quotations from this edition.

for the throne of Athens. His religious attitude reinforces his
position as an outsider. His attitude is exclusive. He sees himself
as one apart. Consequently he is resented by other members of
society; also, as it turns out, by Phaedra and Theseus. When
Hippolytus rejects Phaedra's offer and abuses her, Phaedra's reason for striking back at him is 'that his [Hippolytus'] high heart I
may know no arrogant joy at my life's shipwreck' (II. 728–9). And
Theseus' refusal, in his rage, to listen to Hippolytus' defence is
partly motivated by a resentment of what he considers excessive
and hypocritical chastity; distancing himself from others in his
virtue, Hippolytus is misunderstood and arouses resentment. As
a man apart, he also fails to recognize that he is arousing resentment. His exclusiveness prevents sympathetic insight into other
people's attitude to him. Thus he bears responsibility for those
adverse human reactions which are instrumental in his destruction.

There is finally Theseus himself. He can function as Aphrodite's
instrument because he has little or no control over his emotions.
His reaction to his wife's death is a sentimental indulgence in grief
and despair. His reaction to her suicide note is an uncontrolled
outburst of rage. If Phaedra is incontinent when it comes to amorous passion and Hippolytus is the incarnation of continence,
Theseus is incontinent in his grief and rage.

The two pairs of concepts freedom/responsibility and continence/
incontinence can be used by the reader in his constructive work to
grasp the point of the play as a work of art. However, the reader's
constructive work must go further and additional concepts must
be brought in. For the play brings about the defeat of human
happiness and this defeat is ultimately accidental: 'The care of
God for us is a great thing', sings the chorus,

> if a man believe it at heart:
> it plucks the burden of sorrow from him.
> So I have a secret hope
> of someone, a God, who is wise and plans;
> but my hopes grow dim when I see
> the deeds of men and their destinies.
>
> For fortune is ever veering, and the currents of life are shifting,
> shifting, wandering forever.
>
> (II. 1102–10)

Man hopes that there is a divine order, but his hopes are vain. The
gods act not in accordance with a plan but for their own private

reasons, to satisfy their own whims. The defeat of human happiness in *Hippolytus* cannot be construed as serving any higher purpose as it can in, for instance, *King Oedipus* where Oedipus' discovery of his own identity and guilt, and his consequent suffering, can be seen as confirming a divine order where accidents have no place. Aphrodite nourishes an ill-founded grudge against Hippolytus and makes him suffer out of all proportion to the alleged offence. And the action she initiates involves innocent people in the most acute suffering: it requires the death of Phaedra and brings Theseus the deepest misery. There is no reason for the suffering of these people. There is no divine order or purpose which confers meaning on this suffering.

The lack of a divine purpose in a world where human beings are at the mercy of forces beyond their control combine in *Hippolytus* with human weakness to produce tragedy. The tragedy is not merely one of loss and physical suffering, it also has an ethical aspect. It involves two of the characters in *miasma*, pollution, and it involves the destruction of the pure, the unpolluted character. Through their actions Phaedra and Theseus become 'unclean' or 'stained'. 'My hands are clean: the stain is in my heart', Phaedra answers when the nurse asks, 'There is no stain of blood upon your hands?' (II. 316–17). However, the stain later spreads to her hands when she leaves the suicide note accusing Hippolytus of rape. She also contaminates Theseus by getting him to stain his hands with his son's blood. 'And so you leave me, my hands stained with murder', Theseus says to the dying Hippolytus. But the tragedy does not end there. 'No, for I free you from all guilt in this' (II. 1448–9) is Hippolytus' answer to Theseus, and the blame for the tragedy is placed firmly on Aphrodite. This is not merely a matter of placing the blame where it belongs, it is also a positive act of forgiveness and Theseus and Hippolytus are reconciled. The play thus distinguishes morally not only between man and man, but also between man and god. Whatever weaknesses man may have, at least he has the ability to forgive. There is no such virtue among the gods. At the end, man stands superior to the forces that break him in his sympathy and charity.

This brief and simplified description of the theme of Euripides' *Hippolytus* is built up by help of a number of general concepts through which the different features of the play are apprehended and related to each other: freedom, determinism, responsibility, weakness of will, continence/incontinence, sympathy, guilt, human suffering, divine order, purity, pollution, forgiveness, charity, reconciliation. These *thematic concepts*, as they were called in Chapter 10, are constitutive of the theme as identified through the analysis; they provide the core of what the play is *about*, in the sense we elaborated in connection with fiction. They bring into focus aspects, or universals, through which the content can be conceived. In turn they are used to formulate what we have called *thematic statements* about *Hippolytus*. These statements are formulated as part of the appreciation of the play and they refer to that play. Some thematic statements may be given such a form that they appear to be general statements—like Beardsley's 'theses'—applicable to 'human life' or 'the human situation': 'There is no divine order or purpose which confers meaning on human suffering.' Or statements of this form may be extracted from the thematic analysis: 'Human fate and happiness are determined by personality and accident.' But such statements are interpretative judgements whose primary function in this context is that of characterizing a theme.

The general *theme* of the freedom of the will and responsibility does not exist independently of the way in which it is developed in various cultural discourses. It is through these treatments that the theme is defined. It is important to keep this in mind because it focuses attention on the fact that literary appreciation does not involve understanding a literary work as an *exemplum* of a general concept. Rather, apprehending the various aspects and elements of the work through a network of concepts, as the reader does in literary appreciation, involves a mutual interpretation of work and concept. The concepts of freedom, determinism, responsibility, weakness of will, and the rest, organize *Hippolytus* for the reader and enable him to bring its elements together and to see it as a presentation of a general conflict. At the same time, *Hippolytus* provides its own, literary interpretation of the thematic statements—such as 'There is no divine order or purpose which confers meaning on human suffering'—which in turn serve to summarize the interpretation. The value of such statements rests with their value in making sense of the literary work.

Literary appreciation is the appreciation of how a work *interprets and develops* the general themes which the reader identifies through the application of thematic concepts. *Little Dorrit*, says Lionel Trilling in his introduction to that novel, is about society in relation to the individual human will. This is certainly a matter general enough—general to the point of tautology, were it not for the bitterness with which the tautology is articulated, were it not for the specificity, and the subtlety, and the boldness with which the human will is anatomized.[2]

The thematic concepts are, by themselves, vacuous. They cannot be separated from the way they are 'anatomized' in literature and other cultural discourses. And in literary appreciation it is the 'specificity' and 'subtlety' and 'boldness' of the artistic vision, the vision which is apprehended through thematic interpretation, which is the focus of interest. The focus is on the description of the work leading up to the application of the thematic concepts. As the conclusion of a thematic analysis which constitutes the appreciation of the play, one may formulate the thematic statements which have given direction to the interpretation in order to summarize that interpretation. However, this last step is not in itself of overriding importance, for literary appreciation lies as much in the route taken as in the final destination; in this it is directly comparable to metaphorical interpretation. Sometimes producing a final statement, like attempting a summarizing paraphrase of a metaphor, may even be undesirable. Successful appreciation presupposes that the implied theme is recognized, but to *state it* is often to state the obvious, and sometimes a statement using thematic concepts will simply draw attention away from the interpretation which gives these concepts content.

Without being related to a literary work through a specific analysis of that work, thematic concepts and thematic statements are empty. However, thematic concepts and thematic statements can also be developed and interpreted in what we have called other cultural discourses:

I dare be positive that no one will ever endeavour to refute these reasonings otherwise than by altering my definitions, and assigning a different meaning to the terms of *cause, and effect, and necessity, and liberty, and chance.* According to my definitions, necessity makes an essential part of causation; and consequently liberty, by removing necessity, removes also causes, and is the very same thing with chance. As chance is commonly

---

[2] Lionel Trilling, 'Introduction', *Little Dorrit* (Oxford Ill. Dickens; Oxford, 1953), p. vi. See also Stein Haugom Olsen, 'Literary Aesthetics and Literary Practice', in *The End of Literary Theory*.

thought to imply a contradiction, and is at least directly contrary to experience, there are always the same arguments against liberty or free-will.[3]

Hume in this discussion deals with the issues of determinism, free will, responsibility, blame, and guilt. However, he develops his interpretation of these issues through definition and argument. He links the notion of free will with the notion of chance, the notion of necessity with the notion of cause and effect, and argues through examples that responsibility is attributed only in cases where the action is not seen as a product of chance:

But so inconsistent are men with themselves, that tho' they often assert, that necessity utterly destroys all merit and demerit either towards mankind or superior powers, yet they continue still to reason upon these very principles of necessity in all their judgements concerning this matter. Men are not blame'd for such evil actions as they perform ignorantly and casually, whatever may be their consequences. Why? but because the causes of these actions are only momentary, and terminate in them alone. Men are less blam'd for such evil actions, as they perform hastily and unpremeditately, than for such as proceed from thought and deliberation. For what reason? but because a hasty temper, tho' a constant cause in the mind, operates only by intervals, and infects not the whole character. Again, repentance wipes off every crime, especially if attended with an evident reformation of life and manners. How is this to be accounted for? But by asserting that actions render a person criminal, merely as they are proofs of criminal passions or principles in the mind; and when by any alteration of these principles they cease to be just proofs, they likewise cease to be criminal. But according to the doctrine of *liberty* or *chance* they never were just proofs, and consequently never were criminal.[4]

In philosophical discourse of this kind thematic concepts and thematic statements are interwoven in the argument and become meaningful through definition and explanation, through the consequences that are identified and the conclusions that are drawn in the course of the argument. In philosophical discourse thematic statements and thematic concepts are integrated into the discourse itself in a different way from that of the discourse belonging to literary practice. Of course, there are analogies between philosophical and literary discourse. In philosophical works thematic statements and thematic concepts are applied in the discussion of

---

[3] Hume, *A Treatise of Human Nature*, 407.   [4] Ibid. 411–12.

examples just as in literary interpretation they are applied in the discussion of fictional situations. But as was argued in Chapter 15, this does not turn philosophical discourse into literature nor literature into philosophy, no matter how complex the examples become.

Perennial themes

In Kingsley Amis' *Lucky Jim*, Jim Dixon is at one stage described in this way:

> He felt more than ever before that what he said and did arose not out of any willing on his part, nor even out of boredom, but out of a kind of sense of situation. And where did that sense come from if, as it seemed, he took no share in willing it? With disquiet, he found that words were forming in his mind, words which, because he could think of no others, he'd very soon hear himself uttering. (chapter 18)

It is unnecessary here to put a name to those forces which determine Jim's words and actions. They are impersonal forces which he feels he does not control and which push him towards a life in submission to those he admires least and those he positively hates. But these forces do not win. Jim is saved from a tragic fate by *luck*, but not by luck only. When the millionaire Gore-Urquhart offers him a job as his private secretary and thus an escape from 'the situation' which Jim feels controls him, Gore-Urquhart gives a reason for picking Jim:

> It's not that you've got the qualifications, for this or any other work, but there are plenty who have. You haven't got the disqualifications, though, and that's much rarer. (chapter 23)

Jim is saved by his personal qualities. He does not have the weaknesses which will make him an unavoidable victim of those forces which he feels control his life. In *Lucky Jim* luck is still luck in the sense that Jim attains happiness through a series of accidents. But it is *Jim's* luck. If his personal qualities had been different, if he had had the normal disqualifications for the job as Gore-Urquhart's private secretary, he would not have been *Lucky* Jim. Jim is shown to be ultimately free to break out of the situation which he feels controls him, but it is accidental that he is offered the opportunity to escape and it is accidental that he has the personal qualities to make use of the opportunity.

Though these brief interpretative comments no doubt greatly oversimplify the way in which *Lucky Jim* handles the issues of determinism, free will, chance, luck, accident, responsibility, etc., they nevertheless go at least some way towards establishing the applicability of these concepts to the novel. The novel is totally unlike *Hippolytus*, but it can nevertheless be appreciated by applying exactly the same thematic concepts as were applied in the appreciation of *Hippolytus*. The two works give wholly different applications to these concepts, but the thematic concepts themselves are the same. Furthermore, Jim Dixon in Kingsley Amis's *Lucky Jim* can be understood as being the opposite type of character to those the reader meets in Euripides' *Hippolytus* where the weakness of each character *promotes* the tragic outcome of the action. There is, of course, nothing surprising or novel in the observation that two literary works deal with the same theme. The theme of free will and determinism is a central theme in the cultural discourses of the Western tradition, in religious discourse, in philosophy, in social sciences, and in literature. It is what one may call a *perennial theme*.

Perennial thematic concepts define what in Chapter 10 were called *mortal questions* concerned, in Nagel's words, with 'mortal life: how to understand it and how to live it'.[5] They are permanent focuses of interest in a culture because they are unavoidable. The concepts which define these mortal questions are the fingerprints of the culture. They identify the culture and they are permanent. When they change, the culture itself changes. The questions they define may change, and the application of the concepts will develop with changing circumstances, but the concepts themselves remain the same. Perennial thematic concepts do not merely have an everyday use (indeed, many perennial thematic concepts have no everyday use) but they are also interpreted and developed in practices and forms of discourse which the culture has evolved specifically to deal with mortal questions.

The list of concepts employed in the thematic analysis of Euripides' *Hippolytus* can be divided in two parts. The first half of the list comprises concepts like 'freedom', 'determinism',

[5] Nagel, *Mortal Questions*, p. ix.

'responsibility', 'continence', 'weakness of will', 'sympathy', which play a key role in the formulation of central philosophical problems. They have been the focuses of philosophical controversies for more than two millenia, and as these controversies have developed, the concepts have been interpreted and reinterpreted. The second part of this list comprises concepts like 'divine order', 'purity', 'pollution', 'forgiveness', and 'charity' which have received a significance over and above that which they have in everyday use through the role they play in religious belief, ritual, and in theological discourse. These concepts define central theological issues and again all of them have been with us for more than two thousand years. Each of the concepts has undergone transformations but it is still reasonable to see them as defining the same issues, as being at core the same thematic concepts: for example, pollution as it is defined in Greek culture and religion is different from the Christian notion of sin, but they are both interpretations of a common, underlying notion of human corruption. To point this out is not to suggest that perennial thematic concepts receive their definition in philosophical discourse or through the role they play in religious practice and are then borrowed by the reader of literature who wants to appreciate a literary work of art. On the contrary, these perennial thematic concepts achieve the importance they have within the culture, and receive their content, both from the role they play in philosophical discourse and religious practice, on the one hand, and, on the other, from the role they play in literary appreciation. The philosophical or theological uses do not have logical priority over their use in literary appreciation.

Philosophical concepts like 'freedom', 'determinism', 'weakness of will', 'responsibility', 'sympathy', and the like are interpreted and developed not only in philosophical discussion about the nature of the reality to which they refer, but also through their application in the appreciation of works of art like *Hippolytus*, *Lucky Jim*, and *Middlemarch* (where the Lydgate story raises the same question). This is not to suggest that philosophy and literature 'do the same thing' only in different ways, or that literature could, as Matthew Arnold said it would,[6] replace religion. It is not to suggest that literature offers the *exemplum* to philosophy's concepts

[6] 'The Study of Poetry' in *The Complete Prose Works of Matthew Arnold*, ix: *English Literature and Irish Politics*, ed. R. H. Super (Ann Arbor, Mich., 1973), 161–2.

or religion's ethical precepts. It is to suggest that in a literary culture like the civilization of the West, which traces its origins back to ancient Greece, concepts defining mortal questions are filled with meaning beyond that which they have in everyday discourse, and in application to everyday situations, by being the focus of interest in literature as well as being constitutive of other cultural discourses and practices such as philosophy and religion. It is the role which these concepts play in literature, philosophy, and religious practice which makes them perennial thematic concepts, and they acquire their significance because they are fruitful focuses of both intellectual discursive interest or religious practice, and also imaginative creative interest.

The difference between the use of these concepts in literary interpretation and in philosophical and religious discourse was suggested by the example from Hume. It is of the essence of philosophical discourse that it is about issues. These issues are defined through thematic concepts, and philosophical discourse is concerned with the nature of the reality to which the concepts apply. Thus these concepts help constitute philosophy as an intellectual activity. The situation for religious belief and religious ritual is analogous. Religious belief is formulated by the help of concepts which cannot be removed or changed without changing the belief, and the nature of religious ritual is defined through concepts which, if changed, change the nature of the ritual. The interpretation of theological concepts is aimed at increasing the understanding of the reality which they purport to describe.

Literature is attached to thematic concepts only indirectly. The theme of a literary work emerges from the subject it has, the way in which the subject is presented, the rhetorical features used in its presentation, and the structure which it is given. Sometimes thematic concepts suitable for formulating the theme of a work can be found in the text of the work itself, but mostly it is the reader who has to bring these concepts to the work. The connection between the thematic concepts and the literary work is established through the reader's creation of a network of concepts enabling him both to tie together, imaginatively, the different elements and aspects he recognizes the work as having, and to establish what thematic concepts can be applied and how that might be done. It is this constructive labour which is literary appreciation. Literary appreciation is concerned with the application of a set of thematic concepts to a particular literary work. It is not concerned with any further reality to which these concepts might be applied in their other uses. Appreciation, through interpretation, mediates the connection between the work and thematic concepts; but does no more. Literature offers its own alternative realm of application. It offers an imaginative rather than a discursive interpretation of the concepts. And this possibility of applying thematic concepts in literary appreciation makes no direct contribution to philosophical or theological insight, nor is it tied to any such aim. It constitutes its own form of insight, its own kind of interpretation of thematic concepts. The nature of this insight can be analysed by giving a description of how thematic concepts are attached to literary works. But one can do nothing further to throw light on it.

The independence of literary theme from philosophical and theological theme can be illustrated with an example from *Hippolytus*. Central to a thematic analysis of this play is the concept of pollution. But the particular view of the nature of human corruption defined by the concept of *miasma* is no longer theologically interesting. The concept of human corruption has been reinterpreted and the view of human corruption as a stain which can spread, as pollution which can contaminate like a disease, today appears as a metaphorical way of construing human corruption which makes no claim to literal truth. However, the concept of pollution still has interest as a thematic concept in literary appreciation. Interest in this concept is sustained by the fact that it is applicable in appreciation of works like *Hippolytus* which draw on a religious practice where the concept of *miasma* is central, as well as in the appreciation of a host of modern works where the *image* of human corruption as pollution, as disease, is central. 'There is not a drop of Tom's corrupted blood but propagates infection and contagion somewhere', says Dickens in his description of Tom-all-Alone's, the inner-city graveyard in *Bleak House*. From this monument of human iniquity spreads physical and moral pollution throughout the nation, physical pollution that leads to disease functioning as a symbol of moral corruption. Oswald in Ibsen's *Ghosts* inherits his father's moral corruption in the form of syphilis. Examples like this could be multiplied. The interpretation of human corruption as pollution is still with us, but as a literary rather than as a theological or philosophical interpretation. Literary interpretation of human corruption proceeds independently of the way it is interpreted in religious practice or philosophy.

If this argument is correct, it must be concluded that at the same time as there is a special connection between literature and philosophy and literature and religion, these discourses are not overlapping or interchangeable. Looking back to the birth of Western literature in ancient Greece, there is nothing surprising about a special connection: literature, philosophy, and religion all developed in their different ways from myth. And looking at the important position literature occupies among the values of our culture, it is unsurprising that literature should work with themes which are central also to spiritual activities with much the same cultural importance as literature. On the other hand, it must also be concluded that the *dulce et utile* dichotomy, which has provided the framework for every discussion of the relationship between philosophy and literature since Plato, is inadequate. Literature must be worthwhile, but its value does not consist in its being either *dulce* or *utile*. Literature exercises the intellect as well as the imagination, but it does not instruct in the sense in which philosophy can be said to instruct. Literature does not compete with philosophy, nor does it complement it. Literature and philosophy meet in thematic concepts, but it is not a meeting which leads to marriage or even to holding hands. The relationship is a more distant one: literature and philosophy are neighbours in the same important area of a culture.

The notion of a perennial theme is well suited as a core concept in the explanation of the mimetic aspect of literature, that peculiar kind of *aboutness* which characterizes literary works. It makes it possible to clarify the relationship between literature and other cultural practices, such as religion, philosophy, and science, and it provides the starting-point for an account of *how* literature represents central human concerns and important aspects of the human situation. It also opens up an explanation of the high value attributed to literature as a cultural activity, and it suggests a standard for judging literary works. Moreover, the concept of a perennial theme does not commit the reader to a view that assimilates literature to types of discourse the aim of which is to produce true statements, nor does it commit the reader to a view that thematic statements are fictional.

However, the adoption of the notions of perennial thematic

concepts and perennial themes leaves us with two problems. If they are to serve as the basis for a *general* explanation of the mimetic aspect of literature, it has to be established that theme is of the essence of literature; and the fact that many literary works, even if they have themes, do not have perennial themes also has to be accommodated by this explanation.

The essentiality of theme

Assume that a reader failed to attempt, or to make any headway with, a thematic analysis of Euripides' *Hippolytus*. Such a reader might notice the two goddesses and their influence on the action but would not attribute any further significance to them and the influence they have. He might notice Hippolytus' distinction between the naturally pure heart and those who must restrain their desires to remain pure. He might notice Phaedra's distinction between recognizing what is good and acting in accordance with this insight, and he might notice her explicit comment on weakness of will. However, he will not take these passages as having any further relevance for his apprehension of the play. For such a reader the passages will have a local relevance in the immediate context where they occur, but he will not take them out of this immediate context and try to understand them as contributing to the definition of the author's artistic purpose. Such a reader may also recognize Phaedra's essential weakness, her amorous nature and inability to master it, Hippolytus' exclusiveness, and Theseus' repeated over-reactions, but he will not be able to see these weaknesses as together defining a general type of human weakness, as manifestations of continence/incontinence, nor to see them as qualities which contribute in their different ways to a tragic outcome.

A reader, who for some reason fails to pursue the further significance in the play of Aphrodite's control of the outcome of the action and the weaknesses of the main characters; who fails to see the wider application in the play of the thematic concepts introduced into the speeches of Hippolytus, Phaedra, and the chorus; and who could offer no way of seeing the play which would confer thematic significance on its various features, would fail in *appreciation* of the play as a literary work of art. His failure would be

a failure to identify those features which make the work a worthwhile object of appreciation and it would have consequences:
either he must question the adequacy of his own appreciation of
the play or he must dismiss the play as of marginal interest. The
identification of the theme of the play is not incidental to the
apprehension of the play as a literary work. It does not constitute
a further judgement coming in addition to the appreciation of the
work. It is a judgement fixing the very nature of the particular
work in question. Phaedra, described as the woman who falls in
love with her stepson, invites him to her bed, is rejected, commits
suicide, and falsely accuses Hippolytus of rape, is the Phaedra of
the myth and of other plays. Thus described she has no work-
specific qualities. Euripides' Phaedra gains her individuality, her
uniqueness among such other literary and mythical Phaedras as
we know of, through the use to which Euripides puts her, through
the relations in which he places her, through the perspective which
he provides. And this use, these relations, and this perspective are
apprehended through thematic concepts. A minimal description
of Phaedra devoid of thematic concepts is by necessity a limited
description: it represents a lack of perception of what the play
presents to the reader.

Consider next a very different example, by William Blake:

> O rose, thou art sick:
> The invisible worm
> That flies in the night,
> In the howling storm,
>
> Has found out thy bed
> Of crimson joy;
> And his dark secret love
> Does thy life destroy.

It may be argued that a short lyric poem like this requires a different mode of apprehension from a work like *Hippolytus*. Not only
does it not offer the same opportunity for the application of thematic concepts as a tragedy, but the images presented in this poem
address themselves directly to the reader in their concreteness and
do not function in a larger context including action and character.
It is the experience of these concrete images which is important,
and this experience does not involve thematic analysis. This, however, would be a limiting view of such a literary work as 'The Sick

Rose'. While it may be in the nature of the genre that this poem cannot display the same complexity as the vastly longer works belonging to a genre like tragedy, a proper appreciation of the poem would nevertheless have to bring into play something like the following network of concepts:

it is immediately apparent that the rose which sickens is a mortal rose. The human rose is attacked by a worm which possesses a *dark secret* called *love*, and it is an evil power which destroys the life of the rose. The flower is attacked in its *bed of crimson joy*, and this last imageric phrase can only stand for the sexuality of the mortal rose. The argument of the 'Sick Rose' differentiates between *love* and sexuality. Love here is destructive, it is a night-force, one of the links in the chain which binds delight in the 'Earth's Answer'. But sexuality, the experience in the *bed of crimson joy*, is the very centre of the life of the rose. When it is attacked the flower sickens and dies. What then is the *love* which destroys it? Blake uses the word deliberately, and if we think of it as a counter in a commonly played game of communication we shall more clearly see his intention. He uses a personal expression to convey the experience of sexuality because it is a something which he has discovered, as it were, for himself. But if he has discovered it, it is in spite of *love* as it is commonly called. Blake is concerned in this short poem with an incredible area of experience. In it sexuality is revealed as the basis of life, the social concept of love, as something destructive to life. Love in its social definition is a negative creed of secretive joyless forbidding; love in Blake's experience is a vital matter of joy, open and sensuous.[7]

This critical response links together the images and symbols of the poem by bringing them together under different thematic descriptions which are then interrelated in statements about the theme. Leaving aside the question of the *correctness* of this particular interpretation, it is clear that the same type of argument can be applied in connection with the apprehension of this poem as in connection with the apprehension of *Hippolytus*: to construe the rose and the worm literally only, to concentrate on the concreteness of the imagery, is to rob the poem of purpose and meaning.

The consequence of this argument must be that if we find a poem without a theme, then we can do either one of two things: declare that this is not really a work of literature or judge it as an

---

[7] Wolf Mankowitz, 'The Songs of Experience', *Politics and Letters* (1947), repr. in Margaret Bottrall (ed.), *'Songs of Innocence and Experience': A Casebook* (London, 1970), 127–8.

inferior work which does not properly repay attention. Consider for example Ezra Pound's 'In a Station of the Metro':

> The apparition of these faces in the crowd;
> Petals on a wet, black bough.

These two lines appear under their title as a separate poem in editions of Pound's poems. The 'poem' has only these two lines: two descriptions coupled together by the poet to form a unit. Apart from attending to the two images themselves and the juxtaposition in which they are placed there does not seem to be much one can do with the 'poem'. It does not invite construal in thematic terms. No clue is provided in the poem which may indicate that the details of the images and their juxtaposition have some significance, some function beyond that of presenting a juxtaposition of images. Nor was the 'poem' meant to invite or yield to construal in thematic terms. It is an imagist 'poem' written in accordance with a programme for literature which holds that it is a legitimate, important, and independent function of literature to convey directly a fresh impression.[8] Despite the fact that Pound's lines have rhetorical merit, or what one could call literary merit in a wide sense (the images are precise and the juxtaposition is striking), one would hesitate to call them a literary work, a genuine poem. Considered as a piece of literary discourse, the lines give the impression of incompleteness. For a reader who had no knowledge of their origin or of the fact that they are presented under an independent heading in collections of poems, these lines would naturally appear as a fragment, as needing completion; that is, if indeed they are construed as a piece of literary discourse.

As a contrast consider the following two lines:

> Swiftly the years, beyond recall.
> Solemn the stillness of this spring morning.

These lines do not leave an impression of incompleteness, of being fragmentary. Cut off from independent generic information about these lines it is still possible for a reader to justify construing them as an independent poem: they do have a point beyond that of presenting a juxtaposition of two descriptions conveying a

---

[8] See T. E. Hulme, *Speculations* (2nd edn.; London, 1936), 162 ff.

fresh impression, and it is a point which is captured in thematic terms:

Two experiences, two concretions of emotions, are juxtaposed to yield the proportion, 'My feelings of transience are held in tension with my desire to linger amid present pleasures, as the flight of time is in tension with the loveliness of this spring morning'.[9]

This poem has obvious limitations due to its brevity: the contrast *passing time/present moment* remains undeveloped and it is unclear what the poet might have intended to make of it. But this is a defect of a complete poem where the poet has tried to deal with too large a theme in too small a format. Unlike these lines or any poem like 'The Sick Rose', 'In a Station of the Metro' does not yield to thematic interpretation and it is not unreasonable to suggest that the impression of incompleteness which it gives is due to this.

The incompleteness of Pound's lines *together with* the imagist intention that these lines should convey directly a fresh impression rather than yield a theme explain the hesitation to call them a genuine poem, a literary work. The expectation that a piece of writing should be intended to convey directly a fresh impression is at best only contingently related to the literary stance, while the expectation that a piece of writing is intended to have a theme is definitive of it. If it had been part of the imagist intention that the lines should yield a theme, then a reader would have to approach these lines as he approaches Blake's 'The Sick Rose' or any other poem. That is, no question about the logical status of the lines would then arise for him, only questions of value and success. A failure to find a theme would then lead to a negative evaluation of the poem, but there would be no reason for the reader to hesitate about what he is faced with. The intention is constitutive of the logical status of the lines if the intention is unambiguous. However, the imagist intention is not unambiguous. The intention is that these lines should 'convey directly a fresh impression'. This intention is accompanied by a claim that to convey directly fresh impressions is a characteristic function of literature. If one accepts this claim, Pound's lines must be seen as a genuine poem complete in itself because they serve this function. Now if Pound's lines had

⁹ Hugh Kenner, *The Poems of Ezra Pound* (Norfolk, Conn., 1951), 90.

yielded to thematic analysis there would have been no reason to deny them the status of an independent poem which the imagists claim for them by presenting them in a collection of poems under an independent heading (though one might have taken issue with the reason for seeing the lines this way). However, since these lines do not yield to thematic analysis and thus appear incomplete, and since the primary intention is the specific one that they should 'convey directly a fresh impression' rather than the general one that they should be construed as a literary work to be dealt with by the reader accordingly, the status of these lines is left uncertain. If this argument has force, then the expectation that a piece of writing should have a theme is an essential element in the literary stance and therefore an essential element in the definition of literature.

It is of course possible to reject the suggestion that theme is of the essence of literature simply by insisting on the irrelevance of the considerations brought forward in connection with the above examples for the question concerning how literary works are recognized and appreciated. It may be admitted that these considerations do indeed support the assumption that it is possible to extract a theme from perhaps all literary works, even from such types of work which superficially seem unpromising candidates. But, it may be argued, even if it were possible to interpret all literary works by help of thematic concepts, this kind of intellectualist approach is irrelevant to the appreciation of the work as literature. That is, even if it were possible to extract themes from all literary works, all this shows is that theme is *universal* in literature, not that it is *essential* to it. The suggestion that theme is of the essence of literature, it may be argued, gains its plausibility from a prevalent but misconceived, and distorting, intellectualist critical practice which has arisen as a result of the professionalization of literary studies. This argument is, on one level, unanswerable since it insists on the reader's right to make his own choice when it comes to the *use* of literary works. On the conceptual level, however, the argument has already been answered by the detailed considerations previously advanced grounded in the institution and its constitutive conventions: although one might use literary works as one likes that in itself does not affect the concept of literature, which is not merely arbitrarily characterized.

Moreover the argument usually rests on a false contrast between what is taken to be an over-intellectualized response to literature based on theme and, by implication, some more affective, emotional or imaginative, response. But the claim for the essentiality of theme in a definition of literature, far from denying a role for the imagination, in fact insists on it, both at an authorial level and at the level of literary appreciation. Furthermore, there is nothing in the account that precludes emotional or other affective responses to the content of literary works; indeed a clear place for such responses was afforded in our account of fiction. But affective responses, while they might aid the identification of theme, are not essential to it. Nor do they have an integral place in an explanation of the mimetic aspect of literature.

Topical themes

Perennial themes and perennial thematic concepts are constant focuses for various types of culturally important discourses over the history of a culture. They are not technical or specialist concepts in the sense of being defined exclusively within some discipline which has come into existence at a specific time. However, even given their cultural rootedness, it is not obvious that perennial concepts figure in all literary interpretations. First, there is a type of interpretation that will make use of a technical vocabulary taken from a discipline outside literary criticism. This century has seen the establishment of fairly powerful theoretical 'schools' in literary criticism which recommend that literary interpretation should employ conceptual frameworks which are not only not generally known to an educated public, but which are dependent for their significance on special theories about the human mind, society, language, etc. Since any one of these conceptual frameworks requires special knowledge which in principle cannot have been available to all interested readers of literature (literature has a vastly longer history than any of these theories) they cannot be constitutive of literary appreciation. Such *esoteric interpretative concepts* do not contribute to the diversity of *thematic* concepts which is in question here. They are not logically on a level with thematic concepts which are constitutive of appreciation, and they

pose problems of a different order from the problems under discussion here.[10]

More important from the point of view of the present discussion
is the use in the appreciation of literary works of a certain type of
concept—in contrast to perennial concepts—well exemplified in a
familiar style of modern fiction. We will explore the use of such
concepts by looking at Malcolm Bradbury's *The History Man*.[11] In
this novel the reader is introduced to the Kirks, 'a well-known
couple', who as the book starts, have decided to give a party:

The Kirks have, in fact, had a party at just this time of the year—the
turning-point when the new academic year starts, new styles are in, new
faces about, new ideas busy—for the past three autumns; and, if it had
been anyone else but the Kirks, you might have said it was a custom or
tradition with them. But the Kirks are very fresh and spontaneous people,
who invest in all their activities with high care and scruple, and do nothing just because it has been done before; indeed they are widely understood not to have such things as customs and traditions. If the Kirks
happen to have thought of a party, well, they have thought of it innocently, afresh, and from a sense of need. Evolving time signals mysteriously to those who are true citizens of it; the Kirks are true citizens of the
present, and they take their messages from the prevailing air, and answer
them with an honest sense of duty. They are, after all, very busy people,
with many causes and issues, many meetings and conspiracies, many
affairs and associations to attend to; indeed they are very lucky to catch
each other in like mind, very lucky to catch each other at the same time
in the same house at all. But they do know a need when they see one, and
here they are, together in their own kitchen, and the idea comes, it is not
clear from whom, above all, in fact, from the force of the times. (1–2)

The Kirks are a radical couple and belong to a group of people
who see themselves in heroic terms. Howard, the radical sociolo-
gist, conceives of himself as 'The History Man', the true midwife
of historical events which will lead to the fall of the bourgeoisie
and the realization of the radical ideals of the Kirks. Howard lives
by the historicist thesis that every event can be seen as a step
towards the final act of history as conceived in radical mythology.
In the present passage, Bradbury takes this heroic, historicist

---

[10] Some of the problems that arise in connection with the application of
such concepts have been dealt with in Olsen, 'On Unilluminating Criticism' and
'Criticism and Appreciation', both in *The End of Literary Theory*.

[11] All page citations in the text are from Malcolm Bradbury, *The History Man*
(London, 1978).

thesis and applies it to the Kirks' decision that it is time to send out invitations to their annual autumn party. He places this trivial decision in the same heroic and historicist perspective which Howard, by help of 'a little Marx, a little Freud, and a little social history' (22), always uses to explain and legitimize his actions. For with Howard 'you need to know all this to explain anything'.

You need to know the time, the place, the milieu, the substructure and the superstructure, the state of and the determinants of consciousness, and the human capacity of consciousness to expand and explode. (23)

Bradbury dismisses all common-sense descriptions of the decision to give the party (it is not due to anything as banal as custom or tradition), and he places it in the frame of reference in which the Kirks themselves place their actions to show that they are histori- cal necessities. Radical historicism is thus reduced *ad absurdum*.

The satire directed at the attitudes and the actions of the Kirks is violent. Bradbury insists on the grotesque and meaningless as well as on the ridiculous in his treatment of these attitudes and actions. Barbara is 'a tireless promoter of new causes (Women for Peace, The Children's Crusade for Abortion, No More Sex for Repression' (3). 'Women for Peace', in its meaningless generality, a parody of the names of 'people's movements', is juxtaposed with the grotesque 'Children's Crusade for Abortion' and the simply meaningless 'No More Sex for Repression'. And there is a hard tone to the satire. The Kirks are presented as moral monsters exploiting the established morality with its basis in moral sympa- thy to promote their own radical cause:

When you visit the Kirks, there is always a new kind of Viennese coffee- cake to eat, and a petition to sign. And, as for the Kirks together, the well-known couple, they are a familiar pair in the high-rise council flats, going up and down in the obscenity-scrawled Otis lifts, hunting out in- stances of deprivation to show the welfare people, of careless mother- hood to take to the family planning clinic; in the council offices, where they throw open doors behind which officials sit to thrust forward, in all their rebuking and total humanity, the fleshed-out statistic, the family that has not had its rights, not had just benefits, not been rehoused; and in the town in general, raising consciousness, raising instructive hell. (3–4)

The Kirks are shown up as less interested in the realities of social deprivation than are the officials whom they try to 'show' the human situation behind the statistics. They use social deprivation to promote their own cause, hunting out 'instances' which they can use to raise 'instructive hell'. And the purpose of this is to project themselves as radical heroes.

In Bradbury's novel the radical myth about 'The History Man' becomes for Howard a total, all-embracing mode of understanding. It forces him always to view human beings as objects that can be used or whose states and relationships can be *explained* in social terms. This myth protects him against sympathetic human insight and prevents him from getting involved emotionally and from ever reacting with moral sympathy. The myth governs all his relationships. Howard sees all women as sexual *objects* which he can 'liberate' so as to make them available for his advances. His old friend from his student days, Henry Beamish, who teaches psychology at the same university as Howard, has marital difficulties and generally what one calls existential problems. He is a lovable and sympathetic person, and is in a situation where he needs compassion and friendship. However, Howard's only reaction is to serve up those descriptions and those 'solutions' which his pseudo-scientific sociological theories ('a little Marx, a little Freud, and a little social history') dictate for cases like Henry. His reaction is predictable and without any touch of personal feeling. And when a person refuses to be used by Howard or when he cannot be subsumed under the explanation provided by the myth, Howard has no other option than to ignore him. Thus, when the Kirks prepare their party, they learn that a guest from a previous party has committed suicide and left a note with the words 'This is silly' (15), Barbara, who has not quite reached Howard's state of emotional frigidity, is shocked. However, Howard simply dismisses the suicide as uninteresting for them. It has no place in his radical, optimistic historicism. And when Barbara continues to insist that the suicide is of interest to them because they themselves have existential problems of the same type as the victim, she threatens Howard's myth and thus also his personality. Howard's reaction to this threat is to argue *ad hominem* simply to stop Barbara from saying anything more. Howard meets existential and intellectual challenges only on his own premises. When other people provide the premises, he dismisses them. And if he cannot dismiss them, he does everything he can to destroy whoever threatens him. One of his conservative-minded students accuses Howard (justifiably) of giving marks on a political basis. In response, Howard catches him in an intrigue where the student is dismissed from the university and Howard himself appears as the radical hero who has been a victim of persecution.

The narrator in *The History Man* presents Howard Kirk in a vocabulary which would have been acceptable to Howard himself, given the premisses of this radical myth. His treatment of women, of Henry, of the suicide, of the conservative student, and all the other characters in the book, are not described as irresponsible and monstrous but as intelligent and smart. Howard appears on the whole as cleverer, smarter, and more brazen than the other characters. He is therefore successful in almost everything he does and he dominates both the institutions and the individuals in his environment. What is more, these individuals too are targets for Bradbury's satire. The impression of the moral and intellectual inadequacy of these institutions and individuals, which is established through the fact that Howard dominates them, is thus reinforced through the narrative technique. The result is a picture of a society whose institutions and individuals are seriously threatened because they do not have sufficient moral and ethical resources to withstand an aggressive radicalism that builds on a shameless opportunism and a shallow rationalism. It is a picture of a society in an intellectual and ethical crisis, and it is a pessimistic picture in so far as Howard is the dominating figure.

Bradbury develops his characterization of the Kirks and their radical ideas by placing them as key figures in the radical student movement that took its inspiration from the events in Paris in 1968 and made a considerable impact in the United States and Western Europe at the end of the 1960s and the beginning of the 1970s. The Kirks are thus defined as a cultural and political phenomenon, and their actions and attitudes must be understood in terms of the ideas of this radical movement. The title of the novel focuses on the main idea in the ideology that is the object of Bradbury's satire: the notion that the task of the real radical is to be the collaborator of history and promote the events that will lead to the New Radical Jerusalem. It is the obsession with this idea that makes Howard an effective threat to traditional institutions and values. At the time the History Man phenomenon seemed to be of great social significance, at least to those who belonged to institutions caught up in the events. Whether they accepted or rejected the ideas of the radicals, 'sixty-eighters' had the impression that their ideas posed a significant challenge to established old-fashioned values, and that the old institutions and relationships embodying these values faced imminent or ultimate collapse. However, within a decade the student revolt had been replaced by radical conservatism and after fifteen years the aggressive young generation were 'yuppies' rather than radical academics. After twenty years the fundamental premisses of the whole political debate and the fundamental features of the political scene itself have been changed beyond recognition. 'The History Man' idea has returned to the dark corners of the junior common room, if it existed even there. It no longer seems a threatening phenomenon or even an interesting idea.

This general point can be reinforced through a scrutiny of particular episodes. Consider for example the following description of a departmental meeting in the Social Sciences Department at Watermouth University:

Benita Pream's alarm has pinged at 14.00 hours, according to her own notes; it is 14.20 before the meeting has decided how long it is to continue, and whether it is quorate, and if it should have the window open, and 14.30 before Professor Marvin has managed to sign the minutes of the last meeting, so that they can begin on item 1 of the agenda of this one, which concerns the appointment of external examiners for finals: 'An uncontentious item, I think,' says Professor Marvin.

It is 15.05 before the uncontentious item is resolved. Nobody likes the two names proposed by Professor Marvin. But their dissents are founded on such radically different premises that no two other names can be proposed from the meeting and agreed upon. A working party is suggested, to bring names to the next meeting; no one can agree on the membership of the working party. A select committee of the department is proposed, to suggest names for the members of the working party; no one can agree on the membership of the select committee. A recommendation that Senate be asked to nominate the members of the select committee who will nominate the members of the working party who will make proposals for nominations so that the departmental meeting can nominate the external examiners is defeated, on the grounds that this would be external interference from Senate in the affairs of the department: even though, as the chair points out, the department cannot in any case nominate external examiners, but only recommend names to Senate, who will nominate them. A motion that the names of the two external examiners originally recommended be put again is put, and accepted. The names are put again, and rejected. A motion that there be no external examiners is put, and rejected. Two ladies in blue overalls come in with cups of tea and a plate of biscuits, and place cups in front of all the people present. A proposal that, since the agenda is moving slowly, discussion continue during tea, is put and accepted, with one abstainer, who takes his cup of tea outside and drinks it there. The fact that tea has come without an item settled appears to have some effect: a motion that Professor Marvin be allowed to make his own choice of external examiners, acting on behalf of the department, is put and accepted. Professor Marvin promptly indicates that he will recommend to Senate the two names originally mentioned, an hour before; and then he moves onto the next item. (154–5)

This, of course, is great fun. It is excellent satire, sharply observed with just the right amount of exaggeration. It is also a severe criticism of the modern university, as represented by the new social sciences, as an institution whose members are without discipline or self-criticism, unable to maintain the traditional intellectual norms which the university is supposed to defend. And as the episode progresses, the consequences of this weakness become clear. Howard is able to manipulate the meeting for his own purposes: to prepare a situation which can be used as a focus for 'radical indignation'. The object of criticism here is limited: the university as represented by the social scientists. The satire appeals, above all, to teachers in the humanities, like Bradbury himself, who have social scientists, their pseudo-science and their jargon, as their 'pet hate'. It also appeals to a broader public outside the university that, not least because of the events of 1968 and their consequences, sees the university as a place for incompetent do-nothings in need of professional and moral tutelage. However, the satire has no broader meaning. It is not informed and animated by a general, universally interesting theme which would appeal to all reflective people.

This absence of a broader meaning is not due to the fact that this example is a piece of satire. Consider the following passage from another satirical work:

Being one Day abroad with my Protector the Sorrel Nag, and the Weather being exceeding hot, I entreated him to let me bathe in a River that was near. He consented, and I immediately stripped myself stark naked, and went down softly into the Stream. It happened that a young Female Yahoo standing behind a Bank, saw the whole Proceeding; and inflamed by Desire, as the Nag and I conjectured, came running with all Speed, and leaped into the Water within five Yards of the Place where I bathed. I was never in my Life so terribly frighted; the Nag was grazing at some Distance, not suspecting any Harm. She embraced me after a most fulsome Manner; I roared as loud as I could, and the Nag came galloping towards me, whereupon she quitted her Grasp, with the utmost Reluctancy, and leaped upon the opposite Bank, where she stood gazing and howling all the time I was putting on my Cloathes. (*Gulliver's Travels*, 'A Voyage to the Country of the Houyhnhnms', chapter 8)

The object of satire here is neither Gulliver nor the Yahoos, but what they both represent: human nature. The female Yahoo is inflamed by desire, a desire which is not essentially different from that of human beings, but which is disgusting and frightening because the Yahoos are filthy and stinking brutes without reason or normal cognitive emotions. Gulliver, whose only difference from the Yahoos is that he has reason, rejects the advances of the Yahoo in horror because he considers himself a creature much superior to the Yahoos. Gulliver thus displays human pride, refusing insight into this aspect of his nature and assuming falsely that he is not a Yahoo in this respect. However, it is only the coldly rationalistic Houyhnhnms that have no sexual passion. When 'the Matron Houyhnhnms have produced one of each Sex, they no longer accompany with their Consorts' (chapter 8). Gulliver aspires, foolishly, to their condition.

The interpretation of the passage from *Gulliver's Travels* differs from the interpretation of *The History Man* in the same way as the interpretation of the latter differs from the interpretation of *Hippolytus* and *Lucky Jim*: in the concepts one has to employ to understand it. Concepts like 'sexual passion', 'pride', and 'human nature' are perennial thematic concepts. They can be used to formulate thematic statements of a much broader and more general human interest than the problems and themes which can be formulated by notions like 'the lack of intellectual standards among modern academics'. In general this is what distinguishes *Gulliver's Travels* from *The History Man*. The concept of 'The History Man' is tied to social and political circumstances which have changed, and so the concept has lost much of its interest. On the other hand, pride and the bestial and brutish aspect of human nature, which are part of the theme of 'A Voyage to the Country of the Houyhnhnms' in *Gulliver's Travels*, are examples of central human concerns. Human beings have agonized endlessly over their physical and brutish nature and their tendency to unjustified, dangerous, and offensive pride, in literature, philosophy, and religious discourse. And the continuing interest of *Gulliver's Travels* is due to concern with these themes.

One may call the theme of *The History Man* a *topical theme*. A topical theme is a formulation of problems and issues of particular interest to a group of people (a society, a class, a religious group, a political group, a social group, any special interest group) for a certain period. These problems and issues are defined by reference to a historical and social situation in which that group of people sees itself or society as a whole as being caught up in, at that particular time. Problems and issues of this type are often of burning interest to the group and may involve conflicts between subsections of the group. When, however, the group construes the situation in which it finds itself as changed, these problems and issues lose their interest for the group. Thus it is part of the definition of a topical theme that it is transitory. A topical theme, like a perennial theme, can be formulated in different types of discourse, but these types will on the whole be other than those where perennial themes appear: in propaganda pamphlets, in political speeches and debates, in philosophical articles or theses, in essays in various social sciences and humanistic disciplines.

Consider an example which today is less emotionally charged than that of the phenomenon of the intellectual New Left of the late sixties and early seventies: the 'Condition-of-England' question in the early Victorian period. This issue was one of the most hotly debated social and political questions from the 1830s onward. It arose out of an observable social situation. The rapid industrialization of Britain from the beginning of the nineteenth century had the effect of quickly increasing the distance between the rich and the poor at the same time as it altered the relationship between the wealthy and the workers so that it became a purely economic relationship in which the worker was no more to the factory-owner than a piece of machinery. There was, says one historian,

the presence (irrespective of any historical comparison) of abject poverty, and its contrast with the affluence of the relatively rich; of the seeming degradation of the physical environment and massing of people into over-crowded cities; and of the apparent worsening of relationships between poor and rich, employed and employer.[12]

Thus the issue involved more than the level of wages:

It is . . . not unreasonable to view the Condition-of-England question in the early nineteenth century (when cities grew more rapidly than ever before or since) as one that related to the environment of living as much as to the level of real wages. It was a matter of social relations and outlook, personal confidence and self-fulfilment, security and the quality of day-to-day life.[13]

Among the constellations of concepts that were used to define the 'Condition-of-England' theme were concepts like 'rapid industrial-ization', 'poverty, its causes and cure', 'overcrowded cities', 'the rich and the poor', 'social responsibility (of manufacturers for the workers)', etc. The theme was dealt with endlessly in various forms of discourse, in political pamphlets, in socialist works like Frederick Engels' *The Condition of the Working Classes in England in 1844*, in works of economists based on the impersonal data from local statistical societies, in politically and culturally critical essays like those of Thomas Carlyle, and, of course, in a host of minor novels, like those of Disraeli and Elizabeth Gaskell, as well as in some major novels like Dickens' *Hard Times*. But when the social con-ditions changed, the 'Condition-of-England' question became the focus of historical interest rather than of passionate involvement, and the problem in its specific form of that period disappeared from view.

Themes and value

The distinction between perennial and topical concepts is rough-and-ready but is nevertheless useful in characterizing further the mimetic aspect of literature. Adopting the literary stance towards a work involves being prepared to make an effort to recognize the qualities making the literary work a worthwhile object of appre-ciation. To adopt the literary stance therefore is to be ready to

[12] Barry Supple, 'Material Development: The Condition of England 1830–1860', in Laurence Lerner (ed.), *The Victorians* (London, 1978), 65–6.
[13] Ibid. 64.

make an effort to see a text as expressive not of just any theme, but of such a theme as maximizes the aesthetic reward it offers to the reader. An interpretation of a literary work employing perennial thematic concepts is superior to one employing merely topical thematic concepts exactly in that it defines a richer and more rewarding experience of the work than does the latter. A literary work, in effect, is only as rewarding as the interpretation(s) it can sustain.

It is possible to see *Lucky Jim* as a novel of class-conflict within an academic setting, or as being simply about 'the boorishness provoked by an insufferable sham culture in a provincial backwater',[14] but it gives the novel another dimension and a deeper significance if one concentrates on the perennial thematic concepts indicated in the title of the novel and in the descriptions of Jim's thoughts, and tries to apprehend the novel as a whole through these concepts. Literary appreciation thus always involves an attempt to apprehend the theme of a work using such thematic concepts as come closest to being perennial thematic concepts. If an interpretation using perennial concepts seems artificial or strained or implausible or ill-supported then consequences must be drawn about the literary value of the work itself. Topical thematic concepts can function as stepping-stones in a hierarchy of descriptions leading up to a more general description in perennial thematic terms, but a formulation of theme which does not go beyond the level of topical thematic concepts undermines the aesthetic significance of the work.

Consequently, a literary work which can only be interpreted by help of topical thematic concepts has a limited interest. It has an interest only for a limited group of people at such a time as they find the issues with which the work deals important, and for such people as for whatever reason are interested in this group, its history, or its opinions. It is an artistic weakness in a work to support only concepts of such limited interest. This is exactly the problem with *The History Man*. As a literary work, as a work of art, it seems unsatisfactory. The satire is brilliant, the formal artistry is excellent. The novel is well structured, sharply focused, coherent, uses a variety of literary devices to increase both local and structural complexity, etc. It is the ideas which this form

---

[14] W. W. Robson, *Modern English Literature* (Oxford, 1970), 154.

organizes that give rise to the problem. 'The History Man'-theme simply does not seem of sufficient existential or moral interest to develop a poetic vision of lasting value. The idea of 'The History Man' is of interest only in the context of the student revolt of the 1960s. The consequence is that Bradbury's book, though still readable, seems dated, the satire too violent and cruel, and the pessimism verging on the neurotic.

The same considerations apply to the 'Condition-of-England' novels. Elizabeth Gaskell's *Mary Barton* was one of several novels written on the 'Condition-of-England' question. In that novel John Barton, George Wilson, and their families, the Carsons, etc., are all representatives of the parts in the conflict between rich and poor, the parts in the confrontation between the two nations. 'Mrs Gaskell's strength in *Mary Barton*', says Stephen Gill in his Introduction to the Penguin edition,[15] 'is that she manages to capture within a limited range of effects some sense of the really fundamental issues of the social situation in the 1840s.' On the other hand, Stephen Gill maintains, comparing *Mary Barton* with Dickens' *Bleak House*, 'Mrs Gaskell does not have the intense imagination which could see in the *fact* of a disease an emblem of essential truths about society'.[16] The thematic concepts which are sufficient to characterize adequately the 'fundamental issues of the social situation in the 1840s' are not those in which 'essential truths about society' can be expressed. To see in a fact the emblem of a general condition, and to shape that fact so as to create a profound characterization of this general condition, is what Dickens does in most of his novels. In *Bleak House* the dominant fact is the Court of Chancery, and the description it is given necessarily involves social comment on this institution in Dickens' day. 'I mention here', says Dickens in his Preface to the novel, 'that everything set forth in these pages concerning the Court of Chancery is substantially true, and within the truth.' However, today this social comment seems incidental to the Court's general significance as a metaphor for the society which supposedly civilized people have created for themselves. There is nothing like this in *Mary Barton*. Mrs Gaskell's descriptions of social facts do not

---

[15] Elizabeth Gaskell, *Mary Barton* (Harmondsworth, 1970), 21.
[16] Ibid. 13. The disease in *Bleak House* spreads out from Tom-all-alone's, the inner-city graveyard, and its environment where people live like the rats that carry the disease.

have this deeper significance. And this lack of a deeper significance affects the novel's stature as literature. *Mary Barton* 'survives', says Walter Allen, 'largely as an historical document illustrating early Victorian attitudes to a social problem and the early Victorian fear, which amounted almost to hysteria, of the poor'.[17] *Mary Barton* fails as literature because it does not get significantly beyond a treatment of merely topical themes.

A work with a theme which can be formulated only in topical thematic terms is artistically or aesthetically weak. It is aesthetically weak because it lacks universality: it does not deal with mortal questions. It is, at this point, worth returning to the issue of the cognitive status of literature. We argued earlier that to attribute a perennial theme to a literary work was not to attribute to it a universal *truth*. It can be even more readily recognized that the criticism that a work fails to deal with perennial themes, i.e. that it deals exclusively with topical themes, involves no reference to truth. The criticism of *The History Man* is not that it fails in truth, fails to make true statements, or fails to be true to life. On the contrary, as effective satire the reader recognizes its essential truth to the actual phenomenon it satirizes. The criticism is that it fails in *universality*. What is at issue here is not a 'correspondence' between the work and reality, but the nature of the concepts which can be used to define the theme.

That to express an exclusively topical theme is a serious aesthetic weakness in a literary work may be difficult to acknowledge. A work on a topical theme will normally appeal to, and draw a marked response from, a relatively wide contemporary audience. Such works will, to some, appear as 'relevant', actively engaging important political issues, while to others as shocking or outrageous. *The History Man* with its popular success and serialization on television found a contemporary audience on these premises. It is in many ways a typical case. Much of the acclaim which modern literature receives is based on its treatment of topical themes, like the liberation of women, the rise of black consciousness, the working-class experience, the emptiness of suburban life, and so on. Because an interest in a topical theme is often linked not only with some idealistic belief but also with what a reader believes to be in his own interest, such issues as topical

[17] Allen, *The English Novel*, 185.

themes define have an urgency and arouse passions which make it difficult to recognize that such themes are not of *universal* interest. However, a work which expresses an exclusively topical theme, will not stand 'the test of time', but will become dated and of historical rather than literary interest. It will fail to become a part of the canon of literary works which constitutes the literary heritage.

It should be emphasized that the presence of a topical theme is not in itself an aesthetic weakness. For a topical theme can be an element in the development of a perennial theme. In William Golding's *Darkness Visible*[18] one third of the book is a description of the development of a girl, Sophy Stanhope, from the age of ten to about twenty-one. When she is twenty-one, she plans and participates in the execution of a terrorist attack on a fashionable school for rich boys in order to kidnap one of these boys. Golding describes the growth of the attitudes, beliefs, and urges that finally move her to plan this action. Sophy rejects the intellectual values of her father (a chess commentator and writer of books on chess), the values of normal education (she drops out of school), normal social values (social status, financial security, marriage), and ultimately also all moral values. Sophy is ten in 1967 and her story is brought to a close in 1978. The dates and her attitudes place her as a well-known period phenomenon. She is a representative of that considerable class of youngsters who came from solid, middle-class homes but who rejected their background, were unable to find any alternative set of values, and therefore turned to violence as a satisfaction in itself. If Sophy has no ideology of violence, if she does not become a *political* terrorist, her twin sister Antonia does, and in the final act of violence they act together. Placing Sophy in that class of youngsters who in the seventies either turned to terrorism or became drop-outs (Sophy does both) is necessary to interpret *Darkness Visible* correctly, and not to make Sophy into something more than she is.

However, to stop with this topical theme would be to miss the nature of the vision that the novel presents. Golding only uses this topical theme as a basis for a perennial theme. Sophy, having rejected all conventional values, does not merely find emotional satisfaction in violence (though she does this too: she is a sadist),

[18] Page citations are from William Golding, *Darkness Visible* (London, 1979).

but also meaning and purpose. When she is between thirteen and fourteen years old, Sophy hears a talk on the radio about the universe 'running down' (131). She takes this snatch of cosmological theory and makes it her own view of the universe:

'Everything's just running down. Unwinding. We're just—tangles. Everything is just a tangle and it slides out of itself bit by bit towards something that's simpler and simpler—and we can help it. Be a part.'

'You've got religion. Or you're up the wall.'

'Being good is just another tangle. Why bother? Go on with the disentangling that will happen in any case and take what you can along the way. What it wants, the dark, let the weight fall, take the brake off—'

A truth appeared in her mind. *The way towards simplicity is through outrage.* But she knew he would not understand.

'It's like the collapse of sex.'

'Sex, sex, there's nothing like sex! Sex forever!'

'Oh yes, yes! But not the way you mean—the way everything means, the long, long convulsions, the unknotting, the throbbing and disentangling of space and time on, on, on into nothingness—'

And she was there; without the transistor she was there and could hear herself or someone in the hiss and crackle and roar, the inchoate unorchestra of the lightless spaces.

'On and on, wave after wave arching, spreading, running down, down, down—'

The leaden roofs of the school came back into focus then moved out of it as she stared up into Gerry's worried face.

'Sophy! Sophy! Can you hear me?' (166–7)

Here Sophy links her personal rejection of all values with what she thinks is the cosmic movement of the universe: the universe 'runs down', 'unwinds', 'slides out of itself', towards a darkness and nothingness which is the final goal of all history. One can participate in this movement by rejecting all positive values and by doing the outrageous deed, breaking all taboos in violence: 'The way towards simplicity is through outrage.' So Sophy is not simply a drop-out and a terrorist. She is the modern witch, the woman who sells herself to the forces of darkness. In the quoted passage she loses consciousness as she yields completely to that darkness. Her view of the universe is apocalyptic, and she finds a role for herself in helping to bring about the apocalypse. And she is identified by the character that is her polar opposite in the novel as the whore of Babylon. We are here in the midst of themes that have been central in religion and literature for as long as these have existed. The theme of the apocalypse, of man's fall and his evil nature, is developed further in other parts of the book together with the theme of man's uncertain insight into his own situation. In *Darkness Visible* the topical theme of the origin and nature of the drop-out or the terrorist consciousness serves in the establishment of perennial themes. It is in this respect that *The History Man* fails. In other words, the criticism that a literary work expresses an *exclusively* topical theme is not to criticize it for something it possesses but for something it lacks: a perennial theme.

To say about a work that it expresses an exclusively topical theme is to characterize its content. However, it is not *a criticism of its content* but of the work as art. It is a criticism of the possibilities which a work offers for interpretation of the *subject* which it presents. A work which expresses an exclusively topical theme offers an interpretation of its subject which relies on concepts the content of which are fixed by a community's conception of a social/historical situation. In *The History Man* the whole of chapter 2 and a large part of chapter 3 give the reader 'The Kirk Story', a description but also an interpretation of how the Kirks have become what they are. The interpretation is Howard Kirk's own interpretation, the application of 'a little Marx, a little Freud and a little social history' to his and Barbara's story. The concepts that are used in this interpretation are fixed by the radical mythology which Bradbury satirizes. Bradbury does not offer a different interpretation of these concepts from that offered by this mythology. Nor does the novel offer any possibilities for establishing an alternative set of concepts of which the radical mythology of the Kirks could be seen as offering an instantiation and interpretation.

A work which presents an exclusively topical theme is thus, on one level, weak in imaginative force: it rehearses a fixed, known interpretation of an experience rather than offering an imaginatively profound interpretation. Again, Golding's *Darkness Visible* can be used as a contrast, as an example of a work that offers the opportunity of an imaginatively profound interpretation of its subject. In *Darkness Visible* Sophy's total nihilism, her rejection of all moral and intellectual values, develops as an awareness that there is a black hole at the back of her head, a black tunnel, and that her real self sits at the mouth of this tunnel and looks at the world. This black tunnel is not merely a place of retreat. It is a source of activity, a 'cone of black light'. It is the place of 'the thing which really is nameless', 'this ambushed separateness from which comes all strength' (134). Sophy connects this tunnel with other aspects of her experience. She connects it with her urge to evil:

She shut her eyes with sudden excitement. She made a connection that seemed exact between this new feeling and an old one, the one of the rotten egg, the passionate desire to be weird, to be on the other side, desire for the impossibilities of the darkness and the bringing of them into being to disrupt the placid normalities of the daylight world. With her front eyes shut it was as if those other eyes opened in the back of her head and stared into a darkness that stretched away infinitely, a cone of black light. (134)

The darkness of the tunnel is both the darkness of primeval unsocialized human nature and the darkness of evil as it is understood in a culture based on Christian values. Indeed, the two are inseparable. And in the passage quoted previously Sophy makes a further connection between outrage and the running down of the universe towards a final nothingness; and as she loses consciousness, the darkness within becomes identical with the darkness of 'the lightless spaces'. It becomes, that is, cosmic darkness. Darkness, in *Darkness Visible*, also has a number of further connotations. It is the darkness of Milton's hell:

> No light, but rather darkness visible
> Served only to discover sights of woe,
> Regions of sorrow, doleful shades, where peace
> And rest can never dwell, hope never comes
>   That comes to all . . . (*Paradise Lost*, I, 63–7)

It is also the darkness of the underworld which mortal man cannot penetrate: '*Sit mihi fas audita loqui*' ('May it be permitted me to speak of those things heard'), Virgil's words before Aeneas enters the underworld, is the epigram of the book. It is because darkness acquires these many connotations and connections that the common and contemporary experience which is the principal subject of the book is not merely given an interpretation as a topical theme, but develops a far deeper significance. Through the central symbol of darkness, with these further ramifications, the contemporary experience is made representative of more universal human concerns.

There is also another side to the profound imaginative interpretation here. When a work like this is perceived to express a perennial theme, the subject is perceived as organized through a set of perennial thematic concepts, as in this case, 'evil', 'primeval human nature', 'chaos', 'the meaningfulness of experience', etc. But the work is not merely interpreted through these concepts. For, as was pointed out earlier, the work can also be understood as offering an interpretation (a distinctive literary interpretation) of those general problems and issues which give the concepts focus. A work expresses a perennial theme both when it can be interpreted through, and when it itself interprets, perennial thematic concepts. A work that expresses an exclusively topical theme fails to be original and profound in this way.

Theme in non-literary fiction

The explanation of the mimetic aspect of literature in terms of theme raises a problem. It may be argued that perennial themes are not confined to great or good literary works and can indeed be found also in works of fiction that one would hesitate to honour with the name of 'literature'. In fact, it may be argued, large parts of the pulp fiction market seem to be concerned with love and hate and jealousy, with right action and death, with the struggle between good and evil, etc. Consequently, since literature shares this thematic aspect with other types of fiction, the concepts of 'theme' and 'perennial theme' cannot be used to explain how the humanly interesting content which confers on literary works their special value and cultural prestige is constituted.

There are two related answers to this problem. The first is that theme is not *found* in a literary work but *elicited*. It emerges as a result of the reader taking up the literary stance towards a text; again this recalls the parallel with the 'metaphorical process'. Taking up the literary stance a reader tries to identify a theme in a work and then proceeds to tie this theme to the literary work through an interpretation which constitutes an appreciation of the work, and which fills the thematic concepts and statements with significance by showing how they can be applied to the fictional situations of the work. Through this interpretation the reader supports his initial hypothesis about the theme he believes the work to present. Non-literary fictions are constituted as non-literary by the way in which they are read: the reader does not adopt the literary stance towards them, and therefore does not elicit and support a theme through an interpretation. Non-literary works of fiction are not presented to the reader as literature; the reader is not invited to take up the literary stance to them. This is a social and cultural fact: pulp fiction is intended to be undemanding and relaxing, to satisfy needs for excitement and romance through vicarious experience. It belongs to, and is offered to the reader as, a different *function category* from literature. Neither Ian Fleming nor his publisher present the James Bond stories as novels dealing with the universal themes of good and evil in the world and in the human soul.

However, this can only be the first stage of an answer to this problem. For once literary practice is established with its constitutive conventions and concepts, the literary stance can be adopted towards *any* text. Though a reader may not normally attempt to elicit a theme from non-literary fiction, he might do so, if he chose. Consequently, the problem that a theme can be found also in many, or even most, texts which most readers would hesitate to identify as literary works remains. The second stage of the answer must come in response to this formulation of the difficulty, and it can take as its point of departure the two reasons why a text comes to be seen as a non-literary work of fiction rather than a literary work. First, non-literary works of fiction are intended to serve a much simpler function than is demanded of a literary work: broadly that of stimulating the imagination, for example to satisfy needs for excitement and romance. Secondly, if the reader should adopt the literary stance towards them, they do not yield what a literary work is expected to yield. That is, even if it is possible to elicit a theme from a non-literary work of fiction, this theme is not *realized*, but simply left as a vacuous cliché. What makes it ridiculous to see the James Bond stories as a saga of the struggle between good and evil forces of the world is not merely that the stories present a conflict between characters painted in black and white. Indeed, nothing could be more black and white than the paradigmatic story of the struggle between good and evil, the biblical story of the struggle between God and Satan. And in Golding's *Darkness Visible*, a major literary work dealing with this perennial theme, Golding takes considerable pain to present one of the protagonists, Matty Windrove, as wholly innocent and the other, Sophy Stanhope, as wholly evil. It is rather that the Bond stories do not *develop* a concept of either good or evil at all. The reader is simply *told* that Bond's adversaries are evil and is expected to see Bond as the enemy of these evil characters, as the hero who saves civilization from their evil acts. At the same time, 007 acts much in the same way as his adversaries, only he is cleverer, wittier, and more resourceful. There is no imaginative development of either good or evil. The concepts are not differentiated and filled with any content beyond such clichés as even the least reflective reader possesses prior to reading the work.

The literary work develops theme through literary form, through diction, metaphor, symbol, description of setting, presentation of character, parallels, contrasts, various other features of structure, point of view, etc. It is this merging of theme and form, this emergence of theme from form, that makes literary interpretation of a literary work necessary and literary appreciation possible. If, when a reader adopts the literary stance towards a work of fiction, this appreciation is aborted, if it fails to take place, because this work does not have the formal features that develop theme, and if the work at the same time serves, and is intended to serve, another function, then there is no good reason for labelling it a literary work. This is not an empirical point, but a conceptual one. If a critic succeeded in showing that a work of fiction so far regarded as non-literary, for example, *Dr No*, did yield to an interpretation which developed nuanced concepts of good and evil by attaching these concepts to the subject of the work and the formal features of the presentation of the subject, then he would have demonstrated that *Dr No* is a literary work. In fact, attempts to show that such-and-such a work of fiction does develop a serious theme and therefore is literature are part of the process of revaluation that is a constant feature of criticism. This is an activity that purifies the canon and brings new works into it.

Theme and the mimetic dimension

The aim of the discussion of the last four chapters has been to explore what in Chapter 10 was called *the mimetic dimension of literature*. The point of departure was that literature as a cultural institution attains its value because of its humanly interesting content and the unique way it develops that content. It was suggested that this is not simply a fact about literature, but an essential part of the concept of literature itself: to construe something as a literary work, to adopt the literary stance towards a text, is to construe it as being intended to convey a content of the appropriate kind. This content, it has been argued in this chapter, can be theoretically characterized through the concept of theme. The mimetic aspect of literature is its thematic aspect. The concept of theme has two advantages. It permits the theorist to account for the cognitive status and value of literature without invoking the notions of truth and reference which are so problematic in connection with literary works. A theme is not the kind of entity that can be true or false. Rather it is *interesting* or *uninteresting* and thus fits with the intuition of an 'interesting content'. And the concept of theme permits an explanation of how the value of a work is dependent upon the *kind* of concerns with which a literary work deals: i.e. whether its theme is perennial or merely topical. This explanation can be understood as a clarification of the traditional requirement that a literary work to be great or good must have universal significance, and the view that a literary work that fails to present a content with universal significance is inferior.

One may, of course, question how far it is useful to distinguish between what is universally interesting and what is true. The concept of 'truth' like the concept of 'meaning' is a chameleon concept that blends easily into a number of different discursive environments. It does not sound strange to talk about 'imaginative truth', nor need it be objectionable if all that is meant is that literature realizes themes. Certainly there is one grave drawback with dismissing the notion of 'truth' and cognate terms such as 'insight' and 'knowledge' as possible characterizations of the cognitive function of literature. These are honorary terms that would increase the value and prestige of literature as a cultural practice, placing it firmly among a group of other activities the value of which no one would doubt and the prestige of which no one would attack. If literature could be held to yield truths or knowledge any doubt about its being an activity worthy of attention would be banished. However, the adoption of these terms to characterize the mimetic aspect of literature would not change the realities as we have tried to outline them in this chapter.

There are, moreover, also good reasons for avoiding terms like 'truth', 'knowledge', and 'insight'. These concepts invite the theorist to assimilate the cognitive value of literature to that of philosophy, history, and science, and it raises the temptation to see imaginative truth and literary insight as having the same epistemological status and as being subject to the same logical constraints as philosophical, historical, or scientific truth. Consequently, the better way is to dispense with the use of these concepts altogether.

The question might also be asked whether what has been explained in this chapter can usefully be characterized as 'the mimetic aspect' of literature. It might be argued that the expression 'mimetic aspect' is only fruitfully used to characterize a more direct representational relation between work and world, on the paradigm perhaps of the 'mirror of nature'. As we have identified it, the principal representational quality of literary works resides in a kind of 'aboutness'—explained as thematic content—akin to that applied to fiction. In this respect at least we have emphasized the fictional aspect of literary works. And this, it might be contended, weakens the idea of a true representation. By substituting a thematic aspect for a genuine mimetic aspect in explaining the cognitive value of literature, the objection runs, we have failed to account for the requisite 'direct representational relation' between work and world.

The point here is partly terminological and to that extent can be conceded. However, the terminology has a purpose. The explanation provided in this chapter is intended as an alternative to more standard accounts of literary representation—as 'novelistic truth', propositional content, metaphorical truth, subjective knowledge, or moral philosophy—as discussed in previous chapters. It is intended to answer the problem about the cognitive value of literature, to develop a coherent and consistent account of the traditional demand that literature to be good and great must have a content of universal interest. It is an attempt to answer the same question as Aristotle addresses when he praises poetry for transcending the particularities of history, or as Samuel Johnson addresses when he says that 'Nothing can please many, and please long, but just representations of general nature.'[19] If the present account seems to

---

[19] Samuel Johnson, 'Preface to Shakespeare' (1765) in *The Yale Edition of the Works of Samuel Johnson*, vii: *Johnson on Shakespeare*, ed. Arthur Sherbo (New Haven, Conn., 1968), 61.

stretch the notion of mimesis, it is because the debate about the positive relationship between the world and the work, which must be present to guarantee a universally interesting content, has already stretched the concept. Moreover, though our account does not posit a direct relationship between the literary work and the world, it does establish that there is an indirect relationship: it ties the literary work to other cultural discourses through the concept of 'theme'. In this way the account does provide for a strong and positive relationship between literature and 'life', and it places literature among those cultural practices where it rightfully belongs.

17

Fiction, Literature, and Value

Locating value

The accounts we have presented of both fiction and literature might each be labelled institutional accounts. We have argued that works of fiction as well as literary works, fictional as well as literary language, are identifiable and intelligible only within the context of practices defined by specific conventions and concepts. Neither works of fiction nor works of literature, neither fictional nor literary texts or discourse, have formal features, semantic or syntactic, that define them as fictional or literary. Indeed there are no inherently fictional or literary features of texts or discourse. It follows then that any value ascribed to fiction and to literature cannot be located in a set of features which fictional or literary texts possess in virtue of being these types of text. Value is not inherent in discourse or in texts. It emerges only by seeing a text as either fictional or literary, i.e. in taking up the fictional or literary stance to the text. One can then see it as serving more or less well the purpose or purposes served by the practice.

The present account has also developed what we have called a no-truth theory of literature as well as fiction. We have argued that whatever the purpose of fiction and literature may be, it is not 'truth-telling' in any straightforward sense. Both fiction and literature may contain truths, explicitly or implicitly, and even make truth-claims, but such claims are, we have argued, incidental to the central purposes of either type of discourse. This closes off probably the most traditional, albeit the most contentious, avenue in the search for a place to locate the value of fiction and literature, and it leaves still unsolved the problem of how fictional and literary value are constituted. One way out of this problem is to adopt what may be called a no-value view of fiction as poststructuralist and deconstructionist theories have done. A no-value view need not, and indeed mostly does not, deny that fiction has any value at all, or claim that value is radically and individualistically subjective. Rather it locates value in the function which fictional works perform for a social group (a community) at any given time. It holds that there is no such thing as literary value *per se*, independent of the instrumental values attached to works of fiction at specific points in history. What makes the 'no-value' designation appropriate is precisely that it denies any specifically literary value with a claim to universal acceptance among the broadly defined community of those who read literature and thus participate in literary practice. The group for which the value arises is always a subgroup of these serious readers. It can be small or large, relatively enduring or last as a group only a short time: value is relative to the situation of a community at a place and time, relative to the 'historical situation' in which the community finds itself:

the so-called 'literary canon', the unquestioned 'great tradition' of the 'national literature', has to be recognized as a *construct*, fashioned by particular people for particular reasons at a certain time. There is no such thing as a literary work or tradition which is valuable *in itself*, regardless of what anyone might have said or come to say about it. 'Value' is a transitive term: it means whatever is valued by certain people in specific situations, according to particular criteria and in the light of given purposes.[1]

If one accepts this no-value view of literature then all that is possible in literary theory is a historiography of value, a history of reception and judgements. No universally valid logic of value judgements is possible. Indeed, the types of value which literary works have for different social groups will not be commensurable. Nor will the value judgements of one social group necessarily be even intelligible to other groups. The only possible 'debate' between these different communities would be a power-struggle where argument is reduced to mere persuasion or coercion.

The first comment to make about the no-value view is that it fails to address the problem of how to explain the cultural fact against which it polemicizes: that there are practices of fiction and literature which are seen by the practitioners as ancient practices, serving to ground a tradition. The statement that 'There is no such thing as a literary work or tradition which is valuable *in itself*' is a truism. No human practice is valuable 'in itself'. However, it does not follow that there is no value or set of values that is universally

---

[1] Eagleton, *Literary Theory*, 11.

valid for all those who adopt the practice. Anyone who adopts the practice of using money comes to share in the common purpose of that practice and to ascribe 'monetary value' to the currencies in use. The theoretical problem here is whether there are in fact needs, purposes, and interests served by the practice which are sufficiently universal in character to explain the apparent fact that literary fiction has a culturally central place and, certainly in the case of European culture, has occupied that place for almost as far back as literary culture can be traced.

The second problem for the no-value view is that it has no way of explaining why there is a relatively stable list of canonical works of literature. There is constant revaluation along the margins of the canon, but no one seriously questions whether a canon of literature should include Homer, Aeschylus, Sophocles, Euripides, Aristophanes, etc., i.e. the 'great names' of literary history. What the no-value theory does is to assume without much argument the instability of the canon and to stress historiographical explanations of how these works came to be included in it. There may, of course, be interesting historiographical explanations of how a work became famous or 'accepted', but the history of reception does not explain the existence of a canon. What is surprising about the canon is how quickly it sheds works of little value and the assured position and common appreciation of the value of those that remain. A historiographical explanation of how a particular work or author came to be included in the canon and stay there that makes no reference to the value of those works within the practice is simply inadequate in that it does not provide any reason for us, as readers, to see these works as part of the canon.

The third problem with the no-value view is that it runs together needs, purposes, and interests that can be identified independently of the existence of a practice, and needs, purposes, and interests that are defined through a practice, and that are therefore not recognizable independently of the practice. Eagleton's formulation 'whatever is valued by certain people in the light of given purposes' apparently assumes that what is valued is identifiable under some description which does not necessarily assign value to these things. However, if 'literature' and 'literary work' are evaluative concepts, i.e. if identifying a text as literature is to assume that it will yield a certain value if apprehended through the conventions of the institution, then that value is constituted by the practice itself. Moreover, this value is also constitutive of the concept of literature. This creates a logical problem for the no-value theory which dissolves the unitary concept of literature that gives meaning to the claim that different communities of practitioners assign different values to literature and therefore build different canons of literature. If literature is an evaluative concept then it would be a consequence of the no-value view of literature that the idea of a common universal value for whatever was valued by all these different communities under the label 'literature' could not arise. The no-value view is therefore, in logic, bound to a descriptive concept of literature. Since the theories which would advocate the no-value view would also reject an essentialist account of literature (indeed that is why these theories so easily identify fiction with literature) they would be committed to the view that 'literature' is whatever a community decides to call literature. This position, however, simply means that one abdicates all theoretical responsibility by denying the phenomena that one sets out to explain, not least the existence of a highly valued canon.

The institutional theory we have developed cannot locate the value of fiction or literature *in* the work of fiction or literature itself but must connect it to the practices which define works of these kinds, among other things asking what purpose these practices serve. We have denied that literary value can be located in a truth-telling function. At the same time we have argued that 'literature' is an evaluative concept, which bears with it a commitment to some sort of universalist view of value (at least in the case of literature). We now have to offer an account of value that tries to answer the questions and preserve the distinctions which the no-value view ignores, while also offering an explanation of how literature can have universal value.

The first step is again to insist on the distinction between fiction and literature. The fact that, as we argued in Chapter 10, 'fiction' is a descriptive concept while 'literature' is an evaluative concept does not mean that fiction has no value but it does mean that the value of fiction has to be located externally to the practice of telling fictional stories. There is nothing inherently valuable—or indeed harmful—in the practice of fictive utterance, conceived minimally as an invitation to make-believe. The value of fiction, such as it is, must be located in whatever further purposes the practice serves but these purposes are not defined *by the practice*. They will not be communal or social purposes shared among the community of practitioners but rather context-specific purposes determined by the utterer or author of the fiction on a particular occasion. Montaigne's fables are works of fiction with a didactic purpose. This purpose is only one among others for which works of fiction *may* be used and the purpose of teaching a specific lesson may be served by other types of discourse and other actions than just utterances: a didactic purpose, being neither necessary nor sufficient for fictionality, is not intrinsic to fictive utterance. It seems, then, that a work of fiction can be judged on two levels. First, it can be judged according to how well it serves the context-specific purpose for which it is told. Then that purpose itself can be judged as good or bad in its specific context, an assessment which will characteristically be of a moral or social nature.

Because 'literature' is an evaluative concept, an account of literary value will be more complicated. Since literary value is constituted through the practice, an account of literary value will be an account of the practice itself. We provided such an account of certain aspects (the *mimetic* aspect) of the practice in the last chapter. Moreover, since the purposes and interests which literature serves are internal to the practice, an evaluation of these purposes and interests will be a totally different type of assessment from the one used to assess the purposes, needs, and interests served by the practice of fiction. While it is clear that the purposes, needs, and interests served by literature cannot be severed from other spheres of human life and human activity their interrelation with these spheres will be less direct than in the case of fictional discourse. Evaluating the purposes, needs, and interests served by literary practice is evaluating what Wittgensteinians would call 'a form of life'. Literature is embedded in the value-scheme of our culture just as are certain other intellectual and artistic activities. Discussing its value will involve an attempt to map out how it is embedded in our culture, how it is interrelated with other human activities and interests and, finally, trying to imagine what a culture without literature would be like. This is clearly too large a question to be faced in full here but there is room for some comments on the problem of value both with regard to fiction and with regard to literature.

The value of fiction

Since fiction is not an evaluative concept and the practice of fiction—conceived through the conventions of fictive utterance and the fictive stance—does not define or constitute a certain type of value, there is no canon of great fictional works as such, no great tradition of fiction which embodies the values of the practice. But this being so, we must try to say something about what purposes, interests, and needs fiction or fictive utterance does characteristically serve. Why is it that story-tellers create and present fictive states of affairs as prompts to the imagination? It is not enough—at least in the pursuit of the values of fiction—to answer that they seek to supplement, guide, and stimulate the imaginations of their readers or listeners, though that is no doubt true. We need to ask what further purposes are achieved or sought in doing *that*. After all, as we argued in Chapter 6, there can be harmful as well as beneficial promptings of the imagination. It may be useful to divide these purposes under four broad headings: entertainment, instruction, artistic purpose, and what might be called a mythic purpose. The first three are purposes obviously served by works of fiction. The fourth heading is meant to cover such needs and interests as are not necessarily identifiable as context-specific purposes. Since all are external to the practice of fiction, a discussion of them will not add to our understanding of the practice itself. With the exception of the artistic purpose served by fiction in literature, which has been a central focus of earlier chapters, we shall therefore comment only briefly on each of these types of purpose.

Entertainment can be subdivided into further broad groups such as escape, relaxation, vicarious experience and excitement, and arousal (the list is not meant to be exhaustive). Each of these purposes can themselves be judged as worthy or unacceptable but each work of fiction can also be judged according to how well it performs its function. In the case of entertainment the purpose must be defined with reference to audience, and success is only relative to audience. What will entertain a five-year-old child will not necessarily entertain a mature adult. With regard to the various types of entertainment which a work of fiction may be aimed at serving, they are historically viewed with suspicion rather than approval. It would be outside the scope of this book to discuss the worthiness of the various types of entertainment. But it is worth noting that the purposes, needs, and interests seryed by fiction need not be unequivocally laudable in order to provide sufficient reason for the persistence of the practice of telling fictional stories. Escape, relaxation, arousal, vicarious experience and excitement are generally sought and have been so throughout history. One may try to disguise these purposes and needs behind more laudable and grander functions of fiction, such as the didactic and mythic functions, but as an element in an explanation of the persistence and centrality of the practice of telling stories, entertainment is no less valid than instruction and myth-building.

We do not here need to go deeper into the question of why fiction is entertaining. It may seem artificial to separate, as we have done, entertainment from a mythic purpose that fiction may have since entertainment value may, at least in part, be constituted through the presentation of model characters with which readers can identify, i.e. role or gender models that confirm their prejudices, stereotypes which enforce already settled evaluations and norms, etc. There is a large body of commentary about fiction, both written and screen-fiction, that works with this basic assumption and that assumes that the persistence and pervasiveness of the practice of telling fictional stories are due to this fact. This commentary assumes that fiction is used to create modern myths serving, for example, the purposes of the hegemonic classes by reinforcing acceptance of existing class, racial, or gender patterns. Much of this discussion tends to be conceptually and psychologically naïve in that it neither discusses what it might mean for someone to identify with a character in fiction, nor makes reference to any organized research which might provide some sort of empirical background for generalizations about identification with, and the influence on behaviour of portrayals of, fictional characters.[2] The discussion of why certain types of escape, vicarious

---

[2] A typical recent example is Harriet Hawkins, *Classics and Trash. Traditions and Taboos in High Literature and Popular Modern Genres* (London, 1990). Much of the speculation makes interesting reading, but it remains speculation and naïve speculation at that. The following is the sort of statement that is typical for this type of writing:

'Yet apart from such atavistic stuff as the most chauvinistic American fantasies are made of, there seems no reason why, in an everincreasingly complex, specialised, technological culture, the succession of male role models produced by the Dream Factory since the Second World War (up to and including the American

experience, etc. are entertaining while others are not, again falls outside the scope of this book.

The second general purpose which we identified for the practice of fiction, instruction, can also be easily subdivided into various types of instruction: moral, social, religious, and what one may call pragmatic instruction, stories told to make a point about the solution of a problem in everyday life. The moral fable is a genre that serves the first of these purposes. The periodical essay as developed by Addison and Steele largely served the function of social instruction and it did make use to a large extent of fictional stories. There is a huge production of Christian popular literature the purpose of which is religious instruction. However, none of these purposes is dependent upon any one special genre since they are defined independently of any genre.

The evaluation of the single work of fiction in relation to the purpose of instruction is more complicated than evaluation of entertainment. In entertainment the criterion of value is grounded in the achieved result. In instruction the criterion of value is both achieved result, manner of presentation and quality, or content of message. An effective presentation can be judged as such even when the achieved result is poor. Very often one does not know what the achieved result is simply because no systematic attempt has been made to enquire into the effect of a didactic fiction. Moreover, didactic fiction is always subject to evaluation of the message itself. Stories which give useless or wrong solutions, stories which teach the wrong type of behaviour or pernicious moral doctrine will not serve the purpose of instruction well. However, in contrast to the general function of entertainment which has historically been looked upon with suspicion and disapproval, the instructive purpose of fiction has always been held to be highly laudable, to be the sugar coating on the bitter pill of wisdom, etc. Again the interest in or need for instruction is such a basic need

man's man's favourite cousin from Australia, Crocodile Dundee) has reinforced the same, ego-reassuring, albeit ultimately pathetic male fallacy, just as the more urbanised and middle-class many Americans became in real life, the less urbane, and the more brutally macho and primitive became Hollywood's male icons' (19).

There is no distinction made here between the fictional models offered by the films and the 'chauvinistic American fantasies'. The fictional characters are taken to be the public embodiment of these fantasies.

that it can be taken to provide one reason why the practice of fiction has persisted, though fiction does not play such a central role in instruction that it would be sufficient to explain its pervasiveness. From a theoretical point of view, interest in the instructive or didactic capacities of fiction lie, on the one hand, in the rhetorical ploys used to persuade or manipulate and, on the other, in the special ways in which fiction uses imaginative involvement and point of view to enhance its teaching potential. We looked at some of the issues surrounding the latter in Chapters 5 and 6.

What we have called, for lack of a better word, the *mythic purpose* of fiction is meant to cover the sort of ordering function that theorists have seen fiction as serving through its narrative element (as discussed in Chapter 9). This is not so much a context-specific purpose, but is seen as a basic epistemological need served by fiction. Works of fiction present stories with a clear order, with a beginning, middle, and end, a satisfactorily ordered experience. They project an order on to a set of events that in real life would present no such order. So fundamental is the need for the ordering of experience into a coherent, meaningful whole that works of fiction, with their special capacities for narrative structuring, can come to seem indispensable—and perhaps inherently valuable. It is an argument we have come across before. The notion of order here should not be confused with that of artistic structure, the unity of the work of art. That structure and that unity is, at least in part, defined through theme, while the order of fiction is the order of a narrative sequence prior to the definition of any theme. A typical example of such order can be found in the detective story where all the events fall into place as the investigator at the end sums it all up for us, in front of his assembled gallery of suspects. A whole range of popular fiction is constituted by such well-made, well-ordered stories. However, the mythic purpose is, like the other purposes for which fiction is used, external to the practice. It is neither a necessary nor a universal feature of a work of fiction that it should serve to structure experience beyond that of its own imaginary states of affairs.

The attribution to fiction of a mythic function—i.e. having the function of structuring and explaining experience—is speculative and non-empirical. Some works of fiction, indeed some genres of fictional works, display the sort of order that the postulated mythic purpose would require. And one might point to other human practices that are aimed at creating the sort of order in experience analogous to that created by these fictional stories. The natural sciences try to impose order on the observed physical universe, the various social sciences attempt to make human social behaviour intelligible. History endeavours to organize the past into an intelligible order. And many people tend to organize their past through stories that give an appearance of direction and purpose in their lives. Coupled to the increased knowledge of how humans organize their perception and how brains organize impulses, all this may add up to a case for postulating a basic epistemological need for ordering that fiction can be seen as serving. However, even if one accepts that certain fictional stories are a manifestation of such a basic epistemological need, this is more a feature of narrative than fiction *per se*; the fact that fiction also serves this function is not strongly explanatory of the persistence and pervasiveness of the practice of telling fictional stories. Moreover, in the absence of individually declared and communally defined purposes, and again given the fact that the display of such order is not constitutive of fiction, the attribution of this function to fictional stories will remain speculative.

The value of literature

The concept of literature is an evaluative concept and an expectation of value and strategies for revealing that value are a definitive part of the literary stance. Of course as most literary works are also works of fiction the values of fiction will also be present in those works of literature. But the features derived from the fictional status of a work, though they might contribute to, will not define such *literary* value as the work possesses. As we have emphasized throughout the fictive stance is not the same as the literary stance.

Literary value is defined by the concepts and conventions of literary practice, and these determine the two major features of a literary work: its creative-imaginative aspect and its mimetic aspect. It is within these aspects that literary value is located. The two are interrelated. The mimetic aspect of the literary work, constituted by theme, is dependent for its realization on the subject and its form which together constitute the creative-imaginative aspect of the work. A theme can be elicited from almost any work of fiction, but it is realized and receives its development through the way in which it is presented. However, the mode of presentation cannot by itself constitute a theme as serious and worthwhile. Literary value emerges in appreciation as an identified interrelation between the two aspects. One central, characteristic purpose defined by the literary practice and served by the literary work is to develop in depth, through subject and form, a theme which is in some sense central to human concerns and which can therefore be recognized as of more or less universal interest. Appreciation and consequent evaluation of the individual literary work is a matter of eliciting and supporting the identification and development of a 'perennial theme'.

Since 'literature' and 'literary work' are evaluative concepts, there exists, as one should expect, a canon of literature, a great tradition, that embodies the values of the practice. The concept of literature is defined by the values which the works of the tradition embody. A radical revision of the canon would not be merely a modification of what in our culture is considered as valuable: it would be a rejection of literature itself. None of the present-day attacks on the canon admit this. They argue as if it were meaningful and possible to have alternative canons or alternative concepts of literature, to replace the list of canonical works with another but still retain the central place of literature in the culture. It is, of course, possible to argue for an *end* to literature, but if one does one should recognize what one is doing. The *defence* of the canon, on the other hand, normally takes the approach that the values embodied in the works of the canon are fundamental values that define our societies as *civilized* societies. These values are, according to this type of defence, identifiable without reference to the works of the canon and their importance can be recognized by the role they play in the lives of the single individual and the community:

How then are we to go on as persons to manifest and sustain our being in the world? From what landmarks in our course can we take our bearings? The readings [of the four literary works] that follow approach these questions by sorting through and balancing competing accounts of the roles in our lives of universal principles and demands of our nature, themselves associated with our autonomy, on the one hand, and the effects and demands of particular projects and relationships rooted in our connectedness to nature and society, on the other. The texts under study are preoccupied with conflict and its resolution, between principle and practice, universality and particularity, *Moralität* and *Sittlichkeit*, and Kantian and Hegelian moral philosophy.[3]

However, this theorist argues as if literature provided answers to serious questions that we have to address in our own lives, questions that exist for us independently of the existence of literary practice. The problem with this type of defence from our point of view is that it demands a concept of what may be called 'true-versions' of themes that we have argued in detail cannot be sustained in any substantive form.[4]

In our remarks on literature in the first section of this chapter we suggested a way of answering the question of how to appraise the purposes defined by literary practice. We argued in Chapter 16 that literary works offer their own, literary, interpretations of the themes they present and that these interpretations have only an indirect link with real-life situations, since the situations presented in literary works are defined uniquely through artistic means (style, structure, etc.). However, it is arguable that the importance of literature, its cultural value, is not dependent on or defined by any relation to *externally* defined themes but that it consists in the way in which the practice of literature is *embedded* in our culture. Literature is not merely a response to already defined existential problems, nor an expression of already felt and accepted moral and social values. It is one of the ways in which these existential problems, as well as social and moral values, are defined and developed for us. It is a familiar conception of philosophy that attributes to it the task of formulating and suggesting solutions to problems of knowledge, morality, and metaphysics, of giving substance and precision to questions within these areas. These

---

[3] Richard Eldridge, *On Moral Personhood: Philosophy, Literature, Criticism, and Self-Understanding* (Chicago, 1989), 4.

[4] Eldridge manages to produce convincing readings of the works he discusses by avoiding this question. He simply answers the question about theme without asking the question whether the readings really do provide 'sound' answers to his questions. How problematic the assumption of true-versions of themes can become for someone who insists that literature has to be ethically sound, is well illustrated by Wayne C. Booth's *The Company We Keep: An Ethics of Fiction* (Los Angeles, 1988). Compare e.g. his way of reading *Emma* (*The Company We Keep*, 426–35) with Eldridge's way of reading *Pride and Prejudice* (*On Moral Personhood*, 141–80).

questions may spring from our activities in daily life, but they do not receive perspicuous formulation and substance there. The problems as problems become fully constituted only within philosophical discourse. We now want to suggest that literature functions analogously: it develops themes that are only vaguely felt or formulated in daily life and gives them a 'local habitation and a name'. In the culture that goes back to ancient Greece, literature has developed into a special kind of cognition that has come to constitute, in part, the themes that have become central in the culture. Daily life is disorderly and unorganized. Literary works of art organize described universes in such a way that thematic concepts receive a content when applied to that universe.

Consider again an example of a work presenting a situation which can be thematized by using concepts related to the 'freedom of the will/determinism' theme. Here is a description of Ephraim Tellwright in Arnold Bennett's *Anna of the Five Towns*:[5]

This surly and terrorizing ferocity of Tellwright's was as instinctive as the growl and spring of a beast of prey. He never considered his attitude towards the women of his household as an unusual phenomenon which needed justification, or as being in the least abnormal. The women of a household were the natural victims of their master: in his experience it had always been so. In his experience the master had always, by universal consent, possessed certain rights over the self-respect, the happiness, and the peace of the defenceless souls set under him—rights as unquestioned as those exercised by Ivan the Terrible. Such rights were rooted in the secret nature of things. It was futile to discuss them, because their necessity and their propriety were equally obvious. Tellwright would not have been angry with any man who impugned them: he would merely have regarded the fellow as a crank and a born fool, on whom logic or indignation would be entirely wasted. He did as his father and uncles had done. He still thought of his father as a grim customer, infinitely more redoubtable than himself. He really believed that parents spoiled their children nowadays: to be knocked down by a single blow was one of the punishments of his own generation. He could recall the fearful timidity of his mother's eyes without a trace of compassion. His treatment of his daughters was no part of a system, nor obedient to any defined principles, nor the expression of a brutal disposition, nor the result of a gradually acquired habit. It came to him like eating, and like parsimony. He belonged to the great and powerful class of house-tyrants, the backbone of

---

[5] Page citations in the text are from Arnold Bennett, *Anna of the Five Towns* (Harmondsworth, 1978).

the British nation, whose views on income-tax cause ministries to tremble. If you had talked to him of the domestic graces of life, your words would have conveyed to him no meaning. If you had indicted him for simple unprovoked rudeness, he would have grinned, well knowing that, as the King can do no wrong, so a man cannot be rude in his own house. If you had told him that he inflicted purposeless misery not only on others but on himself, he would have grinned again, vaguely aware that he had not tried to be happy, and rather despising happiness as a sort of childish gewgaw. He had, in fact, never been happy at home: he had never known that expansion of the spirit which is called joy; he existed continually under a grievance. The atmosphere of Manor Terrace affected him, too, with a melancholy gloom—him, who had created it. Had he been capable of self-analysis, he would have discovered that his heart lightened whenever he left the house, and grew dark whenever he returned; but he was incapable of the feat. His case, like every similar case, was irremediable. (127)

Tellwright's behaviour towards his daughters is here presented as instinctive. This is not merely stated but given depth through a series of comparisons, by linking his behaviour to the behaviour of his father and uncles, by linking him humorously to 'the great and powerful class of house-tyrants, the backbone of the British nation, whose views on income-tax cause ministries to tremble', by spelling out his attitudes to the 'domestic graces of life', 'happiness', and by presenting the effect of his attitudes and mood on himself. Ultimately Tellwright is seen as a victim of forces beyond his control which have formed his personality, a personality from which he cannot escape because these forces have also made him incapable of self-analysis ('His case, like every similar case, was irremediable'). This is only a part of the presentation of Tellwright, who appears in most of the chapters in the book. This description thematizes the behaviour that we are shown in the other chapters; it interprets this behaviour for us. The presentation of Tellwright complements the presentation of all the other major characters in the book: they, too, appear as victims of forces beyond their control. Their situations are all different: Titus Price commits suicide as he fails economically and morally; Henry Mynors succeeds in everything he wants to do, even in marrying Anna, but even in his success he is a victim:

Had he guessed what perhaps hung on that answer, Mynors might have given it in a tone less callous and perfunctory. Could he have seen the tightening of her lips, he might even afterwards have repaired his error by some voluntary assurance that Willie Price should be watched over with a benevolent eye and protected with a strong arm. But how was he to know that in misprizing Willie Price before her, he was misprizing a child to its mother? He had done something for Willie Price, and considered he had done enough. His thoughts, moreover, were on other matters. (211)

This is the moment when he finally loses any possibility of possessing Anna's love. But his personality, what he is, prevents him from seeing what is involved. His personality even distorts his perception, as he fails to note the 'tightening of the lips'.

And there is Anna herself. Unlike her father and Henry Mynors, she is capable of self-analysis and sees what is wrong with the community she enters into, and why she will never become a member of that community in spirit though she is integrated socially. Nevertheless, she cannot break away and change her fate:

Some may argue that Anna, knowing she loved another man, ought not to have married Mynors. But she did not reason thus; such a notion never even occurred to her. She had promised to marry Mynors, and she married him. Nothing else was possible. She who had never failed in duty did not fail then. She who had always submitted and bowed the head, submitted and bowed the head then. She had sucked in with her mother's milk the profound truth that a woman's life is always a renunciation, greater or less. Her's by chance was greater. Facing the future calmly and genially, she took oath with herself to be a good wife to the man whom, with all his excellences, she had never loved. (235)

Anna of the Five Towns organizes a described universe in such a way that the reader who applies concepts like 'freedom of the will', 'determinism', 'victim of external forces beyond human control' in the appreciation of that work will come to see how, in that universe, human beings are controlled by external forces. There is no similar order in the real world that will make these concepts meaningful in this way. Daily life does not offer the sort of visible connections that artistic narrative defines. These connections emerge in the artistic presentation of the subject.

What we suggest is that the ideas constituting the large themes of our culture, the mortal questions, are in part literary ideas. Outside works like *Anna of the Five Towns* we have no coherent *vision* of what determinism means. There are other types of discourse, philosophical and theological discourse among others, that offer different kinds of coherent interpretations of such concepts.

These discourses do not compete with literature, but complement it. Furthermore, when we identify 'large' themes in daily life, they tend to be literary themes. We then tend to view reality in artistic terms, either in terms of a particular work to which we have given some attention, or in terms of an artistic technique that we have come to appreciate. This is why it is so tempting to do what Wittgensteinian theorists do and ascribe a learning effect, in the sense of an eye-opener effect, to art. However, seeing life in terms of art is an optional extra that is only sometimes useful and mostly does not occur. Mostly, we simply do not meet the grand themes in trivial daily life.

This is why it is so devastating for literature if artistic unity and coherence should come to be seen as undesirable constructions which prevent the free play of the meanings of the text. With the free play of the meanings of the text, we are back in the essentially unordered triviality of daily life. If art comes to be seen essentially as full of contradictions and incoherence as daily life itself, amounting to nothing much, 'a tale full of sound and fury, signifying nothing', then this is the end of art. Art is then as trivial as daily life, as void of great themes, as boring and inconsequential. And we do not need a realm of art that simply duplicates the triviality of life.

The quality of our cognition of themes and thematic concepts is dependent upon the quality of the literature we read. No doubt, as we have acknowledged, grand themes can be elicited from most fictions, but most fictions make the grand themes only grand clichés. An audience fed on fictions like *Dynasty* will only have simple conceptions of human conflict and human attachment. There may be a coherent vision in such works, with clear choices, but very little for the mind to grapple with and develop. The result is an alternative kind of triviality. It makes no demands on either the intellectual, emotional, or moral nature that are not also made in daily life with its simple choices and short-term goals. For literature like philosophy challenges the reader to make his own construction, to invest time and effort in reaching a deeper insight into the great themes, though this insight is 'literary'.

There is no further move we can now make to defend literary practice or any other cultural practice. Literary practice is embedded in the value-scheme of our culture in the sense that it is one of the practices that define what we hold to be important and valuable. Why we should hold these themes and concerns to be valuable is partly answered by pointing to the fact that we are human beings who are born and die, who are self-reflective, who love and hate, who live in society with other people. But this answer can only be partial. For there are themes and values that go well beyond this basic situation, such as a concern for justice and for moral rights, a concern for art and the artist, a concern for what sort of universe we live in. These are simply things we care about and always seem to have cared about. And this is where the argument stops. To go further would be to start another book in another field.

Bibliography

ÅHLBERG, LARS-OLOF, *Realismbegrepp i litteratur och konst: En idéhistorisk och konstfilosofisk studie.* Acta Universitatis Upsaliensis: Aesthetica Upsaliensia, 4 (Uppsala, 1988).

ALLEN, WALTER, *The English Novel* (Harmondsworth, 1958).

APPIGNANESI, LISA, and MAITLAND, SARA (eds.), *The Rushdie File* (London, 1989).

ARISTOTLE, *The Works of Aristotle*, translated into English under the editorship of W. D. Ross, viii (2nd edn.; London, 1928), xi (London, 1946).

ARNOLD, MATTHEW, *The Complete Prose Works of Matthew Arnold, ix: English Literature and Irish Politics*, ed. R. H. Super (Ann Arbor, Mich., 1973).

AUERBACH, ERICH, *Mimesis: The Representation of Reality in Western Literature*, trans. Willard R. Trask (Princeton, NJ, 1953).

AUSTIN, J. L., 'Truth', *Proceedings of the Aristotelian Society*, Suppl. Vol. 24 (1950), 111–28; repr. in *Philosophical Papers*.

—— *Philosophical Papers* (Oxford, 1961).

—— *How To Do Things With Words* (Oxford, 1962).

—— *Sense and Sensibilia* (Oxford, 1962).

AVNI, ORA, *The Resistance of Reference* (Baltimore, 1990).

BACH, KENT, *Thought and Reference* (Oxford, 1987).

BARRETT, CYRIL (ed.), *Collected Papers on Aesthetics* (Oxford, 1965).

BARTHES, ROLAND, 'Writing: An Intransitive Verb', in *Image-Music-Text*.

—— *Image-Music-Text*, essays selected and translated by Stephen Heath (London, 1977).

—— 'The Reality Effect', in *The Rustle of Language*.

—— *The Rustle of Language* (Oxford, 1986).

BEARDSLEY, MONROE C., 'The Metaphorical Twist', *Philosophy and Phenomenological Research*, 22 (1962), 293–307.

—— 'Metaphor', in Paul Edwards (ed.), *Encyclopedia of Philosophy*.

—— 'Metaphor and Falsity', *Journal of Aesthetics and Art Criticism*, 35 (1976), 218–22.

—— 'Aesthetic Intentions and Fictive Illocutions', in P. Hernadi (ed.), *What is Literature?*

—— 'Metaphorical Senses', *Nous*, 12 (1978), 3–16.

—— *Aesthetics: Problems in the Philosophy of Criticism* (2nd edn.; New York, 1981).

—— 'Fiction as Representation', *Synthese*, 46 (1981), 291–313.

BEARDSLEY, MONROE C. and SCHUELLER, HERBERT (eds.), *Aesthetic Inquiry: Essays on Art Criticism and the Philosophy of Art* (Belmont, Calif., 1967).

BEARDSMORE, R. W., *Art and Morality* (London, 1971).

—— 'Learning from a Novel', *Philosophy and the Arts.* Royal Institute of Philosophy Lectures, vi (1971–2) (London, 1973).

—— 'The Limits of Imagination', *British Journal of Aesthetics*, 20 (1980), 99–114.

BELSEY, CATHERINE, *Critical Practice* (London, 1980).

BENNETT, JONATHAN, *Linguistic Behaviour* (Cambridge, 1976).

BENTHAM, JEREMY, *Bentham's Theory of Fictions*, ed. C. K. Ogden (2nd edn.; London, 1951).

BINKLEY, TIMOTHY, 'On the Truth and Probity of Metaphor', *Journal of Aesthetics and Art Criticism*, 33 (1974), 171–80.

BLACK, MAX, *Models and Metaphors: Studies in Language and Philosophy* (Ithaca, NY, 1962).

—— 'More about Metaphor', in Andrew Ortony (ed.), *Metaphor and Thought.*

BLACKBURN, SIMON, *Spreading the Word* (Oxford, 1984).

BLOCKER, GENE H., 'The Truth about Fictional Entities', *Philosophical Quarterly*, 24 (1974), 27–36.

BLOOM, HAROLD, *Yeats* (New York, 1970).

BOOTH, WAYNE C., *The Rhetoric of Fiction* (Chicago, 1961).

—— *The Company We Keep: An Ethics of Fiction* (Los Angeles, 1988).

BORUAH, BIJOY H., *Fiction and Emotion* (Oxford, 1988).

BOTTRALL, MARGARET (ed.), *'Songs of Innocence and Experience': A Casebook* (London, 1970).

BOYD, RICHARD, 'Metaphor and Theory Change: What is "Metaphor" a Metaphor For?', in Andrew Ortony (ed.), *Metaphor and Thought.*

BRINKER, MENAHEM, 'Verisimilitude, Conventions, and Belief', *New Literary History*, 14 (1983) 253–67.

BROOKS, CLEANTH, *The Well-Wrought Urn* (2nd edn.; London, 1968).

BROOKS, PETER, *Reading for the Plot: Design and Intention in Narrative* (New York, 1985).

CAMP, JOSEPH L., 'Why Attributions of Aboutness Report Soft Facts', *Philosophical Topics*, 16 (1988), 5–30.

CARNAP, RUDOLF, 'Empiricism, Semantics and Ontology', in Leonard Linsky (ed.), *Semantics and the Philosophy of Language.*

CARROLL, NOËL, 'Art, Practice and Narrative', *The Monist*, 71 (1988), 140–56.

—— 'Interpretation, History, and Narrative', *The Monist*, 73 (1990), 134–66.

CASCARDI, ANTHONY J., *Literature and the Question of Philosophy* (Baltimore, 1989).

CASTAÑEDA, HECTOR-NERI, 'Fiction and Reality: Their Fundamental Connections', *Poetics*, 8 (1979), 31–62.

CEBIK, L. B., *Fictional Narrative and Truth: An Epistemic Analysis* (Lanham, Md., 1984).

CHARLTON, WILLIAM, 'Is Philosophy a Kind of Literature?', *British Journal of Aesthetics*, 14 (1974), 3–16.

CHATRABARTI, ARINDAM, 'Two Problems in the Ontology of Fictional Discourse', *Journal of Indian Council of Philosophical Research*, 1 (1983), 139–59.

CLEGG, JERRY S., 'Some Artistic Uses of Truths and Lies', *Journal of Aesthetics and Art Criticism*, 31 (1972), 43–7.

CLEVE, JAMES VAN, 'Foundationalism, Epistemic Principles, and the Cartesian Circle', *Philosophical Review*, 88 (1979), 55–91.

CLOSE, A. J., '*Don Quixote* and the "Intentionalist Fallacy"', *British Journal of Aesthetics*, 12 (1972), 19–39.

COHEN, L. J., 'The Semantics of Metaphor', in Andrew Ortony (ed.), *Metaphor and Thought*.

—— and MARGALIT, A., 'The Role of Inductive Reasoning in the Interpretation of Metaphor', in Donald Davidson and Gilbert Harman (eds.), *Semantics of Natural Language*.

COLERIDGE, SAMUEL TAYLOR, *Biographia Literaria*, ed. J. Shawcross (Oxford, 1907).

COLLETT, ALAN, 'Literature, Criticism and Factual Reporting', *Philosophy and Literature*, 13 (1989), 282–96.

COOPER, DAVID, *Metaphor* (Oxford, 1986).

CULLER, JONATHAN, *Structuralist Poetics* (London, 1975).

—— *On Deconstruction: Theory and Criticism after Structuralism* (London, 1983).

—— *Framing the Sign* (Oxford, 1988).

CURRIE, GREGORY, 'What is Fiction?', *Journal of Aesthetics and Art Criticism*, 43 (1985), 385–92.

—— 'Fictional Truth', *Philosophical Studies*, 50 (1986), 195–212.

—— 'Works of Fiction and Illocutionary Acts', *Philosophy and Literature*, 10 (1986), 304–7.

—— 'Fictional Names', *Australasian Journal of Philosophy*, 66 (1988), 471–88.

—— *The Nature of Fiction* (Cambridge, 1990).

DAVIDSON, DONALD, 'What Metaphors Mean', *Critical Inquiry*, 5 (1978), 31–47; repr. in *Inquiries into Truth and Interpretation*.

—— *Inquiries into Truth and Interpretation* (Oxford, 1984).

—— and HARMAN, GILBERT (eds.), *Semantics of Natural Language* (Dordrecht, 1972).

DENNETT, DANIEL C., 'Beyond Belief', in Andrew Woodfield (ed.), *Thought and Object: Essays on Intentionality*.

460 BIBLIOGRAPHY

DENNETT, DANIEL C., *The Intentional Stance* (Cambridge, Mass., 1987).

DERRIDA, JACQUES, 'Limited Inc.', *Glyph*, 2 (1977), 162–254.

DESCARTES, RENÉ, *The Philosophical Writings of Descartes*, i, trans. John Cottingham, Robert Stoothoff, and Dugald Murdoch (Cambridge, 1985).

—— *The Philosophical Writings of Descartes*, ii, trans. John Cottingham, Robert Stoothoff, and Dugald Murdoch (Cambridge, 1984).

DEVITT, MICHAEL, *Realism and Truth* (Princeton, NJ, 1984).

—— 'Rorty's Mirrorless World', *Midwest Studies in Philosophy*, 12 (1988), 157–77.

DIAMOND, CORA, 'Having a Rough Story about What Moral Philosophy Is', *New Literary History*, 15 (1983–4), 155–70.

DIJK, TEUN A. VAN (ed.), *Pragmatics of Language and Literature* (The Hague, 1976).

DONNELLAN, KEITH, 'Reference and Definite Descriptions', *Philosophical Review*, 75 (1966), 281–304.

—— 'Speaking of Nothing', *Philosophical Review*, 83 (1974), 3–32.

DORTER, KENNETH, 'Conceptual Truth and Aesthetic Truth', *Journal of Aesthetics and Art Criticism*, 48 (1990), 37–51.

DUMMETT, MICHAEL, 'Truth', in George Pitcher (ed.), *Truth*.

—— *Truth and Other Enigmas* (London, 1978).

EAGLETON, TERRY, *Literary Theory: An Introduction* (Oxford, 1983).

EATON, MARCIA M., 'Good and Correct Interpretations of Literature', *Journal of Aesthetics and Art Criticism*, 29 (1970), 227–33.

—— 'The Truth Value of Literary Statements', *British Journal of Aesthetics*, 12 (1972), 163–74.

—— 'Liars, Ranters, and Dramatic Speakers', in B. R. Tilghman (ed.), *Language and Aesthetics: Contributions to the Philosophy of Art* (Lawrence, Kan., 1973).

—— 'On Being a Character', *British Journal of Aesthetics*, 16 (1976), 24–31.

EDWARDS, PAUL (ed.), *Encyclopedia of Philosophy* (London, 1967).

ELDRIDGE, RICHARD, *On Moral Personhood: Philosophy, Literature, Criticism, and Self-Understanding* (Chicago, 1989).

ELGIN, CATHERINE Z., *With Reference to Reference* (Indianapolis, 1983).

ELLIOTT, R. K., 'Poetry and Truth', *Analysis*, 27 (1966–7), 77–85.

ELLIS, JOHN, *Against Deconstruction* (Princeton, NJ, 1990).

EVANS, GARETH, *The Varieties of Reference* (Oxford, 1982).

FALCK, COLIN, *Myth, Truth and Literature* (Cambridge, 1989).

FEAGIN, SUSAN L., 'The Pleasures of Tragedy', *American Philosophical Quarterly*, 20 (1983), 95–104.

FEIGL, H., and SELLARS, W. (eds.), *Readings in Philosophical Analysis* (New York, 1949).

FODOR, JERRY, 'Methodological Solipsism Considered as a Research Strategy in Cognitive Psychology', in *Representations*.

—— *Representations* (Cambridge, Mass., 1981).

FOGELIN, ROBERT J., *Figuratively Speaking* (New Haven, Conn., 1988).

FOOT, PHILIPPA (ed.), *Theories of Ethics* (Oxford, 1967).

FOWLES, JOHN, *A Maggot* (London, 1985).

FREGE, GOTTLOB, 'On Sense and Reference', in *Philosophical Writings of Gottlob Frege*, trans. and edited by Peter Geach and Max Black (Oxford, 1970).

—— *Posthumous Writings*, edited by Hans Hermes, Friedrich Kambartel, and Friedrich Kaulbach (Oxford, 1979).

GABRIEL, GOTTFRIED, 'Fiction—A Semantic Approach', *Poetics*, 8 (1979), 245–55.

GALE, RICHARD M., 'The Fictive Use of Language', *Philosophy*, 46 (1971), 324–39.

GENETTE, GERARD, 'Boundaries of Narrative', *New Literary History*, 8 (1976–7), 1–15.

GOLDMAN, ALAN H., 'Fanciful Arguments for Realism', *Mind*, 93 (1984), 19–38.

GOODMAN, NELSON, 'About', *Mind*, 70 (1961), 1–24.

—— *The Languages of Art* (London, 1969).

—— *Ways of Worldmaking* (Brighton, 1978).

—— 'On Starmaking', *Synthese*, 45 (1980), 211–15.

—— 'Fiction for Five Fingers', *Philosophy and Literature*, 6 (1982), 162–4.

—— *Of Mind and Other Matters* (Cambridge, Mass., 1984).

GRAFF, GERALD, *Literature Against Itself: Literary Ideas in Modern Society* (Chicago, 1979).

GRICE, H. P., 'Meaning', *Philosophical Review*, 66 (1957), 377–88; repr. in *Studies in the Ways of Words*.

—— 'Utterer's Meaning and Intentions', *Philosophical Review*, 78 (1969), 147–77; repr. in *Studies in the Ways of Words*.

—— *Studies in the Ways of Words* (Cambridge, Mass., 1989).

GUTHRIE, JERRY L., 'Self-Deception and Emotional Response to Fiction', *British Journal of Aesthetics*, 21 (1981), 65–75.

HAACK, SUSAN, 'Realism', *Synthese*, 73 (1987), 275–99.

HACKING, IAN, *The Emergence of Probability* (Cambridge, 1975).

HARRÉ, ROM, 'Narrative in Scientific Discourse', in Cristopher Nash (ed.), *Narrative in Culture*.

HARRISON, ROSS, *Bentham* (London, 1983).

HART, H. L. A., 'A Logicians' Fairy Tale', *Philosophical Review*, 60 (1951), 198–212.

—— *The Concept of Law* (Oxford, 1961).

HARTMAN, GEOFFREY, *Criticism in the Wilderness* (New Haven, Conn., 1980).

HAWKES, TERENCE, *Structuralism and Semiology* (London, 1977).

HAWKINS, HARRIET, *Classics and Trash: Traditions and Taboos in High Literature and Popular Modern Genres* (London, 1990).

HAWTHORN, JEREMY, *Unlocking the Text* (London, 1987).

HEINTZ, JOHN, 'Reference and Inference in Fiction', *Poetics*, 8 (1979), 85–9.

HEMMINGS, F. W. J. (ed.), *The Age of Realism*. The Pelican Guide to European Literature (Harmondsworth, 1974).

HEMPEL, CARL, 'Comments on Goodman's *Ways of Worldmaking*', *Synthese*, 45 (1980), 193–9.

HENLE, PAUL, 'Metaphor', in Paul Henle (ed.), *Language, Thought and Culture*.

—— (ed.), *Language, Thought and Culture* (Ann Arbor, Mich., 1965).

HEPBURN, RONALD W., 'Poetry and "Concrete Imagination": Problems of Truth and Illusion', *British Journal of Aesthetics*, 12 (1972), 3–18.

—— 'Art, Truth and the Education of Subjectivity', *Journal of Philosophy of Education*, 24 (1990), 185–98.

HERNADI, P. (ed.), *What is Literature?* (Bloomington, Ind., 1978).

HEYL, BERNARD C., 'Artistic Truth Reconsidered', *Journal of Aesthetics and Art Criticism* 8 (1950), 251–8.

HOBBES, THOMAS, *Leviathan* (London, 1651).

HOBSBAUM, PHILIP, *A Theory of Communication* (London, 1970).

HORWICH, PAUL, *Truth* (Oxford, 1990).

HOSPERS, JOHN, *Meaning and Truth in the Arts* (Chapel Hill, NC, 1946)

—— 'Literature and Human Nature', *Journal of Aesthetics and Art Criticism*, 17 (1958–9), 45–57; repr. in Monroe C. Beardsley and Herbert Schueller (eds.), *Aesthetic Inquiry: Essays on Art Criticism and the Philosophy of Art*.

—— 'Implied Truths in Literature', *Journal of Aesthetics and Art Criticism*, 19 (1960–1), 37–46.

—— (ed.), *Introductory Readings in Aesthetics* (New York, 1969).

HOWELL, ROBERT, 'Fictional Objects: How They Are and How They Aren't', *Poetics*, 8 (1979), 129–77.

HRUSHOVSKI, BENJAMIN, 'Fictionality and Fields of Reference', *Poetics Today*, 5: 2 (1984), 227–51.

HULME, T. E., *Speculations* (2nd edn.; London, 1936).

HUME, DAVID, *A Treatise of Human Nature*, ed. Selby-Bigge (Oxford, 1888).

—— *Enquiry Concerning Human Understanding*, ed. Selby-Bigge (Oxford, 1893).

—— *Essays, Moral, Political and Literary* (Oxford, 1963).

IHWE, JENS F., and RIESER, HANNES, 'Narrative and Descriptive Theory of Fiction. Some Contemporary Issues', *Poetics*, 8 (1979), 63–83.

INWAGEN, PETER VAN, 'Creatures of Fiction', *American Philosophical Quarterly*, 14 (1977), 299–304.

—— 'Fiction and Metaphysics', *Philosophy and Literature*, 7 (1983), 67–77.

ISENBERG, ARNOLD, 'The Problem of Belief', *Journal of Aesthetics and Art Criticism*, 13 (1954–5), 395–407; repr. in Cyril Barrett (ed.), *Collected Papers on Aesthetics*.

JAMES, HENRY, *'The Art of Fiction' and Other Essays* (New York, 1948).

JOHNSON, SAMUEL, *The Yale Edition of the Works of Samuel Johnson*, vii: *Johnson on Shakespeare*, ed. Arthur Sherbo (New Haven, Conn., 1968).

JONES, JOHN, *On Aristotle and Greek Tragedy* (London, 1962).

KANT, IMMANUEL, *Critique of Pure Reason*, trans. Norman Kemp-Smith (London, 1963).

KAPLAN, ABRAHAM, 'Referential Meaning in the Arts', *Journal of Aesthetics and Art Criticism*, 12 (1953–4), 457–74; repr. in Monroe C. Beardsley and Herbert Schueller (eds.), *Aesthetic Inquiry: Essays on Art Criticism and the Philosophy of Art*.

KENNER, HUGH, *The Poems of Ezra Pound* (Norfolk, Conn., 1951).

KERMODE, FRANK, *The Sense of an Ending* (Oxford, 1967).

—— *Essays on Fiction* (London, 1983).

KETTLE, ARNOLD (ed.), *The Nineteenth-Century Novel: Critical Essays and Documents* (London, 1972).

KILLHAM, JOHN, 'A Novel's Relevance to Life', *British Journal of Aesthetics*, 11 (1971), 63–73.

KITTAY, EVA FEDER, *Metaphor* (Oxford, 1987).

KNOWLES, DUDLEY, and SKORUPSKI, JOHN (eds.), *Virtue and Taste: Essays on Politics, Ethics and Aesthetics in Memory of Flint Schier* (Oxford, 1993).

KOETHE, JOHN, 'Putnam's Argument Against Realism', *The Philosophical Review*, 88 (1979), 92–7.

KRIEGER, MURRAY, 'In the Wake of Morality: The Thematic Underside of Recent Theory', *New Literary History*, 15 (1983–4), 119–38.

KRIPKE, SAUL, *Naming and Necessity* (Oxford, 1980).

LAMARQUE, PETER, 'Truth and Art in Iris Murdoch's *The Black Prince*', *Philosophy and Literature*, 2 (1978), 209–22.

—— 'How Can We Fear and Pity Fictions?', *British Journal of Aesthetics*, 21 (1981), 291–304.

—— 'Metaphor and Reported Speech: In Defence of a Pragmatic Theory', *Journal of Literary Semantics*, 11 (1982), 14–18.

—— 'Fiction and Reality', in Peter Lamarque (ed.), *Philosophy and Fiction: Essays in Literary Aesthetics*.

—— 'Bits and Pieces of Fiction', *British Journal of Aesthetics*, 24 (1984), 53–8.

—— 'Philosophical Theories of Metaphor', *Studies in Philosophy* (University of Tsukuba, Japan), 10 (1984), 1–13.

LAMARQUE, PETER, 'The Puzzle of the Flash Stockman: A Reply to David Lewis', *Analysis*, 47 (1987), 93–5.

—— 'Critical Discussion of David Novitz, *Knowledge, Fiction and Imagination*', *Philosophy and Literature*, 13 (1989), 365–74.

—— 'Make-Believe, Ontology and Point of View', in Richard Woodfield (ed.), *Proceedings of the xith World Congress of Aesthetics*.

—— 'Narrative and Invention: The Limits of Fictionality', in Cristopher Nash (ed.), *Narrative in Culture*.

—— 'Reasoning to What is True in Fiction', *Argumentation*, 4 (1990), 99–112.

—— 'Essay Review of Kendall Walton *Mimesis as Make-Believe*', *Journal of Aesthetics and Art Criticism*, 49 (1991), 161–6.

—— 'In and Out of Imaginary Worlds', in Dudley Knowles and John Skorupski (eds.), *Virtue and Taste: Essays on Politics, Ethics and Aesthetics in Memory of Flint Schier*.

—— Review of Gregory Currie, *The Nature of Fiction*, *Philosophical Quarterly*, 42 (1993), 253–6.

—— (ed.), *Philosophy and Fiction: Essays in Literary Aesthetics* (Aberdeen, 1983).

LAWRENCE, D. H., 'Morality and the Novel', repr. in David Lodge (ed.), *20th Century Literary Criticism* (London, 1972).

LEAVIS, F. R., *Anna Karenina and Other Essays* (London, 1967).

—— *The Living Principle: English as a Discipline of Thought* (London, 1975).

—— *The Critic as Anti-Philosopher: Essays and Papers*, ed. G. Singh (London, 1982).

LEBOWITZ, MICHAEL, 'Creating Characters in a Story-Telling Universe', *Poetics*, 13 (1984), 171–94.

LERNER, LAURENCE, *The Truest Poetry* (London, 1960).

—— (ed.), *The Victorians* (London, 1978).

—— (ed.), *Reconstructing Literature* (Oxford, 1983).

LEVIN, S. R., 'Concerning What Kind of Speech Act a Poem Is', in Teun A. van Dijk (ed.), *Pragmatics of Language and Literature*.

LEWIS, DAVID, 'Truth in Fiction', *American Philosophical Quarterly*, 15 (1978), 37–46.

LEWIS, H. D., 'On Poetic Truth', *Philosophy*, 21 (1946), 147–66.

LINSKY, LEONARD (ed.), *Semantics and the Philosophy of Language* (Urbana, Ill., 1952).

—— (ed.), *Reference and Modality* (Oxford, 1971).

LODGE, DAVID, *The Modes of Modern Writing* (London, 1977).

—— *Small World* (Harmondsworth, 1984).

—— (ed.), *20th Century Literary Criticism* (London, 1972).

LOEWENBERG, INA, 'Creativity and Correspondence in Fiction and in Metaphors', *Journal of Aesthetics and Art Criticism*, 36 (1978), 341–50.

LYAS, COLIN, 'The Relevance of the Author's Sincerity', in Peter Lamarque (ed.), *Philosophy and Fiction: Essays in Literary Aesthetics*.

McCLOSKEY, DONALD N., 'Storytelling in Economics', in Cristopher Nash (ed.), *Narrative in Culture*.

McCORMICK, PETER, 'Moral Knowledge and Fiction', *Journal of Aesthetics and Art Criticism*, 41 (1982–3), 399–410.

—— *Fictions, Philosophies and the Problems of Poetics* (Ithaca, NY, 1988).

MACDONALD, MARGARET, 'The Language of Fiction', *Proceedings of the Aristotelian Society*, Suppl. Vol. 28 (1954), 165–84; repr. in Cyril Barrett (ed.), *Collected Papers on Aesthetics*.

MAN, PAUL DE, *Allegories of Fiction: Figural Language in Rousseau, Nietzsche, Rilke and Proust* (New Haven, Conn., 1979).

—— *Blindness and Insight: Essays in the Rhetoric of Contemporary Criticism* (2nd edn.; London, 1983).

MANKOWITZ, WOLF, 'The Songs of Experience', *Politics and Letters* (1947), repr. in Margaret Bottrall (ed.), *'Songs of Innocence and Experience': A Casebook*.

MARGOLIS, JOSEPH, 'Literature and Speech Acts', *Philosophy and Literature*, 3 (1979), 39–52.

—— 'Fiction and Existence', *Grazer Philosophische Studien*, 19 (1983), 179–203.

—— 'The Logic and Structure of Fictional Narratives', *Philosophy and Literature*, 7 (1983), 162–81.

MARTIN, GRAHAM DUNSTAN, *Language, Truth and Poetry* (Edinburgh, 1975).

—— 'A New Look at Fictional Reference', *Philosophy*, 57 (1982), 223–36.

MARTIN, R., and SCHOTCH, P., 'The Meaning of Fictional Names', *Philosophical Studies*, 26 (1974), 377–88.

MELLOR, D. H., 'On Literary Truth', *Ratio*, 10: 1 (1968), 150–68.

MEW, PETER, 'Metaphor and Truth', *British Journal of Aesthetics*, 11 (1971), 189–95.

—— 'Facts in Fiction', *Journal of Aesthetics and Art Criticism*, 31 (1973), 329–37.

MIALL, DAVID S. (ed.), *Metaphor: Problems and Perspectives* (Brighton, 1982).

MILL, JOHN STUART, *Autobiography* (Oxford, 1924).

MILLER, ARTHUR, *Timebends: A Life* (New York, 1987).

MILLER, RICHARD W., 'Truth in Beauty', *American Philosophical Quarterly*, 16 (1979), 317–26.

MITCHELL, JULIAN, 'Truth and Fiction', *Philosophy and the Arts*. Royal Institute of Philosophy Lectures, vi (1971–2) (London, 1973).

MITCHELL, W. J. T., *Against Theory* (Chicago, 1985).

—— (ed.), *On Narrative* (Chicago, 1981).

Moi, Toril, *Sexual/Textual Politics: Feminist Literary Theory* (London, 1985).

Moorman, Mary, *William Wordsworth: A Biography. The Early Years 1770–1803* (Oxford, 1957).

Mounce, H. O., 'Art and Real Life', *Philosophy*, 55 (1980), 183–92.

Murdoch, Iris, *The Sovereignty of Good* (London, 1970).

Nagel, Thomas, *Mortal Questions* (Cambridge, 1979).

—— *The View From Nowhere* (Oxford, 1986).

Nash, Cristopher, 'Literature's Assault on Narrative', in Cristopher Nash (ed.), *Narrative in Culture*.

—— (ed.), *Narrative in Culture: The Uses of Storytelling in the Sciences, Philosophy and Literature* (London, 1990).

Nelson, William, *Fact or Fiction: The Dilemma of the Renaissance Storyteller* (Cambridge, Mass.; 1973).

Newsom, Robert, *A Likely Story: Probability and Play in Fiction* (London, 1988).

Nietzsche, Friedrich, *The Complete Works of Friedrich Nietzsche: The First Complete and Authorized Translation.* ii, ed. Oscar Levy (London, 1909).

Norris, Christopher, *Deconstruction: Theory and Practice* (London, 1982).

—— *The Deconstructive Turn: Essays in the Rhetoric of Philosophy* (London, 1983).

—— *The Contest of Faculties* (London, 1985).

Novitz, David, 'Fiction, Imagination and Emotion', *Journal of Aesthetics and Art Criticism*, 38 (1979–80), 279–88.

—— 'Fiction and the Growth of Knowledge', *Grazer Philosophische Studien*, 19 (1983), 47–68.

—— *Knowledge, Fiction and Imagination* (Philadelphia, 1987).

Nussbaum, Martha Craven, 'Reply to Gardiner, Wollheim, and Putnam', *New Literary History*, 15 (1983–4), 201–8.

—— *The Fragility of Goodness: Luck and Ethics in Greek Tragedy and Philosophy* (Cambridge, 1986).

—— *Love's Knowledge: Essays on Philosophy and Literature* (Oxford, 1990).

Nuttall, A. D., *A New Mimesis: Shakespeare and the Representation of Reality* (Oxford, 1983).

Ohmann, Richard, 'Speech Acts and the Definition of Literature', *Philosophy and Rhetoric*, 4 (1971), 1–19.

Olsen, Stein Haugom, *The Structure of Literary Understanding* (Cambridge, 1978, 1985).

—— 'Understanding Literary Metaphors', in David S. Miall (ed.), *Metaphor: Problems and Perspectives*, 36–54.

—— 'Why Does Hedda Gabler Marry Jörgen Tesman?', *Modern Drama*, 28 (1985), 591–610.

—— *The End of Literary Theory* (Cambridge, 1987).

ORTONY, ANDREW (ed.), *Metaphor and Thought* (Cambridge, 1979).

PARSONS, TERENCE, *Nonexistent Objects* (New Haven, Conn., 1980).

PASKINS, BARRIE, 'On Being Moved by Anna Karenina and *Anna Karenina*', *Philosophy*, 52 (1977), 344–7.

PATEY, DOUGLAS LANE, *Probability and Literary Form* (Cambridge, 1984).

PAVEL, THOMAS G., *Fictional Worlds* (Cambridge, Mass., 1986).

PHILLIPS, D. Z., *Through a Darkening Glass: Philosophy, Literature, and Cultural Change* (Oxford, 1982).

PITCHER, GEORGE (ed.), *Truth* (Englewood Cliffs, NJ, 1964).

POLLARD, D. E. B., 'Fiction and Modality', *Philosophy and Phenomenological Research*, 35 (1974–5), 472–83.

—— 'On Talking "about" Characters', *British Journal of Aesthetics*, 16 (1976), 366–9.

PRADO, C. G., *Making Believe: Philosophical Reflections on Fiction* (Westport, Conn., 1984).

PRICE, KINGSLEY BLAKE, 'Is the Work of Art a Symbol?', *Journal of Philosophy*, 50 (1953), 485–503.

PRINCE, GERALD, *Narratology: The Form and Functioning of Narrative* (The Hague, 1982).

PUTNAM, HILARY, 'The Meaning of "Meaning" ', in *Philosophical Papers, ii: Mind, Language and Reality.*

—— *Philosophical Papers, ii: Mind, Language and Reality* (Cambridge, 1975).

—— 'Literature, Science, and Reflection', *New Literary History*, 7 (1975–6), 483–92; repr. in *Meaning and the Moral Sciences.*

—— *Meaning and the Moral Sciences* (London, 1978).

—— 'Reflections on Goodman's *Ways of Worldmaking*', *Journal of Philosophy*, 76 (1979), 603–18.

—— *Philosophical Papers, iii: Realism and Reason* (Cambridge, 1983).

—— 'Is There a Fact of Matter about Fiction?', *Poetics Today*, 4 (1983), 77–82.

—— 'The Craving for Objectivity', *New Literary History*, 15 (1983–4), 229–39.

—— 'Taking Rules Seriously: A Response to Martha Nussbaum', *New Literary History*, 15 (1983–4), 193–200.

—— 'A Comparison of Something with Something Else', *New Literary History*, 17 (1985–6), 61–80.

QUINE, WILLARD VAN ORMAN, *From a Logical Point of View* (2nd rev. edn.; New York, 1961).

—— *The Ways of Paradox and Other Essays* (New York, 1966).

—— 'Quantifying In', in Leonard Linsky (ed.), *Reference and Modality.*

QUINTON, ANTHONY, *The Divergence of the Twain: Poet's Philosophy and Philosopher's Philosophy*, A Lecture to Mark the Official Opening of the Centre for Research in Philosophy and Literature, University of Warwick, 8 October 1985 (Centre for Research in Philosophy and Literature, University of Warwick, 1985).

RADFORD, COLIN, 'How Can We Be Moved by the Fate of Anna Karenina?', *Proceedings of the Aristotelian Society*, Suppl. Vol. 69 (1975), 67–80.

—— 'Tears and Fiction: A Reply to Weston', *Philosophy*, 52 (1977), 208–13.

RAMSEY, F. P., 'Facts and Propositions', in George Pitcher (ed.), *Truth*.

RAPHAEL, D. D., 'Can Literature Be Moral Philosophy?', *New Literary History*, 15 (1983–4), 1–12.

—— 'Philosophy and Rationality: A Response to Cora Diamond', *New Literary History*, 15 (1983–4), 171–8.

RAWLS, JOHN, 'Two Concepts of Rules', *Philosophical Review*, 64 (1955), 3–32; repr. in Philippa Foot (ed.), *Theories of Ethics*.

REDDY, MICHAEL, 'The Conduit Metaphor', in Andrew Ortony (ed.), *Metaphor and Thought*.

RÉE, JONATHAN, 'Timely Meditations', *Radical Philosophy*, 55 (1990), 31–9.

REID, LOUIS ARNAUD, 'Art, Truth, and Reality', *British Journal of Aesthetics*, 4 (1964), 321–31.

RICHARDS, I. A., *Principles of Literary.Criticism* (2nd edn.; London, 1926).

RIFFATERRE, MICHAEL, 'Interpretation and Descriptive Poetry: A Reading of Wordsworth's "Yew Trees" ', in Robert Young (ed.), *Untying the Text: A Post-Structuralist Reader*.

—— *Fictional Truth* (Baltimore, 1990).

ROBSON, W. W., *Modern English Literature* (Oxford, 1970).

RODWAY, ALLAN, *The Truths of Fiction* (London, 1970).

RORTY, RICHARD, *Philosophy and the Mirror of Nature* (Princeton, NJ, 1979).

—— *Consequences of Pragmatism: Essays 1972–1980* (Brighton, 1982).

—— 'Unfamiliar Noises: Hesse and Davidson on Metaphor', *Proceedings of the Aristotelian Society*, Suppl. Vol. 61 (1987), 283–96.

—— *Contingency, Irony, and Solidarity* (Cambridge, 1989).

—— 'Just One More Species Doing its Best', *London Review of Books*, 13: 14, 25 July 1991.

ROSEBURY, B. J., 'Fiction, Emotion and "Belief" ', *British Journal of Aesthetics*, 19 (1979), 120–30.

ROUSE, JOSEPH, 'The Narrative Reconstruction of Science', *Inquiry*, 33 (1990), 179–96.

ROUTLEY, RICHARD, 'Some Things Do Not Exist', *Notre Dame Journal of Formal Logic*, 7 (1966), 251–76.

—— 'The Semantical Structure of Fictional Discourse', *Poetics*, 8 (1979), 3–30.

RUSHDIE, SALMAN, 'Salman Rushdie Writes to Rajiv Gandhi', in Lisa Appignanesi and Sara Maitland (eds.), *The Rushdie File.*

RUSSELL, BERTRAND, *Logic and Knowledge*, ed. R. C. Marsh (London, 1956).

—— *An Inquiry into Meaning and Truth* (London, 1962).

RYAN, MARIE-LUARE, 'Fiction, Non-Factuals and the Principle of Minimal Departure', *Poetics*, 8 (1980), 403–22.

—— 'Fictions as a Logical, Ontological, and Illocutionary Issue', *Style*, 18 (1984) 121–39.

RYLE, GILBERT, 'Imaginary Objects', *Proceedings of the Aristotelian Society*, Suppl. Vol. 12 (1933), 18–43; repr. in *Collected Papers*, ii.

—— *Collected Papers, ii: Collected Essays 1929–1968* (London, 1971).

SAINSBURY, MARK, *Russell* (2nd edn.; London, 1985).

SAUSSURE, FERDINAND, *Course in General Linguistics*, trans. Wade Baskin (rev. edn.; London, 1974).

SCHAFER, RAY, 'Narration in the Psychoanalytic Dialogue', in W. J. T. Mitchell (ed.), *On Narrative.*

SCHAPER, EVA, 'Fiction and the Suspension of Disbelief', *British Journal of Aesthetics*, 18 (1978), 31–44.

SCHEFFLER, ISRAEL, 'The Wonderful Worlds of Goodman', *Synthese*, 45 (1980), 201–9.

SCHIER, FLINT, 'Tragedy and the Community of Sentiment', in Peter Lamarque (ed.), *Philosophy and Fiction: Essays in Literary Aesthetics.*

SCHIFFER, STEPHEN, *Meaning* (Oxford, 1972).

—— *Remnants of Meaning* (Cambridge, Mass., 1987).

SCHMIDT, SIEGFRID, 'Fictionality in Literary and Non-Literary Discourse', *Poetics*, 9 (1980), 525–46.

—— 'The Fiction is that Reality Exists', *Poetics Today*, 5: 2 (1984), 253–74.

SCHOLES, ROBERT, 'Language, Narrative, and Anti-Narrative', in W. J. T. Mitchell (ed.), *On Narrative.*

SCRIVEN, MICHAEL, 'The Language of Fiction', *Proceedings of the Aristotelian Society*, Suppl. Vol. 28 (1954), 185–96.

SCRUTON, ROGER, *Art and Imagination: A Study in the Philosophy of Mind* (2nd edn.; London, 1982).

SEARLE, JOHN R., *Speech Acts: An Essay in the Philosophy of Language* (Cambridge, 1969).

—— 'Reiterating the Differences: A Reply to Derrida', *Glyph*, 1 (1977), 198–208.

—— *Expression and Meaning: Studies in the Theory of Speech Acts* (Cambridge, 1979).

SELLARS, WILFRED, 'Presupposing', *Philosophical Review*, 63 (1954), 197–215.

SESONSKE, ALEXANDER, 'Truth in Art', *Journal of Philosophy*, 53 (1956), 345–53.

SHELLEY, PERCY BYSSHE, *A Defence of Poetry*, ed. Albert S. Cook (Boston, 1890).

SIRRIDGE, MARY J., 'Truth from Fiction?', *Philosophy and Phenomenological Research*, 35 (1974–5), 453–71.

SKINNER, QUENTIN, 'Motives, Intentions and the Interpretations of Texts', *New Literary History*, 3 (1972), 393–408.

SKULSKY, HAROLD, 'On Being Moved by Fiction', *Journal of Aesthetics and Art Criticism*, 39 (1980–1), 5–14.

SÖRBOM, GÖRAN, 'Imitation and Art', in Richard Woodfield (ed.), *Proceedings of the xith International Congress in Aesthetics*.

SPARSHOTT, F. E., *The Structure of Aesthetics* (Toronto, 1963).

—— 'Truth in Fiction', *Journal of Aesthetics and Art Criticism*, 26 (1967), 3–7.

STANZEL, F. K., *A Theory of Narrative* (Cambridge, 1984).

STEINBERG, DANNY D., and JAKOBOVITS, LEON A., *Semantics: An Interdisciplinary Reader in Philosophy, Linguistics and Psychology* (Cambridge, 1971).

STEINMANN, MARTIN, 'Poetry as Fiction', *New Literary History*, 2 (1971), 259–81.

—— 'Rortyism', *Philosophy and Literature*, 12 (1988), 27–47.

STERN, J. P., *On Realism* (London, 1973).

STRAWSON, P. F., 'On Referring', *Mind*, 59 (1950), 320–44; repr. in *Logico-Linguistic Papers*.

—— 'Truth', *Proceedings of the Aristotelian Society*, Suppl. Vol. 24 (1950), 129–56; repr. in *Logico-Linguistic Papers*.

—— *Introduction to Logical Theory* (London, 1952).

—— 'Reply to Mr Sellars', *Philosophical Review*, 63 (1954), 216–31.

—— 'Identifying Reference and Truth-Value', *Theoria*, 30 (1964), 96–118; repr. in *Logico-Linguistic Papers*.

—— *Logico-Linguistic Papers* (London, 1971).

STROUD, BARRY, *The Significance of Philosophical Scepticism* (Oxford, 1984).

SUPPLE, BARRY, 'Material Development: The Condition of England 1830–1860', in Lawrence Lerner (ed.), *The Victorians*.

TALLIS, RAYMOND, *In Defence of Realism* (London, 1988).

—— *Not Saussure: A Critique of Post-Saussurean Literary Theory* (London, 1988).

TARSKI, ALFRED, 'The Semantic Conception of Truth and the Foundation of Semantics', *Philosophy and Phenomenological Research*, 4 (1944), 341–75; repr. in H. Feigl and W. Sellars (eds.), *Readings in Philosophical Analysis*.

THEOBALD, D. W., 'Philosophy and Fiction: The Novel as Eloquent Philosophy', *British Journal of Aesthetics*, 14 (1974), 17–25.

TILGHMAN, B. R. (ed.), *Language and Aesthetics: Contributions to the Philosophy of Art* (Lawrence, Kan., 1973).

TODOROV, TZVETAN, 'All against Humanity', review of Robert Scholes, *Textual Power: Literary Theory and the Teaching of English* (New Haven, Conn., 1985), *Times Literary Supplement*, 4 October 1985.

TRILLING, LIONEL, 'Introduction', *Little Dorrit* (Oxford Ill. Dickens; Oxford, 1953).

TRIMPI, WESLEY, 'The Ancient Hypothesis of Fiction: An Essay on the Origins of Literary Theory', *Traditio*, 27 (1971), 1–78.

—— 'The Quality of Fiction: The Rhetorical Transmission of Literary Theory', *Traditio*, 30 (1974), 1–118.

URMSON, J. O., 'Dramatic Representation', *Philosophical Quarterly*, 22 (1972), 333–43.

—— 'Fiction', *American Philosophical Quarterly*, 13 (1976), 153–7.

VAIHINGER, HANS, *The Philosophy of 'As If'*, trans. C. K. Ogden (2nd edn.; London, 1935).

WALSH, DOROTHY, 'The Cognitive Content of Art', *Philosophical Review*, 52 (1943), 433–51; repr. in Eliseo Vivas and Murray Krieger (eds.), *The Problems of Aesthetics* (New York, 1953).

—— *Literature and Knowledge* (Middletown, Conn., 1969).

WALTON, KENDALL L., 'Pictures and Make-Believe', *Philosophical Review*, 82 (1973), 283–319.

—— 'Fearing Fictions', *Journal of Philosophy*, 75 (1978), 5–27.

—— 'How Remote are Fictional Worlds from the Real World?', *Journal of Aesthetics and Art Criticism*, 37 (1978–9), 11–23.

—— 'Appreciating Fiction: Suspending Disbelief or Pretending Belief?', *Dispositio*, 5 (1980), 1–18.

—— 'Fiction, Fiction-Making and Styles of Fictionality', *Philosophy and Literature*, 7 (1983), 78–88.

—— Review of Nicholas Wolterstorff, *Works and Worlds of Art*, *Journal of Philosophy*, 80 (1983), 179–83.

—— 'Do We Need Fictional Entities? Notes towards a Theory', in *Aesthetics: Proceedings of the Eighth International Wittgenstein Symposium* (Vienna, 1984), 179–92.

—— *Mimesis as Make-Believe* (Cambridge, Mass., 1990).

WARNOCK, MARY, *Imagination* (London, 1976).

WATT, IAN, *The Rise of the Novel: Studies in Defoe, Richardson and Fielding* (London, 1967).

WEBER, RONALD, *The Literature of Fact: Literary Nonfiction in American Writing* (Athens, Oh., 1980).

WEITZ, MORRIS, *Philosophy of the Arts* (Cambridge, Mass., 1950).

—— 'Truth in Literature', *Revue internationale de philosophie*, 9 (1955), 116–29; repr. in John Hospers (ed.), *Introductory Readings in Aesthetics*.

WELLEK, RENÉ, *Concepts of Criticism* (New Haven, Conn., 1963).

WESTON, MICHAEL, 'How Can We Be Moved by the Fate of Anna Karenina?', *Proceedings of the Aristotelian Society*, Suppl. Vol. 69 (1975), 81–93.

WHITE, HAYDEN, *Topics of Discourse: Essays in Cultural Criticism* (Baltimore, 1978).

—— ' "Figuring the Nature of Times Deceased"; Literary Theory and Historical Writing', in Ralph Cohen (ed.), *Future Literary Theory* (New York, 1989).

WICKER, BRIAN, *The Story-Shaped World, Fiction and Metaphysics: Some Variations on a Theme* (London, 1975).

WILLIAMS, BERNARD, 'Getting it Right', *London Review of Books*, 11: 22, 23 November 1989, 3, 5.

WILSON, CATHERINE, 'Literature and Knowledge', *Philosophy*, 58 (1983), 489–96.

WISDOM, JOHN, *Logical Constructions* (New York, 1969).

WOLTERSTORFF, NICHOLAS, 'Worlds of Works of Art', *Journal of Aesthetics and Art Criticism*, 35 (1976), 121–32.

—— *Works and Worlds of Art* (Oxford, 1980).

WOODFIELD, ANDREW (ed.), *Thought and Object: Essays on Intentionality* (Oxford, 1982).

WOODFIELD, RICHARD (ed.), *Proceedings of the xith International Congress in Aesthetics* (Nottingham, 1990).

WOODS, JOHN, *The Logic of Fiction: A Philosophical Sounding of Deviant Logic* (The Hague, 1974).

WOOLF, VIRGINIA, *Collected Essays,* ii (London, 1966).

YOUNG, ROBERT (ed.), *Untying the Text: A Post-Structuralist Reader* (Boston, 1981).

Index